PATERNOSTER THEOLOGICAL MONOGRAPHS

The Triune God
and the Charismatic Movement

A Critical Appraisal from a Scottish Perspective

PATERNOSTER THEOLOGICAL MONOGRAPHS

A full listing of titles in this series and
Paternoster Biblical Monographs
appears at the end of this book

PATERNOSTER THEOLOGICAL MONOGRAPHS

The Triune God and the Charismatic Movement

A Critical Appraisal from a Scottish Perspective

Jim Purves

Foreword by Parush Parushev

PATERNOSTER

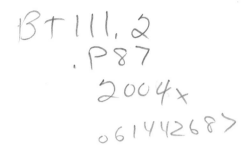

British Library Cataloguing in Publication Data
A catalogue record for this book is available from the British Library

ISBN 1–84227–321–3

Typeset by the author
Printed and bound in Great Britain
for Paternoster
by Nottingham Alpha Graphics

Series Preface

In the West the churches may be declining, but theology—serious, academic (mostly doctoral level) and mainstream orthodox in evaluative commitment—shows no sign of withering on the vine. This series of *Paternoster Theological Monographs* extends the expertise of the Press especially to first-time authors whose work stands broadly within the parameters created by fidelity to Scripture and has satisfied the critical scrutiny of respected assessors in the academy. Such theology may come in several distinct intellectual disciplines—historical, dogmatic, pastoral, apologetic, missional, aesthetic and no doubt others also. The series will be particularly hospitable to promising constructive theology within an evangelical frame, for it is of this that the church's need seems to be greatest. Quality writing will be published across the confessions—Anabaptist, Episcopalian, Reformed, Arminian and Orthodox—across the ages—patristic, medieval, reformation, modern and counter-modern—and across the continents. The aim of the series is theology written in the twofold conviction that the church needs theology and theology needs the church—which in reality means theology done for the glory of God.

Series Editors

David F. Wright, Emeritus Professor of Patristic and Reformed Christianity, University of Edinburgh, Scotland, UK

Trevor A. Hart, Head of School and Principal of St Mary's College School of Divinity, University of St Andrews, Scotland, UK

Anthony N.S. Lane, Professor of Historical Theology and Director of Research, London School of Theology, UK

Anthony C. Thiselton, Emeritus Professor of Christian Theology, University of Nottingham, Research Professor in Christian Theology, University College Chester, and Canon Theologian of Leicester Cathedral and Southwell Minster, UK

Kevin J. Vanhoozer, Research Professor of Systematic Theology, Trinity Evangelical Divinity School, Deerfield, Illinois, USA

To Jennifer
my wife and partner in all that is beautiful and true

Contents

Foreword   **xiii**

Foreword — xiii

Preface and Acknowledgements — xvii

Abbreviations — xix

General Introduction — xxi

Chapter 1 The Charismatic Movement in Scotland — 1

1.1   Introduction — 1

1.2   Before 1964 — 2

1.3   1964-74 — 6

1.4   After 1974 — 9

1.5   The Historic Churches — 13

1.6   The Church of Scotland — 13

1.7   The Baptist Union of Scotland — 17

1.8   Towards a Theology of the Charismatic Movement — 20

1.9   The Doctrinal Issues — 26

1.9.1   *The Doctrine of the Trinity* — 27

1.9.2   *Pneumatology* — 27

1.9.3   *The Doctrine of the Eucharist* — 28

1.9.4   *Epistemology* — 28

1.9.5   *Ecclesiology* — 29

Chapter 2 Patristic Foundations — 31

2.1   Introduction — 31

2.2   The Apostolic Fathers — 32

2.3   The Pre-Nicene West — 36

2.4   The Pre-Nicene East — 40

2.5   Arius, Nicea and the *Homoousion* — 44

2.6   The Status of the Son — 46

2.7   Relationships Within the Trinity   50
2.8   Developing a Doctrine of Relations   51
2.8.1   *In the East*   51
2.8.2   *In the West*   54
2.9   The Priority of the Immanent Trinity   57
2.10   Foundations for the *Filioque*   59
2.11   The Spirit and Christology   60
2.12   The Spirit and Christian Experience   64
2.12.1   *Gregory of Nyssa*   65
2.12.2   *Augustine of Hippo*   67
2.12.3   *Post-Nicene Developments: A Summary*   68
2.13   The Patristic Bequest: Evolving Pneumatological Structures   70
2.14   Three Patristic Models   72
2.14.1   *The Pre-Nicene Model*   72
2.14.2   *The Eastern Model*   73
2.14.3   *The Western Model*   75
2.15   The Patristic Bequest: An Inheritance   76

Chapter 3 John Calvin   78
3.1   Introduction   78
3.2   The Knowledge of God the Creator   79
3.2.1   *Duplex Cognitio Dei*   80
3.2.2   *Imago Dei*   82
3.3   The Knowledge of God the Redeemer   84
3.4   Man's Union with Christ   87
3.5   The Spirit and Faith   89
3.6   The Spirit and the Sacraments   92
3.7   The Parameters of Orthodoxy   95
3.8   The Spirit and Election   99
3.9   The Spirit as an Epistemic Agent   101
3.10   Calvin's Legacy in Retrospect   108

Chapter 4 The Scots and Westminster Confessions of Faith   112
4.1   Introduction   112
4.2   The Scots Confession: A Survey   113
4.3   The Scots Confession: Commentators   119
4.4   The Westminster Confession: A Survey   121

4.5   The Westminster Confession: Commentators   126
4.6   Summary   130

Chapter 5 Edward Irving   **132**
5.1   Introduction   132
5.2   Irving's Christology   135
5.2.1 *Pneumatological Implications*   137
5.2.2 *Soteriological Implications*   139
5.2.3 *Trinitarian Implications*   141
5.3   Irving's Pneumatology   142
5.4   The Spirit and the Sacraments   149
5.5   Critique   150
5.5.1 *The Spirit and Christology*   151
5.5.2 *The Spirit and the Trinity*   152
5.5.3 *The Spirit and the Doctrine of Election*   153
5.5.4 *The Spirit and the Resurrected Christ*   154

Chapter 6 Thomas F. Torrance   **156**
6.1   Introduction   156
6.2   The Spirit and the Trinity   160
6.3   The Spirit and the Hypostatic Union   164
6.4   The Spirit and the Sacraments   166
6.5   The Person and Function of the Spirit   170
6.6   Critique   174

Chapter 7 Tom Smail and James Dunn   **176**
7.1   Introduction   176
7.2   Tom Smail   176
7.2.1 *The Sovereign Character of God's Prevenient Grace* 177
7.2.2 *The Corporate Context within which the Spirit Operates* 177
7.2.3 *Theology as Trinitarian, with a Christocentric Focus* 178
7.3   *Reflected Glory*   179
7.4   *The Forgotten Father*   181
7.5   *The Giving Gift*   184
7.6   James Dunn   190
7.7   The Priority of Experience   190
7.8   Smail and Dunn in Context   202

Chapter 8 Towards the Trinity   **208**
8.1   Review   208
8.2   The Question of Relationality   212
8.3   An Anthropocentric Reference in Perceiving the Trinity   218
8.4   Relating the Sprit in us to the Spirit in Jesus   222
8.5   The Twofold Procession of the Spirit   225
8.6   The Person and Function of the Spirit   227
8.7   Conclusion   230

Glossary of Theological and Other Specialist Terms   **233**

Bibliography   **237**

Index   **243**

FOREWORD

The title of this book is rather deceptive. Whereas its clear focus upon the Scottish Charismatic Movement implies a location in particular time and space, it is more than a contextual inquiry, in that it narrates a more complex story of the Church's struggle to come to terms with the role of the Spirit in the mystery of the Trinity. In an almost encyclopedic breadth, it spans time and denominational boundaries by reaching to the beginnings of the Christian movement, touching on the origins of the Reformed tradition and reflecting on twentieth-century Pentecostalism and the Charismatic Renewal in the historic churches.

In *The Triune God and the Charismatic Movement: A Critical Appraisal from a Scottish Perspective*, Dr Jim Purves builds upon not only his faith pilgrimage and charismatic experience, as valuable as these are, but also on years of pastoral experience and theological study and reflection within three major forms of ecclesial life in Scotland. Further, he focuses his research within the dominant Scottish Reformed theological tradition, thereby creating a medium and vocabulary that enable him to relate the Charismatic emphasis on suprarational experience to more conventional theological language. The accompanying glossary of theological and specialist terms is quite appropriate for this work.

The first part of the work is a succinct account of a largely western Christian, and particularly Augustinian, line of theological thinking about the nature and the ministry of the Holy Spirit in the complexity of the relationship to the Son; and their relationship to the Father within the Trinitarian understanding of God. From chapter 3 on, the author surveys theological developments in the Calvinist heritage. The inquiry unfolds by juxtaposing contrasting perspectives rather than tracing the developments chronologically; and his analysis illumines a tendency within (Scottish) Reformed theology of subordinating Pneumatology to Christology.

In the last chapter of the book, considering seriously the Charismatic Movement's emphasis upon an immanent experience of God and developing further some Ante-Nicene patristic soteriological insights, Purves presents his own perspective on the working of the Holy Spirit. He moves away from both exclusively Christocentric theological models and currently fashionable emphases on the Social Trinity by redefining the relationality within the Trinity in terms of ontic actuality (the becomingness towards humanity) of the Son and of the Spirit. His revised Trinitarian model emphasises three distinctive characteristics: 1) the bifocal symmetry of the ontic actuality of the Son and the Spirit; 2) the effect of the Spirit in bringing persons to proximate towards the person of Jesus Christ; and, deductively, 3) the two-fold procession of the Spirit from the Father to the incarnate Son and from the Father to humanity, resulting in an eschatological perception the resurrected humanity in Christ.

Advancing further the works of Colin Gunton and John Zizioulas, Purves's pneumatological approach suggests a bifocal symmetry of the Son and of the Spirit in God's salvific economy. His theological model offers a balance between the ontic actuality of the Son in the Incarnation and the immanent becomingness of God in the Spirit towards persons and communities evident in charismatic experience and, concurrently, in the activating of human, eschatological awareness. This is the point at which the revised Trinitarian model departs most radically from the traditional western model and comes closer to the spirit of Orthodox theologizing. Purves argues, however, that the revised Trinitarian model can fit into the framework of the Scottish tradition and accommodate the experience of the Movement in Scotland.

Frankly, I was initially disinclined to accept the invitation to write the Foreword to this study. Could a person with my kind of experience and mindset profit from (not to think of writing about) Dr Purves's research?

For one thing, I come from an ecclesiastical tradition contextually related to Orthodox Christian sub-culture that is generally antagonistic towards extreme expressions of the charismatic gifts, an antagonism re-enforced by the tension created recently by culturally-insensitive Charismatic imports into Eastern Europe. In addition, as with most converts from highly rational and intellectually developed secular ideologies, I am rather skeptical of the grand scholastic claims of universal validity. My limited knowledge of the Church's experience tells me that doctrinal debates and elaborate systematic theological schemata have rarely had a positive bearing on the daily life of the Church. Moreover, I have little affinity with doctrinal Reformed theologizing. A puzzling riddle for me has been, in particular, the weak pneumatology of the theologies of even the best representatives of this otherwise comprehensive school of thought.

Now having read his study, I can give a definitive affirmative answer to my query. Even a biased observer has to agree that a renewed emphasis on the working of the Holy Spirit is an important fact about the current life of the churches across the denominational divide and across the globe. A sensitive openness to the Spirit's immediate presence brings re-vitalization and emotional warmth and strengthens Christian commitment. But at the same time, it is true, at least in Eastern Europe, that spontaneously-emerging Charismatic communities with superficial theological thinking act more like therapeutic emergency units than as an organic whole. Thus, theological reflection on the marvels of the experience of the community gathering in the Spirit is badly needed.

Even if one opts for *doing* theology, as I would prefer, rather than constructing models of how to do it, a convictional model or a map of the process for doing is still needed. Not surprisingly, this map of a particular doing is made intelligible in terms of existing or dominant theological culture. Mutual interpenetration of medium and message is inevitable.

The strength of Purves's research work lies in the masterful blend of experience and contextual language of appropriation. It is a rewarding attempt to expand the Trinitarian and pneumatological insights of the Scottish Reformed tradition to embrace the experience of the Charismatic Movement in Scotland in the 1960s, 70s and 80s. His penetrating analysis provides an excellent example of a much-needed link between the experiential primary theological life of the Church and the well-developed conceptual framework of secondary academic theological discourse.

Dr Purves has accomplished a formidable task in this book. He has worked carefully on relating hard theological thinking with meaningful Christian experience of both an individual and an ecclesial community. While the premises of his work are contextually dependent, he has brought forth important issues for the whole Christian Church. I found Dr Purves's theological reflections refreshing and illuminating. One may not always agree with his assessment or follow his interpretation of a particular event or theological insight, but certainly his stimulating thought will leave no-one concerned with the well-being of the Church indifferent.

Parush R. Parushev
International Baptist Theological Seminary
Prague, Czech Republic
July 2004

PREFACE AND ACKNOWLEDGEMENTS

This work began as an act of pilgrimage. I was converted to a living and vital faith in Jesus Christ during the Charismatic Movement's heyday in Scotland, in 1975. Shortly afterwards, I was introduced to the Reformed faith through the outstanding ministry of the Rev James Philip, of Holyrood Abbey, Edinburgh. So I began my Christian life, both a Charismatic and a student of Reformed truths! Ordained to the Church of Scotland ministry in 1981, I was privileged to serve within that denomination until 1987, when I left to found an independent, Charismatic fellowship. These were heady and exciting, as well as challenging times. It was out of this environment that I began to reflect on the nature of the Trinity and the doctrine of the Holy Spirit, as I came to appreciate the great gulf that appeared to exist between the Christian dogmas I had been tutored in as a theological student and the experience I had entered and saw around me of the Holy Spirit's presence and power.

Having completed and submitted the work for a PhD awarded by the University of Aberdeen in 1994, I really thought that was an end to it. I sensed, in the church atmosphere around me, that battle lines were drawn and trenches dug. But God's grace prevails and times have changed. Ten years on, adopted by the Baptist Union of Scotland where I serve as pastor of a wonderful congregation, I see both a new openness to reviewing the doctrine of the Holy Spirit and an eagerness to redefine the parameters of orthodox theology in ways that will further serve the purposes of our God and the Kingdom of our Lord and Saviour, Jesus Christ. I am delighted that Paternoster Press have now invited me to update and attempt to make the original doctorate more intelligible, that it might be chewed, bitten, digested and goodness knows what else by those who would read it and reflect on the challenges it offers.

This work is not an easy read. Were I a more able writer, it might be; but there it is. Please read it slowly and reflect on it, chapter by chapter. Please also forgive the omission of Scriptural references; although, by way of explanation, it should be said that this work was undertaken not as an exercise in expounding Scriptural truths but as an attempt to draw the reader into serious theological engagement with issues that have led to what I believe to be a deep and serious pathology in the way dogmatic theology has often been used or, more often, ignored in relating Trinitarian Theology to the Charismatic Movement. I am deeply grateful for this opportunity to offer my own reflections to a wider Christian community. It is my prayer that, with all its failings and shortcomings, this study may in some measure bless and stimulate those who seek to engage with the reasoning and argumentation that it contains.

Within the body of the text I have retained transliterated Greek or Latin words and phrases when using technical, theological terms that are integral to my line of reasoning, either offering my own renderings in English or seeking to explain them in a glossary which lays out some of the more technical words and phrases that are used both in this study and in the science of Christian Dogmatics. All omissions and mistakes are entirely my own and I offer my sincere apologies for them all!

Thanks go to those interviewed in the preparation of this work, for their thirst to see growth in both Christlike conformity and Holy Spirit enabling in the church they have loved and served; to my church administrator, Christine Lumsden and Brian Barclay, for reading over the script and suggesting some adjustments in style that, hopefully, make it more intelligible to the general reader; and to Anthony Cross and Jeremy Mudditt of Paternoster Press, for graciously guiding me through the process of preparing this material for publication.

Jim Purves
Bristo Baptist Church
Edinburgh

Abbreviations

Full details of all works cited appear in the Bibliography and, within the text, on the occasion of their first appearance. Thereafter, works are cited in a short form, using either the main title or an abbreviated reference. In the case of series volumes, the first reference may appear as a volume number along with the series abbreviation. Abbreviations are explained as follows:

ANF	*The Ante-Nicene Fathers of the Christian Church*, 9 volumes, A. Roberts and J Donaldson (Editors), Eerdmans, Grand Rapids, 1885.
Clement	*The Apostolic Fathers*, translated by J. B. Lightfoot, MacMillan & Co., London, 1893.
Collected Writings	*The Collected Writings of Edward Irving in Five Volumes*, G. Carlyle (Editor), Alexander Strachan & Co., London, 1865.
FOTC	*The Fathers of the Church*, 109 volumes, Catholic University of America, Washington, 1947 – present.
Hermas	*The Shepherd of Hermas*, translated by C. H. Hoole, Rivingstons, London, 1870.
Ignatius	*The Ante-Nicene Fathers* Vol. 1, A. Roberts and J. Donaldson (Editors), Eerdmans, Grand Rapids, 1884.
Institute	*Calvin: Institutes of the Christian Religion*, 2 volumes, J. T. McNeill (Editor) and translated by F. L. Battles, Westminster Press, Philadelphia, 1960.
NPNF	*The Nicene and Post-Nicene Fathers of the Christian Church*, Second Series, 14 volumes, P. Schaff and H. Wace (Editors), Eerdmans, Grand Rapids, 1891.
Scots Conf.	*Scots Confession*, translated by J. Bulloch, St. Andrew Press, Edinburgh, 1960.
Westminster Conf.	*The Westminster Confession of Faith*, Free Presbyterian Publications, Glasgow, 1973.

General Introduction

In this work, we set out to test the theological validity of the Charismatic Movement's emphasis upon an experience of God that is understood to transcend a rational appreciation of God's Being and acts: an experience held as necessary for forming, in the individual believer, a proper appreciation and enjoyment of the Christian life. The Charismatic Movement has stressed the special significance of the Holy Spirit in bringing about a personal, suprarational experience of God, whereby the Holy Spirit inducts the individual Christian into a sublime, conscious communion with the Divine. This suprarational experience of the Holy Spirit is viewed as properly embracing and affecting the whole being of a person. An individual's rational appreciation and full awareness of God will properly arise out of such an experience: the rational is predicated by the experiential. Our task will be to examine whether such an understanding of the Person and function of the Holy Spirit can be validated without violating the central tenets of orthodox, Trinitarian theology.

In embarking on this study, we set out to chart a course which, beginning with an overview of the Charismatic Movement as it developed in Scotland, proceeds to examine Trinitarian theology as it evolved through the Patristic era, going on from there to trace how the subsequent course of pneumatology, as it was formed in the thought of Calvin and the theology of the Scottish Reformation, led to the establishment of theological perspectives which neither would nor could easily accommodate the experiential emphasis of the Charismatic Movement. In pursuing our thesis we do not seek to provide an extensive review of post-Reformation Scottish pneumatology, nor do we engage in a comprehensive discussion of the contemporary Trinitarian debate, although we will touch on both of these. Rather, we shall attempt to construct a basic, Trinitarian framework which might assist in providing a theological foundation for the possible reconciliation and consolidation of the particular pneumatological insights of the Reformed and Charismatic traditions.

In examining the heart of the Charismatic experience there lies an opportunity to reappraise the Christian perception of God. The Charismatic Movement has, in large measure, spoken in and held to the language of Christian orthodoxy. What has been of special significance is the fresh stimulation the Charismatic Movement has brought to questions over the Person and function of the Holy Spirit. Our study considers the Scottish context, but our conviction is that the issues we will address have relevance to a much wider, continuing debate on the proper relationship between propositional theology, Christian experience and Christian behaviour. Our quest arises out of a concern to address the apparent gulf that exists between the experience of many Christians within the Charismatic Movement and the great tradition of Scottish, Reformed theology. To that end, as we seek to identify the focal theological issues that arise out of the reception of the Charismatic Movement in Scotland, we look to whether an answer to our quest may be shaped from pneumatological perspectives which arise from within the Scottish, Reformed theological tradition.

In chapter 1 we begin by tracing the early development of the Charismatic Movement in Scotland, observing how its development affected and was responded to by the wider church. We will attempt to identify those issues which are pertinent to an understanding of pneumatology in a Trinitarian framework, mapping out an agenda whereby we might address them and formulating the questions which require to be addressed.

In chapter 2 we review the Patristic roots of Trinitarian theology, following the development of early perceptions of the Triune God from the time of the Apostolic Fathers, noting that there is some similarity between Charismatic and pre-Nicene understandings of the Spirit. We will observe how primitive perceptions of the Spirit came to be shaped and changed by the development of Trinitarian theology, these perceptions being continued yet adapted through to the post-Nicene period and the emergence of distinctive Trinitarian models in both west and east.

In chapter 3 we will note how Patristic concerns, centred on the western model of the Trinity, found expression in the pneumatology of John Calvin and led to an increasing emphasis on the function, as distinct from the Person, of the Holy Spirit. Having reviewed the theological basis of Calvin's pneumatology, we will go on to argue that one specific aspect of the Spirit's function comes to dominate other aspects and leads to an imbalance, if not in Calvin, in those who sought to interpret and apply his theological method.

In chapter 4 Calvin's legacy is traced in and compared to the pneumatology of the *Scots Confession* and the *Westminster Confession*. In analysing the perspectives of the two *Confessions*, we will observe how they deal with three functions of the Spirit which can be identified in Calvin's thought: the Spirit as an epistemic agent, the suprarational work of the Spirit and the Spirit as an executor of God's elective decision.

In chapters 5 and 6 the attempts of Edward Irving and Thomas F. Torrance to redress the imbalances which occurred in the Scottish context are examined, set within the theological context of their own times. In particular, we observe how they have interpreted the Person and function of the Spirit in the light of their differing Trinitarian concerns.

In chapter 7 we examine and compare the work of two contemporary theologians who, both having experienced something of the Charismatic Movement, have produced contrasting interpretations of how the Spirit should be viewed within a Trinitarian context. In chapter 8 we conclude our study by framing an alternative model of the Trinity, drawing on our observations both of the Charismatic Movement and the development of pneumatology in the Scottish context. In arguing for a renewed focus on God's salvific economy, we seek after a fresh, Trinitarian understanding whereby we can come to a fuller awareness of the Person and function of the Holy Spirit, as He seeks to be active and present in our lives today.

Chapter 1

The Charismatic Movement in Scotland

1.1 Introduction

How can we best describe or define the Charismatic Movement as it appeared in Scotland? We are faced with a phenomenon, rather than as a structured or homogeneous organisation. Although structures did evolve as the Movement grew and time passed, the Charismatic Movement's beginnings are not to be traced in a self-conscious attempt to orchestrate or organise a new theological perspective but are to be seen as arising from a common cause embraced by individuals who, in coming together to form relationships with one another, shared a suprarational experience of the Holy Spirit in their lives.

One distinctive characteristic of the Scottish Charismatic Movement is found in that its beginnings are traced not within the sectarian, minority groupings of the Pentecostals but among relationships formed between individual Christians in the historic denominations. Where the beginnings of what became Pentecostalism are commonly identified with events at Azusa Street in 1906, the origins of the Charismatic Movement can most readily be associated with the ministry and influence of Dennis Bennett, whose autobiographical account of his personal renewal in the Holy Spirit, *Nine O'Clock in the Morning*,[1] was to be read widely by many who were looking for a fresh experience of God. Bennett's intimation in 1959, to his Episcopalian congregation of Van Nuys, California, that he had been 'baptised in the Spirit'[2] and had spoken in tongues, marked the beginning of a Movement that would quickly spread throughout North America and into Europe, a Movement which carried, as a central tenet, the importance of the individual Christian experiencing the reality and presence of the Holy Spirit in a direct and personal way. The Charismatic Movement, from its inception, emphasised a reception and experience of the Holy Spirit by the individual Christian.

There were those who perceived, early on, a need to set the Renewal within the corporate context of the church. In England the Fountain Trust was launched in 1964. Its first director, Michael Harper, visited Bennett in the USA

---

[1] First British edition published by Coverdale House, London, 1971.
[2] In Charismatic circles, the expressions 'baptism in the Spirit' and 'the baptism of the Spirit' are treated as synonymous. We will treat them as such throughout our study. Similarly, the Holy Spirit will more commonly be referred to as 'the Spirit'.

in 1965. With the declared object of promoting renewal within the whole church, the Fountain Trust that year commenced publication of the magazine *Renewal*. Ten years later, an anniversary edition of the magazine would boast that no 'new church party' had been formed by the Trust.[3] This call to a general, renewed corporate awareness of the Holy Spirit in the church, as distinct from individual experience, was not, however, the only one to be sounded in 1964. That same year the American, explicitly Neo-Pentecostal organisation for Christian laity, the Full Gospel Business Men's Fellowship International (FGBMFI), held its first British conference in London. The emphasis of the FGBMFI was unashamedly individualistic, encouraging men and women towards faith in Christ and personal renewal in the Holy Spirit. At its outset, the Charismatic message could not readily be distinguished from the Pentecostal.

Indeed, the early message of the Charismatic Renewal, despite its origin among members of historic denominations, was unambiguously Neo-Pentecostal. Participants and publications alike promoted the belief that there might occur a distinctive experience in the individual believer's life which could be termed 'the baptism in the Holy Spirit', accompanied by glossolalia. Both FGBMFI meetings and Bennett's book typified the sense of the Movement, focusing on a shared testimony of God working to produce this effect, in a direct and experienced way, in the believer's life.[4] Theological reflection was not an issue. What appeared to matter was experience of God, not theological comprehension of Him.

While the amorphous nature of the Charismatic Movement makes its early developments difficult to define, we can attempt to trace an evolution of thought within the Movement as it appeared in Scotland. Specifically, two events, the formation of the Fountain Trust in 1964 and the founding of Scottish Churches Renewal in 1974, punctuate and act as watersheds for the development of the Movement within the Scottish context. Consequently, we can divide our review of the Charismatic Movement's development into three periods: before 1964, 1964-74 and after 1974.

1.2   Before 1964

Prior to 1964 and the first effects of the Charismatic Movement's development

---

[3] *Renewal*, 53, (1974), p. 3.
[4] The centrality of 'giving a testimony', which is an account of personal conversion or seminal Christian experience, or the account of an individual's 'baptism in the Spirit' remains a central feature of FGBMFI meetings. In Bennett's book, the initial two chapters centre on the need for vitality in the faith and how this can be found in the life of Christians today. This potential is discussed through the use of a distinctively narrative, biographical style. In chapter 3, entitled 'It came with the Package', Bennett clearly identifies glossolalia as a sign of 'baptism in the Spirit'.

in the USA, the legacy of Pentecostalism, as it arose in the early years of the twentieth century, had limited influence in the Scottish context, bringing more influence to bear on smaller groupings than on the larger denominations. This fact is reflected in the limited growth of Pentecostal denominations in Scotland. Although there were some significant moves forward in the early years of the Pentecostal Movement, as in the establishment of the Kilsyth church and the labours of Donald Gee,[5] the influence of Pentecostals was largely restricted to the centres of urban population. The Pentecostal Movement was a pioneering and homogeneous movement, highly evangelistic in its ethos. This homogeneity was a strength; but, when placed in the context of a nation such as Scotland, it meant that Pentecostalism came to be seen as a largely foreign import, gaining little social recognition. It is no coincidence that the main impetus for Pentecostal church growth took place in growing urban situations, where society was less structured and settled. For our purposes, of more significance was the influence which the early Pentecostals had upon groupings which already held an emphasis upon spiritual experience of and personal encounter with the Holy Spirit. A representative of this strain is found in Hugh Black, a school teacher and a founder of the Struthers Memorial Church in Greenock.[6]

Black, born in 1923 and raised in Brethren circles, dated his 'baptism in the Holy Spirit' to 1943. This experience was, for Black, to be interpreted in Pentecostal terms, as it was accompanied with the sign of glossolalia. For Black such an experience did not denote the beginning of the Christian life or communion with the Holy Spirit; but the 'baptism in the Holy Spirit' ushered in a deeper realisation of the Christian's true inheritance in Jesus Christ. Christian life itself is rooted in a conscious, personal realisation of salvation: a personal assurance of faith which was, for Black, essential and basic to the Christian life. The Pentecostal experience is but the crowning of faith, a flowering and deeper realisation of our rightful inheritance in union with Jesus Christ.

Through Black we can detect the presence of earlier theological strains in the Scottish context which, in some measure, served to prepare the way for the appearance of the Charismatic Movement. Firstly, there is the adoption of an anthropocentric reference to conversion, with an emphasis on the responsibility of the individual in making a response to the 'offer' of salvation. This is reflected in Black's thought in a way that marks him as typical of his

---

[5] The establishment of a Pentecostal work at Kilsyth in 1908 is recorded in Gee's history of the Pentecostal Movement, *Wind and Flame,* Heath Press, Croydon, 1967. Gee, a leading British Pentecostal, was from 1920 to 1930 the pastor of a Pentecostal congregation at Bonnington Toll, Leith.

[6] Black has published a number of devotional works. His publishing house is named 'New Dawn Books' of Greenock. His principal works are *Reflections on the Baptism of the Holy Spirit* (1987), *The Clash of Tongues with Glimpses of Revival* (1988) and *Reflections on the Gifts of the Holy Spirit* (1988).

generation, through a stress on the Finneyite conversion experience. This is a theological perspective of Christian conversion expressed in Finney's immensely popular work, *Lectures on Revivals of Religions*, the influence of which was sealed, in Scotland, through the Second Great Awakening of 1859. For Finney, Christians are as guilty for not having the Spirit, where He is experientially absent from their lives, as sinners are for not repenting; in fact, more so. As Christians have more light, they are so much the more guilty for not having the Spirit, for

> All beings have a right to complain of Christians who have not the Spirit. You are not doing the work of God, and he has a right to complain. He has placed his Spirit at your disposal and if you have it not, he has a right to look to you and hold you responsible for the good you might do, did you possess it....[7]

The action of God is seen in the cooperative agency of the Holy Spirit present with and joined to the individual Christian. The initiative in maintaining and deepening communion between the Christian and God does not lie in God's hands but with the individual. Certainly, Finney identifies certain reasons as to why the Spirit of God might not dwell with men, such as when their moral attitude is wrong: moral laxity will inhibit the work of the Spirit of God.[8] It is, however, within the capacity of man to come to the point where the Holy Spirit can be known and recognised in the believer's life. Where there is a problem bringing this about, it occurs through a resisting of the Spirit by the individual, rather than a reticence on the part of God to reach out.

Because of this foundational, Finneyite understanding of the Spirit at work in the individual Christian life, Black's perception of the 'baptism in the Holy Spirit' was interpreted as an experience of the Spirit which was subsequent to Christian conversion and distinguishable from the ongoing presence and work of the Spirit that commences at the time of the conversion experience. An understanding of the ongoing work of the Spirit was strengthened by the influence of Holiness theology, itself founded on the Perfectionist theology of John Wesley. Black emphasised personal holiness in a way consonant with the Keswick Convention's tradition of teaching a gradual increase in sanctification.[9] This conviction regarding the need to seek after the Spirit was crowned with the expectation of a further Pentecostal 'baptism in the Spirit'.

Other features, however, are to be found in Black's thought. We find the influence of Black's association with Duncan Campbell, a key figure in the

---

[7] C. Finney, *Lectures on Revivals of Religions*, W. G. McLoughlin (Editor), Harvard University Press, Cambridge, Mass., 1960, p. 122.

[8] Finney, *Lectures on Revivals of Religions*, p. 111.

[9] The notion of sudden and instantaneous sanctification, a view preferred in American Holiness traditions that served as the precursors of modern Pentecostalism, had limited impact in Scotland.

Lewis Revival.[10] Campbell's own theology[11] helps us understand the complex weave of features present in Black's thought. From 1958 to 1966, Campbell was the Principal of the Faith Mission Training Home and Bible College in Edinburgh. Campbell also emphasised the importance of personal holiness but added to it the need for a sovereign work of God's Spirit in bringing revival to the nation. Campbell acknowledged that it is the redemptive work of Christ which saves us from the forces of hell but stressed that central to the Christian message was the necessary response of faith which must be accompanied by a consecration to holiness of life. Revival is related to holiness among Christians, for the Christian is entrusted with manifesting Christ's character in the world.

Although Campbell believed in sanctification as a process, he also affirmed the validity of a definite experience of the Spirit subsequent to conversion that would assist and aid in this process of sanctification. Campbell himself did not associate this with a specifically Pentecostal doctrine of glossolalia; yet for Black, Campbell's perception of an experience of the Spirit subsequent to conversion was readily married to a Pentecostal understanding of the Holy Spirit at work in an experience which itself was subsequent to the conversion experience. Black concluded that 'baptism in the Holy Spirit' was an experience bringing help in holiness, enabling the cause of Christian revival and deeper intimacy with God. Such an experience, if valid, could hardly be held as anything other than a vital feature of the Christian life.

To summarise, four strands of thought can be traced in Black, illustrative of an understanding of the Holy Spirit which was present prior to 1964 and which would affect the Charismatic Movement's early development in Scotland. Firstly, we find the Finneyite stress on the volition of individual Christians in looking to receive not only salvation but also in being open to a greater reception and working of the Holy Spirit within their lives. Secondly, we can trace the effect of the Holiness Movement, in stressing the need for personal holiness and the individual's responsibility in seeking after Christian perfection. Thirdly, we note a belief that this further pursuit of the Spirit's enabling, far from being for selfish satisfaction, was necessary for the furthering of the Christian cause. Fourthly, we see a type of Pentecostalism that looked for a reception of the Spirit in a manner which brought deeper intimacy with God, expressed through speaking in tongues, or glossolalia.

Black's thought and writings can be described as Neo-Pentecostal in that they represented in the Scottish context the confluence of Finneyite, Holiness and Revivalist thinking married to a Pentecostal pietism which found, in glossolalia, a renewed and deep expression of intimacy with God. In this way

---

[10] Black was involved with Campbell in the later stages of the Lewis Revival of 1949-52, the most recent account of which is the work by Colin and Mary Peckham, *Sounds from Heaven*, Christian Focus, Fearn, 2004.

[11] Discussed in A. Woosley, *Duncan Campbell: A Biography*, Hodder & Stoughton, London, 1974.

the Pentecostal message, with its distinctive emphasis on an experience of the Spirit subsequent to conversion, could be the more easily integrated into strains of thought already present in Scotland, albeit mainly in a non-conformist setting. At the heart of this message lay the conviction that life with God, wherein God reveals Himself through His involvement with Christians, is to be experienced by the Christian in a manner which affirms a suprarational function of the Spirit, yet, at the same time, in a way which is consciously perceived and appreciated by the Christian believer.

To what degree was suprarational experience, in this context, taken as self-evidently experience of God? Black understood that Christian conversion, involving a confessional element, precedes 'baptism in the Spirit'. An emphasis on the suprarational experience of the Spirit is not the exclusive foundation of his theology of the Spirit. At the same time suprarational experience, as well as the formation of faith and holiness, is construed as integral to the ministry of the Holy Spirit. It is the presence of this characteristic, the propriety of an ongoing, suprarational experience of divine activity, rather than stress upon a distinctive moment of personal conversion or seminal experience subsequent to Christian conversion, which would provide the continuity linking this period of Neo-Pentecostalism with later developments in the Charismatic Movement within Scotland.

1.3   1964-74

The early Charismatic Movement was both individualistic and Neo-Pentecostal. It was individualistic in that the beginnings of the Charismatic Renewal in Scotland were characterised by an emphasis on the renewal of individuals in their Christian experience, seeking to bring them into a deeper, experiential awareness of and walk with God. Concern at this stage was not with broader, ecclesiological issues. The means of effecting this renewal was seen by participants to be the Pentecostal experience, applied to the lives of individuals. The early Charismatic Movement was Neo-Pentecostal and in this sense the message of Charismatic renewal, as brought to Scotland in the early 1960s, was not a new one. The difference lay in the constituency to which the message was addressed and by whom it was received. A portion of the historic church was opened, for the first time, to the influence of Pentecostal teachings presented in a fresh way.

The significance of the Fountain Trust's institution in 1964 lay not only in that it marked the appearance of a clearly Charismatic organisation in Britain but that it sought to supplement the Neo-Pentecostal stress on personal renewal with the promotion of corporate renewal within the historic denominations. The Fountain Trust's stress on renewal in the Holy Spirit was not restricted to a Pentecostal perspective. It opened the way for the Charismatic Movement to evolve out of its Neo-Pentecostal origins. With Anglicans as its first general secretary and trustees, the Fountain Trust's basic aims[12] indicated a commitment not only to the experience of individual renewal in the Holy Spirit but to a wider mandate which would embrace the corporate dimension of the church, both in its local and universal expressions.

In Scotland a Charismatic perspective on the work of the Spirit that looked beyond the individual was slower to emerge, although the ethos of the Fountain Trust was readily endorsed by participants of Charismatic Renewal within the historic Scottish churches. The beginnings of a Charismatic theology of the Spirit in Scotland can best be traced in the accounts of individuals who were influenced by the new emphases that the Charismatic Movement brought.

One such man was Brian Casebow who, in 1959, was inducted into the Church of Scotland charge of St. Margaret's, Motherwell. Casebow had contact with students at New College, Edinburgh, through his friendship with a theological student, Gordon Strachan. Some students were receiving the American Neo-Pentecostal journal, *Trinity*.[13] Casebow recalls how, by 1961, he felt a growing thirst for the Holy Spirit's reality.[14] It was at this time that he found himself looking to and embracing the Charismatic message, accepting the Pentecostal teaching on the 'baptism of the Spirit' and the demonstrative place of glossolalia, although not yet himself speaking in them. This latter phenomenon first occurred for Casebow in May 1963, while he was alone and at prayer in his study. Another minister affected at this time was the then pastor of Springburn Baptist Church, David Black. Black's first awareness of the Pentecostal message and a thirst for what it promised had come after his introduction to the Springburn charge in 1963. During a meeting which he attended, held in Scottish Churches' House in 1964, David Black was prayed for, first by Hugh Black and, after the meeting, by the Baptist Ken Dougal and the Presbyterian Tom Smail. Thereafter, Black recalls, he experienced what he identifies as a 'baptism in the Holy Spirit':

---

[12] Peter Hocken, in his study on the early development of the Charismatic Movement in England, comments that 'the Fountain Trust was devised as, and functioned strictly as, a service agency'. He goes on to note that the three aims of the Fountain Trust were:

1. To encourage Christians of all churches to receive the power of the Holy Spirit and to glorify Christ by manifesting in their lives the fruit and gifts of the same Spirit, so that they may enrich their worship, strengthen their witness and deepen their fellowship.
2. To encourage local churches to experience renewal in the Holy Spirit and to recover the full ministry of the Holy Spirit including that of healing.
3. To encourage Christians to expect and pray for worldwide revival.

P. Hocken, *Streams of Renewal*, Paternoster Press, Exeter, 1986, p. 125.

[13] *Trinity* was first published in 1961 by The Blessed Trinity Society, which was founded in 1960 by Jean Stone, a member of Bennett's congregation in California. The publication was committed to a Pentecostal theology, in that it viewed glossolalia as a sign of the 'baptism in the Holy Spirit'.

[14] Recorded interview: 9 May 1991.

It was psychologically releasing and was a total experience: from that point onward I could never have doubted the reality of God.[15]

There was no apparent intent, at this point, of seeking to establish a Pentecostal foothold within the traditional churches. On the contrary, there was continued fellowship and support among those seeking, in the broader sense, a suprarational experience of God both within and beyond the Charismatic constituency. This is demonstrated in the case of Tom Smail, inducted into the Church of Scotland charge of Thornley Church, Wishaw, in 1962. Smail was influenced by a group of members from his congregation who, on visiting the island of Iona, had met Keith Edwards, a member of the Iona Community from a Gorbals charge, who had himself entered into the Charismatic experience. A subsequent visit to Thornley Church by Edwards occasioned Smail's own introduction to the Neo-Pentecostal message. From that time there developed a group of young ministers, variously influenced by the message which was being freshly promulgated from the USA, who began to meet together to share and discuss their common experience, going on to conduct public, monthly meetings in and around the Motherwell area.[16] In 1964 this group extended its first invitation to Dennis Bennett and Jean Stone to attend public conferences in Scotland, thereby settling the main pattern of early Charismatic influence.

In summary, it can be said that in the period 1964-74 the evolving character of the early Charismatic Movement was best reflected in the ethos of the Fountain Trust, in seeking to promote the spiritual renewal both of the individual Christian and of the churches to which 'renewed' individuals belonged. What distinguished the emerging Charismatic Renewal from Pentecostalism was that it sought to encourage spiritual renewal within the denominational structures in which its participants found themselves. Through to the early 1970s, there appears to have been a positive expectation by participants of the Charismatic Renewal that the growing Movement would have a decisive effect on the spiritual renewal of historic churches throughout the land and, subsequently, in the stirring of revival in the nation. Observers also found signs of hope within the Charismatic Movement for the church at large. As Dr. Horace Walker of the Church of Scotland Home Board noted during his speech at the 1973 General Assembly stewardship debate, there appeared to be evidence of fresh spiritual experiences among young people affected by the Charismatic Movement. What was needed was 'a fresh baptism of the Holy Spirit, a new Pentecost'.[17] The potential of the Charismatic

---

[15] Recorded interview: 5 February 1990. As with Casebow, this experience occurred for Black during a time of private and personal devotion.

[16] Evening meetings with local congregations would comprise a time of praise, followed by personal testimony of experiencing the Spirit. Thereafter, questions would be invited from the congregation to the panel of ministers.

[17] Editorial, *Renewal*, (45), 1973, p. 3.

Movement was apparent. Positive expectation was at its height.

1.4   After 1974

The first development of a peculiarly Scottish dimension to the Charismatic Renewal came in 1971, with a meeting held in the Renfrew Church Centre. This was organised by David Black who in 1974 became the first director of Scottish Churches Renewal. Black's appointment reflected the hope that there might occur within the Scottish context what had been accomplished by the Fountain Trust through its successful promotion of spiritual renewal in England.[18] The effect of the Charismatic message upon the churches was now, however, beginning to change. There had arisen some cases of schism between those who had welcomed the new, experiential emphasis and those who opposed it. Some participants of the Renewal became aware that this called for a greater degree of sensitivity towards those who would not embrace the Neo-Pentecostal doctrine of subsequence, if the declared intent of promoting Charismatic renewal within the established churches was to be sustained. This was reflected in the declared aims of the Scottish Churches Renewal, or SCR.[19] The omission of any reference to a specific experience of 'baptism in the Holy Spirit', accompanied by glossolalia, was understandable, given that the second stated aim of SCR was to seek after 'a balanced faith which seeks to avoid the dangers of fanaticism and division'.

It was felt that, where the Charismatic message emphasised experience of the Spirit and not the momentary distinctions of conversion and 'baptism in the Spirit', the message could be absorbed into the theological traditions within which the participants stood. This intent was confirmed by a statement, contained in the first newsheet issued by SCR, that

---

[18] It was at the time noted in *Renewal* that Black had been appointed to 'an organisation similar to the Fountain Trust which has been set up in Scotland to serve the churches north of the border in spiritual and charismatic renewal'. *Renewal*, (54), 1974, p. 4.

[19] The four stated aims of SCR were:

  1. The renewal of the life of the Christian church in Scotland by the recovery of the full ministry of the Holy Spirit in the body of Christ.

  2. To encourage Christians to know the release of the power of the Holy Spirit in their lives and to glorify the Lord Jesus Christ by manifesting the fruit and gifts of the Spirit so that, by a balanced faith which seeks to avoid the dangers of fanaticism and division, they may enrich their worship, strengthen their witness and deepen their walk with God.

  3. To endeavour by all means to serve the local churches, recognising that spiritual renewal must operate at the local level.

  4. To encourage Christians to pray and prepare for revival in Scotland.

It is not the intention to form an organisation as such, or to pressurise anyone into
a particular theology or viewpoint of the Baptism of the Holy Spirit ...[20]

Optimism over the potential of the Charismatic Movement was to be found not
only among participants. The expectation of the Charismatics, of playing a role
in the renewal of the historic churches,[21] was complemented by a belief among
some ecumenical leaders that the Charismatics had something genuine to
contribute. A positive response was made by SCR to a proposition coming from
the executive committee of the Scottish Council of Churches, that an advisory
group be appointed to aid SCR;[22] and that this group be gathered under the
auspices of the Mission, Development and Unity Committee of the Scottish
Council of Churches.

This attempt to graft the Charismatic Renewal into the mainstream of
Scottish ecumenism came as the mid-1970s marked the high point of the
Charismatic Movement in Scotland. Conferences were held at St. Andrews in
the summers of 1976, 1977 and 1978 with, as guest speakers, American
Episcopalians Dennis and Rita Bennett. Jim Graham, an expatriate Scottish
Baptist from Goldhill in the south of England, appeared with Scottish speakers
such as David Black and the Roman Catholic Mark Dilworth. In 1976, at the
first of the residential conferences at St. Andrews, the speakers included Dennis
Bennett and Pentecostal Cecil Cousen. In 1977 the SCR issued the first edition
of the periodical *Scottish Renewal* and David Black, as director of SCR, went
on an exploratory visit to Charismatic churches in the USA in February of that
year. Expectancy and energy were the hallmarks of the time.

Other factors, however, were beginning to shape the Charismatic Movement
in Scotland. With the advent of SCR there came a growing sensitivity both to
an apparent rejection of spiritual renewal by many within the historic
denominations, as well as a growing awareness of further developments in the
USA, England and Scotland which married the Charismatic Movement to
newly-evolving church structures. In particular, this was seen in the developing
'house church movement' and in the practice of 'shepherding',[23] both in the
USA and in England. Not all were hostile to this ecclesiological dimension
being superimposed on the earlier emphasis of personal, individual renewal,
which had been the hallmark of the 1960s. As David Black commented on his

---

[20] *SCR Newsheet*, May 1974.

[21] The editorial in *Renewal*, 54 (1974), noted that SCR 'is affiliated to the Mission,
Development and Unity committee of the Scottish Council of Churches, which now
recognises that the Charismatic Movement has a vital role to play in the ecumenical
movement'.

[22] Black commended the proposal to the SCR interim advisory committee in a letter of 5
September 1975. He believed that this link would help in 'the development of our aims
throughout Scotland'.

[23] A hierarchical, authoritarian form of church life, where an individual 'shepherd' is
given spiritual authority over the life of other Christians.

return from the USA trip, there appeared to be a positive side to the new emphases, especially evident in the ministries of Bob Mumford and Derek Prince, where there arose

> a discipline which can only be beneficial to the church. While here in the U.K. the 'house churches' follow this emphasis, it is also seen in the teaching of many historic churches, and recently a number in Scotland have indicated their recognition and acceptance of this 'shepherding'.[24]

Part of the difficulty was a growing tension and impatience in some quarters at what was felt to be a lack of response from the historic churches towards the Charismatic Movement's message of spiritual renewal. If the Charismatic Movement had a message from God to be received by Christians and the church, why was this not happening? As Black comments at the end of his report,

> God can bypass ministers and churches when they refuse to be open to 'what the Spirit is saying to the churches'.[25]

So it is that, by the turn of the 1980s, we see an increasing sense of frustration arising from the Charismatic constituency, in not being able to carry its message to the centre of church life in the nation. The reasons for that were perhaps not all one sided. As the then chairman of the Charismatic coordinating group mooted, prior to a meeting in 1982,

> Do we create suspicion among our neighbours because we attach too much importance to the gifts of the Spirit? Is our theology too 'woolly'? Are there still not Charismatic groups that universalise the particular and insist that everyone must experience baptism of the Holy Spirit as a 'second blessing' or that all must be able to speak in tongues?[26]

When SCR agreed to disband in 1984, it was clear that many of the hopes for integrating the Charismatic Movement into the mainstream of Scottish church life had been dashed by the inability of the developing Charismatic Movement to find the acceptance it had looked for. Instead, what occurred was a growth in splinter groups and parachurch organisations to accommodate those who wished to pursue a Charismatic emphasis, free from the fetters of traditional, ecclesiastical structures.[27]

---

[24] Black's Report to SCR, p. 7.
[25] Black's Report to SCR, p. 8.
[26] In a letter from Stewart Lang to Jim Rennie, 25 February 1982.
[27] At the SCR coordinators' meeting of 21-22 February 1984, it was noted that the number of local SCR prayer groups had diminished. The growing influence of four other groups was suggested as being a factor in this: the FGBMFI, the Lydia Fellowship, the Catholic Charismatic Renewal and the emergence of new, independent Fellowships.

The ministry of Hugh Clark, the leader of the largest of the new, charismatic churches,[28] lay in this latter category. Brought up in a Salvation Army home in the Motherwell area, Clark was deeply influenced by the ministry of Elim Evangelist Alexander Tee and, at the age of eighteen, entered the Pentecostal experience of 'baptism in the Spirit' accompanied by glossolalia. His growth in the Elim Church continued until, in the 1970s, his musical and organisational skills were combined in directing a Scottish production of the Christian musical, 'Come Together'. This catalyst formed a group of people which grew until, in 1981, Clark left the Elim Church and founded a new, independent church in Coatbridge, moving to the present building, the King's Centre in Motherwell, in 1986. In the growth of experimental ministry, first as part-time, lay pastor of the Coatbridge Elim Church, Clark looked for support from others who had developed in the Charismatic tradition; and this was readily provided from among the more developed Charismatic Movements in the USA and England.[29] A similar story is found in the case of Stewart Brunton, founding leader of the Gate Fellowship in Dundee. Brunton gained help in the mid-1970s from men such as Hugh Black of Greenock, but later looked south to England, developing links with the pioneering church work of the House Church leader, Gerald Coates. Throughout the independent, Charismatic churches in Scotland we see the lines of dependency stretching to the USA and England, with a limited degree of consolidation within Scotland itself.[30]

This brief review of the Charismatic Movement's development in Scotland has outlined the appearance, growth and demise of a movement for spiritual renewal in the Christian church. The apparent failure of the Charismatic Movement in achieving its goal of national, Christian renewal is the issue that provides the motivation for this study. What theological considerations might there have been in aiding and abetting this divorce of the new, Charismatic churches from the mainstream of the Scottish church; and to what degree can such factors be attributed to pneumatological suppositions and Trinitarian perceptions adhered to among the churches in the land? What are the critical, theological issues which the Charismatic Movement raises when viewed from within the theological framework of the Scottish context? Before attempting to address these questions, we will first have to note how the Charismatic Movement was viewed by the wider Scottish church.

---

[28] The King's Church, Motherwell.

[29] Clark developed early contacts with Mike Pussey of the independent King's Church in Aldershot. In the 1970's contact was made with Derek Prince in Fort Lauderdale, Florida, the home of *New Wine* magazine and the 'shepherding' group, Christian Growth Ministries, of which Prince was a member.

[30] Some attempt at uniting the separate strands of independent Charismatic churches in Scotland has been made, principally by Hugh Clark, under the auspices of the 'Charismatic Leaders Conferences'. This attempt has met with limited success.

1.5   The Historic Churches

Within the Scottish context, the advent of the Charismatic Movement evoked a considered response and discussion from within both the Church of Scotland and the Baptist Union of Scotland. Other parts of the church in Scotland were also affected. From the early 1970s, the influence of the Charismatic Movement could be traced within the Roman Catholic church, enjoying the approval of both Cardinal Gray and Archbishop Winning. The Roman Catholic movement, however, remained principally a movement of laity[31] and, theologically, was largely absorbed within the liturgical framework of the denomination. As Mark Dilworth, the late Abbot of the Benedictine Abbey at Fort Augustus and an early participant within the Charismatic Movement in Scotland observed,

> What Catholics mean by this so-called 'baptism in the Holy Spirit' is that the Sacramental Baptism and Confirmation they have already received begin to have the transforming effect they are supposed to have. The Holy Spirit was there but his power was dormant; now it is released. No new sacrament has been received; any laying on of hands is simply a visible sign that the bystanders were praying earnestly. We are quite clear on the point. Baptism and Confirmation are sacraments; prayer for the release of the Spirit, with or without the laying on of hands, is not.[32]

Where the Charismatic Renewal has led to the emergence of a Charismatic Renewal Fellowship within the Scottish Episcopal church, developments there mirrored and were largely shaped by the Charismatic Renewal within the Church of England, not by Scottish sources. It is from within the Church of Scotland and the Baptist Union of Scotland that we can most clearly identify an attempt to respond to the theological issues raised by the Charismatic Movement in Scotland. We begin by looking at the response from the larger of the two denominations, the national Church of Scotland.

1.6   The Church of Scotland

The Charismatic Movement's growing influence was brought to the attention of the Church of Scotland's General Assembly at a time when the Kirk was engaged in a period of major review and reappraisal. In 1971 the 'Committee of Forty' was appointed with the remit,

---

[31] Mark Dilworth estimated that some 1% of practising Scottish Catholics are members of the Catholic Renewal, with some 5% of the clergy involved.
'Renewal and Scottish Catholics in Renewal', *Renewal* 86 (1980), p. 29.
[32] Unpublished paper by M. Dilworth, 'Charismatic Renewal and Scottish Catholics', undated, p.11.

to interpret for the church the purpose towards which God is calling His people in Scotland, to investigate and assess the resources of the church in persons and in property for the fulfilment of this purpose, and to make recommendations for the reshaping of the life and structure of the church.[33]

The previous year had seen the first moves towards a review of the *Westminster Confession*'s status within the Kirk. It appeared that there was a growing atmosphere of openness to change. At the General Assembly of 1972, it was proposed and accepted that

The General Assembly instruct the Panel [on Doctrine] to examine afresh the doctrine of the Holy Spirit, with particular reference to the gifts of the Spirit and in the light of the contemporary Charismatic or Neo-Pentecostal movement, and to report to the Assembly in 1974.[34]

A working party was set up by the Panel on Doctrine and an interim report was presented in 1973.[35] The interim report made it clear that certain criteria in considering the Charismatic Movement had been identified and were to be used in compiling the final report.[36] The first of these was an understanding of the function of the Holy Spirit. While acknowledging that the church can and does at times resist the prompting of the Holy Spirit, it was to be clearly stated that Reformed theology saw the Holy Spirit's ministry as testifying to the ascended Christ, revealing His presence and present reality to the church. Specifically, the 'real presence' of Christ in the eucharist was cited as an example of this ministry. Secondly, it was laid down in the interim report that the Spirit was to be understood as coming to the whole church, which is the body of Christ. Any understanding of the gifts of the Spirit had to be set within the wider context of the church's corporate nature and Christ's lordship over it. Thirdly, it was made clear that specific manifestations of the Spirit's presence should be interpreted within the context of the Spirit's role of harbinger of peace. Neo-Pentecostalism might well be found to have a place within the church; but it was not the decisive indicator of the Spirit's presence.

   That there was a reference in the interim report to the widespread influence of the Charismatic Movement across the worldwide church was significant. As we noted earlier with reference to relations between SCR and the Scottish Council of Churches, in some quarters of the Kirk the Charismatic Movement was seen as a new and possibly potent vehicle in the pursuit of a deeper ecumenism: this factor alone would have commended its further investigation

---

[33] *Assembly Reports*, 1971, p.829.

[34] *Assembly Reports*, 1972, p.18 (coloured section).

[35] *Assembly Reports*, 1973, pp. 219-20. The interim Report of the Panel, on 'The Work and Gifts of the Holy Spirit', made clear that its concern with the Charismatic Movement arose out of the Movement's contemporary, ecumenical significance.

[36] *Assembly Reports*, 1973, p. 220.

to many who otherwise were not inclined towards Pentecostalism in either their devotional outlook or experience. The very inter-denominational character of the Charismatic Movement's gathering momentum gave rise to hope that here was a powerful, common denominator that might help in bringing revival to the whole, universal Church.

At the same time, this very openness towards the Charismatic Movement could well have given rise to another difficulty, in failing to encourage a dispassionate, critical appraisal of the emphasis on suprarational experience which lay at the heart of the Charismatic Movement's appeal. An optimistic hope of consolidating the vitality of the Charismatics within the theological *status quo* of the church might obscure the real areas of divergence between a pneumatological perspective, which held that the church, as a corporate entity, had received the gift of the Spirit, and one that focused on the individual within the church as an experiencer of the Holy Spirit, who blows where He wills.

The Panel on Doctrine was well aware of the challenge which the Charismatic Movement presented in the area of ecclesiology. The opening section of the final Report[37] in 1974 acknowledged the Panel's indebtedness to two earlier reports, both from American Presbyterian churches, which had recently been published.[38] These reports had critiqued the Neo-Pentecostal perception of the Holy Spirit's Person and work. From this starting point, the Panel appears to have looked at the Charismatic Movement as a Neo-Pentecostal phenomenon appearing within the historic churches. On that basis, the Panel's Report went on to preface its assessment of Neo-Pentecostalism with four observations.[39] In the first place, it was affirmed that there could be no place for tritheism, in treating the Holy Spirit independently of the Father and the Son. Secondly, a clear and legitimate association, although not identification, should be made between the presence and work of the Holy Spirit and the presence and witness of the church. Thirdly, any understanding of 'baptism in the Holy Spirit' should not usurp the priority of water baptism as the church's rite of initiation; nor, fourthly, should the acceptance of spiritual gifts associated with 'baptism in the Holy Spirit' be taken as inferring that less significance should be attached to other gifts present and manifest within the church. There could be no place for an elitist notion of a 'spiritual' church within the church catholic.

Having established its viewpoint that the theology of the Charismatic Movement was primarily Neo-Pentecostal, the Report proceeded to a broad review of Pentecostalism's understanding of the Person and work of the Holy Spirit followed by a critique of Neo-Pentecostalism, drawn from various sources, including the Reformer John Calvin and the nineteenth century

---

[37] Report of the Panel on Doctrine on *The Charismatic Movement within the Church of Scotland*, in *Assembly Reports*, 1974, pp. 167-83.

[38] *Assembly Reports*, 1974, p. 167.

[39] *Assembly Reports*, 1974, pp. 165-6.

Scottish preacher Edward Irving. The Report's observations were wide ranging, seeking to address what were perceived to be varying issues raised by the Charismatic Movement. On some issues it reserved judgement.[40] On its central recommendations it was clear. The import of the Report's initial observations, noting the Charismatic Movement as an apparent challenge to orthodox Trinitarian thought and a threat to the proper marriage of pneumatology to ecclesiology, was reinforced. Neo-Pentecostal practices were, where possible, to be accommodated. Erroneous or potentially divisive theology was not.

While the 1974 Report grasped the ecclesiological question as the central issue, other questions did, however, remain unanswered. To what degree was it correct to assume that the Charismatic Movement was, as seen in the Scottish context, a Neo-Pentecostal phenomenon? In taking its starting point from the American reports, the 1974 Church of Scotland Report did not appear to recognise those developments, which we have noted through the 1960s and into the 1970s, within the contemporary, Scottish Charismatic Movement. The Report's main weakness lay in its assumption that Charismatic and Neo-Pentecostal were synonymous terms: an assumption which, as we have noted, was not necessarily true of the Scottish Charismatic Movement as it developed in the period after 1964. Moreover, by assuming that an emphasis on the suprarational experience of the Spirit implied a 'doctrine of subsequence', the Report treated this as synonymous to holding to a doctrine of 'entire sanctification' or Christian perfectibility and concluded,

> that this implies the rejection of the Reformed rediscovery of the biblical truth of *simul iustus et peccator*.[41]

It was unfortunate that an appraisal of the Charismatic Movement should be confused with a critique of Neo-Pentecostalism, leading to the Report's conclusion that the Charismatic emphasis on suprarational experience was to be understood in terms of a 'theology of subsequence'. The Charismatic message was presented as bringing a focus on the Spirit, rather than on the object of His operation, the Lord Jesus Christ. On this basis, the 1974 Report concluded that there was a danger of dichotomising the grace of God between that found in Christ and that present in the work of the Spirit.[42] As a later report of the Panel on Doctrine commented in 1976,

---

[40] E.g. on the helpfulness of identifying ecstatic utterances as demonic or otherwise. *Assembly Reports*, 1974, p. 179.

[41] *Assembly Reports*, 1974, p. 169.

[42] 'Pentecostals emphasise, not the oneness of God, but his threeness. [For them] the Holy Spirit has an existence of his own, and it is the encounter with the Holy Spirit, apart from and beyond the encounter with Christ, which makes the Christian's life complete'. *Assembly Reports*, 1974, p. 170.

The panel's remarks [in 1974] on the 'theology of subsequence', which were the main thrust of the Report, were generally commended by the Presbyteries.[43]

A more fundamental difficulty, however, arose not out of a misunderstanding but through an omission. By addressing the Charismatic Movement in Scotland as Neo-Pentecostal, with the accompanying inference that the underlying perception of the Spirit's work to be found therein was Pentecostal, the Report did not face a more basic challenge: that the Charismatic Movement's apparent success invited a reappraisal of how we can properly describe the Holy Spirit's presence and present activity within the church and among Christians. The Charismatic Movement spoke of experiencing the Holy Spirit. On this matter, concerning how we can speak of the Spirit as present and experienced both by the church and the individual in the immediate sense, the 1974 Report remained silent.

1.7   The Baptist Union of Scotland

The Baptist Union of Scotland provides us with an interesting contrast to the Kirk in the manner of its reception and understanding of the Charismatic Movement. While sharing many of the suppositions of the Kirk's Reformed tradition, the Baptists had been more heavily influenced by Finneyite convictions and that hybrid of Reformed and Wesleyan theology, rooted in the experience of mid-nineteenth century American revivalism, which was represented in the 1955 'All Scotland' Crusade of Billy Graham. In the early 1970s the Church of Scotland, in the face of declining attendances and falling membership, had sought to engage in a process of self-appraisal. The problems which precipitated this were not, however, unique to the national church. The Baptists, as with other parts of the church catholic in Scotland, were experiencing difficulty. The 1977 Scottish Baptist Assembly agreed to consider

necessary new structures to accommodate existing growth and to facilitate the achievement of Growth Goals adopted. It committed us to a radical rethinking...[44]

Against this background, at a time when denominational identity and purpose were in need of both reappraisal and reaffirmation, the Scottish Baptist Union's Doctrine and Inter-Church Relations Group was given the remit of considering

the doctrine of the church as the body of Christ, and especially the place of the fivefold ministry: to take into account the 'shepherding movement' and to consider the relation of water and Spirit baptism.[45]

---

[43] *Assembly Reports*, 1976, p. 140.
[44] Extract from the presidential address to the Scottish Baptist Assembly of 1978. *Scottish Baptist Year Book*, 1979, p. 93.

As the nature of the remit betrays, this analysis, which was effectively a report on the Charismatic Movement, was precipitated by developing events within Scotland. As in the case of the Church of Scotland's Report, the Baptist approach to the Charismatic Movement was reactive. Where the Baptist Union report differed was in the nature of those problems to which it reacted, problems which arose from the development of the Charismatic Movement in Scotland throughout the 1970s. Two features dominated the Baptist Union report.

Firstly, there was the reaction to a threat, perceived as present within the Charismatic Movement, to Baptist congregational identity and unity. Neo-Pentecostal pneumatology, in moving the focus from the central act of believers' baptism onto 'the baptism in the Holy Spirit', appeared to challenge Baptist ecclesiology, rejecting a Baptist conviction that all baptised believers were fully possessed of the Holy Spirit and thereby enabled, through the congregational meeting, to discern together God's will. For Scottish Baptists, congregational government was a principle which lay at the heart of church polity. This was further threatened by a growing association, in the 1970's, of the 'Shepherding Movement' with the new, independent Charismatic church structures in Scotland. In these new churches there had emerged some degree of acceptance of strong, oligarchical structures, a trait which, although possibly acceptable within Presbyterian and Episcopal circles, contrasted strongly with a Baptist emphasis on congregational government.[46]

Secondly, a reaction against the Charismatic emphasis on experiencing the Holy Spirit arose because such an experience was not associated with either conversion or believers' baptism. Where, through an absorption of strains in Holiness teaching and Finneyite revivalism, the Baptists were not uncomfortable with an emphasis on experiencing God, this had come to be focused on a conversion experience, consummated in the act of believers' baptism. Consequently, the report to the Scottish Baptist Assembly strongly reacted to a Neo-Pentecostal emphasis on glossolalia[47] as a criterion for determining the Holy Spirit's presence in the believer's life. Unlike the earlier Church of Scotland report, the Baptist Union report did not explicitly discount the notion of 'entire sanctification'; but the understanding that there might be a

---

[45] *Scottish Baptist Year Book*, 1979, p. 99.

[46] The perceived threat to congregationalism was reflected in the 1979 Report, where it was suggested that 'a great deal of caution should be exercised when new and totally unfamiliar ideas are thrust upon the local church, especially as new revelations, and all such new elements need to be tested by their conformity to Christ ... if the body is uniform or dominated by one member, then it is not a body in its true sense'. *Scottish Baptist Year Book*, 1979, pp. 99-102. Alex Russell, a Baptist pastor who was at one time a coordinator for SCR, warns of the danger of 'authoritarianism, isolation and confusion' in the 'non-denominational' fellowships in an article entitled, 'Grass not so green in non-denominational fellowships' in *Scottish Baptist*, December 1984, p. 18.

[47] *Scottish Baptist Year Book*, 1979, pp. 99-100.

further, seminal experience of the Spirit, posterior to baptism, was not acceptable.

This stress on an individual's experience of the Holy Spirit posed a threat to the unity of congregations which had, hitherto, found their congregational identity in the shared conversion experience of their members and in the practice of believers' baptism. Congregational independency, the active participation by members in Christian service, a simple biblical fundamentalism: these were emphases common to both Baptist churches and Charismatic groups. Baptist disavowal of both ecclesiological and credal formulae made their churches possibly more vulnerable than other denominational groupings to inroads by Charismatic elements who claimed, along with Baptists, both an experience of the grace of God and divinely appointed forms of church government, appealing to Biblical authority as a mandate for their teaching. Not least for these reasons, it was necessary for the Baptist Union of Scotland to take a stand against Charismatic teaching. This stand was made on the issue of the Spirit and experience, focusing on the Charismatic emphasis on experiencing the Spirit outwith the context of either conversion or baptism. This reaction is evidenced by a pamphlet version of the 1979 report, which states that

> the strong emphasis on experience and immediate revelation (vital though these are) may have led to a neglect of Scripture as the supreme source of truth and ground of authority.[48]

Where, in the face of the threat posed by the Charismatic Movement, the place of suprarational experience was minimised and appeal was made to the authority of Scripture, the Baptist Union retreated from facing questions which arose from Finneyite and Holiness influences latent within its own tradition, issues relating to the Person and function of the Spirit as encountered by Christians today. Instead of examining fundamental tenets of pneumatology, appeal was made to the high ground of the Spirit's revelational work and questions of Biblical hermeneutics. Traditional *theologoumena*, in this case the association of the conversion experience and baptism with the presence of the Holy Spirit were, however, difficult to defend in the face of those who claimed both Biblical authority and immediate, fresh inspiration given by the Holy Spirit. This was especially so in Baptist circles where, although normally implicitly accepted as based on Biblical authority, such *theologoumena* were, as we have already noted, detached from the safeguards of confessional formulae or supervisory, ecclesiastical structures.

Throughout the 1980s, as awareness of the Charismatic Movement continued to grow, tensions continued within the Baptist Union of Scotland. On

---

[48] *Scottish Baptists and the Charismatic Renewal Movement*, Baptist Union of Scotland Publications, undated, p. 4.

the one hand, there was a vitality which the Charismatic Movement appeared to offer the church. On the other hand, there were accepted viewpoints regarding the propriety of congregational government and the manner of the Spirit's operation upon and within the church. Certainly, for some, the whole issue of experiencing the Holy Spirit would better have been avoided. One contributor to *Scottish Baptist* cautioned, on observing that the Charismatics appeared to detach themselves from traditional Baptist values,

> Let us beware of a movement which flourishes best where the Bible is least known and which causes such terrible division within the ranks of Christian churches and fellowships today... .[49]

Despite the strength of such sentiments, the need to remain continually open to the prompting and movement of the Holy Spirit was generally accepted and recognised within the denomination. As Peter Barber, the then general secretary of the Scottish Baptist Union, observed in his annual report of 1981,

> We need as churches and individuals to know a greater openness to the Spirit. It is a pity that squabbling over the Charismatic Movement among believers has tended to close minds and lives to all that God wants to do among His people by the Spirit.[50]

The difficulty lay in understanding what, in practice, this 'openness' actually meant. Where fresh experience of the Holy Spirit led to an emphasis on individualism at the expense of congregational unity, it was to be rejected.

1.8   Towards a Theology of the Charismatic Movement

We have identified the hallmark of the Charismatic Movement as an emphasis on personal, suprarational experience of the Holy Spirit. In this experience, the Holy Spirit inducts the Christian into a conscious communion with the Divine. The Holy Spirit is understood to embrace and affect the whole being of man, with a deeper appreciation of God arising as a consequence to this experience. How, though, is this to be understood theologically? More particularly, what has it meant to those who have emphasised it? An answer to this question is not easily come by. A general difficulty encountered by interested observers who have sought to make an intelligent appraisal of the Charismatic Movement has been the apparent disinclination among its participants to address pertinent, theological issues. This failure has not necessarily been due to an anti-theological attitude. The nascent Charismatic Movement, as found in the Scottish context, owned a genealogy which was hidden in Wesleyan foundations: John Fletcher had spoken of 'baptism of the Holy Spirit' as an

---

[49] S. Pendrich, 'Is God doing a new thing?', in *Scottish Baptist*, December 1982, p. 12.
[50] *Scottish Baptist Year Book*, 1982, p. 32.

experience of personal assurance of spiritual well-being in his work, *Entire Sanctification*. A perception of the Spirit applying the benefit of salvation that was filtered through the influences of Finneyite, Holiness, Revivalist and Pentecostal thinking could be traced, albeit one foreign to the main, Reformed tradition of Scottish theology. There was, however, among exponents of Charismatic practice, an apparent lack of engagement with the Scottish Reformed theological tradition.

This failure among the Charismatics to engage with the Reformed tradition was married together with the assumption made by their critics that the Charismatic Movement was but Neo-Pentecostalism in another guise. Such an assumption was understandable. The first standard account of the Charismatic Movement to be published in Britain was Michael Harper's *As at the Beginning*, published in 1965. In this work, Harper sought to establish a case for the Charismatic message by claiming continuity between the Pentecostal and Charismatic Movements as part of an ongoing work of the Holy Spirit, affirming that the message of both Movements was biblical and catholic. The timing was significant, in that Harper's book came on the market around the same time as the English edition of the first, critical analysis of the Pentecostal Movement, made by a Norwegian, Nils Bloch-Hoell.[51] The works of Harper and Bloch-Hoell were of the greater significance in that they addressed an area of theology, pneumatology, in which there had been little recently published work. Lesslie Newbigin's *The Household of God*, published in 1953, had identified the Pentecostal, along with the Catholic and Protestant, as being one of three main streams which constituted modern Christianity; but although other biographical works were available at the time,[52] the works of Harper and Bloch-Hoell were the first reflective works available to the British reader since the beginnings of the Charismatic Movement. The concurrence of a work of critical reflection on the now well-established, worldwide Pentecostal movement with the publication of a popular commendation of this new wave of Neo-Pentecostalism which was rising in the historic churches meant that there was, understandably, an association to be made between Pentecostalism and the Charismatic Movement.

Should it be the case that the Charismatic Movement's perspective on the Person and function of the Holy Spirit is distinguishable from that of Neo-Pentecostalism, on what basis can we establish what were the particular, theological implications of the Charismatic Movement as it found expression in the Scottish context? In that we have identified an emphasis on suprarational experience as the Charismatic Movement's distinguishing feature, it becomes

---

[51] N. Bloch-Hoell, *The Pentecostal Movement*, Universitetsforlaget, Copenhagen, 1964. The original Norwegian edition was published in 1958.

[52] The most significant being the Neo-Pentecostal work of John Sherrill, *They Speak with Other Tongues*, Hodder & Stoughton, London, 1965; and David Wilkerson, *The Cross and the Switchblade*, Random House Inc., New York, 1963.

necessary for us to create a basic theological framework and vocabulary in order to relate this emphasis on suprarational experience to more conventional theological language. In doing this, we can identify and seek to develop four characteristics of the Charismatic Movement's emphasis on experiencing God. These four characteristics are identified, in brief, as follows:

- Experiencing God means more than rationally appreciating either God or any event through which we experience God.
- Experiencing God enhances our rational appreciation of God.
- Experiencing God is construed primarily in terms of experiencing the Holy Spirit.
- Given the emphasis on experiencing God, considerable importance is attached to Christian relationships, both with God and among Christians.

We now examine these characteristics in more detail.

- *Experiencing God means more than rationally appreciating either God or any event through which we experience God*

It is not enough to explain the nature of God in propositional or rational language, whether that language be phrased in terms of God's positive attributes (cataphatic terms), or in descriptors of what He is not (apophatic terms). The primary means of God communicating His present reality to us cannot be understood by propositional language alone. We can only apprehend God in so far as He comes to us or actualises His own Being towards us. This communication of God to us we will describe as the *ontic actuality* of God, defined, for the purpose of our thesis, as *the becomingness of God towards us in His own Being*. God is known and met with by us through His ontic actuality. This institutes our ability to meet with Him and constitutes our ability to speak of Him. Our speech about Him cannot contain or wholly communicate His ontic actuality. Our speech, or rational appreciation of God, arises as a consequence of our meeting with His ontic actuality. Throughout this thesis, our primary concern will be with the ontic actuality of the Spirit, in discussing how it is that the Spirit is made manifest in Christian experience. At the same time, we will make reference to the ontic actuality of the Son, by which we understand His Incarnation and historic manifestation in the person of Jesus Christ. Ultimately, our interest will lie in resolving how we can speak of God's ontic actuality as that which is expressed both in the ontic actuality of the Son, as met with in the Incarnation, and the ontic actuality of the Spirit, as realised in Christian experience.

For the Charismatic, the primary means of realising the ontic actuality of God is through present experience. God's communication to us is a communication of His Being actualised towards our Being. It is this meeting, of His Being towards our Being, which is the essence of the Christian life. The appropriation of rational or propositional truth regarding God is understood to arise out of this meeting with God in His ontic actuality. Such a meeting with God is not irrational nor lacks the possibility of rational explication. It is better described as suprarational. Our apprehension of God is constituted through our suprarational experience of Him, whereby we appropriate God's ontic actuality. This suprarational appropriation of God provides us, in turn, with that apprehension of God out of which we speak of Him in rational terms.

This perspective can best be illustrated from accounts given by some leaders within the Charismatic Movement. Stewart Brunton, of the Gate Fellowship, records his 'baptism in the Holy Spirit' in the following terms:

> I had an experience of God such as I had never known in my life; I became aware of a close relationship with God....I cannot really pinpoint the exact moment when [speaking in tongues] happened, I just know that events took place and I can just recall that experience of going home in the car and we were in air: God was so real![53]

In the experience and belief of some of the Charismatics, glossolalia comes as a spontaneous accompaniment to the 'baptism in the Holy Spirit'. Hugh Clark speaks of an experience whereby, while lying on his bed one night, he

> pressed through to the Lord [in prayer] and He came and filled the room with glory and I discovered that I was speaking in tongues.[54]

This accompaniment of glossolalia is, however, far from universal. For Brunton, the glossolalia followed some two weeks later. The manifestation of glossolalia did not prove the validity of the 'baptism in the Holy Spirit', for the experience, of itself, was accepted as self-validating. Likewise, David Black, in specifically repudiating the notion that glossolalia is a necessary sign of the 'baptism in the Holy Spirit', affirms that the main characteristic of those baptised in the Holy Spirit is,

> a sense of the reality of God.....the dimension is deepened in the 'baptism of the Holy Spirit'.[55]

In Black's understanding, this heightened awareness of God is accompanied by a reception of the gifts of the Holy Spirit; but these are identified by Black as consequential to rather than essential characteristics of the 'baptism in the Holy Spirit':

> These gifts are dormant, they are there; in some people they are not dormant, some people are using them although they are not baptised in the Holy Spirit.....but the 'baptism in the Holy Spirit' widens and deepens the expression of

---

[53] Recorded interview: 5 December 1989.
[54] Recorded interview: 17 November 1989.
[55] Recorded interview: 24 November 1989.

these gifts, and they come in greater power and authority through the 'baptism of the Holy Spirit'.[56]

Likewise, for Brian Hayes, the critical feature which characterises the 'baptism of the Holy Spirit' is not the manifestation of glossolalia. For Hayes, glossolalia is to be seen as the most easily exercised of the Spirit's gifts and is of help in liberating or releasing Christians in their operating with other gifts of the Holy Spirit. There is no question of glossolalia being a necessary proof of the Holy Spirit's presence.[57]

What we see as crucial to the perception of these Charismatics is not an identifiable, seminal point of experience, described as a 'baptism in the Holy Spirit', but a present, ongoing experience of the Holy Spirit. The consensus is perhaps best expressed by Clark when he states,

> I am an experiencer of God. Through my experience of His work in my life, I then hopefully arrive at some understanding of what it is all about.[58]

Does the theological apparatus of the Scottish Reformed tradition allow for dialogue with such a perception of God, a perception that is construed primarily in suprarational terms? One of our tasks in pursuing our thesis will be to examine whether an understanding of the ontic actuality of the Spirit has been hindered or enhanced through the development of pneumatology, as it has come to find expression in the Scottish context. In order to develop our thesis we will attempt to build on the concept of God's Being as experienced in His ontic actuality, God relating Himself to us in such a way that allows us to gain a suprarational appreciation of Him.

• *Experiencing God enhances our rational appreciation of God*
Clark's presentation of His understanding of experience brings us to our second characteristic of Charismatic theology. We saw that, for the Charismatic, the primary means of realising the ontic actuality of God is through suprarational experience. Rational awareness and understanding of God's revelation is seen to follow on from suprarational experience. Implicit in this is the suggestion that the greater our experience of God, the greater will be our appreciation of God's truth. Where rational appreciation of God arises from a meeting with Him in our experience, then the greater our experience of God, the greater will be our understanding of Him.

Given this emphasis on experience, in what way can a viable connection be made between experience and any propositional, theological truths held in

---

[56] Recorded interview: 24 November 1989.

[57] Recorded interview: 20 November 1989. Brian Hayes, a former Elim Pentecostal pastor, formerly senior elder of the Edinburgh Christian Fellowship and now leader of Edinburgh Christian Family Church.

[58] Recorded interview: 17 November 1989.

conjunction with that experience? Certainly, this is a weak point which we will have to address in our study. Where experience is held as the essential quality of the Christian life, confessional orthodoxy becomes a secondary issue. This weakness is, in practice, protected by a characteristic of the Charismatic Movement in Scotland: the implicit acceptance of a fundamentalist interpretation of Scripture. While clear criteria of connection are not established, the experience of God is treated as a predicate for the possession of Scriptural authority and dogma, which in turn are seen as validating Charismatic experience. Perhaps for this reason, where the possession of Scriptural truth is itself seen to arise out of that primary experience of God, there is a disinclination to form further theological statements, which could only be of a secondary and auxiliary nature. Certainly, this would help explain a disinclination among Charismatics to form clearly explicated expressions of faith in matters of belief and practice. Precedence is given to experiencing the God who reveals Himself in Christ, in preference to formulating theological statements about Him. Orthodoxy is not to be overturned; but orthoexperience takes precedence. A framework of objective truth is seen to be present in the Scriptures: yet what matters, above all, is that these truths are made personal and immediate in the believer's life, through the action of the Holy Spirit.

- *Experiencing God is construed primarily in terms of experiencing the Holy Spirit*

A third characteristic of the Charismatic Movement was that experience of God should be seen primarily in terms of experiencing the Holy Spirit. This undoubtedly arose partly from the language of Neo-Pentecostalism, which the Charismatic Movement adopted in speaking of the 'baptism in the Holy Spirit'. There is no obvious indication, however, as to what this means in Trinitarian terms. To what degree is it legitimate to speak of the Holy Spirit, as distinct from the other Persons of the Trinity, as met with in our personal experience? The Charismatic Movement does not address this question directly. The main concern has been to encourage engagement with the Holy Spirit, rather than reflect on His relationship to the Father and the Son.

- *Given the emphasis on experiencing God, considerable importance is attached to Christian relationships, both with God and among Christians*

The fourth distinctive characteristic which we identified as arising from the Charismatic emphasis on suprarational experience of the Holy Spirit concerns the importance attached to relationship. Experience of God is seen as arising from an objective reality, a meeting with God which is founded on the action of God Himself towards us. An alternative way of describing the Charismatic emphasis is to perceive it not in terms of experience - which can carry connotations of unlicensed subjectivity - but of relationship. Consequently, possession of the truth of God depends on our being in right relationship with Him; and our ability to develop and sustain an appreciation of truth depends on our being in right relationship with those others who also share an experience of God in His ontic actuality.

So it is that, among the Charismatics, ecclesiology arises out of an emphasis on sustaining a proper matrix of relationships with God and other Christians. The church is not primarily a *means* of grace, but an *expression* of grace. As Hugh Clark comments,

> We are talking about an environment of New Testament living that is conducive to people entering into the fullness of the Holy Spirit.[59]

Having noted these four characteristics of the Charismatic Movement's emphasis on experiencing God, let us now go on to offer four questions which will shape our theological investigation and which we will review once again at the end of our study. Firstly, what does it mean to speak of God in His ontic actuality? Does the theological apparatus of the Scottish Reformed tradition allow for dialogue with a perception of God that is primarily suprarational? One of our tasks, in developing our thesis, will be to examine whether an emphasis on the ontic actuality of God is compatible with traditional, theological descriptors of God as Trinity. Secondly, there is a need to explore whether it is theologically legitimate to speak of the Holy Spirit, as distinct from the Father and the Son, as He who meets with us in His ontic actuality. Thirdly, in so far as we identified that a relationship must exist between suprarational experience and rational appreciation of God, what is the precise nature of this relationship? Is it legitimate to make suprarational experience a predicate for rational appreciation of God? Finally, we will have to ask whether the importance attached to relationship, both with God and with other Christians, is of help in assisting us to pursue our examination into the Person and function of the Holy Spirit.

While these questions are of importance and will need to be addressed by us, attention first has to be given to those doctrinal issues which arose out of the Charismatic Movement's impact on the wider Scottish church and the reactions which we noted, from the reports of the Church of Scotland and the Baptist Union of Scotland, in our review of the Charismatic Movement's development in Scotland. It is to these matters that we now turn our attention.

1.9   The Doctrinal Issues

In order to assess whether or not the Charismatic Movement, as it appears in Scotland, has a contribution to make towards a Christian appreciation of God, we must address the doctrinal issues that arose from our brief review of the Movement's interaction with the Church of Scotland and the Baptist Union of Scotland. Whatever the merit of the issues raised, the fact that they arose at all

---

[59] Recorded interview: 17 November 1989.

indicates that some doctrinal points were under question, an examination of which might help us come to a better understanding of both the Holy Spirit and the Triune Being of God.

We might usefully identify and arrange the issues under five headings: the doctrine of the Trinity, pneumatology, the doctrine of the eucharist, epistemology and ecclesiology.

1.9.1   The Doctrine of the Trinity

The question of how a concentrated focus on the Holy Spirit might affect a proper understanding of the Trinity was raised by the Church of Scotland reports of 1973 and 1974. The 1973 interim report raised the issue of the relationship between the Holy Spirit and the risen Christ. In what way do we understand the manner of the Holy Spirit's testimony to Christ? Is there not a danger, as mooted in the 1974 report, that a preoccupation with the Spirit might lead to a failure in relating His ministry to the Person of Jesus Christ; and having cut an understanding of the Spirit away from a Christocentric axis, would this not possibly lead to tritheism? How are we to understand the ministry of the Holy Spirit and our participation therein, whilst retaining a proper regard to the Trinitarian nature of God as Father, Son and Holy Spirit? A focal concern in the Church of Scotland reports was that too much regard to the Spirit would, if held in isolation from the Son, diminish a proper appreciation of God's Trinitarian nature. We must therefore explore whether it is possible to develop an understanding of the ministry of the Holy Spirit while continuing to hold that the centre of the Gospel is in Jesus Christ. Can we speak specifically about the Son and the Spirit and at the same time give proper regard to the Trinitarian nature of God as Father, Son and Holy Spirit?

We begin our exploration of this theme in chapter 2, reviewing the development of a Trinitarian pneumatology through the Patristic period. We will observe there how our perception and expectation of the Holy Spirit is critically affected both by our approach to Christology and the manner in which we seek to describe the Trinitarian nature of God.

1.9.2   Pneumatology

It was in our review of Hugh Black's understanding of the Holy Spirit that we first came across the question of whether a supposedly suprarational experience of God is self-evidently an experience induced by the Spirit of God. In the Baptist Union report of 1979, the question of the Christian's participation in and reception of the Holy Spirit was addressed. What does it mean to talk of 'receiving the Holy Spirit', whether at conversion, baptism or any other point in the Christian life? In our study, it will be necessary to ask in what way the Scottish Reformed tradition has understood the Holy Spirit's activity and engagement in the life of Christians. We will have to assess the adequacy of whatever understanding we find; and ask whether we can legitimately speak of different functions of the Holy Spirit in a manner that does not detract from the unitary character of His Person.

Having begun our examination of pneumatology by reviewing, in chapter 2, the ways in which alternative Trinitarian models allow us differing perspectives on the Holy Spirit, we will go on in chapter 3 to examine Calvin's understanding of the Holy Spirit's Person and function, having regard both to his understanding of the Trinity and also God's salvific involvement with mankind. In chapter 4 we will further explore how this understanding of Calvin was shaped, in the confessional formulae of the post-Reformation Scottish context, into a distinctive, pneumatological perspective, proceeding through chapters 5 and 6 to see how this is interpreted in the writings of two leading Scottish theologians, one of the nineteenth century and one of the twentieth century.

1.9.3   The Doctrine of the Eucharist

In the Church of Scotland 1973 interim Report, specific reference was made to the universal significance of the eucharist throughout the Christian church in affirming the presence of Christ in the midst of His people. Given the Charismatic emphasis on meeting with the ontic actuality of God, in what way can the eucharist offer an understanding of the presence of Christ and the Spirit that is compatible with or complementary to a Charismatic perspective? In order to address this question, we will need to form some understanding of the eucharist as it has been understood within the Scottish context. We will set about this task by noting, within chapter 3, Calvin's understanding of Christ and the Spirit's presence within the eucharist, proceeding through chapter 4 to note how that was received in credal form, specifically in the *Scots* and *Westminster Confessions* in Scotland. In chapters 5 and 6 we will go on to note two developed, post-Calvinistic interpretations of the significance of the eucharist to a Trinitarian theology.

1.9.4   Epistemology

What activity of God is necessary to allow us to respond to Him and to describe His Being and activity? Is our perception of God to be rooted in our own understanding of Him, or is there some other basis from which we need to speak? For a Neo-Pentecostal, such as Hugh Black of Greenock, treating the 'baptism in the Holy Spirit' as part of a doctrine of subsequence allowed the making of a rational, confessional statement to be acceptable prior to any further experience of the Spirit. For a Charismatic, such as Hugh Clark of Motherwell, suprarational experience of God's ontic actuality provides, in itself, the basis of a rational explication of God and His dealings with man. How are we to construe the relationship between awareness of God, as born out of a suprarational experience, and the revelational significance of the Holy Spirit in illumining man's understanding of God? The Charismatic Movement's emphasis on suprarational experience invites us to reappraise our Christian basis for knowing God and forming a rational, cognitive faith in Him.

Having noted in chapter 3 something of Calvin's approach to epistemology, we will proceed through chapters 4, 5 and 6 to trace the way in which a rational, cognitive faith has been related to the ontic actuality of the Spirit. In chapter 7 we will examine two alternative approaches which have been forged in the light of the Charismatic Movement, one emphasising the priority of human experience and the other the objective nature of God's revelation in Christ, proceeding in the final chapter to offer some suggestions as to how suprarational experience can best be related to a rational and cognitive faith in terms of the Spirit's ontic actuality.

1.9.5 Ecclesiology

The question was raised in the Baptist Union report of 1979, as to the relationship of baptism as the accepted means of initiation into the church and the Charismatic experience as bringing a special endowment of the Spirit for ministry. This reflected a more fundamental question which had been raised in the 1973 Church of Scotland interim report. What is the relation of the Spirit's coming to the individual, as over against the whole church? Again, the 1974 report had demonstrated a central concern with the character of the Spirit's relationship to the church. This question, as to the relationship between individual and corporate reception of the Spirit, will need to be addressed.

In chapter 7, in looking at the work of two Scottish theologians who have both been affected by the Charismatic Movement and who offer radically different interpretations of the manner by which we can speak of the individual's and the church's participation in the Holy Spirit, we will explore further the relationship between the church's corporate participation in and the individual's reception of the Holy Spirit.

In the final chapter of our study we will return to address the four questions arising from the characteristics, noted in section 1.8, which we identified as belonging to the Charismatic Movement and coming from its emphasis upon suprarational experience of the Holy Spirit. From there, we will go on to explore whether it is possible to construct a theological understanding of the Holy Spirit and the Trinity which represents the essential character of the Charismatic Movement in a manner which can be understood from the Scottish theological perspective.

In asking whether the theological apparatus of the Scottish Reformed tradition allows for dialogue with a perception of God that is founded on suprarational experience, we will have to resolve whether it is helpful to speak of God in terms of His ontic actuality. One of our tasks in the final chapter will therefore be to ask whether our understanding of the ontic actuality of the Spirit is aided by any contemporary, theological explorations into the nature of God as Trinity. Specifically, we will seek to develop a model of the Trinity which might help us resolve the tension between a suprarational experience of the Spirit and a rational, cognitive faith in Christ. Our ability to tackle this issue, which exposes the weakest point in the Charismatic Movement's understanding of the Holy Spirit, will be a decisive factor in evaluating whether a legitimate Charismatic and Trinitarian theology of the Spirit can be had and applied in the Scottish context.

Chapter 2

Patristic Foundations

2.1 Introduction

In this chapter we seek to trace the emergence of a doctrine of the Spirit in the Patristic era. In sections 2.2-4 we begin by looking at the pre-Nicene era, that period which falls between the time of the Apostles and the Council of Nicea in 325 AD. We observe how a perception of God, arising from a focus on His salvific economy, came to be influenced and affected by various considerations. In sections 2.5-7 we discuss those tensions which, arising from conflicting interpretations of Christology, led to a clash between Arian and Nicene perspectives. In sections 2.8-10, we go on to argue that the consequent ascendancy of the Nicene perspective led to a greater focus on and exploration of the Immanent Trinity, accompanied by a weakened understanding of the Holy Spirit within God's salvific economy. In section 2.11 we suggest that the agenda set by the defence and explanation of the Son of God's full divinity, in the *homoousion* of the Nicene Creed, was not necessarily helpful for the subsequent development of pneumatology. We note in sections 2.12-13 that, in both west and east, a continued focus on the Immanent Trinity in post-Nicene Trinitarian thought led to a further obscuring of the Spirit's salvific economy. We summarise our observations in section 2.14 by offering some Trinitarian models which can be taken to represent pre-Nicene, post-Nicene western and post-Nicene eastern positions, concluding our study of the Patristic bequest in section 2.15.

In entering the world of pre-Nicene Christianity, we are confronted with a pattern of understanding and speaking of the Holy Spirit, together with the Father and the Son, quite different from that found among those engaged in the Scottish debate over the Charismatic Movement. Where the question of retaining a proper Trinitarian perspective on the Holy Spirit appeared a matter of real concern in the Scottish context, we are faced in the early pre-Nicene period with an absence of any clearly formulated Trinitarian structure. In framing an overview of Patristic developments that shaped pneumatology within a Trinitarian context, we can attempt to trace an understanding of how the Holy Spirit came to be perceived, theologically, in His relation to the Father and to the Son. This, hopefully, will assist us in assessing how we can present an understanding of the Person and function of the Spirit which adequately conveys that suprarational, experiential emphasis of the Charismatic Movement, while maintaining a Trinitarian perspective on the Spirit.

2.2   The Apostolic Fathers

One of the striking features of early pre-Nicene thought, as expressed in the writings of the Apostolic Fathers (those leaders and theologians of the church who were the immediate successors of the Apostles), was the manner in which the Holy Spirit could be spoken of and referred to without being presented as a rival to or detractor from Jesus Christ; and that this could occur within a context where there was no clearly defined ontological framework through which Father, Son and Holy Spirit were viewed in their relationship as Persons of the Holy Trinity. For this reason the heterogeneous writings of this sub-apostolic period, while offering no systematic account of the Spirit nor demonstrating any clear evolution towards an understanding of Trinitarian ontology, offer a perspective on the Holy Spirit which is of interest to our study. These writings exhibit, albeit in a scattered and erratic manner, an early appreciation of the Holy Spirit's Person and function. In them we meet with a view of God's economic action which is not rationalised or relativised but which focuses on God as He is made known in His salvific economy. Such a perspective on the Spirit is not dissimilar to that which we observed among Charismatics, where we discerned an emphasis on apprehending God only as He comes to us, or as He actualises His own Being towards us: a communication of God which we described as the ontic actuality of God.

Although we cannot trace a systematic exposition of the Spirit in the Apostolic Fathers, what we can do is to identify, by the manner in which the writers make mention of the Spirit, something of their awareness and appreciation of His Person and function. Among the Apostolic Fathers, the predominant approach in presenting an understanding of the Spirit was to draw on various texts by means of direct quotation from the Scriptures, thereby forming a series of observations or statements. There is no evidence of a Trinitarian model being used to explain the operations of the Spirit or any relation of the Spirit to the Father and the Son outwith God's salvific economy. What is apparent is an appreciation of both the illuminatory action of the Holy Spirit, related to Jesus and directed towards the church, and the Spirit's integral involvement in the self-revelation of God, attracting worship along with the Father and the Son.

In the *Shepherd of Hermas*,[1] a popular work within the early church,[2] the Spirit is presented as immediate to human experience, dwelling in people as in

---

[1] An early date for this work is assumed. For discussion of this see F. L. Cross, *The Early Christian Fathers*, Duckworth, London, 1960, pp. 23-24

[2] Irenaeus treats *Hermas* as if it were Biblical Scripture, in *Against Heresies* 4.20.2

a vessel,[3] possessing an identity distinct from mankind[4] and not restricted by them.[5] At the same time, *Hermas* sees the Spirit as harmonising with and finding expression through the devout person.[6] He who indwells the devout is 'the Holy preexistent Spirit, which created the whole creation'.[7] While affirming these characteristics of the Spirit, *Hermas* parallels this with a description of the Son. While it is the Spirit who indwells men, the Son guards over them. It is the Son who has purified their sins by labour, much hardship and has shown them the paths of life.[8]

The need to make a further distinction between the respective roles of the Spirit and the Son does not arise. There is no discussion on how the Spirit was active, through the Incarnation, in the Son Himself. The relation of the Logos and the Holy Spirit in the person of Jesus Christ is not discussed.[9] Instead, the focus is on the salvific work of the Son on behalf of man, complemented by the ongoing indwelling of the Holy Spirit. In this, it is the activity of God, acting in and on humanity, that finds emphasis. There may be a lack of differentiation in the relationship of the Son to the Spirit in God's salvific event; but the clarification of such a distinction was not the concern of *Hermas*.

This perspective on the Holy Spirit, as integral to but undifferentiated within God's salvific economy, is further illustrated by Clement, who acknowledges the Holy Spirit as one who searches out mankind in the depths,[10] entering people[11] and granting them assurance.[12] Again, where a relationship between Christ and the Spirit appears to be assumed and unexpounded, Clement places his emphasis on the Spirit as He who declares the truth of God and Christ Jesus,[13] inspiring men to do the same:[14] not simply as an agent of truth, but as imparter of it. Likewise, in *The Martyrdom of Polycarp*, the Spirit is an imparter, acknowledged as He who grants incorruption[15] and Himself the object of doxological praise.

While the revelatory and declaratory aspects of the Spirit's works appear at

---

[3] *Commandment* 3, in *The Shepherd of Hermas*, translated by C. H. Hoole, Rivingstons, London, 1870, p. 44.
[4] *Commandment* 5.1ff., *Hermas*, p. 51.
[5] *Commandment* 5.2, *Hermas*, p. 53.
[6] *Commandment* 11, *Hermas*, pp. 70-71.
[7] *Similitude* 5.6, *Hermas*, pp. 97-98.
[8] *Similitude* 5.6, *Hermas*, pp. 97-98.
[9] Some have taken this as indicating an ambiguous attitude towards God as Trinity: see Glimm, Marique and Walsh, *The Apostolic Fathers*, CUA, Washington, 1947, p. 230.
[10] In *1 Corinthians* 28, where Clement quotes from Psalm 139, in *The Apostolic Fathers*, translated by J. B. Lightfoot, MacMillan, London, 1893, p. 69.
[11] *1 Corinthians* 8, *Clement*, p. 60.
[12] *1 Corinthians* 42, *Clement*, p. 75.
[13] *1 Corinthians* 8, 16 and 22, *Clement*, pp. 60, 63 and 67.
[14] *1 Corinthians* 47, 57, *Clement*, p. 77.
[15] *Martyrdom* 14, *Clement*, p. 208.

the forefront of the Apostolic Fathers' witness, the interpolation of a broad range of Scriptural concepts into these early theological works, in descriptions of the Spirit, demonstrates an understanding of other aspects of the Spirit's function as integral to His workings. Again, in the work of Ignatius, the illuminatory role of the Spirit is the most oft cited,[16] yet there is a broad understanding of the Spirit active in ways that are other than epistemic. He is the conceiver of Jesus,[17] inseparably united with believers,[18] cooperator with the Son yet distinct from Him.[19] The Spirit is the enabler[20] and comforter of man,[21] the agent of incorruption and empowering.[22] While a specific theology of the Spirit is not yet developed, the Spirit is seen to stand as a strong link and connection between mankind and God.

In all of this and despite the fact that some of the sub-apostolic writings have little or nothing to say on the Holy Spirit,[23] we can detect an awareness of the ontic actuality of the Spirit. In facing us with a perspective on the Being of the Holy Spirit as present and active among Christians and the church, there is an understanding of the Spirit phrased in terms of God's salvific economy. Certainly, at this stage in the development of Trinitarian thought, descriptions of relations between the Father, Son and Holy Spirit are not yet concretised. At the same time, it should be conceded that some relation appears to be held as axiomatic, in that the Spirit is construed as active, not in isolation from but in unity with, the Father and the Son. This is illustrated in Ignatius, where we find a portrayal of the ontic actuality of the Spirit in *Ephesians* 9. In this passage, Ignatius describes the Spirit in terms of His dynamic interaction with the Father and the Son, the actuator of the mission of Christ in the lives of Christians:

> From his power Jesus Christ will deliver you, who has founded you upon the rock, as being chosen stones, well fitted for the divine edifice of the Father, and who are raised up on high by Christ, who was crucified for you, making use of the Holy Spirit as a rope, and being borne up by faith, while exalted by love from earth to heaven, walking in company with those that are undefiled.[24]

---

[16] *Ephesians* 4, 8, 9 and 15; *Magnesians* 9; *Philadelphians* 3 and 7, in *The Ante-Nicene Fathers* Vol. 1, A. Roberts and J. Donaldson (Editors), Eerdmans, Grand Rapids, 1884, pp. 50, 52, 53 and 56; 62; 81 and 83.
[17] *Ephesians* 18, *Ignatius*, p. 57.
[18] *Magnesians* 15, *Ignatius*, p. 65.
[19] *Trallians* 1, 6, *Ignatius*, p. 68.
[20] *Romans* 8, *Ignatius*, p. 77.
[21] *Philadelphians* 4, *Ignatius*, p. 81.
[22] *Philadelphians* 6, 7, *Ignatius*, p. 83.
[23] Such as the *Didache*, which stresses the Christian call to moral order, rather than reflecting on the enabling help of the Spirit.
[24] The quotation is taken from the longer version of the text: see *Ignatius*, p. 53. Lightfoot detects the analogy, in Ignatius' thought, of a 'lifting machine', where 'the

Here we see that the revelatory action of the Spirit as a function of a broader perception of the Spirit's work, integral to God's ontic actuality and His salvific economy towards man. The Spirit is not viewed in isolation but is seen as active in outworking the intent of the Father through the salvific triumph of the resurrected Son. However, as with the developing pneumatology of the Charismatic Movement in Scotland, early pre-Nicene pneumatology did not evolve in an environment free from outside influences. Although it is not until the writings of Justin Martyr that the first, explicit note of apologetical engagement with contemporary Greek thought is heard,[25] it was inevitable that some interaction should occur with the dominant philosophical framework of the age. What was not immediately apparent was that conflict would arise between a perspective which held, on the one hand, to the ontic actuality of God in His salvific economy and, on the other, to the dualism inherent within the framework of Platonic philosophy. Justin, speaking of the Father, Son and Holy Spirit united as the object of our doxology,[26] distinguishes the Son as second to 'the true God Himself', the prophetic Spirit holding third place.[27] Here, the sense of ontic actuality in the dynamic economy of Father, Son and Holy Spirit is married to a perception of a priority within God which owes its genesis to a notional separation of God from man: this Justin specifically associates with Plato.[28] As such, Justin's emphasis lies not with the ontic actuality of the Spirit, but on the Spirit's mediatory agency between God and man: a rational power, proceeding from God.[29] The Spirit may be viewed as operating to testify to the Son.[30]

While the work of the Spirit appears to remain unchanged from earlier descriptions, in that the Spirit brings mankind understanding of God, there is a change in perception of the Spirit's mode of operation. Justin presents the Spirit as the mediator, or agent, of the transcendent God. Justin's polemical intent causes him to minimise any direct association of the Spirit with Absolute Deity. So it is that in his *Hortatory Address to the Greeks*, Justin can convey an understanding of the descent and energy of the Spirit;[31] yet at the same time, by identifying the Spirit with categories native to Platonic thought, as he does in

---

framework, or crane, is the Cross of Christ; the connecting instrument, or rope, is the Holy Spirit; the motive power, which acts and keeps the machine in motion, is faith; the path, upon which the spiritual stones are raised that they may be fitted into the building, is love'. *The Apostolic Fathers*, Pt.2, Vol.2, Sct.1, MacMillan, London, 1885, p. 54.

[25] Justin's work, while apologetical, was not a polemic against Greek thought. H. von Campenhausen remarks that Justin found in Plato an intellectual bridge and ally: *The Fathers of the Greek Church*, Pantheon, New York, 1959, p. 15.

[26] *1st Apology* 6, *ANF*, Vol. 1, p. 164.

[27] *1st Apology* 13, *ANF*, Vol. 1, pp. 166-67.

[28] *1st Apology* 60, *ANF*, Vol. 1, p. 183.

[29] *Dialogue with Trypho* 61, *ANF*, Vol. 1, p. 227.

[30] *Dialogue with Trypho* 32, 36, 38 and 74, *ANF*, Vol. 1, pp. 210, 213 and 235.

[31] *Address to the Greeks* 8, *ANF*, Vol. 1, p. 276.

associating the Spirit with 'virtue' in Plato's *Dialogue with Meno*,[32] he also, albeit unwittingly, invites the adoption of a subordinationist view of the Spirit.

This is not to say that Justin perceives the Spirit as a created Being, separate from God: yet, in emphasising His function as mediatory, the focus is taken away from the Person or Being of the Spirit and is placed upon His function. A stress on the Spirit's agency invites a particularisation of His function, whereas a stress on the Spirit's ontic actuality might have served better to retain a focus on His Being. A subtle distinction is introduced in how the Spirit is perceived. The context is no longer simply one of divine immediacy combined with some functional distinction between the Son and the Spirit. Added to this now are concepts of transcendence associated with the noetic-sensible divide of Platonism and abstracted, relational distinctions as to the manner in which Father, Son and Spirit are construed together.

2.3   The Pre-Nicene West

In Irenaeus we are faced with a writer who traces a distinctive work undertaken by the Spirit, distinguishing within God's salvific economy the ontic actuality of the Holy Spirit from that of the Son.[33] Given that his main works are in the form of *Against Heresies*, an exposure of the Valentinian Gnosticism that was invading his church, and *Proof of the Apostolic Preaching*, a catechetical summary of Christian belief, we meet in Irenaeus with one who is not yet concerned, as others would later be, with innovative, apologetic thinking.[34] This makes Irenaeus' contribution to our tracing of early pneumatology all the more significant, for his understanding is presented in a context where the preservation and proper presentation of the Christian kerygma is a focal issue.

In seeking to understand Irenaeus' perception of the Spirit and His operation within God's salvific economy, we might usefully make a distinction between the work undertaken by the Holy Spirit (*opus operandi*), which has a clearly Christocentric reference, and the means whereby this work is made effective (*modus operandi*). The *modus operandi* of the Spirit appears to be perceived by Irenaeus in terms of the ontic actuality of the Spirit, the Person and function of the Spirit being both dynamic and immediate towards the human condition. In Irenaeus' understanding, the primary *opus operandi* of the Spirit is to testify to the Son.[35] As was the case with the Apostolic Fathers, this perception is founded on passages from the New Testament Scriptures. The Spirit comes to

---

[32] *Address to the Greeks* 32, *ANF*, Vol. 1, pp. 286-87.

[33] A fuller discussion of Irenaeus' perception of the Spirit and how it contrasts to that of Justin is found in J. A. Robinson, *St. Irenaeus: the Apostolic Preaching*, MacMillan, New York, 1920, pp. 24-68.

[34] F. L. Cross remarks that *Against Heresies* appears untidy and unsystematic: *The Early Christian Fathers*, pp. 111-12.

[35] *Against Heresies* 3.16, *ANF*, Vol. 1, pp. 440-44.

the Son[36] and also to the church, that the church might be fruitful in her relationship with the Father and the Son, whose image and superscription the church bears by the Spirit.[37] While the Spirit's operation bears reference to the Son, it is complementary to and not to be confused with the mission of the Son.[38] The Son and the Spirit are the two 'hands of God',[39] separately assigned[40] functions in the work of salvation and sanctification.[41] In this way, we can say that the Spirit fulfils His *opus operandi*. Consequently, the *modus operandi* of the Spirit is to be found in the Spirit's own, ontic actuality expressed in and on the lives of men, this action being distinct from yet complementary to that of the Son. As the Spirit renews and vivifies the church, the church is made inseparable from the Spirit's presence, because of her contingency upon the Spirit. The Spirit confirms faith and acts as the guarantee of our salvation, nourishing the faithful as a babe is nourished at its mother's breasts.[42] The Spirit may be spoken of, in the same breath, as the agent both of revelation and of sanctification;[43] but distinguished in His *modus operandi* from the Son, to whom He testifies.

What we appear to meet with, in Irenaeus, is a perception of the Spirit at work that is rooted in the Spirit's ontic actuality, the realisation of His Person and a relationship with us which is from the Father towards us. In Irenaeus, a concern with the ontological identity of the Trinity has not yet developed in that there is no apparent concern with relations within the immanent Godhead outwith God's salvific economy towards man. There is, however, the presence of an economic Trinitarian perspective in that, while acknowledging and holding to the monarchy of the Father and the specific, salvific mission of the Son, Irenaeus maintains an understanding of the Spirit distinguished, in His ontic actuality, from both the Father and the Son. This is founded on the salvific economy of God. Irenaeus betrays no interest in establishing an understanding of God to and within Himself, removed from His salvific economy towards man.

It is no surprise, then, to find that Irenaeus emphasises the present operation of the Holy Spirit in the church,[44] nor that he marries the complementary work

---

[36] *Against Heresies* 3.17.1, *ANF*, Vol. 1, p. 444.

[37] *Against Heresies* 3.17.3, *ANF*, Vol. 1, p. 445.

[38] Robinson concludes that 'the teaching of St. Irenaeus as to the relation of the Holy Spirit to the Incarnation is vague, perhaps even transitional... . He seems to prefer to think of a cooperation of the Word of God and the Wisdom of God - the two hands of God to whom the creation of the first formed man was due ...', *St. Irenaeus: The Apostolic Preaching*, pp. 66-67.

[39] *Against Heresies* 5.1.3, *ANF*, Vol. 1, p. 527.

[40] *Against Heresies* 4. pref.4, *ANF*, Vol. 1, p. 463.

[41] *Against Heresies* 4.38.3, *ANF*, Vol. 1, pp. 521-22.

[42] *Against Heresies* 3.24.1, *ANF*, Vol. 1, p. 458.

[43] *Against Heresies* 4.1.1, *ANF*, Vol. 1, p. 463.

[44] *Against Heresies* 2.32.4, *ANF*, Vol. 1, p. 409.

of the Son and the Spirit through explaining that the location wherein the activity of the Spirit may be met with (*locus operandi*) is the church, the body of Christ on earth:

> For this gift of God has been entrusted to the church, as the breath of life to created man, to the end that all members by receiving it should be made alive.....For where the church is, there is the Spirit of God; and where the Spirit of God is, there is the church and every kind of Grace.[45]

We might say that, for Irenaeus, the separately assigned functions of the Son and the Spirit coincide in the church. In terms of Trinitarian economy, the church represents the confluence of the Son and Spirit in their work, as it is assigned to them by the Father. Without the church there would be no ready means of explaining the relation of the Son and the Spirit.

At the very outset of the Patristic era, we are presented with an understanding of the Spirit which is founded not on a Trinitarian model explicated in terms of relationships within God's immanent Being; but one that is rooted in God's engagement with us. The revelation of God is met with in the ontic actuality of God at work in His salvific economy towards mankind, realised both in the Incarnation of the Son and in the continued action of the Holy Spirit towards us. To describe the ontological relationship of Father, Son and Spirit in terms other than those denoted in this economic action is neither urgent nor helpful, in that it is in God's salvific economy that God is met with by man.

In the apologetic writing of Justin we did, however, see the vulnerability of this Trinitarian perspective when confronted with the dualism of Platonic thought and its axiom of an ontological gulf between God and man. It is not surprising that this problem appears, from our analysis so far, not to have significantly figured among pre-Nicene writers in the Latin West. As we shall see in the next section, the problem was more acute in the Greek East, among those who had to address more urgently the agenda presented by the framework of Greek thought. What is apparent in the Latin West is a growing emphasis on the church as an organised, corporate identity, the proper *locus operandi* of the Holy Spirit's operation. The Spirit is identified most readily by the nature of His operation in the church. In Hippolytus' primary work, *The Apostolic Tradition*, his perspective of the Roman Church presents an understanding of the Spirit as active among two separate groups: the ecclesiastical hierarchy and the people. Hippolytus' perception is of the Spirit dealing, in and through the whole church, with a defined and structured identity. Likewise Novatian, in the work written prior to his schism, the *Treatise concerning the Trinity*, saw the church as perfected and completed by the gifts of the Holy Spirit. The one qualification that appears to be placed on the ontic actuality of the Spirit, in the

---

[45] *Against Heresies* 3.24.1, *ANF*, Vol. 1, p. 458.

Latin West, is one arising from an evolving ecclesiology. In Cyprian of Carthage, who formulated the doctrine, *outside the church there is no salvation*,[46] we see a development of Irenaeus' earlier association of the Spirit's *modus operandi* with the church as *locus operandi*, a stress being placed on the oneness of the church; and hence on the activity of the Holy Spirit in and through the church:

> The church is one and indivisible: therefore there cannot be a church among the heretics. The Holy Spirit is one, and cannot dwell with those outside the community; therefore the Holy Spirit has no place among the heretics.[47]

Apart from defining the context wherein the Spirit's presence might be recognised, this early ecclesiological development did little to impede the pre-Nicene West from retaining an emphasis on the ontic actuality of the Spirit. This is further evidenced in the work of the other great western writer of this early period, Tertullian.[48] In *Against Praxeas*, Tertullian speaks of the Son as 'proceeding' from the Father, a term which later orthodoxy would restrict to the Holy Spirit. In seeking to repudiate the monarchian contention that God is undifferentiated, Tertullian uses language which, once the agenda set by Platonic thought had been absorbed, would have suggested to later orthodoxy a subordinationist doctrine of the Son. For Tertullian, however, the question of the Son's subordination was not an issue; his focus was elsewhere:

> We...believe that there is one only God, but under the following dispensation, or economy, as it is called, that this one only God has also a Son, His Word, who proceeded from Himself, by whom all things were made, and without whom nothing was made.[49]

Here we see the representation of the salvific economy of Father and Son without a desire to enquire further into the nature of God. Consequently, because Tertullian does not address the issue from the perspective of God's immanent Being but from that of God's salvific economy, Tertullian appears to be unaware as to how his presentation can leave the way open to charges of subordinationism. Tertullian is content to posit the relationship of the Trinity in

---

[46] '*Extra ecclesiam nulla salus*'.

[47] *Epistle* 74.4, in *The Early Christian Fathers*, edited and translated by H. Bettenson OUP, London, 1956, p. 271.

[48] J. Danielou notes that Tertullian, in emphasising the common *testimonium animae*, presented a theology which was 'essentially an attempt to set in order the different realities known through reason and faith. It is, in other words, a kind of phenomenology, implying a direct apprehension of these realities...', *The Origins of Latin Christianity*, DLT, London, 1977, p. 344.

[49] *Against Praxeas* 2, in *The Writings of Tertullian*, Vol.2, T & T Clark, Edinburgh, 1870.

various analogies, illustrating the 'procession' which comes from the Father. Thus, in commenting on the monarchian position in *Against Praxeas*, Tertullian states,

> I am, moreover, obliged to say this, when they contend for the identity of the Father, and the Son and Spirit, that it is not by way of diversity that the Son differs from the Father, but by distribution: it is not by division that He is different but by distinction; because the Father is not the same as the Son, since they differ one from the other in the mode of their being (*modulo*). For the Father is the entire substance, but the Son is a derivation and portion of the whole, as He Himself acknowledges: 'My Father is greater than I.' In the psalm His inferiority is described as being 'a little lower than the angels.' Thus the Father is distinct from the Son, being greater than the Son, in as much as He who begets is one, and He who is begotten is another; He, too, who sends is one, and He who is sent is another; and He, again who makes is one, and He through whom the thing is made is another.[50]

Where the writers of the pre-Nicene West faced the challenge of monarchianism through stressing the salvific economy of God, they were simply emphasising that which was natural to their perspective on God. They were not engaged in developing a Trinitarian perspective which would lead towards the ontological isolation of the divine from the human or the noetic from the sensible. This latter problem was the challenge that first faced the theologians of the pre-Nicene East, to whom we now turn.

2.4   The Pre-Nicene East

In turning to examine developments in pneumatology and moves towards an evolved Trinitarian perspective in the pre-Nicene East, we are faced with the question of how influential the pervading backdrop of Platonic thought was in setting a framework wherein early Trinitarian theology would be forged.

J. P. Mackey in his study, *The Christian Experience of God as Trinity*, detects an emanationalist and subordinationist model of God present in both Christian and non-Christian traditions in the pre-Nicene period,[51] arguing that the specific content of Trinitarian thought was formed, through a process of modification and development, within the wider context of Greek traditions and thinking.[52] Mackey traces this process in both the pre-Nicene East and West: Tertullian, for example, is clearly implicated, in his 'theology of the Three',[53] as one who has drunk deep at the well of Greek thought. While we would not

---

[50] *Against Praxeas* 9, *The Writings of Tertullian*, Vol.2, p. 349.

[51] J. P. Mackey, *The Christian Experience of God as Trinity*, SCM, London, 1983, p. 130.

[52] *The Christian Experience of God as Trinity*, p. 104.

[53] *The Christian Experience of God as Trinity*, p. 127.

dispute that the parallels which Mackey draws between Christian and non-Christian traditions are highly persuasive we would, however, wish to raise a question. Mackey identifies that a common factor in both Christian and non-Christian traditions lies in seeking to preserve an understanding of the immutability of the One, or God. Our concern has led us in a different direction. Our desire to trace developments in the manner in which the Spirit's economy was seen in relation to the Father and the Son has directed us not towards identifying a stress on the immutability of the One, but to note the ontic actuality of God expressed through the salvific action of both the Holy Spirit and the Son. We must therefore ask whether such a concern and emphasis on the salvific economy of both the Son and the Spirit arises from the priority of maintaining a subordinationist perspective in their relationship to the One, or whether it possibly stems from a desire to preserve another, more primitive motif: that the manner by which God relates to us is in and through His ontic actuality, expressed through the ministry of both the Son and the Holy Spirit. Certainly, Mackey's identification of immutability as a decisive factor and our theme of ontic actuality are not mutually exclusive; but, on the other hand, they are not necessarily to be held together. For the moment we note Mackey's case but reserve judgement on whether it is necessary to embrace it in the pursuit of our thesis.

Certainly, in Clement of Alexandria, the effect and influence of contemporary modes of Greek thought in his communication of the Christian message was such as to produce a synthesis barely recognisable as Christian.[54] From another perspective, however, it was hardly surprising that the problem of apparent syncretism should arise. The Christian kerygma, with its soteriological emphasis, was concerned with God's salvific economy and not with the philosophical issues which were the main concern of Platonic thought.[55] Where the focus of early Christian theology lay upon the salvific economy of God and the implications of this for the Christian community, there was less interest in the question that arrested the Greek mindset, that of the ontological nature of God's Being. Consequently, where there had been, in the church, no early development of or concern over an understanding of God's identity in terms of His immanent, ontological Being, it was likely that the ready-made philosophical and ontological suppositions available from both middle-platonism and neoplatonism would be transplanted into Christian thought. Such

---

[54] A. Meredith detects a particular reverence for Plato in Clement, faith being understood as a building of the knowledge of God, the pursuit of self-perfection as man's aim. Meredith opines that there is no substantial difference between Clement's perception of prayer and Plato's understanding of private, intellectual contemplation: 'Clement of Alexandria', in *The Study of Spirituality*, edited by C. Jones, G. Wainwright and E. J. Yarnold, SPCK, London, 1986, pp. 112-15.

[55] The distinction between soteriological and philosophical emphases is noted by T. A. Hart in chapter 1 of 'Incarnation and Apotheosis', PhD thesis, Aberdeen , 1989.

a development was most likely to occur, as we would contend it did, within the Eastern church. The problem arising from this development was that it turned the focus in understanding God away from His salvific economy onto the philosophical conundrum regarding the essential nature of God's Being. The effect of this would be of seminal importance for the development of Trinitarian theology, where the pre-Nicene emphasis on the ontic actuality of the Son and the Holy Spirit as expressions of God's salvific economy had to be interpreted and reaffirmed in a way that would assert their involvement and participation in the Father's divinity.

The difficulties arising from this tension can be seen in the work of Clement's successor in Alexandria, Origen. For Origen, the Spirit is the teacher and revealer of God, illumining the Scriptures[56] and working holiness among Christians,[57] acting in unison with the Father and the Son in the Trinity's purpose of saving mankind.[58] This perspective on the ontic actuality of the Spirit is qualified by Origen's attempt to integrate his understanding of the Spirit into a Trinitarian ontology where Father, Son and Spirit are identified according to their particular functions in God's salvific economy;[59] yet are immanently related to one another in a way that can be affirmed as eternal to God Himself.[60]

Where Tertullian appeared to hold to the economy of the Trinity as his basis for considering the identity of God, Origen also wishes to speak of the Trinity's economy; however, his dualistic perspective, set within the Platonic framework, constrains him. Origen's reflection on the construction of the eternal generation of the Son by the Father takes us into a scheme of thinking which engages the philosophical question of God's own immanent, ontological identity. This is evident in the manner of Origen's speech regarding the Spirit and His relation to the Father and the Son. He can, on the one hand, emphasise

---

[56] *On Principles* 1.3.1, in *The Writings of Origen*, Vol.1, T & T Clark, Edinburgh, 1869, p. 33.

[57] *On Principles* 1.3.8, *The Writings of Origen*, Vol.1, p. 41.

[58] 'It seems proper to inquire what is the reason why he who is regenerated by God unto salvation has to do both with Father and Son and Holy Spirit, and does not obtain salvation unless with the cooperation of the entire Trinity; and why it is impossible to become partakers of the Father and the Son without the Holy Spirit'. *On Principles* 1.3.5, *The Writings of Origen*, Vol.1, p. 37.

[59] B. Drewery identifies that in Origen's thought, 'the grace of the Father applies to all creation; the grace of the Son to all rational beings; but the grace of the Holy Spirit is restricted to the saints - the regenerate'. *Origen and the Doctrine of Grace*, Epworth Press, London, 1960, p. 172.

[60] In *On Principles* 1.3.4, Origen can identify that 'although something else existed before the Holy Spirit, it was not by progressive advancement that He came to be the Holy Spirit ... for if this were the case, the Holy Spirit would never be reckoned in the unity of the Trinity, i.e. along with the unchangeable Father and His Son, unless He had always been the Holy Spirit'. *The Writings of Origen*, Vol.1, pp. 36-37.

the Spirit's place in eternity, with the Father and the Son.[61] At the same time, Origen's emphasis on the economy of the Spirit leads him to explore the nature of the Spirit's relation to the Father and the Son.[62] The same issue arises in Origen's analysis of the Son's relation to the Father and the apparent subordinationism that results.[63]

Scholarly opinion has taken varying approaches to Origen's apparently Platonising tendencies. Mackey, understandably, identifies Origen as the most notable of the pre-Nicene subordinationists.[64] Kelly has argued that, although Origen's attempt at making ontological distinctions within the Triune God may cause him to appear as subordinating the Son and the Spirit to the Father, this is acceptable as merely a corollary to the graded hierarchy of Platonism.[65] Crouzel, on the other hand, has suggested that despite the influence of middle-platonism, Origen was seeking to render a model of the Trinity that was dynamic, preserving an understanding of the Father's continual generation of the Son, while insisting on the eternal nature of that generation;[66] and goes on to note that if Origen is to be accused of subordinationism, it is but a subordination within the economic action of the Godhead.[67] Crouzel makes three observations in justifying his analysis. He maintains that for Origen, firstly, the Father is the origin of the other two Persons and initiator of the Trinity. Secondly, the Son and the Spirit are agents *ad extra* of the Trinity. Thirdly, the mediating role of the Son rebounds onto His inner Being: 'the subordination for which Origen was blamed, which is also found in the other ante-Nicenes ... was not in contradiction with orthodoxy because it does not express an inequality of power ... but rather expresses realities which orthodoxy of necessity recognises, origin and mediation.'[68] More recently R. D. Williams, in his sympathetic reappraisal of Arius' standing in a tradition of pre-Nicene, Alexandrian theology, expresses the opinion that, for Origen, the Son's definitive function is to manifest the Father, the Son having no other reality except for this.[69]

Whatever precise interpretation we bring to Origen, what is apparent is an attempt to preserve an appreciation of the salvific economy of God. This was married to a growing need to make philosophical exploration of what that meant for the immanent, ontological Being of God as Trinity. The tension

---

[61] *On Principles*, Preface 4, *The Writings of Origen*, Vol.1, p. 3.

[62] *Commentary on John* 2.73-88, *The Fathers of the Church*, Vol. 80, translated by R. E. Heine, CUA, Washington, 1989, pp. 113-17.

[63] *On Principles* 1.2.10, *The Writings of Origen* Vol.1, pp. 28-30.

[64] Mackey, *The Christian Experience of God as Trinity*, p. 129.

[65] J. N. D. Kelly, *Early Christian Doctrines*, 5th Edition, A & C Black, London, 1985, pp. 127-28.

[66] H. Crouzel, *Origen*, T & T Clark, Edinburgh, 1989, p. 187.

[67] *Origen*, pp. 188ff.

[68] *Origen*, p. 203.

[69] R. D. Williams, *Arius: Heresy and Tradition*, D L T, London, 1987, pp. 143-44.

arising between these two factors came to dominate the theological arena of the third and fourth centuries. For our purposes, the question that matters is how the issues addressed in the ensuing debate helped or hindered the church in developing a Trinitarian model that expresses the reality of God as Father, Son and Holy Spirit, while also maintaining an understanding of the Spirit's ontic actuality in His dealings with men.

2.5   Arius, Nicea and the *Homoousion*

It is now necessary to mention the significance of Arius, for our understanding of the nature and effects of the theology propounded by Arius and his school will have a decisive role in determining our interpretation of later developments in Trinitarian theology and on the place given to the Holy Spirit in the Trinitarian models which evolved through and beyond the Nicene period. It is generally acknowledged that it was the teaching of Arius and his party, regarding the subordinate nature of the Logos, which triggered the credal formulations of Nicea in 325 and Constantinople in 381. That is in formulating a statement, at Nicea, on the Son's eternal relationship to the Father and, at Constantinople, on the Spirit's relationship both to the Father and to the Son, the church was engaged in tackling the problems arising from the teaching of the Arians.

Where did Arius' subordinationist teaching come from? Or rather, what were Arius' central concerns? Mackey identifies the Arian position as continuing pre-Nicene subordinationist/emanationalist perspectives, whilst rejecting essentialist language regarding the Being (*ousia*) of the Three.[70] In other words, the central issue which arose in the Arian controversy was not that traditionally understood and stated by Kelly,[71] that what is at issue is the status of the Logos and His relation to the Godhead. The central issue in Mackey's view lay with the appropriateness or otherwise of introducing essentialist language in describing our perception of the Three. This point made by Mackey is important, for it helps in highlighting an effect of the Arian debate. The Arian debate moved attention away from a pre-Nicene perspective on God's salvific economy to one where, among the post-Nicene theologians, much attention was given towards seeking how, firstly, the relationship of the Father and Son and then, secondly, their relationship to the Holy Spirit could be identified in terms of one *ousia*, or *homoousion*. As Mackey opines,

> I cannot personally see that the *homoousios* did any more than gradually - as it moved towards the meaning of identity of substance - threaten to destroy an older model, on which its protagonists nevertheless persistently, if surreptitiously, prove

---

[70] *The Christian Experience of God as Trinity*, p. 131.
[71] *Early Christian Doctrines*, p. 223.

themselves dependent whenever they wish to secure their inner-divine distinctions from disappearance.[72]

The question arises as to what Arius' opponents, the protagonists of the *homoousion*, were attempting to preserve. Was it, in fact, a pre-Nicene subordinationist/emanationalist perspective, newly married to categories of essentialist thought? Or was it something else: an emphasis on the salvific economy, the ontic actuality of God, whereby the Trinity of Father, Son and Holy Spirit could be affirmed not only as united in action but, in the face of Greek dualism, also as One in Being? At the same time, could it be that the concern of the Arians was not simply a defence of God's immutability but, against the pervading environment of Greek thought, the preservation of a pre-Nicene emphasis on the salvific economy of God and the actual involvement of the Son - and the Spirit - in the Creation? From this perspective, it is not the notion of God's immutability, albeit present in the interpretative framework, which lies at the heart of things; but the investment of God in His salvific economy, expressed in His ontic actuality. Fundamental to the appreciation of both Arius' protagonists and antagonists was the ontic actuality of the Triune God towards man.

Following this line of thought, we would moot the possibility that the subordinationist position of Arius arose out of a search, among both pro and anti-Nicenes, for a means of communicating the salvific economy of the Trinity against the backdrop of a metaphysical climate that inhibited an understanding of God in terms of His ontic actuality. We suggest that Arius' understanding of the Logos arose, in some part, out of a desire to stress the salvific economy of God, expressed through the humanity of Christ and the participation of the Logos in human nature. As R.P.C. Hanson noted in his study into the origins of Trinitarian theology, Arian theology was conceived of to convey the truth of a God who really suffers: that the Logos is, in fact, not immutable.[73]

Certainly, Arius' approach contrasted to that of Athanasius, whose emphasis lay on the shared Being (*homoousion*) of the Father and the Son. In this regard, it might be asked whether Athanasius and Arius both represent strains of thought true to the pre-Nicene tradition but falling on opposite sides of an ontological divide, between the Creator and the created, absorbing a dualism which had been superimposed onto their understanding of the Triune God by neoplatonic thought. Where Athanasius' stress on the *homoousios* of the Father and the Son focused on the divine unity within God's *ousia*, Arius looked more towards the unity of the Logos with the created, human nature of Christ. Within his own Trinitarian understanding Athanasius himself wrestled, as we shall see, with the problem of how he might best maintain an understanding of God's

---

[72] *The Christian Experience of God as Trinity*, p. 165.
[73] R.P.C. Hanson, *The Search for the Christian Doctrine of God*, T & T Clark, Edinburgh, 1990, p. 121.

salvific economy; yet his focus lay on the shared *ousia* of the Father and the Son. Consequently, it could be said that the victory of the *homoousion* party at Nicea proved to be a decisive step towards the development of a growing focus on ontological relationships within God's immanent Being, with less attention being given to the priority of the Triune God's salvific economy. This does not make us conclude, though, that Nicea forced the church to turn her back on an emphasis on the salvific economy of God. For our purposes, it means that a developing perspective on the Spirit would be shaped around the immanent relationship perceived as existing, through the *homoousion*, between the Father and the Son.

2.6   The Status of the Son

As Williams concludes in his study on Arius, the precise nature of Arius' relation to contemporary non-Christian philosophy can only remain speculative:[74] yet Arius, in seeking to define the relation of the Logos to an immutable God, stood in a tradition of Alexandrian thought reaching back to Origen.[75] In tackling the nature of the relationship of the Father to the pre-incarnate Logos, Arius worked towards an understanding of the soterial significance of the Son within a framework built on the foundation of Plato's dualist cosmology.[76] Arius' great antagonist, Athanasius, engaged the questions raised by the Platonic divide with a similar concern to maintain a soteriological focus to the theological debate; yet in Athanasius we meet most clearly with the declaration that it is in the Being of the Son Incarnate that we apprehend the Triune God. Ontologically, the Son Incarnate is for Athanasius the *locus operandi* of the Trinity's self-revelation to man, through His salvific economy:

> If then for our sake he sanctifies Himself, and does this when he is become man, it is very plain that the Spirit's descent on him in the Jordan was a descent upon us, because of His bearing our body. And it did not take place for promotion to the Word, but again for our sanctification, that we might share His anointing.....For when the Lord, as man, was washed in the Jordan, it was we who were washed in Him and by Him. And when he received the Spirit, we it was who by him were made recipients of it.[77]

The question arises, however, as to whether Athanasius actually related his prioritising of the Son's ontic actuality to a developed understanding of the Trinity's immanent Being; or whether his emphasis on the event of the Incarnation was but a development of an earlier, pre-Nicene emphasis on the salvific economy of God towards man. Is it correct to conclude, on the basis of

---

[74] *Arius: Heresy and Tradition*, p. 230.
[75] *Arius: Heresy and Tradition*, pp. 143-44.
[76] *The Search for the Christian Doctrine of God*, pp. 121ff..
[77] *Against the Arians* 1.47, *NPNF*, Vol.4, p. 333.

his advocacy of the *homoousion* and opposition to Arius, that Athanasius thought in essentialist terms? Can we agree with T. F. Torrance that Athanasius provides, through his focus on the event of the Son's Incarnation, a key to eternal relations and distinctions within the immanent Being of God?[78]

Certainly, within the thought of Athanasius, there is a clear emphasis on the association and unity between the Father and the Son that finds expression in the *homoousion*. This, given Athanasius' polemic against the Arians, was hardly surprising. At the same time, this does not imply that Athanasius had developed a model of the Trinity which combined an understanding of the incarnate Son's consubstantial relationship to the Father with a perception of a developed, ontological matrix of relationships between Father, Son and Holy Spirit. It cannot be assumed that relationships that are held to be true of God in the event of His salvific economy should predicate a perception of God as He is in His immanent Being.[79] God may have been perceived by Athanasius as possessing a dynamic within His own Being;[80] yet to speak of Athanasius as having a developed perception of Trinitarian relationships, described in terms of God's immanent Being, is quite another matter. Athanasius can demand an ontological centring of the Son's relationship to the Father in the event of the Incarnation, as he does in *Against the Arians*; but this is not the same as providing a key to a full Trinitarian theology in which the relation of Father, Son and Holy Spirit are formed in an integrated model of God's immanent Being. In order to gain an insight into Athanasius' understanding of the Spirit, we should perhaps look to *Letters to Serapion* rather than in *Against the Arians* where Athanasius is preoccupied with the *homoousion*. In so doing we find that, in *Letters to Serapion*, the stress lies on the self-giving of God in His salvific economy, depicted most vividly in Athanasius' illustration of water from a fountain. Here, the Father is shown as a fountain, the Son as a river and our drinking of the Spirit as our drinking of Christ: a salvific economy in movement *from* the Father, *through* the Son and *in* the Spirit.[81] Certainly, Athanasius' identification of the salvific economy preserves a coherent picture

---

[78] Torrance states, 'Quite clearly, Athanasius' approach to the doctrine of the Holy Spirit took its start and controlling norm from the revealing and saving acts of God in the incarnate *parousia* of His only begotten Son in Jesus Christ, and moved through the *homoousios to Patri* to its ultimate grounds in the eternal relations and distinctions within the one *ousia* of the Godhead'. T. F. Torrance, *The Trinitarian Faith*, T & T Clark, Edinburgh, 1988, p. 304.

[79] Torrance argues that it is Epiphanius who later develops Athanasius' position, so that the 'enhypostatic realities and distinctive properties of the Father, Son and Holy Spirit always remain the same in the equality and consubstantiality of the Holy Trinity'. *The Trinitarian Faith*, pp. 224-26.

[80] See *The Search for the Christian Doctrine of God*, p. 423.

[81] *Letters to Serapion* 1.19, in *Letters to Serapion*, C. R. B. Shapland (Trans.), Epworth, London, 1951, pp. 108-13.

of the One Triune God at work[82], Athanasius ever mindful of the need to preserve an understanding of the integrity of God in Triunity,

> a Triad, holy and complete confessed to be God in Father, Son and Holy Spirit, having nothing foreign or external mixed with it ... and it is consistent and in nature indivisible, and its activity is one.[83]

Athanasius does not, however, develop his understanding of the Triune relationship beyond this point; and we may well be led to conclude that, in *Letters to Serapion*, while concerned with combating the *Pneumatomachi*'s error of extending the Arian perception of the Son to the Holy Spirit, Athanasius was also seeking to do no other than preserve a pre-Nicene understanding of God's salvific economy towards us. Shapland, in his commentary on *Letters to Serapion*, opines that the precise relation of the Son to the Spirit is opaque[84] for, as Hanson also notes, the manner in which Athanasius perceives the relation of the Spirit to the Son is not dogmatic.[85] In stressing the *homoousion*, Athanasius may call for the centre of our focus to be on the Incarnation as the true basis for our appreciation of God; but it cannot be deduced from this that he had, or wished to develop, a clear understanding of the Trinity's immanent Being. J Pelikan rightly observes that Athanasius, having set his scheme of Trinitarian thought upon the notion of Christ as *homoousion*, had no need to develop an understanding of the relationship of the Spirit to the Son.[86] In this regard, we need to be conscious of the danger of interpolating into Athanasius' thought conclusions about the nature of those relationships existing between Father, Son and Holy Spirit which arose from a later stage of Trinitarian theology.

This said, from Athanasius, we gain a principle that would be implicitly assumed in later Chalcedonian orthodoxy: that where our knowledge of God is determined through His salvific economy towards us, this interaction is in and through the Son. Epistemologically, knowledge of the Holy Spirit becomes

---

[82] *Letters to Serapion* 1.14, pp. 93-94.

[83] *Letters to Serapion* 1.28, pp. 134-35.

[84] 'The action of the Godhead, as [Athanasius] understands it, derives from the Father and is accomplished through the agency of the Son in the Spirit. It must be admitted that he does not make altogether clear what he means by "in the Spirit"'. *Letters to Serapion*, pp. 36-37.

[85] 'At *Orations against the Arians* 3.24 [Athanasius] says openly that the Son does not share in the Spirit in such a way that this sharing ensures his abiding in the Father, but rather he receives the Spirit from the Father. There is certainly no doctrine of the *nexus amoris* here! In two places Athanasius is ready to apply the term *homoousion* to the Spirit (Letters to Serapion 1.27 and 2.6); he is not known to do this elsewhere.' Hanson, *The Search for the Christian Doctrine of God*, p. 752.

[86] J. Pelikan, *The Emergence of the Catholic Tradition*, University of Chicago Press, Chicago, 1971, p. 214.

contingent on the Incarnation of the Son and the *homoousion*. The Spirit is not to be apprehended by us outwith our apprehension of the Son. At the same time, we note that Athanasius was seeking to affirm the real status of the Spirit, whom he perceived as being part of an interrelated salvific economy towards us, from the Father, through the Son and in the Holy Spirit, for as,

> the Son is an only-begotten offspring, so also the Spirit, being given and sent from the Son, is himself one and not many, nor one from among many, but Only Spirit. As the Son, the living Word, is one, so must the vital activity and gift hereby he sanctifies and enlightens be one perfect and complete.[87]

Were we, however, to try to develop a Trinitarian model from the theology of Athanasius we would be faced with an interpretative model acutely vulnerable to misrepresentation. The danger, implicit in Athanasius' affirmation of the Father-Son *homoousios*, was that the place of the Holy Spirit within the Trinity be formulated exclusively in terms of that Father-Son relationship. A stress on the vicarious sanctification of our humanity, in and through the Incarnation of the Logos, could leave us with a Trinitarian model of God viewed within His own immanence, allowing no peculiar action of the Spirit to complement that of the Son, but subsuming the action of the Spirit entirely within the activity of the Son's Incarnation.[88]

Against this background, we must wonder what Athanasius would have made of the additional comments on the Holy Spirit added to the Nicene creed by the Nicene-Constantinopolitan formula of 381 AD.[89] Most probably a simple affirmation acknowledging the economy of the Spirit actualised, or proceeding, from the Father would have been quite acceptable to him; but it seems unlikely that Athanasius would have anticipated developments which were to introduce internal distinctions within the eternal Being of God, in the immanent relations of Father, Son and Holy Spirit. Where the Council of Nicea affirmed the *homoousion* of the Son, the further qualification as to the status of the Holy Spirit, made at Constantinople, arose from the need to affirm the deity of the Spirit over against those who extended the logic of Arianism from the Son to the Spirit. This extension of the Arian position, which Athanasius argued so powerfully against in *Letters to Serapion*, led to an emphatic association being made by the pro-Nicenes between the Spirit and the union of Father and the Son, an association which found expression in the

---

[87] *Letters to Serapion* 1.20, pp. 116-17.

[88] Here, we are sympathetic towards Hanson where he opines that Athanasius 'has almost no concept of the Spirit's function except to be a kind of understudy to the Son ... we miss in Athanasius' account any serious understanding of the distinct function of the Holy Spirit in salvation'. *The Search for the Christian Doctrine of God*, pp. 751-52.

[89] 'Who proceeds from the Father, Who with the Father and the Son is jointly worshipped and jointly glorified, Who spoke through the prophets'. *Creeds, Councils and Controversies*, edited by J. Stevenson, SPCK, London, 1973, p. 335.

Constantinopolitan creed of AD 381.

At the same time, we must note what the Constantinopolitan formula did not state. The Spirit is not presented as *homoousion* with the Father and the Son. Why such restraint? Was it simply because of the strength of continuing Arian sympathies? Or was it, perhaps, also due to the ongoing tension of working through, on the one hand, implications regarding the ontological integrity of the uncreated One, whilst still retaining a perspective on the ontic actuality inherent within the salvific economy of the Triune God? The need to defend the integrity of the Triune God invited a development of thought which a perspective founded on the salvific economy could not provide. Although both Athanasius and Arius wished to give theological expression to God's ontic actuality, the work of Arius, rooted as it was in a popular, Platonic framework, sadly demanded that his antagonists address him from the same perspective. The development of doctrine in the post-Nicene period was firmly moved into a framework of thought fashioned by the philosophy of Plato.

2.7   Relationships Within the Trinity

Where ontological questions were brought to the forefront of theological debate within the church, further development of theological understanding was called for on two fronts. The challenge of Arius required an affirmation of the Son's deity as equal to that of the Father's. The challenge of monarchianism demanded that some form of differential be introduced to explain the immanent Being of the Trinity. Unfortunately, this 'war on two fronts' led to hermeneutical problems. Countering Arius involved a response that apparently affirmed, through the *homoousion* of the Father and the Son, the unity of God's Being. On the other hand, the threat of monarchianism required that differentials be introduced to the church's perception of God. Needless to say, tensions could and did arise when an attempt was made to establish the place of the Spirit within the context of an ontological debate which was essentially binitarian, focused on the relation of the Father to the Son.

We see something of these tensions in Cyril of Jerusalem. Cyril could affirm that,

> The Holy Spirit is a most mighty power, a being divine and unsearchable. He is a living, intelligent being, the sanctifying power of all things made by God through Christ.[90]

Cyril recognised the dynamic, complementary action of the Spirit and the Son. At the same time he was wary, as were many others, of prying into the inner sanctity of the Triune God. Not only the Arians disliked the *homoousion*. For

---

[90] *Catechetical Lectures* 16.3, in *The Later Christian Fathers*, edited and translated by H. Bettenson, OUP, London, 1974, p. 37.

Cyril, the effect of introducing differentials into the relationship of the Trinity was not to affirm the deity of the Son, but to challenge the integrity of God:

> The Father gives to the Son; and the Son communicates to the Holy Spirit......The Father through the Son, with the Holy Spirit, confers all His gifts; the gifts of the Father are none other than those of the Son and those of the Holy Spirit. For there is one salvation, one power, one faith; one God the Father; one Lord, his only begotten Son; one Holy Spirit, the Paraclete. It is enough to know these things; do not be curious about the Spirit's nature or *hypostasis*....it is enough for salvation to know that there is a Father, a Son and a Spirit.[91]

Is it possible that there was a reticence, in formulating a more refined pneumatological perspective, which was born out of the introduction of the *homoousion* to the debate on the relationship of the Father to the Son? The affirmation that the Son is consubstantial with the Father had not been without controversy. Not all were prepared to sacrifice an appreciation of the salvific economy of the Trinity by introducing further distinctions within the Trinity; and early experience, especially around Nicea's debates on the Son, had not sharpened appetites for further, unnecessary acrimony over the Holy Spirit. It cannot be forgotten that Constantinople's declaration on the Holy Spirit, that 'He proceeds from the Father', was disarmingly simple and brief. Whatever, it was certainly the case that by the time the status of the Spirit had become an issue, when, around 360, the reasoning applied among the Arians to the Logos was also applied to the Spirit by those labelled *Pneumatomachi* (Spirit-fighters) by their opponents, the interpretative framework which was to lead not only to the pneumatological amplification of Nicea at Constantinople but also to the Christological formula of Chalcedon had already been set. A developing doctrine of the Spirit within the Trinity was to follow the pattern set through the debate over the Son.

2.8   Developing a Doctrine of Relations

2.8.1   In the East

In the period following the Council of Nicea, three great theologians of the East, Gregory of Nazianzus, Basil of Caesarea and Gregory of Nyssa, are collectively referred to as the Cappadocians. Although they do not offer a singular, cohesive model of the Trinity, their thought and theological process marks an important stage in the development of a doctrine of the Immanent Trinity. This is sometimes referred to as the Doctrine of Relations or, from the sixth century and more popularly in the work of John of Damascus in the eighth century, as the doctrine of perichoresis. It is to Cappadocian stage of development that we now turn.

Was it possible to speak of differentials within God without introducing

---

[91] *Catechetical Lectures* 16.24, *The Later Christian Fathers*, p. 38.

subordination? Gregory Nazianzen gave what was to be the classic statement on the matter: that the Father is the Begetter and the Emitter, the Son the Begotten and the Holy Spirit the Emission, all three being coeternal, with this procession taking place beyond time. An appeal to the atemporal, immanent relation of God's Being seemed to circumvent the difficulties of subordinationism. The difficulty lay in that the early tradition of Trinitarian understanding was formed not out of a perspective of God's Triune Being as immanent to Himself, but of God's reality as He is in His salvific economy, in the ontic actuality of the Son and the Spirit. An appeal to the atemporal Being of God did not automatically fit with a Trinitarian understanding generated from the salvific economy.

The arising tensions can be seen in the writings of Basil of Caesarea. Basil appealed, with the Nazianzen, to the atemporality of God as a ground for affirming the relationship of the Father and the Son. In his work, *On the Holy Spirit*, he affirmed,

> But noone is so senseless as to say that the Maker of the worlds is posterior to the Father, when the fact is that the natural conjunction of the Son and the Father admits of no dissociating interval of time.[92]

Basil, however, was unhappy to abstract his speech and relegate his knowledge of the Trinity to atemporal reality alone. Basil also retained the language and emphasis of the salvific economy:

> I testify to every man who confesses Christ, and denies God, that Christ will profit him nothing; or, if he call upon God, and does not acknowledge the Son, that his faith is in vain; and if a man rejects the Spirit, I tell him that his faith in the Father and the Son will be futile, for he cannot even have that faith without the presence of the Spirit. For he who does not believe the Spirit does not believe in the Son; and He who does not believe in the Son does not believe in the Father.....For it is not possible to worship the Son but by the Holy Spirit, nor is it possible to call upon the Father but by the Spirit of adoption.[93]

While seeking to affirm the Son's substantial equality with the Father, Basil appeared to allow for the salvific economy of the Trinity to be translated into terms descriptive of the immanent Being of God. It was not that Basil was unaware of the opposite danger to monarchianism, that of sub-numeration, with the introduction of 'three orders' of God: he stressed that while knowledge of God is from the Spirit, through the Son and to the Father, the Three are met with in a oneness of action which defies separation.[94] While constrained to

---

[92] Basil of Caesarea, *Basil the Great on the Holy Spirit*, translated by G. Lewis, Religious Tract Society, London, 1888, p. 35.
[93] *Basil the Great on the Holy Spirit*, p. 59.
[94] *Basil the Great on the Holy Spirit*, p. 94.

defend the integrity of the Trinity in the face of Arian attack, Basil was well aware of where an abstraction in our perception of the Trinity could lead to. This sensitivity, both to the salvific economy of the Trinity and a reticence in abstracting concepts of God, is possibly the reason behind Basil's reluctance to describe the Spirit as *homoousios* with the Father.

On the other hand, it should be conceded that Basil, in making the distinction between the *ousia* of God and the *hypostases* of the Father, Son and Spirit,[95] appears to be seeking after a Trinitarian model which also affirms the ontological integrity of God in terms of God's immanent Being. Basil uses the relationality of the Persons to qualify the nature of the substance.[96] Clearly, any understanding of the Spirit's ontic actuality is affected by this. A stress on the relational unity of the Trinity within the immanent Being of God could diminish an appreciation of the ontic actuality of the Spirit in the salvific economy.

For the Nazianzen the Spirit could be described as the Emission, in dealing with mankind the Trinity is 'as three suns might be joined to each other, producing one mingled light'.[97] For Gregory of Nyssa, as we will demonstrate in section 2.12, the focus also turns towards the oneness of the Trinity, apprehensible in unity of Being, separate from man. A Trinitarian model which posits the nature of God's immanent Being begins to take priority over an understanding of God based on the ontic actuality of the Son and Spirit in their salvific economy.[98]

To summarise, we can say that the Cappadocians, despite their acknowledged role in tackling the ontological issues arising from a focus on the Immanent Trinity, were still aware of the need to maintain some understanding of the Trinity's salvific economy. It may well be that, as Hanson hazards,[99] they were less concerned with the doctrine of the Incarnation than was Athanasius; but this does not mean, as Torrance has suggested, that they were any less driven by soteriological considerations.[100] Rather, the great difficulty facing the Cappadocians was that they had to address the question of God's immanent Being within a philosophical framework which, because its concern was not

---

[95] 'I shall say that the substance (*ousia*) is related to subsistence (*hypostasis*) as the general to the particular ... Father, Son and Holy Spirit, in the complete and perfect *hypostasis* of each person so named'. *Epistles* 214.4, *The Later Christian Fathers*, p. 77.

[96] 'Therefore in respect of the Godhead we acknowledge one *ousia*, so as not to give a different account of being ... We must confess our faith by adding the particular to the general'. *Epistles* 236.3, *The Later Christian Fathers*, pp. 77-78.

[97] *Orations* 31, *The Later Christian Fathers*, p. 115.

[98] Torrance takes a contrasting view of the Cappadocians, interpreting them as introducing a retrogressive relativism into the enhypostatic unity of the Trinity, through suggesting that there is a 'causation of being' of the Son and the Spirit from the Father. *The Trinitarian Faith*, p. 246.

[99] *The Search for the Christian Doctrine of God*, pp. 731 and 733.

[100] *The Trinitarian Faith*, p. 313.

intrinsically soteriological, did not insist that the development of a Trinitarian model be rooted in and developed through the ontic actuality of the Word made flesh in Jesus Christ and the present experience of the Holy Spirit grounded in the Spirit's ontic actuality. This failing was perhaps not immediately evident in the Trinitarian thought of the Cappadocians themselves, among whom a coherent, systematic presentation of relationships between the Persons of the Trinity remained undeveloped.[101] The Cappadocians did, however, help to further prepare the foundation for a later Trinitarian model in the East which appeared to present a disjunction between the Immanent and Economic Trinity. For the West, they helped to provide a framework for the development of the crucially influential Trinitarian thought of Augustine. It is to the development of this latter Western strain that we now turn our attention.

2.8.2   In the West

It was Hilary of Poitiers, the first writer in Latin to address the issue of the Trinity since Tertullian, who through his work *De Trinitate* brought to the West of the Empire the cogency of argument against the Arians that he had sampled in the East; and at the same time imported the concepts which had dominated the *homoousion* debate in the East to the West. Hilary's work *De Trinitate*, despite its title, had little to say about the place of the Spirit. For Hilary, the primary issue to be addressed was the relationship between the Father and the Son. In so far as the Spirit illumines and directs our thinking towards that relationship, we participate in Him. Even then, that participation in the Spirit is qualified, for

> It is not necessary to speak of Him in whom we must believe together with the Father and the Son who begot Him. Indeed, in my opinion there should not be any discussion about whether He is. He is, since as a matter of fact He is given, accepted, and obtained, and He, whom in our profession we must join with the Father and the Son, cannot be separated in such a profession from the Father and the Son.[102]

Later in the work, when affirming the usefulness of the term *homoousios*, Hilary concludes,

---

[101] Alternatively, the Cappadocians have been interpreted, through presenting a relational model of the Trinity, as possessing a more developed perspective on the Trinity than some who were to follow: see C. Gunton, 'Augustine, the Trinity and the Theological Crisis of the West', *Scottish Journal of Theology* (43.1), 1990, pp. 44-45.

[102] Hilary of Poitiers, *De Trinitate* 2.29, *FOTC*, Vol. 25, pp. 57-58.

it is revealed that God the Father and God the Son are clearly one, not by a union of person, but by the unity of nature (*non unione personae, sed substantiae unitate*).[103]

The affirmation of the Son's consubstantiality with the Father leads Hilary to affirm, regarding the procession of the Holy Spirit, a harmony of the Father with the Son,

And He who proceeds from the Father will send the Spirit of truth from the Father. Hence there is no longer an adoption where a procession is revealed.[104]

The reason for this affirmation, regarding the Spirit, is Christological: Hilary's primary concern is to make a statement regarding the Son's, not the Spirit's, relation to the Father. So it is, in the following section, Hilary can affirm,

Nor will I now infringe upon any one's liberty of thought in this matter, whether they may regard the Paraclete Spirit as coming from the Father or from the Son.[105]

Yet in relating the Spirit to the Son in the Spirit's economy towards us,[106] Hilary defines the Spirit on the basis of the community which exists between the Father and the Son.[107] In Hilary we see the legacy of the Eastern theological framework, born out of the crisis of Nicea and its ensuing developments, transported to the West. What is of interest is that, despite the priorities of the *homoousion* debate and the need to affirm the Trinity's transcendence, there remains in Hilary a reticence to abandon a pre-Nicene perspective of the Spirit's ontic actuality:

I cannot describe Him whose words to me are beyond my power of description. Just as from the fact that Your Only-Begotten was born from You all ambiguity in language and difficulty in understanding are at an end and only one thing remains, that He was born, so, too, in my consciousness I hold fast to the fact that your Holy Spirit is from You, although I do not grasp it with my understanding.[108]

In what way, then, did the theologians of the West differ from the Cappadocians and their guarded development of an ontological model of the Trinity? We detected a desire among the Cappadocians to affirm the integrity of God's Triune, immanent Being, qualified by a continued adherence to a pre-Nicene understanding of God's ontic actuality. This found expression through stressing the Incarnation of the Son and the action of the Holy Spirit, met with

---

[103] *De Trinitate* 4.42, *FOTC*, Vol. 25, p. 131.

[104] *De Trinitate* 8.19, *FOTC*, Vol. 25, p. 289.

[105] *De Trinitate* 8.20, *FOTC*, Vol. 25, p. 289.

[106] *De Trinitate* 8.30, *FOTC*, Vol. 25, pp. 297-99.

[107] *De Trinitate* 9.73, *FOTC*, Vol. 25, pp. 395-96.

[108] *De Trinitate* 12.56, *FOTC*, Vol. 25, p. 542.

in His emission from the Father. In the West, on the other hand, a factor that would speed the development of an abstracted Trinitarian model was the desire to affirm the place of the Spirit within the ontological unity of God. Such an affirmation would bring the focus of theological attention more fully onto the place of relations within the Trinity.

It is in the work of Ambrose, *The Holy Spirit*, that we see a development in formulating a doctrine of God which was expressed in terms of His immanent Being rather than one formulated out of God's salvific economy. Ambrose's intent was to affirm the oneness of operation found in the action of the Trinity, thereby affirming the status of the Spirit alongside that of the Father and the Son.[109] Certainly, for Ambrose it was enough to affirm the unity of Triune operation,[110] with the simple qualification that any form of Sabellianism is wrong.[111] His theology, in affirming the unity of the Spirit's action with the operation of the Father and the Son, did not in itself predicate further speculation into the nature of God's Being, or present a doctrine of relations as explicit as that later formulated in the East by John of Damascus;[112] yet it did invite further definition as to the nature of internal relationships within the immanent Being of God. This process was accelerated when combined with another important development that took place in the West: the early emphasis on the doctrine of the church. For Ambrose, this meant marrying a model of the Trinity, One in operation, with an understanding of the church and her sacraments as the *modus operandi* of the Trinity's action towards us:

> Not only is there one operation everywhere on the part of the Father and the Son and the Holy Spirit, but also one and the same will, one calling and one giving of commands, which may be seen in the great and saving mystery of the church.[113]

> Therefore the Father sanctifies, the Son also sanctifies, and the Holy Spirit sanctifies, but the sanctification is one, because the baptism is one, and the grace of the sacrament is one.[114]

The path towards reversing the relationship of subject and predicate, whereby a model of the Immanent Trinity might be given precedence over the economic model of the Son and Spirit's ontic actuality, had been well prepared. It is in Augustine of Hippo that we see this development of the Immanent Trinity and the Spirit construed therein most forcefully expressed.

---

[109] Ambrose of Milan, *The Holy Spirit* 1.11-12, *FOTC*, Vol. 44, pp. 79-80.

[110] *The Holy Spirit* 1.12-13, *FOTC*, Vol. 44, pp. 82-83.

[111] *The Holy Spirit* 1.13, *FOTC*, Vol. 44, p. 84.

[112] For a fuller discussion of the doctrine of relations and a contemporary, experimental development to this approach, *vide* P. S. Fiddes, *Participation in God*, DLT, London, 2000, especially pp. 71ff..

[113] *The Holy Spirit* 2.10, *FOTC*, Vol. 44, p. 131.

[114] *The Holy Spirit* 3.4, *FOTC*, Vol. 44, p. 163.

2.9 The Priority of the Immanent Trinity

The influence of Augustine on the subsequent development of Trinitarian thought in the West cannot be questioned: neither can the fact that the significance of his contribution is interpreted in many differing ways. Of recent commentators, Colin Gunton's analysis of Augustine has been among the less sympathetic. At the heart of his criticism, Gunton detects a neoplatonic strain in Augustine's thought that fails to engage with the full significance of the Incarnation. Gunton views Augustine as building an analogical understanding of the Trinity founded not on the relatedness of the Triune persons in their salvific economy but upon an understanding of the substantial Being of God supported by the relationship of the Triune persons, yet not constituted by that relationship.[115] Gunton does not view Augustine's perception of God's immanent Being as properly founded on the salvific economy. Consequently, Gunton perceives Augustine's understanding of the Spirit as deficient in that inadequate hypostatic weight is given to it, thereby detracting from the personal distinctiveness of the Spirit within the Trinity.[116] Mackey, while no less critical of Augustine in recognising his devaluation of the Incarnation[117] and a neoplatonic dualism present in Augustine's writings, is more sympathetic towards Augustine's attempts at fashioning an understanding of the Trinity which would affirm a perception of the Triune God compatible with the Nicene *homoousion*. Mackey does not dispute Augustine's use of 'substance language';[118] but sees this as arising from the legacy of Nicea and the consequent reaction to a subordinationist / emanationist model, a reaction quickened by the Arian controversy. Within that context, Mackey detects a vestige of the earlier economic emphasis in Augustine's preference 'for the wisdom of the inner man as source of an image of the Triune God';[119] but sees Augustine being carried along, with others, towards a focus on the immanent Being of God in contrast to the pre-Nicene emphasis on economy.

Augustine's preference for a theology of substance, formed consciously or otherwise, is illustrated in the following extract from *De Trinitate*:[120]

Father, Son, and Holy Ghost mean a divine unity in an inseparable equality of one and the same substance, and are therefore not three Gods but one God: though the Father has begotten the Son, and therefore He who is the Father is not the Son; the Son is begotten from the Father, and therefore He who is the Son is not Father; the

---

[115] 'Augustine, the Trinity and the Theological Crisis of the West', pp. 45-6.
[116] 'Augustine, the Trinity and the Theological Crisis of the West', p. 55.
[117] *The Christian Experience of God as Trinity*, p. 158.
[118] *The Christian Experience of God as Trinity*, p. 153.
[119] *The Christian Experience of God as Trinity*, p. 162.
[120] 'On the Trinity'.

Holy Spirit is neither Father nor Son, but only the Spirit of Father and Son, himself co-equal with both and belonging to the unity of the Trinity.[121]

Augustine's starting point appeared to lie not with the ontic actuality of the Son and the Spirit in God's salvific economy. Rather, it lay with the ontological priority of God's immanent Being, prior to and determinative of all revelation. Augustine perceived the divine Fatherhood as a relation within the immanent Triunity of God: not one specifically related to the economy of the Son and the Spirit. An understanding of ontological relationships within the Trinity is not contingent upon a perception of the Father, Son and Spirit formed from their salvific economy.

That the salvific economy of God is not constitutive of His internal nature does not mean that relational factors, for Augustine, are unimportant: they are vital to a proper understanding of God. The Father is the source in that the Son is begotten of Him and the Spirit proceeds from Him.[122] However, the essential basis of these relationships is founded not on the Trinity's salvific economy but out of the Trinity's immanent Being. In this sense, it is the relationships that are true of the Trinity within Himself which become prescriptive of our proper comprehension of God's nature. This is not to say that Augustine did not allow the association of particular attributes of Deity with the different persons of the Trinity; but such is not the same as associating distinctive economic functions with the ontic actuality of the Son and the Holy Spirit. As Augustine explains,

> Yet there is good reason why in this Trinity we call none Word of God but the Son, none gift of God but the Holy Spirit, none of whom the Word is begotten and from whom the Holy Spirit originally proceeds, but God the Father. I add the word 'originally,' because we learn that the Holy Spirit proceeds also from the Son. But this is part of what is given by the Father to the Son, not as already existing without it, but given to Him as all that the Father gives to His only begotten Word, in the act of begetting. He is begotten in such wise that the common gift proceeds from Him also, and the Holy Spirit is Spirit of both. And this distinction in the indivisible Trinity is not to be admitted in passing, but to be observed with all diligence. For hence it comes that the Word of God is by a special fitness called also the wisdom of God, though both the Father and Holy Spirit are wisdom. If then one of the three is by special fitness to be named charity, the name falls most appropriately to the Holy Spirit. And this means that in the incomposite and supreme being of God, substance is not to be distinguished from charity; but substance is itself charity, and charity is itself substance, whether in the Father or in the Son or in the Holy Spirit, and yet by special fitness the Holy Spirit is named charity.[123]

---

[121] Augustine of Hippo, *De Trinitate* 1.7, in *Library of Christian Classics*, Vol. 8, translated by J. Burnaby, SCM, London, 1965, p. 19.

[122] *De Trinitate* 5.15.

[123] *De Trinitate* 15.29, *Library of Christian Classics* Vol. 8, pp. 158-59.

Again, Augustine's understanding of 'special fitness' is traced not through the salvific economy but in the analogy of God's true nature that is formed in our understanding. Indeed, it is fundamental to a proper understanding of Augustine to see that his Trinitarian model is formed on an analogical perception of the Trinity's ontological Being, rather than on the salvific economy, or ontic actuality, of the Son and the Holy Spirit. Certainly, there is some correlation between God's self revelation and our awareness of His ontological reality; but the association is far from being unambiguously causal.[124]

For Augustine, our understanding of God comes neither from the present ontic actuality of the Spirit nor from the Incarnation of the Son. The focus is now on a Triune interaction, the ontological reality of God's immanent Being, appreciated by us and independent of the moment of revelation in the Incarnation. In Augustine, the evolution of a Trinitarian model accessible to Platonic categories of thought and expression is completed. The maxim *opera Trinitatis ad extra sunt indivisa*[125] has been realised.

2.10 Foundations for the *Filioque*

The significance of Augustine to our study is due not only to his place within the evolving Trinitarian thought of the fourth century, but because of the legacy which he would leave in Western Trinitarian thought through his perception of the Holy Spirit as *vinculum*[126] between the Father and the Son. Augustine, while operating within a neoplatonic framework, preserved an insight into the economy of God through identifying the Spirit as proceeding principally from the Father. The accretion that Augustine now adds is that, being begotten of the Father, the Son also receives from the Father, that the Spirit should proceed from the Son also.[127] That is, the Spirit proceeds from the Father and from the Son.

That the *Filioque* clause, expressing this Western perception, does not find formal acceptance within the western text of the Nicene-Constantinopolitan creed until eleventh century[128] should not obscure the fact that the theological foundations for this were laid much earlier. As we noted in Hilary of Poitiers, the engagement by Latin theologians with the implications of the *homoousion* debate led to an affirmation of a common substance (*substantia*) as belonging to the Father and the Son. Where the language of substance was used to

---

[124] J. Burnaby contends that Augustine's understanding of the Divine is structured only indirectly on God's self revelation. *Library of Christian Classics*, Vol. 8, p. 126.
[125] 'The operations of the Triune God are, when viewed from the outside, indivisible'.
[126] 'bond'.
[127] *De Trinitate* 15.17.29.
[128] By Pope Benedict VIII. The early use of the *Filioque* in the West can be traced in the Athanasian creed and in the Canons of the Council of Toledo in AD 589.

develop a theology of God's immanent Being, it was understandable that the Spirit be construed in terms of the substantial relationship of the Father to the Son. In addition, that growing emphasis that was traced in Ambrose, upon the church and her sacraments as not only the *locus* but also the *modus operandi* of the Spirit, invited a perspective which viewed the Holy Spirit as the communicator of God's presence to the body of Christ, the church.

We would suggest that three features can therefore be identified in causing Augustine's motif of the Spirit as *vinculum* to emerge as a dominant model in the development of later Western Trinitarian thought. Firstly, Augustine's use of the neoplatonic framework invited a dualistic perspective on the Trinity. Despite both the contemporary triadic, economic outlook of neoplatonism and the continuing presence of a primitive, pre-Nicene Christian emphasis on the salvific economy within Augustine's understanding, Augustine's recourse to an analogical model in communicating an understanding of the immanent Triunity of God invited a view of the Spirit expressed in analogical terms, thereby reinforcing a separation between our perception of the Spirit and our experience of Him. Secondly, the Western use of the language of substance invited an affirmation of the Spirit's Being which was expressed in terms of the substantial relationship of the Father and Son, rather than an identification of the Spirit in His own ontic actuality. Thirdly, a stress on the church, the body of Christ, as the *modus operandi* of the Spirit, enhanced the attraction of viewing the Spirit as the 'bond of love' between the immanent Godhead and the body of Christ on earth.

2.11   The Spirit and Christology

Athanasius may well have been a significant figure in ensuring that the Son was given His place in Chalcedonian orthodoxy; but is it possible that Athanasius' own Christology and Alexandrian heritage prejudiced him from facing the full issue of Christ's humanity and the work of the Spirit therein? We suggested earlier that, in seeking to do no other than preserve a pre-Nicene understanding of God's salvific economy towards us, there arose a lack of clarity in Athanasius' distinction of the Spirit from the Son. In emphasising the *homoousion* did Athanasius, albeit unconsciously, fail to retain an understanding as to the vital place of the Spirit's ontic actuality, realised in the vicarious humanity of Christ?

Athanasius, as the great proponent of Nicene orthodoxy, emphasised the essential ontological gulf which exists between the Divine and the created, while maintaining that the redemption of mankind is brought about through the bridge of the Incarnation and the sharing of the human, created condition by the Son of God. It needs to be asked, however, whether Athanasius' preoccupation with affirming the *homoousion* led him to allow insufficient scope for the work of the Holy Spirit, expressed and realised in and through Christ Jesus. More than that, could it be that his perception of the Logos' relationship with the humanity of Christ preempted his developing a proper understanding of the Holy Spirit's action in and through the humanity of Christ?

Certainly there were constraints on Athanasius. The legacy which stemmed from the condemnation of the third century Antiochene bishop, Paul of Samosata, who refused to allow for a distinction within the Godhead and who employed the term *homoousios* in identifying the union of the Father with the Son,[129] meant that Athanasius had to be especially clear, when speaking of the *homoousion*, as to the distinction between the Father and the *Logos ensarkos*. The consequent price, in emphasising the investment of the Son of God in Christ as *Logos ensarkos*, could well have been an obscuring of Christ's human soul. An over-emphasis on the place of the Logos within the humanity of Christ might detract from a developed understanding of the Holy Spirit's mission within the humanity of Christ; yet a stress on the role of the Spirit could be mistaken as a failure to appreciate the distinction of the Father and the Son within the *homoousion*. It may well be that Athanasius was sensitive to this problem and wished to avoid the charge of presenting a Father/Son - Spirit binitarianism.

On the other hand there is the further danger, in reading Athanasius, of interpolating into his thought an understanding of the Being of the Logos which was foreign to him. It may well be that Athanasius' understanding of the *Logos ensarkos* implied for him the activity of the Spirit. What Athanasius understood by personhood within the Trinity is a moot point; but it was unlikely to carry the individualistic connotations associated with later, Cartesian thought.

Given these qualifications, it does remain important to ask, as A. Grillmeier does, to what extent Athanasius adopts a *Logos-sarx* framework which both fails to take account of the ontic actuality of the Holy Spirit and lacks a realistic appreciation of the humanity of Christ. An over emphasis on the inhomination of the Logos could obscure both the true humanity of Christ and the work of the Holy Spirit within that humanity.

Grillmeier's suggestion is that there is the potential in Athanasius to underestimate the 'human' in Christ, in a manner similar to Apollinarius, although avoiding the final conclusions of the latter.[130] Should Grillmeier be correct, we would have to recognise that there is a pneumatological effect which arises from such a Christology. There is the possible danger, within Athanasius' Alexandrian heritage, that the priority given to the activity of the Logos in the Word-man could subrogate the role of the Holy Spirit, demoting it to that of a secondary work, containing and restricting the Spirit's activity to that which occurs within the assumptive role of the Logos.

---

[129] *Arius: Heresy and Tradition*, p. 161.

[130] 'The idea of the positive, vital and dynamic influence of the Logos on the flesh of Christ ... tends not just to conceal the soul of Christ, but also to exclude it all together ...'. A. Grillmeier, *Christ in Christian Tradition*, Vol. 1, Mowbrays, London, 1975, pp. 325-26.

The effect of such a priority being given to the *Logos-sarx* model can be seen in the conflict which has been characterised as existing between the Alexandrian and Antiochene schools of Christology. As Wallace-Hadrill observes, the emphasis upon the reality of Christ's humanity, the hall-mark of Antiochene theology, arises from a reaction to docetism.[131] This is important if, in stressing the humanity of Christ, it is Antiochene spirituality which has emphasised the imitation of Christ in devotional and religious life.[132]

Such a commendation of the Antiochene emphasis places Athanasius in a poor light if, as Louth suggests, it is true that Athanasius displays an anti-mysticism that is rooted in a perception of the human soul that will not allow it to be seen, in any way, as co-natural with God or co-eternal with Him.[133] Could this be the legacy which arises from the grounds of Grillmeier's complaint against Athanasius and the Alexandrian position? Whatever, it was the influence of the Alexandrian stress on the *Logos-sarx* which would condition, within a Trinitarian context, the developing theology of the West and provide the parameters of acceptable orthodoxy in the East; and, in turn, fashion an understanding of the Spirit's role in relation to the Son.

This is not to say that all Alexandrians were implicated in the error of Apollinarius: there was a danger seen by others, such as Gregory of Nyssa, in denying the presence of a human soul in Christ. However, as Grillmeier observes in reviewing the problems which he sees as arising out of the Alexandrian tradition, the slowness in recognising the implications of Christ's full humanity among the Fathers of the East in the fourth century suggests that they may have failed properly to acknowledge the full humanity of Jesus.[134]

The question of whether or not the humanity of Jesus was given its true place is properly directed to Gregory of Nyssa. Even allowing for the defence against Apollinarianism that Gregory felt it necessary to engage in, does he give enough credence to the active humanity of Christ Jesus?

The hub of Gregory's Christology can perhaps best be seen in the following extract from *Against Eunomius* 5.5:

> The godhead 'empties itself' in order that it may come within the capacity of the human nature; the humanity is renewed by becoming divine through the commixture with the divine....As fire that often lies hidden below the surface of wood is not observed by the senses of those who see or even touch the wood, but

---

[131] D. S. Wallace-Hadrill, *Christian Antioch: A Study in Early Christian Thought in the East*, CUP, Cambridge, 1982, p. 20.

[132] Wallace-Hadrill notes that 'It is of central importance to the Antiochene conception of religion that the victory must be that of the human will over the temptation to disobedience'. *Christian Antioch: A Study in Early Christian Thought in the East*, p. 161.

[133] A. Louth, *The Origins of the Christian Mystical Tradition*, OUP, Oxford, 1981, p. 78.

[134] *Christ in Christian Tradition*, Vol. 1, p. 343.

is manifest when it is kindled into flame; so...he who, because He is the 'Lord of Glory', thought nothing of that which men think shame, and concealed, as it were, the members of his life beneath his bodily nature in fulfilling the divine plan by means of his death, kindled it to flame again by the power of his own godhead, turning into life that which had been brought to death, pouring that limited first fruit of our nature into the infinity of his divine power. Thus he *made it to be that which he himself was*, making the form of the servant to be Lord, the human son of Mary to be Christ, him who was crucified through weakness to be life and power, and making all that is reverently conceived as belonging to God the Word to be also in that which the Word assumed; so that those properties no longer seem to be in either nature by way of distinction and division. *Rather it seems that the perishable nature is re-created by commixture into the divine, since the divine prevails over it; and thus it partakes of the power of the Godhead; as if one should say that a drop of vinegar mixed in the ocean is turned into sea by that mixture*, since the natural qualities of the liquid do not remain in the infinity of the prevailing element.... That which as crucified because of weakness has itself become, through the prevailing power of him who dwelt within it, what the indweller is in fact and title, namely, Christ and Lord.[135]

What is of interest here is the role assigned to the Logos. Such is the active subordination of the humanity of the flesh to the divinity of the Logos, that there is little place for either human initiative and assent in the actions of Christ, or a place for the activity of the Spirit in the life of Christ. The priority of action would appear to lie in the latent power of the indwelling Logos.

Moreover, can we discern, in the passages italicised, a key to the mystical theology of Gregory? Where the humanity of Christ is subordinated to the activity of the Logos, this leads to a spiritual theology that can indeed speak of people being 'brought into' the presence of God, but which finds it far harder to comprehend an activity of the Spirit reaching out to the humanity of Jesus. His humanity, and ours, is made to be a passive spectator in the drama of redemption, as the priority of the Logos' activity is affirmed.

Gregory, of course, was not essentially concerned with formulating a theology of the Spirit, other than to defend the Spirit's place within the uncreated Trinity. The circumstances of apologetic debate did not require him to explore the implications of the salvific economy of the Spirit. This said, his mystical theology and understanding of our experience of God does appear to arise out of his prior doctrine of immutability and a necessary ontological separation of mankind and deity, the created and the uncreated.

It is the understanding of the Spirit within a dualistic, mystical theology of the Trinity that we now turn to consider.

---

[135] *Against Eunomius* 5.5, *The Later Christian Fathers*, pp. 138-39. Italics mine.

2.12   The Spirit and Christian Experience

In tracing the developing understanding of the Spirit within the context of Trinitarian models in the Patristic era, we have observed an evolution in thought. Moving from a perspective, present in the Apostolic Fathers, which allowed for the ontic actuality of the Spirit's economy, we saw the development of a theology where the Spirit's action was not only distinguished but differentiated from the ontic actuality of the Son's historic, salvific mission. This differentiation was largely due to Christological considerations, the effect of which was to reinforce a perception of the Spirit whereby His Person and function were construed as logically consequential to the ontology of the Son's relation to the Father. In stressing the soterial mission of the Son and His relationship to the Father, an understanding of the Spirit came to be founded on an understanding of the Father - Son relationship: something of this was seen in Athanasius. Add to this the growing tendency of the post-Nicenes, evident among the Cappadocians, to stress the ontological gulf between mankind and God, and we arrive at a Trinitarian model which obscures the pre-Nicene perception of a salvific economy expressing the ontic actuality of the Son and the Spirit. Where, in the Apostolic Fathers, the Spirit was seen as present to mankind in His ontic actuality, by the fourth century we can detect an increasing emphasis on the ontological gulf between God and man, presenting an understanding of the Spirit which increasingly stressed His place within the immanent Trinity and the perichoretic character of the Triune God's activity.

To what degree was this evolution in Trinitarian thought accompanied by a change in presenting an understanding of the Spirit's mission: away from His ontic actuality, revealing the very Being of God to us, towards something new and in contrast to the emphasis of the pre-Nicene tradition? In tackling this question, it is necessary to make some further mention of neoplatonism and its presentation of the relationship of mankind to God. The distinction made between the noetic and sensible in facilitating an understanding of human identity was integral to the Platonic understanding of the One and the evolution in thought which occurred through to the neoplatonic perspective of God. Throughout Platonism, middle-platonism and neoplatonism was the perception of an ontological gulf between God and man. Although developments of Plato's original thesis might come to see this gulf bridged by various mediating agents, the Platonic tradition held as fundamental to its perspective a disjunction between the Creator and creation. That part within a person, by which the Divine could be perceived and understood, was the noetic. Through this part of a person the *nous*, or supreme spiritual reality, could be apprehended.

It was this conceptual framework which facilitated a defence against the Arian threat, itself the product of neoplatonism's inability to marry the Creator and the created in the person of Jesus Christ. By building on the concept of man's noetic nature, in addition to and complementary to his sensible nature, the case could be made for the human apprehension of God in His immanent Being. More particularly, it allowed for the argument that Jesus Christ, the Son of God, should be construed as *homoousios* with God the Father, one in *ousia*, or Being, with God. The interpretation of this, noetically, could be applied to the status of the Son outwith the moment of the Incarnation. The affirmation of the Son Incarnate as *homoousios* with the Father was the result of an ability to construe, noetically, the prior or transcendent unity that exists between the Father and the Son. This logic could easily be extended to the Spirit. The question which concerns us is the degree to which the distinction between the noetic and sensible robbed the church of a proper appreciation of the Spirit's ontic actuality.

Gregory of Nyssa and Augustine of Hippo are two theologians, from the East and the West respectively, who present us with Trinitarian models which evolved beyond a perception of the Holy Spirit within God's salvific economy into one where their understanding of the Holy Spirit is integrated into an ontological model of God's immanent Being. We look to them in asking the question whether there can be detected a neoplatonic influence in their thought which might seek to disallow an acknowledgement of direct, ontic action by the Spirit upon the sensible nature of man. Thereafter, we will look briefly at Denys the Areopagite.

2.12.1   Gregory of Nyssa

For Gregory, the life of spiritual growth consisted of three successive stages: the way of light, the knowledge of God within 'the mirror of the soul' and knowledge of God in the darkness. This third stage is critical. As Danielou notes,[136] it is here that the impotence of man's power to know the divine essence becomes evident: indeed, the highest form of contemplation is awareness of this inaccessibility. This is illustrated from the *Life of Moses*:

> What now is the meaning of Moses' entry into the darkness and of the vision of God that he enoyed in it? ...The sacred text is here teaching us that ... as the soul makes progress, and by a greater and more perfect concentration comes to appreciate what the knowledge of truth is, the more it approaches this vision, and so much the more it sees the divine nature is invisible. It thus leaves all surface appearances, not only those that can be grasped by the senses but also those which the mind itself seems to see, and it keeps on going deeper until by the operation of the spirit it penetrates the invisible and incomprehensible, and it is there that it sees God. The true vision and the true knowledge of what we seek consists precisely in not seeing, in an awareness that our goal transcends all knowledge and is everywhere cut off from us by the darkness of incomprehensibility. Thus that profound evangelist, John, who penetrated into this luminous darkness, tells

---

[136] *From Glory to Glory:Texts from Gregory of Nyssa's Mystical Writings*, edited and translated by H. Musurillo, with an introduction by J. Danielou, John Murray, London, 1962, p. 26.

us that no man hath seen God at any time, teaching us by this negation that no man - indeed, no created intellect - can attain knowledge of God.[137]

For Gregory, the spiritual quest is one of continued ascent and transformation towards the immutable God. This is a quest into deeper 'darkness', as we come closer to God who is Spirit and whose very reality defies explanation and description within our material senses. This ascent into darkness is truly entrance into an awareness of the infinite realms of God's reality: yet it is not to be interpreted as a proximation to the essence of God's own Being. It is a deeper and deeper appreciation of God as exterior to our senses.[138] The gulf that separates the created from the Creator is, for Gregory, one that does not invite the realisation or possibility of a substantial, ontological interaction between mankind and God. This is illustrated in the following extract, out of Gregory's *From Dove to Dove*:

> the divine nature is simple, pure, unique, immutable, unalterable, ever abiding in the same way, and never going out of itself. It is utterly immune to any participation in evil and thus possesses the good without limit, because it can see no boundary to its own perfection, nor see anything that is contrary to itself. When therefore it draws human nature to participate in its perfection, because of the divine transcendence it must always be superior to our nature in the same degree. The soul grows in its constant participation in that which transcends it; and yet the perfection in which the soul shares remains ever the same, and it is always discovered by the soul to be transcendent to the same degree.[139]

Certainly this advance of the human soul is, for Gregory, experiential; but it is an experience induced within man's subjective being, rather than an experience of the Being of God Himself. One image used is that of vertigo, as in the *Commentary on Ecclesiastes*, where Gregory describes the incomprehensibility of God's Being; and that, becoming aware of such,

> the soul, slipping at every point from what cannot be grasped, becomes dizzy and perplexed and returns once again to what is co-natural to it, content now to know merely this about the Transcendent, that it is completely different from the nature of things that the soul knows.[140]

For Gregory, to speak of God as Spirit is to emphasise the ontological separation of Deity from mankind's sensible awareness. It is because God is Spirit that He is inaccessible to our senses. God is not only inaccessible to

---

[137] *From Glory to Glory*, p. 29.

[138] 'God remains forever beyond, and the soul must constantly move forward. So it is that the man who sees God will constantly be drawn into more and more of His reality, an infinite quest through the "luminous darkness"'. *From Glory to Glory*, p. 55.

[139] *From Glory to Glory*, p. 190.

[140] *From Glory to Glory*, pp. 127-28.

mankind's comprehension; He is, Himself, beyond the possibility of participation in mankind's sensible existence.

In this respect, there does appear to be demonstrated in Gregory's thought a dualism between spirit and matter, reflected in an emphasis on the immutability of God. Certainly, Gregory may have come to qualify the philosophical perspective of a Platonic divide between mankind and God, through introducing a soteriological aspect to the act of contemplation, in the process of sanctification:[141] this, however, highlights the absence of any direct participation by mankind in the ontic actuality of the Holy Spirit. Direct apprehension of and communion with the Spirit is not possible for man, where the Spirit's Being is restricted to a communion within the Trinity, which may well be expressed in ontological terms of God's immanent Being, but which is without an ontic actuality expressed towards mankind. In this sense, there is no direct experience of God possible in apophatic theology.

2.12.2 Augustine of Hippo

Where a desire to stress the transcendence of God led, in the East, to the development of apophatic theology, the path in the West took a different course. Louth identifies the basis for Augustine's understanding of the Spirit and the Trinity as lying in the *Confessions*, further developed in *De Trinitate*.[142] In the earlier work Louth detects the influence of neoplatonism but sees a move by Augustine, in *De Trinitate*, to ground his understanding of the Trinity more clearly on the Incarnation. The adoption of a Christocentric model does not, however, mean that the salvific economy of the Trinity is central to Augustine's thought. Rather the significance of the Incarnation lies in that mankind, as *imago Dei*,[143] is seen as an image of the Incarnate One, Christ the Word of God, who Himself is the true image of God. As such, the image of God in man's rational soul is Trinitarian.[144] It follows that renewal for the Christian is a renewal in the image of and participation with the Trinity of God. Renewal is renewal into the image of God, through a growing realisation of the truth of the Trinity disclosed in the heart of the believer.

Spiritual renewal does not lie within the province of the Spirit, expressed through His ontic actuality realised in the Christian's life. Rather it is associated with a quickening of man's noetic awareness and a growing awareness of a sensibly remote God. Thus it is in Book 14 of *De Trinitate* that Augustine speaks of the renewal of the mind, through the contemplation by mankind of the true image of God. Burnaby, commenting on this, notes that this leads us to an understanding of man's true end lying, not in action, but in the renewal of

---

[141] *From Glory to Glory*, p. 47.
[142] Louth, *The Origins of the Christian Mystical Tradition*, p. 145.
[143] 'Image of God'.
[144] Louth, *The Origins of the Christian Mystical Tradition*, p. 147.

his mind.[145]

Augustine, while adopting a dualism similar to Gregory through stressing the ontological integrity of the Trinity over against man's createdness, avoids a model of the Trinity which centres on the salvific economy of God or is contingent upon the ontic actuality of the Son or the Holy Spirit. However, he undertakes a quite different approach to that of Gregory in formulating an understanding of mankind's communion with God. While, in the East, this understanding was developed through the *via negativa*[146] of apophatic theology, Augustine builds his system on the use of analogical language, finding a parallel to the immanent relations of the Trinity within man's rational soul. In this, we can say that Augustine's model of the Trinity and his understanding of that model reflected in the human mind leads to an emphasis on the facility of mankind's intellectual faculty in apprehending the truth of God. Since the human person was made in the image of the whole Trinity, Augustine sought to discern, in mankind's make up, patterns of relationship to aid understanding of the Trinitarian relations. However, while this model served to strengthen an understanding of God's Being within Himself, use of the analogical method could lead to an understanding of the Trinity where our appreciation of God's Triune Being arises primarily out of our rationality.[147] In such a case, the perichoretic oneness of God can become accepted as axiomatic, rather than an as a means of contesting for the substantial unity of God. That the doctrine of perichoresis owed its ultimate origin to the pre-Nicene perception of God's salvific economy, expressed through the ontic actuality of the Son and the Holy Spirit, could easily be lost sight of.

2.12.3   Post-Nicene Developments: A Summary

The Trinitarian models of Gregory and Augustine appear to differ. Gregory's understanding of the soul's ascent towards God prefigures and provides a basis for the later development in the East, through Symeon and Gregory Palamas, of a theology that spoke of our engagement with the *energeia*,[148] or external manifestation of the Trinity, without an engagement with God in His own, immanent Being. Such an understanding of the Trinity stood in contrast to the relational model of Augustine, which was to be discovered imprinted on mankind's rational self-consciousness. However, these differences can obscure how much the differing perspectives of Augustine and Gregory share in common. Both approaches have at their heart a dualism that separates the Being

---

[145] 'Augustine like Plotinus insists that the true end of man is not action but contemplation; and this means that the perfect image of God can only be found in the mind at worship'. *Library of Christian Classics*, Vol. 8, p. 29.

[146] 'the negative way'.

[147] This point is made by C. Gunton, in chapter 3 of *The Promise of Trinitarian Theology*, T & T Clark, Edinburgh, 1991.

[148] 'Energies'.

of God from the sensible existence of mankind, restricting mankind's appreciation of God to the realm of the noetic, whereby the possibility of direct, sensible communion with the Spirit is obscured. The cross-fertilisation of Gregory's perspective with that of Augustine, through Denys the Areopagite, which was later to help form the basis for Western medieval mystical theology, did little to change a problem that was endemic to the theology of both the East and the West and which would, in its turn, condition the pneumatological perspective of the larger part of the modern church. Augustine's emphasis on perceiving the Trinity through the use of analogy prepared the way towards a later Western emphasis on man's intellectual faculty in maintaining communion with God. This, together with an emphasis, shared with the East, on the Trinity's transcendence and ontological immutability, helped to ensure that the earlier stress on the economy of the Spirit was further obscured.

At this point, Pseudo Dionysius deserves mention, not only because of his significance in providing a key to the later integration of Western and Eastern mystical theology, but also because he represents the fruit of post-Nicene thought, in communicating the ontological integrity of an undifferentiated Trinity. Where *Mystical Theology* is the key to Denys, then the fulcrum of his theology lies in the opening prayer of that short work:

> Trinity!! Higher than any being,
>   any divinity, any goodness!
>   Guide of Christians
>   in the wisdom of heaven!
> Lead us up beyond unknowing and light,
>   up to the furthest, highest peak
>   of mystic scripture,
>   where the mysteries of God's Word
>   lie simple, absolute and unchangeable
>   in the brilliant darkness of a hidden silence.
>   Amid the deepest shadow
>   they pour overwhelming light
>   on what is most manifest.
>   Amid the wholly unsensed and unseen
>   they completely fill our sightless minds
>   with treasures beyond all beauty.[149]

As with Gregory before him, Denys' focus lies on an ontologically remote Trinity which is the object of both his reverence and desire. Where his understanding of God is gleaned through illumination from the transcendent God who reaches out towards him, that illumination gained is ontologically

---

[149] *The Complete Works of Pseudo-Dionysius*, translated by C. Luibheid, SPCK, London, 1987, p. 135.

removed, in our experience, from the one who is its origin: here we have a foretaste of Gregory Palamas' *energeia*. Denys shows the triumph of the Alexandrian perspective in that he qualifies this lack of ontological differentiation within God by reference to the event of the Incarnation alone. This is demonstrated in *The Divine Names*, where he states,

> They also describe it as a Trinity, for with a transcendent fecundity it is manifested as 'three persons.' This is why 'all fatherhood in heaven and on earth is and is named after it.' They call it Cause of beings since in its goodness it employed its creative power to summon all things into being, and it is hailed as wise and beautiful because beings which keep their nature uncorrupted are filled with divine harmony and sacred beauty. But they especially call it loving towards humanity, because in one of its persons it accepted a true share of what it is we are, and thereby issued a call to man's lowly state to rise up to it. In a fashion beyond words, the simplicity of Jesus became something complex, the timeless took on the duration of the temporal, and, with neither change nor confusion of what constitutes him, he came into our human nature, he who totally transcends the natural order of the world.[150]

Here we see a cumulative, spiritual legacy forged out of Nicea, Constantinople and Chalcedon: a Trinitarian model based on a transcendent God, ontologically unverifiable except in the moment of the Incarnation. In the Cappadocians, we saw the tendency to veil the ontic actuality of the Spirit within the internal dynamic of the Trinity, hidden in a nascent doctrine of perichoresis and behind the mystery of the Christ's two natures, the Divine separate from yet radiating through the human. In Augustine, the revelation of the Trinity takes place through the true *imago Dei*, Christ Jesus. For Denys, we might also ask whether the full implication of that marriage of mankind and God, the Created and Creator, is too easily veiled behind the mystery of Christ's two natures. Does Denys' spirituality, rather than include us, actually exclude us from full participation in the life of Christ? And is there a failure to grasp the full significance of the Christian's calling to a truly Christlike life, enabled not only by the Incarnation but also by a full communion in the Holy Spirit? Such question are integral to the legacy of post-Nicene thought.

2.13 The Patristic Bequest: Evolving Pneumatological Structures

In this chapter we have argued that the first three centuries, prior to the Council of Nicea and the necessary addressing of issues raised by the conceptual challenge of Platonic thought, saw the early church's understanding of the Triune God born out of the salvific economy of God towards mankind, met with in the ontic actuality of both the Son and the Holy Spirit. The Apostolic Fathers appear to have been reticent in defining this experience of and meeting

---

[150] *The Divine Names* 1.4, in *The Complete Works of Pseudo-Dionysius*, p. 51.

with God. The emphasis lay in appreciating that, in the salvific economy of Father, Son and Holy Spirit, there is manifestly one God at work; and that one God is constitutively three. The concern of the pre-Nicene writers, as apologists and guardians of the witness to God's revelation in Christ, was not to formulate an ontological model of God's immanent Being but to present the economic integrity of God's ontic actuality. Their immediate concern was soteriological and not metaphysical. Their concern lay not with the nature of God within His inner Being; rather, it was to present an understanding of the correlated work of Father, Son and Holy Spirit in salvific economy.

The difficulty lay in that, as it became necessary to develop a Christian apologetic towards contemporary society and to formulate a Trinitarian theology which might help Christians better comprehend their faith in God, a change occurred. Although there appears to have been an early stress on the salvific economy of God, the suppositions of Greek thought too easily absorbed the economy of the Christian revelation into the conceptual framework of pagan thought, creating a theological framework which was dependent upon an alien axiom, arising out of a God who was conceived of as immutable and transcendent, largely beyond and outwith the experience of man.

In our study, we noted how Mackey offers a persuasive interpretation of the early Christian experience of God, built around his observations on the interaction of the Christian message with Greek thought. We find ourselves, however, diverging from Mackey's thesis in two areas. Firstly, Mackey argues that the early development of Trinitarian thought took place within the context of Greek thought, the form of Trinitarian thought being derived by a process of modification. While acknowledging the helpfulness of Mackey's study in tracing the reflection of Greek concepts in the evolution of Christian thought and accepting that this environment was formative in shaping the development of Patristic thinking, especially in the post-Nicene period, we would wish to suggest that the ontic actuality of God, in His salvific economy, offers us a primitive perception of the Triune God which is sustained throughout the Patristic period, more prominent in the pre-Nicene era but evident also in the turbulent atmosphere of Nicene and post-Nicene thought.

This leads us to our second point of divergence from both Mackey and a traditional interpretation of the Arian crisis. We would suggest the development of the *homoousion* be viewed not so much as a reaction to the Arian threat but as a parallel development to the Arian emphasis. The Arians identified the Logos as created, thereby associating the Logos more clearly with the created flesh of Jesus. In Nicene understanding, the emphasis of association is between the Logos and the Creator. In both cases, the distinction arises from a dualistic framework. Both Arian and Nicene interpretations can arguably be seen as alternative means of coping with this framework. The pre-Nicene period, from our perspective, is one where Platonic categories are appearing but where there is a nascent, Trinitarian theology that should not be described in subordinationist/emanationalist terms, terms which suggest a Greek mindset.

Rather, we detect a perspective on the Spirit which emphasises the Spirit's present and ongoing ontic actuality, together with the ontic actuality of the Son which is realised in and through the Incarnation.

We have argued that despite the developments that led to affirming firstly, the *homoousion* of the Son and secondly, the *homoousion* of the Spirit, the ontic actuality of the Spirit, as it is perceived in pre-Nicene thought, is not communicated through or defined by the Son. The Son's own ontic actuality is expressed and founded in the Incarnation. Both the Spirit and the Son are evidently related to the Father. There is an appreciation of God met with in the salvific economy and an understanding of God which is soteriological, not ontological. That is, in the pre-Nicene period, there is no clear interest in the issue of God's immanent Being. To put it simply, what matters is man's engagement with the saving God, not his speculations concerning the God who saves. The pre-Nicene focus is upon the ontic actuality of God.

The absorption of Trinitarian awareness into the neoplatonic metaphysical framework invited a conceptual model of God which could lead to a synthesis which was misleading in two respects. It invited a concept of relationality within God, either within a monarchianism which could lead to subordinationism, separating the Son & Spirit from the Father; or to a docetism which could arise from misconstruing the association of the Son with the *ousia* of the Father. Further, an abstracted model of the Trinity could lead to an emphasis on the transcendence of God in His immanent Being. Whichever might arise, an appreciation of the Spirit's ontic actuality would be eroded. Christian attention was taken up in addressing a conceptual framework which was foreign to the Gospel revelation. Certainly, there was a great apologetic challenge, to apply the Gospel to the dominant culture of the time; however, this did not necessarily promote understanding of the Christian experience of God within His church.

In summarising the differing pneumatological perspectives which arise out of Patristic thought, we would seek to identify three frameworks of Trinitarian thought, or Trinitarian models, which have arisen from our review of developments in Patristic pneumatology. These models, whilst generalising, serve the purpose of representing distinctive stages of development in Patristic pneumatology and we shall have occasion to refer to them as we develop our thesis. The first we shall name the pre-Nicene model. The second and third, both post-Nicene, we identify as the Eastern and Western models.

2.14   Three Patristic Models

2.14.1   The Pre-Nicene Model
In section 2.2, in reviewing the sub-Apostolic period, we traced an early appreciation of the ontic actuality of the Spirit. While later post-Apostolic writers also wrestled with attempts to express the salvific economy of God, we observed in section 2.3 that it was Irenaeus who first clearly formulated the

concept of the 'dual procession' of the Son and the Spirit from the Father. This emphasis on the ontic actuality of the Spirit as well as that of the Son did not appear to detract from the central atoning work of Christ Jesus or from an appreciation of the Incarnation as central to the Gospel: the enduring soteriological relevance of Irenaeus' concept of recapitulation,[151] which stressed the soterial inclusiveness of the Son, testifies to that. In forming our pre-Nicene model of the Trinity, we follow this understanding of Irenaeus and represent it as follows:

Father

Son   Spirit

Mankind

The ontic actuality of the Spirit is depicted alongside the work of the Son that is in and through the Incarnation. This work of the Spirit, although integrally involved with that of the Son, is seen to be peculiarly His own and is not to be confused with that of the Son. It is this interpretation of Irenaeus' thought that we describe, throughout this work, as the pre-Nicene model of the Trinity.

2.14.2   The Eastern Model

In speaking of an Eastern model, we refer to the development of a post-Nicene understanding of the Trinity built upon the thought of Athanasius and developed therefrom in the Eastern Church. The distinctive feature detected in Athanasius' thought was that the revelation of God has now been focused on the Incarnate Son, *homoousios* with the Father. The event of the Son's Incarnation becomes the basis of our apprehending God. This does not, in Athanasius' own thought, necessarily detract from the ontic actuality of the Spirit. Rather, it sets the basis of our interaction with God and appreciation of His ontological nature as expressed in and through the Son. With a sharper focus on the Incarnation there arises a parallel interest in the Spirit's action on the Son; but with an obscuring of the Spirit's ontic actuality as realised in our immediate experience. We might represent this Athanasian model as follows:

---

[151] The notion that all of human life, from birth to death, is drawn into and contained by the life of Jesus Christ.

Father

|

Spirit

Son Incarnate

Subsequent to Athanasius, we remain unpersuaded that a developed understanding of relations within the Triunity of God was clearly expressed in the work of the Cappadocians. Certainly, an exploration into the relationality of the Persons and an understanding of relational and temporal differentiation is present, in embryonic form, in the writings of both Basil and the Nazianzen;[152] yet each Cappadocian brings his own distinctive insights into relations within the Trinity. In this, the focus has moved towards the ontological relations of God in His own Being, which we would represent in what we style our Eastern model:

Father

| |

Spirit

Son

The Church

As this model came to be developed in the East, an emphasis on the Triune God's perichoretic identity led to diminishing appreciation of the Spirit's ontic actuality towards man. The nature of the Spirit's Being and function within God's salvific economy becomes secondary. The primary concern became the inner identity of God.

In the post-Chalcedonian East we find a continued growth of an ontological gulf forming between mankind and God. Although only in embryonic form, we have the beginnings of the classic Orthodox[153] understanding of communion with God occurring through the energies - a concept which, although differing in substantive content from that found in the western notion of grace, has obvious parallels in that it distances mankind from the possibility of direct

---

[152] Basil, in his differentiation of the one *ousia* and three *hypostases*; the Nazianzen in his understanding of relations in the Godhead, where the Father is Begetter and Emitter, the Son the Begotten and the Spirit the Emission.

[153] An excellent presentation of Orthodox belief, from a Western evangelical perspective, is found in Donald Fairbairn, *Eastern Orthodoxy through Western Eyes*, Westminster John Knox Press, Louisville, 2002.

participation in the ontic actuality of the Holy Spirit. The Holy Spirit, although not perceived in the analogical terms of Augustine, is made remote and distant from man's immediate experience, as illustrated in the work of Pseudo Dionysius in 2.12. By the time Orthodoxy would reach the fourteenth century, Gregory Palamas could speak of the energies working within us, making us aware of a higher light which, although not communicable to our senses,[154] brings us to contemplate the mystery of God which is beyond all intellectual activity.[155] This we might represent as follows:

The Holy Trinity

Energies

The Communion of the Saints

2.14.3   The Western Model

Among the post-Nicene western theologians, it is Augustine's perception of the Trinity that provides our critical model for understanding future developments in Trinitarian thought. As we saw, the affirmation of the Triune God's one substance as an integrated identity of three persons occurred within a framework that distanced the immanent Being of God from the immediacy of human experience. Further, an analogical understanding of God, accessible to mankind as *imago Dei*, was rooted in a dualistic framework which saw mankind's communion with God founded in humanity's noetic, not sensible, being. At the same time, the West shared that conviction forged out of the Christological disputes of the East, that our interaction with God and appreciation of His ontological nature is brought about in and through the Son and His Incarnation. These features combined with a rapidly evolving and structured ecclesiology in the West to create a pneumatology emphasising the rational nature of the Spirit's work and the facility of man's intellectual faculty in apprehending God's communion with His church through His Spirit. This perspective ushered in an understanding of the Triune economy which moved away from an emphasis on the ontic actuality of the Holy Spirit to a focus upon the ontological unity of the Immanent Trinity and the Spirit as *vinculum Trinitatis*, the bond of love between Father and Son; and, through the Incarnation, the bond of love between God and the church, the body of Christ on earth. This Western model we would represent as follows:

---

[154] Gregory Palamas, *The Triads*, 1.3.5, SPCK, London, 1983.
[155] *The Triads*, 1.3.17.

The Grace of God, expressed in the Incarnation through the Church

2.15   The Patristic Bequest: An Inheritance

In undertaking our review of the Patristic period, we have sought to explore the relationship of the Spirit and His ministry to that of the Son, and their relationship within a Trinitarian understanding of God. One question, arising from chapter 1, was whether too much focus on the Holy Spirit might cause our understanding of the Spirit to be detached from a Christocentric axis. Our study in this chapter now leads us, however, to pose another question in response: how appropriate is it, in fact, to speak of the Spirit with an exclusively Christocentric reference? It was the need to affirm the Son's deity that led to the Nicene *homoousion* and consequent attempts to relate the Spirit to the one *ousia* of the Father and the Son. We have seen, however, that the post-Nicene search for an Immanent Trinity produced its own problems. On the other hand, the pre-Nicene emphasis on the ontic actuality of the Son and the Spirit, as exampled in the work of Irenaeus, seemed to preserve a complementary function of the Son and the Spirit in the salvific economy. While recognising the need for a Christocentric reference, we must question whether it is either necessary or appropriate to frame our understanding of the Spirit's ontic actuality in an exclusively Christocentric manner.

Would a failure to secure a clearly Christocentric reference to the ontic actuality of the Spirit not lead to tritheism? The answer to this challenge would depend on how we conceive of God as Trinity. As we have seen, it is not essential, in interpreting early Christian tradition, to view the Triune God as possessed of a perichoretic identity and function. Augustine's dictum, *opera Trinitatis ad extra sunt indivisa,* arises from a focus upon the immanent Trinity. This alternative is not necessarily to be preferred to a pre-Nicene emphasis on the ontic actuality of the Son and the Spirit in God's salvific economy.

How, then, are we to understand the ministry of the Holy Spirit and our participation therein, while having proper regard to the Trinitarian nature of God as Father, Son and Holy Spirit? From our studies in this chapter we have seen that an answer to this question will depend not only on our expectation of how we should properly relate to the Spirit, but also on what assumptions we bring to our understanding of God as Trinity. In the following chapters, we go on to investigate some of the expectations of the Spirit that have appeared within the Scottish Reformed tradition. In the final chapter, we will once again return to the question of how we might best convey an understanding of the Spirit and our communion with Him.

Chapter 3

John Calvin

3.1 Introduction

In this chapter we come to explore the influences that were to shape an understanding of the Holy Spirit's Person and function within Scottish theology, as they evolved out of the thought and writings of John Calvin, the Reformer whose Trinitarian outlook would shape the development of Scottish pneumatology. We will not lay bare the whole of Calvin's doctrine of the Spirit, nor attempt an extensive review of the considerable amount of scholarly research that has engaged with this area of Calvin's thought. Our hope is to tease out some of the issues that arise, demonstrating not only how Calvin's pneumatology runs in continuity with Patristic Trinitarian concerns but also possesses features which have produced their own problems within the Scottish context.

As with the Patristic period, pneumatology itself was not at the centre of Reformation debate. The Reformers in general saw themselves as apologists and defenders of the Faith, not speculative theologians. As Calvin commented,

> Faith should not cling only to the essence of Christ, so to say, but should pay heed to His power and office. For it would be of little advantage to know who Christ is unless the second point is added of what He wishes to be toward us and for what purpose He was sent by the Father.[1]

Along with a desire to reaffirm and declare the central tenets of the Christian faith, we meet in Calvin a fresh emphasis on the priority of Scripture in formulating theological truths and in shaping guidelines for life, all accessible to human reason and comprehension. For the Reformers it was the rational content of faith which required reaffirmation, standing as it did in contrast to the mystical obscurantism which had come, by the late Middle Ages, to shroud the essential character of the Christian confession. To conclude from this that pneumatology was unrelated to the central tenets of Reformed thought would, however, be misleading. Where the Reformers had come to inherit that Trinitarian model, which we identified in the preceding chapter as the Western

---

[1] J. Calvin, *Commentary on John*, 1.49, translated by T. H. L. Parker, St. Andrew Press, Edinburgh, 1959, p. 43.

model, this affected how the Holy Spirit came to be perceived when new topics of debate were entered into. It is the manner in which John Calvin's use and adaptation of this model affects and helps shape his pneumatology that we now seek to explore.

We begin our exploration of Calvin's pneumatology by reviewing a central theme, mankind's knowledge of God. In section 3.2 we observe how Calvin's perception of the Trinity, and human relationship to the Trinity through Christ, shapes the manner in which he views the Spirit to be at work within humanity, thereby bringing our focus onto the Immanent Trinity. In section 3.3 we argue that Calvin's understanding of the *communicatio idiomatum*[2] and his view of the Incarnation, expressed in the *extra Calvinisticum*,[3] presents us with a Christology arising out of this focus on the Immanent Trinity. We approach Calvin's understanding of man's union with Christ set within this epistemological framework, whereby the Spirit functions not only as *vinculum Trinitatis* but also as agent in effecting, in humanity, an understanding of mankind's union with God in Christ. Consequently, we continue our outline of mankind's substantial union with Christ in section 3.4 and review, in section 3.5, how Calvin's Christocentric focus effects a correlation between the Spirit and faith in bringing man to God through Christ. In section 3.6 we trace a distinct yet complementary understanding of the Spirit at work in the sacraments, going on in section 3.7 to note how Calvin's concern to maintain the parameters of Christian orthodoxy further influences the shape of his pneumatology. Thereafter, having noted in section 3.8 that the work of the Spirit in election arises as a logical development of Calvin's Christocentric concern, we further discuss in section 3.9 how the combination of these various factors has led to the forming of an emphasis upon a particular facet of pneumatology, that of the Spirit functioning as an epistemic agent. We conclude our study of Calvin by noting, in section 3.10, how some aspects of his theological method come to affect subsequent developments in pneumatology.

3.2   The Knowledge of God the Creator

There are two features of Calvin's thought which, married together, are integral components in forming an appreciation of how Calvin understood God to be recognised by man. These features are the twofold knowledge of God (*duplex cognitio Dei*) and man as the image of God (*imago Dei*).

---

[2] The relationship between the divine and human aspects of Christ's nature.

[3] The notion, traced in the writings of Calvin, that while the Son of God fully becomes incarnate in human flesh in the person of Jesus Christ, there is also a manner in which we must continue to speak, even during that time of Christ's earthly life, of the Son of God continuing to abide in heaven.

3.2.1   Duplex Cognitio Dei

The *duplex cognitio Dei* distinguishes between two complementary ways in which God comes to be known by man, through man's knowledge of God as Creator (*cognitio Dei Creatoris*) and as Redeemer (*cognitio Dei Redemptoris*). The distinction is seen most clearly in the editions of the *Institute* published from 1539 through to the final edition of 1559. We shall structure our study of Calvin around the 1559 edition of the *Institute*.[4] Divided into four books, the first was given over to *cognitio Dei Creatoris* and the second to *cognitio Dei Redemptoris*.[5] This distinction is presented by Calvin as a logical one, in that God appears to man first as Creator and then as a Redeemer.[6] At the same time, Calvin stresses that it is through faith in Christ that true knowledge of God is found.[7] Indeed, as he states in his *Commentary on 1 Peter*, a proper perception of God must be founded on Christ, for

> All thinking about God without Christ is a vast abyss which immediately swallows up all our thoughts ... let us, therefore, remember, that Christ is not called the image of the invisible God in vain, but this name is given to Him for this reason, that God cannot be known except in Him.[8]

It is in seeking to understand Calvin's perception of the relationship between *cognitio Dei Creatoris* and *cognitio Dei Redemptoris* that problems can arise. Knowledge of God is found in *cognitio Dei Creatoris* but salvation is founded on *cognitio Dei Redemptoris*. We might say that knowledge of God as Redeemer appears to take epistemological priority; but how is that to be related to the logical priority of *cognitio Dei Creatoris*? The possibility that Calvin is contending for, in some measure, a *theologia naturalis* rather than stressing a knowledge of God through his salvific economy is of interest to us, in that it would affect our interpretation of the significance of a Triune, salvific economy to Calvin's thought. Is it possible that Calvin allows for a human perception of the Triune God outwith man's reception and appropriation of God in His salvific economy?

---

[4] The first edition of the *Institute* was published in 1536 and contained 6 chapters on Law; Faith; Prayer; Sacraments; the five false sacraments; Christian polity. The format, from 1539, appeared to follow the scheme of The Apostles' Creed. Quotations from the 1559 edition cited in this chapter are taken from *Calvin: Institutes of the Christian Religion*, edited by J. T. McNeill and translated by F. L. Battles, The Westminster Press, Philadelphia, 1960.

[5] The four books are entitled: 1. Of the Knowledge of God the Creator; 2. Of the Knowledge of God the Redeemer in Christ; 3. The Mode of Obtaining the Grace of Christ; 4. Of the Holy Catholic Church.

[6] *Institute* 1.2.1.

[7] *Institute* 3.2.6.

[8] J. Calvin, *Commentary on 1 Peter*, 1.20-21, translated by W. B. Johnston, St. Andrew Press, Edinburgh, 1963, p. 250.

The precise nature of the *duplex cognitio Dei* was the subject of a controversy which arose between Barth and Brunner in the mid-1930s and was taken up, more recently, in the work of Parker and Dowey. Dowey, following Brunner's reasoning, locates the *cognitio Dei Creatoris* in two sources, those of the Creation in general and in the doctrine of Scripture, the *cognitio Dei Redemptoris* having Christ alone as its source.[9] Dowey argues that for Calvin the general attributes of God are patent in the world; and Scripture, as a second source of revelation, complements this general revelation. Both the Creation in which we live and Scripture together constitute the grounds for the *cognitio Dei Creatoris*.[10] Dowey's argument follows on the structure of the 1559 edition of the *Institute* where after the first five chapters, in chapters 6-10 of book 1, attention turns from God manifest in his works to the facility of Scripture in helping 'to direct us aright to the very Creator of the Universe'.[11] At the same time, Dowey is clear that this *cognitio Dei Creatoris* is only rightly perceived by those who have grasped the *cognitio Dei Redemptoris*[12] which is in Christ. Parker, on the other hand, denies that in interpreting Calvin any disjunction should be allowed between *cognitio Dei Creatoris* and *cognitio Dei Redemptoris*. A *duplex cognitio* can be identified; but it centres on a distinction, traced by Parker as a theme present throughout the first three books of the *Institute*, between the knowledge of God and a knowledge of ourselves.[13] For Parker, it is in the complementary character of knowing both ourselves and God, not a distinction between the *cognitio Dei Creatoris* and *cognitio Dei Redemptoris*, that Calvin's central theme is to be found. Parker perceives a *duplex cognitio* in Calvin in so far as we are led towards that true knowledge which arises out of a recognition of both God and ourselves.

What is of interest to us in this debate are the differing perceptions of Dowey and Parker as to the Holy Spirit's function within Calvin's thought. Dowey locates the work of the Spirit in the *cognitio Dei Creatoris* as that inspiration which arises from the testimony of the Spirit within man and which, when united to the objective revelation of the Word of God in Scripture, effects a special revelation which is in addition to the general revelation of God the Creator found in His Creation.[14] The Spirit is to be identified at the place of His working an internal testimony within us. Parker, by contrast, understands Calvin as taking a thematic approach throughout the *Institute* in presenting the united action of the Triune God, in Christ and by means of the Holy Spirit, the

---

[9] A. E. Dowey, *The Knowledge of God in Calvin's Theology*, Columbia University Press, New York, 1952, p. 43.

[10] *The Knowledge of God in Calvin's Theology*, p. 146.

[11] *Institute* 1.6.1, p. 69.

[12] *The Knowledge of God in Calvin's Theology*, p. 221.

[13] T. H. L. Parker, *Calvin's Doctrine of the Knowledge of God*, Oliver & Boyd, Edinburgh, 1969, p. 8.

[14] *The Knowledge of God in Calvin's Theology*, p. 124-5.

Word and the Spirit emphatically joined together in the one moment of revelation towards us;[15] and that Calvin refuses to countenance any distinction being made between the receiving of the Word of God and the Spirit.[16]

However we might view this dispute, it serves to introduce to our study of Calvin the problem of determining what function is assigned to the Spirit in Calvin's thought. More particularly, it begs the question as to how, in relation to the *cognitio Dei Creatoris*, Calvin perceives the Spirit to be active. In order to engage with this question we must first investigate Calvin's understanding of how the *cognitio Dei Creatoris* is realised within man, who is made in the image of God (*imago Dei*).

3.2.2   Imago Dei

It is by man as *imago Dei* that God is apprehended; and the proper centre of that image is, for Calvin, in man's soul.[17] Calvin does not identify this *imago* in terms of Augustine's analogical model of the Trinity, expressed in the soul's 'understanding, will and memory'.[18] Rather, Calvin appears to locate the *imago Dei* in the capacity of man to commune with God. T. F. Torrance captures this sense of the Spirit's action as the medium of communication between God and man when he states,

> in Calvin's thought the Spirit stands for the ultimate majesty of God, the ultimate objectivity in which we are carried over from ourselves to knowledge of God out of God, and not out of ourselves.[19]

Whether we can agree with this interpretation of Calvin by Torrance, who is an advocate of the view that the Spirit and the Word should always be correlated in our perception of them, we will return to discuss shortly. We do, however, take up Torrance's point that it is the Spirit who provides us with knowledge of God; and that this knowledge is founded in the faculties of the human soul. The nature of these faculties is more clearly laid out in *Institute* 1.15.7, where Calvin explains,

> that the human soul consists of two faculties, understanding and will. Let the office, moreover, of understanding be to distinguish between objects, as each seems worthy of approval or disapproval; while that of the will, to choose and follow what the understanding pronounces good, but to reject and flee from what it disapproves.[20]

---

[15] *Calvin's Doctrine of the Knowledge of God*, p. 136.
[16] *Calvin's Doctrine of the Knowledge of God*, p. 78.
[17] *Institute* 1.15.3.
[18] This Calvin explicitly rejects in *Institute* 1.15.4.
[19] T. F. Torrance, *Theology in Reconstruction*, SCM, London, 1965, p. 96.
[20] *Institute*, p. 194.

Here is a vital clue in seeking to understand Calvin's mindset and method. It is through the faculty of understanding, or intellect, that man as the *imago Dei* comes to a knowledge of God. Certainly, Calvin has much to say in book 2 of the *Institute* about how this faculty has been corrupted by man's fall. However, this should not detract from the fundamental perception of the Spirit's work that is apparent here: the internal testimony of the Holy Spirit is to be firmly located in man's intellectual faculty.

What then are we to make of Torrance's claim that this knowledge is 'of God out of God, and not of ourselves'?[21] Torrance, in seeking to insist, as Parker did, on the marriage of Spirit and Word, inevitably sees this action of the Spirit as a dynamic accord of the Spirit and Word in revelatory action towards us. However, if we concede that there is some plausibility in Dowey's argument for a *duplex cognitio Dei* wherein the Spirit's inspiration arises from His testimony to man's subjective awareness, then it is possible to view this action of the Spirit, located in the faculty of man's intellect, in a different way. That is, the revelatory action of the Spirit is distinguishable from the Word, in so far as the work of the Spirit in effecting *cognitio Dei Creatoris* is to be distinguished from that of the Spirit in effecting *cognitio Dei Redemptoris*. In such a case, we can find in Calvin a distinguishing of the Spirit from the Word in so far as we can distinguish between the Spirit's action in man's soul, stimulating and informing man's intellect, and the Spirit's action, as He is married to Christ, in communicating an awareness of our redemption in Him. Here, then, is the tension. On the one hand, following Parker, we can identify a marriage between the Spirit and the Word, in that all knowledge of God is forged by the one Spirit. On the other hand, following Dowey, we can distinguish an act of the Spirit which informs man's rational faculty concerning the nature of God, distinguishable from the more clearly defined knowledge of God which comes through His Word and leads us to Christ. There is seen to be an accord between the Spirit and the Word while, at the same time, the Spirit can be seen to work in the faculty of our understanding in a manner distinguishable from the Word.

This tension, arising in Calvin's understanding of the Spirit, can be better understood when we see how Calvin's thought follows on from that earlier Trinitarian tradition which we identified and described as the Western model of the Trinity. In the preceding chapter we presented our case for viewing the Western model of the Triune God's Being, one substance with an integrated identity of three Persons, as occurring within a framework of thought which distanced the immanent Being of God from the immediacy of human experience. We argued that where man's communion with God was expressed in terms of man's noetic, not sensible, being, this helped point the way towards a pneumatology which would emphasise the rational nature of the Spirit's work and the facility of mankind's intellectual faculty in apprehending God's

---

[21] *Theology in Reconstruction*, p. 96.

communion with us; and that this ushered in an understanding of God's Being which moved away from an emphasis on the ontic actuality of the Spirit to a focus upon the ontological unity of the Immanent Trinity and the Spirit as *vinculum*, that bond which unites Christ with his church. From what we have traced of Calvin's perception of the Spirit in the *cognitio Dei Creatoris*, we can identify something of this Western Trinitarian model in his thought. While a bond between the Spirit and the Word can be traced, the Spirit's action can also be distinguished from that of the Word and centred in the Spirit's action upon man as *imago Dei*, within man's soul and intellectual faculty. The Spirit is thus active within the church, turning us towards a fuller knowledge of God through His Word and of God as He is in Himself.

In returning to address our earlier question of how Calvin views the Spirit as effective within the *cognitio Dei Creatoris*, we would contend that the Spirit's work in promoting man's intellectual apprehension of God is, for Calvin, an important aspect of the *cognitio Dei Creatoris*. We might describe the action of the Spirit in this way as that of an epistemic agent, bringing awareness of God to our human intellect. In this respect, a focus on man as *imago Dei* and the importance of man's intellectual faculty in apprehending God, united to an emphasis on Scripture as the 'spectacles' whereby we see God more clearly,[22] does little to invite a perspective of the Spirit which would require us to stress the priority of God's salvific economy and the Spirit's ontic actuality. The focus is turned upon man's intellectual faculty and the facility of the Scriptures in aiding us to come to a clearer understanding of God. Calvin can speak quite clearly of a *cognitio Dei Creatoris* which, by these means, allows us to appreciate and speak of the Triune nature of God's immanent Being.[23] At the same time, we would acknowledge that the Spirit's work in the *cognitio Dei Creatoris* is for Calvin only part of the picture. It is to the second part, the Spirit at work in the *cognitio Dei Redemptoris*, that we now turn.

3.3 The Knowledge of God the Redeemer

Our contention is that Calvin's primary understanding of the Spirit's function arises not out of God's salvific economy and the ontic actuality of the Spirit but is based on an acceptance of the Trinity's revelation as Immanent Trinity, sensibly remote from mankind. This leads to a relegation of the Spirit's role to that of an epistemic agent. Should this view be tenable, then we would expect a parallel to be found in Calvin's dealing with the Son. That is, we would expect to find a Christology that did not stress the ontic actuality of the Son in and through the moment of Incarnation but one which, following the Western Trinitarian model, perceived the Being of the Son primarily in terms of God's immanent Being as Trinity. In this section we investigate whether this is, in

---

[22] *Institute* 1.6.1.
[23] *Institute* 1.13.

fact, the case.

Calvin's Christology requires to be interpreted within his soteriological outlook and his understanding of Christ as Redeemer. As Willis observes,

> The theme which dominates Calvin's Christology is that Christ is to be known fruitfully not in his essence but in his power to save, not as he is invisibly in himself, but as the Father willed him to be towards us and in his office.[24]

Following the *cognitio Dei Creatoris* in book 1, it is in books 2 and 3 of the *Institute* that Calvin engages with the *cognitio Dei Redemptoris*. Whatever the precise dynamics of the *duplex cognitio Dei*, we can affirm that for Calvin true knowledge of God is afforded only through faith in Christ our Redeemer. As Calvin makes clear in his 1559 edition of the *Institute*,

> the whole knowledge of God the Creator that we have discussed would be useless unless faith also followed, setting forth for us God our Father in Christ.[25]

The Christian hope lies in Christ alone.[26] We become children of God through the Son taking what is His and imparting it to us,[27] remedying our disobedience by His obedience[28] and offering of Himself as the true sacrifice.[29] Calvin clearly places his soterial centre in Christ and his Christology is shaped by this. The question we must face is whether Calvin's understanding of knowledge of God, coming through Christ the Redeemer, corresponds to a perception of God formed primarily from the Triune God's action and revelation in His salvific economy. Two features of Calvin's Christology combine in leading us to suggest that it does not. These features are found in Calvin's understanding of the *communicatio idiomatum* and what has become known as the *extra Calvinisticum*.

The *communicatio idiomatum* arose from the interpretation of Chalcedon's Christological formula of Christ as possessed of one nature with two idioms, the divine and the human. What type of communion occurs between these idioms? At one extreme, Luther argued that there was a complete communion of idioms. Zwingli, on the other hand, determined there to be none, the two idioms cohabiting yet independent. Calvin's understanding, expressed in *Institute* 2.14, took a middle course in making a distinction between the divinity and humanity of Christ. Some properties of Christ were to be assigned to His divinity, some to his humanity and some to both.[30] Why, it might be asked, was

---

[24] E. D. Willis, *Calvin's Catholic Christology*, Brill, Leiden, 1966, p. 61.

[25] *Institute* 2.6.1, p. 341.

[26] *Institute* 2.6.3.

[27] *Institute* 2.12.2.

[28] *Institute* 2.12.3.

[29] *Institute* 2.12.4.

[30] *Institute* 2.14.1-2.

this a matter of concern? Such a distinction in Christ's nature was certainly of some help in discussing Christ's physical constitution, but more importantly it effected an understanding of the nature of Christ's presence at the eucharist,[31] a major issue at the time. For our purposes, it also had the effect of inviting a distinction between the full presence of the Son of God as He is found in His transcendence and communion within the immanent Triunity of God and that measure of His divine presence which was present in and through the humanity of Jesus of Nazareth. Calvin's interpretation of the hypostatic union of Christ's humanity and divinity in *Institute* 2.14 is of interest to us when read in conjunction with the last section of *Institute* 2.13, where he lays out what the Lutherans dubbed the *extra Calvinisticum*, stating,

> For even if the Word in his immeasurable essence united with the nature of man into one person, we do not imagine that he was confined therein. Here is something marvellous: the Son of God descended from heaven in such a way that, without leaving heaven, he willed to be borne in the virgin's womb, to go about the earth, and to hang upon the cross; yet he continuously filled the world even as he had done from the beginning![32]

In one sense, the *extra Calvinisticum* did seem to convey a knowledge of Christ which was rooted in the Son of God's ontic actuality, as He is towards us in the Incarnation; yet it also suggests that for Calvin Christ is, in Himself, more than that which is wholly apparent in the Incarnation. Willis, in his defence of Calvin's Christology on this point, argues that Calvin, in presenting us with a view of the eternal Son which is not restricted to the flesh of His humanity, helps us to grasp how the majesty and power of the Son can be joined to that which is weak and limited.[33] In response, it must be asked whether the *extra Calvinisticum* could not also hint at a Calvin who is more comfortable with a noetic view of Christ as Son of God made manifest in the flesh of man; but not as Christ who, in His ontic actuality, is eternally and decisively married to humanity in the Incarnation. Calvin may have explicitly countered a Nestorian notion of 'two persons' in Christ, one who was God and another who was man;[34] but the impression is still given of Calvin looking beyond the moment of the Incarnation to the immanent Being of God and the abiding reality of the Son within an immanent Trinity, beyond that of the Son wholly manifest in the event of the Incarnation.

One other aspect of this should be noted. Willis contends that the positive effect of the *extra Calvinisticum* is to make pneumatology integral to Christology,[35] the avenue of divinity's - and therefore the Spirit's - concourse

---

[31] *Institute* 4.17.31.

[32] *Institute* 2.13.4, p. 481.

[33] *Calvin's Catholic Christology*, p. 63.

[34] *Commentary on John*, 1.20, p. 20.

[35] *Calvin's Catholic Christology*, p. 83.

with Christ's humanity established through the Incarnation of the Son. How positive this is in aiding us towards a perception of God's Triune Being, which might bring us to a clearer appreciation of the Spirit, remains open to question. Certainly, it invites a perspective on the Spirit which views Him as that bond which is between God's immanent Being and the body of Christ on earth; but this is quite different from a Trinitarian understanding of the Spirit which builds on the dynamic, ontic actuality of the Spirit as complementary to a dynamic, ontic actualisation of the Son expressed in the Incarnation. We are, instead, faced with a view of the Spirit which runs the danger of presenting the Spirit's function as consequential and not complementary to the Son's. Calvin's Christology appears to invite the danger of subsuming the ontic actuality of the Spirit within the soteriological significance of the Son's mission. It could easily be interpreted as inviting us to view our communion with the Trinity solely in terms of our reception of the Son in His soterial mission.

To summarise, we can say that in our brief review of Calvin's *cognitio Dei Redemptoris* we have noted a Christology that does not so much stress the ontic actuality of the Son in and through the moment of Incarnation but invites us to look beyond the Triune God manifest in the Son's soterial mission to the Immanent Trinity. In this respect, we have discovered a parallel perspective in Calvin's understanding of the Son to that of the Spirit. Our review of Calvin's *cognitio Dei Redemptoris* would appear to confirm our earlier suggestion that Calvin's understanding of the Spirit's role in activating knowledge of God did not arise from a focus on God's salvific economy and the ontic actuality of the Spirit but continued to stress a view of the Trinity, found in the Western model of the Trinity, which focused on the immanent Being of God. While we would argue that this supports our contention that Calvin treated the Spirit as an epistemic agent in effecting our knowledge of God, we would not argue that this is the only perception of the Spirit present in Calvin: yet it does beg the question as to how Calvin's more general understanding of the Spirit stands in relation to this emphasis on the Spirit's epistemic agency. It may be that the Christological focus brought by Calvin to God's salvific economy implies the presence of the Spirit, active in the *extra Calvinisticum* and the *communicatio idiomatum*; but is this always clear? These are the questions which must exercise our minds as we now turn to examine Calvin's understanding of mankind's union with Christ, expounded in book 3 of the *Institute*.

3.4   Man's Union with Christ

In order to appreciate the teaching on man's union with Christ that is presented in the opening chapters of book 3 of the *Institute*, we must return to that distinction made earlier between the logical order of Calvin's thought, which begins with *cognitio Dei Creatoris* and proceeds to *cognitio Dei Redemptoris*, and the epistemological order which centres on faith in Christ. That is, the centre of knowledge of God, for Calvin, lies in man's response of faith to the soterial mission and manifestation of the Son of God. In this sense, the logical priority of *cognitio Dei Creatoris* is but a preamble to the reverberating truth of *Christus solus*[36]. Man's concourse with God is firmly centred, for Calvin, in and through the coming of Jesus Christ.

Following on the logical order of the *Institute*, book 3 deals with the manner of receiving the grace of God which comes through Christ the Redeemer to those who are His own. What is important to grasp is that Calvin is dealing here with that relationship with God which he sees as belonging to those who are Christ's, that is, the church. Calvin is concerned with the distinctive relation between God and those who belong to Christ, a union with Christ effected through His manifestation and ministry in human flesh whereby we, who are of human flesh, may share and have our part in the benefits of Christ's soterial mission. Calvin is addressing that union which occurs, not between Christ and all flesh, but between Christ and His church. This distinction is important because, in looking to the profound aspects of the Spirit's ministry which Calvin here presents us with, we need to appreciate that we are being shown an understanding of the Spirit active, not upon humanity as a whole, but in and among those who are part of the body of Christ on earth. Calvin is concentrating on an understanding of the Spirit which is founded in and through what has been accomplished, as rehearsed in book 2 of the *Institute*, in Christ's soterial mission. In looking to this relationship, which centres on the consequences of Christ's soterial mission, we shall meet again with a perception of the Spirit which characterises the Western model of the Trinity: that of the Spirit as the bond which is between God and the body of Christ on earth, the church.

These features are evident in the opening section of *Institute* 3.1, where Calvin explains that the Spirit, as one who is a witness by His presence both in heaven and on earth, is the bond between the Christ and the church, 'by which Christ effectually unites us to Himself'.[37] In this respect, it is the Spirit who acts as a seal upon our hearts, affirming in us what Christ has accomplished on our behalf. It may be that the logical order commences with the *cognitio Dei Creatoris* and the epistemological with the *cognitio Dei Redemptoris*; but ultimately it is the same Spirit who is active in bringing our lives into a deeper appreciation of what Christ has done for us. Greater engagement with God therefore comes through our participation in the Spirit, for

> reason itself teaches us to climb higher and to examine into the secret energy of the Spirit, by which we come to enjoy Christ and all his benefits.[38]

This communion in the Spirit is expressed in terms of the church's union

---

[36] 'Christ alone!'
[37] *Institute* 3.1.1, p. 538.
[38] *Institute* 3.1.1, p. 537.

with Christ, not a union between Christ and mankind as a whole. As Calvin states, the church

> stands by God's election, and cannot waver or fail any more than his eternal providence can. Secondly, it has in a way been joined to the steadfastness of Christ, who will no more allow his believers to be estranged from him than that his members be rent and torn asunder.[39]

The questions which we need to address are how it is, for Calvin, that we meet with the Spirit in this union and in what way we can identify the Spirit's presence and action in His affirming us in our union with Christ. We begin by looking briefly at Calvin's understanding of the Spirit's role in effecting faith, extending this to look at the role of the Spirit in prayer. Thereafter we will go on to explore Calvin's understanding of the Spirit within his doctrine of the sacraments.

3.5   The Spirit and Faith

R. S. Wallace, in expounding the central place of faith in uniting us to Christ and inserting us into Christ's body, the church, comments,

> In saying all this about the power of faith, we need in no way take back anything that has already been said about the Holy Spirit as being the sole effective bond between Christ and those united to Him, for it is the principal work of the Holy Spirit to create in the heart of man the faith which unites him to Christ, therefore it is equally true that we are united to Christ by the Holy Spirit alone and by faith alone.[40]

We might say that, as faith arises within our humanity, so the Spirit is active in humanity through that avenue afforded by the soterial mission of the Son and Christ's manifestation in human flesh. As we are brought by the bond of the Spirit into eternal communion with God, so faith is a bond between ourselves and God. As man's communion with the Spirit is founded on Christ's communion with humanity through His life on earth, so our faith is founded on Christ and brought into communion with Him now by the Holy Spirit. As Calvin himself puts it,

> Now we shall possess a right definition of faith if we call it a firm and certain knowledge of God's benevolence towards us, founded upon the truth of the freely

---

[39] *Institute* 4.1.3, p. 1015.
[40] R. S. Wallace, *Calvin's Doctrine of the Christian Life*, Oliver & Boyd, Edinburgh, 1959, p. 21.

given promise in Christ, both revealed to our minds and sealed upon our hearts through the Holy Spirit.[41]

That avenue through which the Spirit operates and faith is active between God in heaven and the body of Christ on earth is one and the same. Is it the case, though, that the Spirit is to be identified with the formation of a rational, cognitive faith and with that alone? Certainly it does appear that, for Calvin, faith is the expression of that which is primarily rational and not suprarational. In that the activity of the Spirit in our hearts gives rise to conscious faith, this is a seal on that which is already apprehended by our minds.[42] However, this action of the Spirit is more than rational, in that its issue is our participation with Christ Himself. Calvin condenses it thus:

> Christ, when he illumines us into faith by the power of his Spirit, at the same time so engrafts us into his body that we become partakers of every good.[43]

How then can Calvin avoid confusing the Person and function of the Spirit with the effect of conscious faith or, at least, associating the two in a manner which does not make the Spirit's ministry synonymous with the production and presence of faith? Faith, residing in us, brings us to look to where Christ is, in heaven; for faith is the bond between us who are on earth and Christ who is in heaven. Using the metaphor of light shining from a source, Calvin perceives faith, even in its weakest form, as bringing our minds into the light of God, as a man might be brought into the light of the sun to 'dwell on its steadfast brightness and .... receive its benefits'.[44] Faith, in mortal man, is the means whereby he is illumined in the knowledge of God's gift of salvation through Christ. In such manner faith, as a bond between man and God, is built on the fundamental work of the Spirit as that foundational bond which is between us and Christ. That faith should be expressed as a bond between man and God - and therefore between man and the Triune God - is contingent upon the priority of the bond formed between God and the church by the Spirit. The bond of faith arises from the bond of the Spirit. The Person and function of the Spirit can therefore be distinguished from conscious faith because the latter can only exist if the former is already present: the presence of faith is contingent on the presence of the Spirit.

This relationship between the Spirit and faith is further illustrated in Calvin's understanding of the Spirit at work in Christian prayer. Calvin sees the Spirit as tutoring us 'to tell us what is right and temper our emotions'.[45] Calvin does not refer explicitly to the Spirit's role as *vinculum* in his treatment of

---

[41] *Institute* 3.2.7, p. 551.
[42] *Institute* 3.2.36.
[43] *Institute* 3.2.35, p. 583.
[44] *Institute* 3.2.19, p. 565.
[45] *Institute* 3.20.5, p. 855.

prayer in *Institute* 3.20; but man's dependency on the mediatorial work of Christ is underlined.[46] Wallace summarises it well when he states,

> The Spirit of adoption is the author of that filial approach in boldness and confident hope in succeeding in our requests which is the distinguishing mark of true prayer.[47]

Our ability to pray in the Spirit arises from our union with Christ and is shaped thereby. The Spirit acts as that bond between us and Christ, our mediator, for by the Spirit we come to participate in Christ's filial approach before the Father.

The priority of this bond, formed between human beings and Christ by the Holy Spirit, can further be illustrated by some of Calvin's comments on the process of sanctification in the Christian life. In his *Commentary on Ephesians* Calvin remarks,

> Such is the union between us and Christ, that in a sense He pours Himself into us. For we are not bone of His bone, and flesh of His flesh, because, like ourselves, He is a man, but because, by the power of His Spirit, He engrafts us into His Body, so that from Him we derive life....[48] It is in vain that men fret themselves to comprehend, by the understanding of the flesh, its manner and character; for here God exerts the infinite power of His Spirit.[49]

The very nature of the Spirit at work as the bond between Christ and his church is, of itself, suprarational: yet for Calvin, it remains the case that the suprarational character of the Spirit's work will always be closely associated with a rational and cognitive faith, in that the work of the Spirit is the restoration of man as the *imago Dei* who, as we noted earlier, has as his crown the intellectual faculty of the soul. This indissoluble association of the bond of the Spirit with the bond of faith is concisely illustrated in Calvin's *Commentary on 2 Corinthians* where he states,

> The whole power of the Gospel depends upon its being made life-giving to us by the grace of the Holy Spirit.... Observe that the purpose of the Gospel is the restoration in us of the image of God which had been cancelled by sin and that this restoration is progressive and goes on during our whole life, because God makes His glory to shine in us little by little.... Our present knowledge of God is

---

[46] *Institute* 3.20.17-20.

[47] *Calvin's Doctrine of the Christian life*, p. 287.

[48] J. Calvin, *Commentary on Ephesians*, 5.31, translated by T. H. L. Parker, St. Andrew Press, Edinburgh, 1965, p. 209.

[49] *Commentary on Ephesians*, 5.32, p. 209.

indeed obscure and feeble in comparison with the glorious vision we shall have at Christ's last appearing.[50]

The sanctifying work of the Spirit in transforming the church and its members inevitably leads to a change in man as the *imago Dei*, a restoration of man's intellectual faculty and a gradual growth in knowledge, through faith, of God. The bond of the Spirit enables the bond of faith.

Calvin does, however, identify another avenue whereby the Spirit is perceived as active. The Spirit, while sustaining faith within the church, reinforces this through His activity in the sacraments. It is to this aspect of the Spirit's work that we now turn.

3.6   The Spirit and the Sacraments

That the sacraments are a vital mark of the church is, for Calvin, largely self-evident. As he states in his prefatory address in the *Institute*, the essential mark of the church is the 'pure preaching of God's Word and the lawful administration of the sacraments'.[51] It is how the sacraments relate to Calvin's pneumatology that invites our attention.

Extensive studies of Calvin's sacramental theology have been written, secondary works to which only brief reference can be afforded in our study. McDonnell, in his study of Calvin's eucharistic doctrine, views pneumatology as the central key to understanding Calvin's doctrine of the sacraments, so much so that Calvin's 'Christology can only be considered pneumatologically'.[52] It is through his doctrine of the Spirit that Calvin comes to an understanding of Christ's presence in the sacraments. Thus, in the eucharist, 'the body and blood are really given, really received, not just union with Christ', and this is effected by the hidden power of the Holy Spirit.[53] Wallace, while more cautiously stressing that there is no localisation of Christ's body or attachment to the earthly elements,[54] notes that the descent of Christ in the eucharist is effected by the Spirit and that Calvin has 'no doubt about the reality and concreteness of the gift of the body and blood of Christ'.[55] As Calvin himself explains, this reception of Christ clearly has a suprarational aspect to it, for

---

[50] J. Calvin, *Commentary on 2 Corinthians*, 3.18, translated by T. A. Smail, St. Andrew Press, Edinburgh, 1964, p. 50.

[51] *Institute*, pp. 24-5.

[52] K. McDonnell, *John Calvin, the Church, and the Eucharist*, Princeton University Press, Princeton, 1967, p. 250.

[53] *John Calvin, the Church, and the Eucharist*, p. 239.

[54] R. S. Wallace, *Calvin's Doctrine of the Word and Sacrament*, Oliver & Boyd, Edinburgh, 1953, p. 208.

[55] *Calvin's Doctrine of the Word and Sacrament*, p. 203.

if anyone should ask me how this takes place, I shall not be ashamed to confess it as a secret too lofty for either my mind to comprehend or my words to declare. And, to speak more plainly, I rather experience it than understand it.[56]

It may be, as McDonnell suggests, that Calvin's stress on the role of the Holy Spirit in the sacrament arises from his resolve not to confuse the ubiquity of Christ with His specific presence in the sacrament;[57] however, Calvin's stress on the role of the Spirit can readily be appreciated when we recall Calvin's regard for the Spirit as that bond which effects and sustains a real union between Christ and ourselves. As we have already observed, for Calvin the event of the Incarnation brings us in our humanity to be united to the exalted Christ through the bond of the Spirit. The question which now faces us is how Calvin's understanding of the Spirit here differs from or complements his emphasis upon the epistemic agency of the Spirit which we detected within the *duplex cognitio Dei*.

That Calvin should relate the sacraments to a rational, cognitive faith should not surprise us. Coming in book 4 and following the methodological order of the *Institute*, the sacraments are to be understood ecclesiologically where the church is construed Christologically. Sacraments are there as an aid to the church whose faith is in Christ,[58] the sacraments ratifying and making more evident the promise of God in Christ[59] and serving as those columns which better support our faith on the Word of God as its foundation.[60] Consequently, the Holy Spirit makes the sacraments effective for us, our hearts being opened where our minds have been illumined by the Spirit,[61] the sacraments effecting a brilliance of illumination communicated from God the Father, 'just as he illumines our bodily eyes by the rays of the sun'.[62]

That the sacraments reinforce a rational and cognitive faith, through an internal work in the believer which complements the external ministration of the sacrament, is well set out in Calvin's short *Summary of Doctrine concerning the Ministry of the Word and Sacraments*.[63] Here Calvin distinguishes man as the external minister and the Holy Spirit as the internal minister. In chapter 2 of the *Summary*, our communion with Christ in the sacrament is identified as being both mystical and spiritual: mystical, in that it is 'incomprehensible to human reason' and spiritual because 'it is effected by

---

[56] *Institute* 4.17.32, p. 1403.

[57] *John Calvin, the Church, and the Eucharist*, p. 257.

[58] *Institute* 4.14.1.

[59] *Institute* 4.14.3.

[60] *Institute* 4.14.5.

[61] *Institute* 4.14.8.

[62] *Institute* 4.14.10, p. 1286.

[63] *Calvin: Theological Treatises*, edited by J. K. S. Reid, The Westminster Press, Philadelphia, 1954. We follow Reid in attributing this work to Calvin (p. 170).

the Holy Spirit'.[64] Where we audibly hear the external spoken word, the Holy Spirit internally effects 'in the hearts of whomsoever he will their union with Christ through one faith'.[65] In baptism, the external sacrament of the water is complemented internally by the endowment of Christ, the Spirit baptising 'with the blood of the spotless Lamb',[66] while in the Supper the Holy Spirit,

> by his secret virtue, feeds the souls of the faithful, both truly and efficaciously, with the body and blood of the Lord unto eternal life, as truly as they know themselves to be nourished for this mortal life by bread and wine.[67]

It is the mystery of the Spirit's action that, for Calvin, reflects the profundity of the Spirit's place as bond between God and man. The very incomprehensibility of the Spirit's action is due to His being that bond which is between Christ and His church. The centre of faith lies with the Saviour, who is the Son; and the action of the Spirit is to bring us deeper into communion with the Son. To this end, the Spirit is both He who enables faith and He who sustains it within the ministration of the sacraments. The mystery of the Spirit's working is appropriate to the anonymity of His function in bonding us to the soterial focus that is in the Son. As Calvin explains, when discussing baptism in the *Institute*, God

> does not feed our eyes with a mere appearance only, but leads us to the present reality and effectively performs what it symbolises.[68]

What is of special interest in the *Summary* is the manner in which this short work demonstrates Calvin's understanding of how the Spirit can be perceived both as initiator and sustainer of our relationship with Christ. The Spirit is active, in a mysterious way, to effect our union with Christ and give birth to faith in men and women. On the other hand it is the Spirit who, as Calvin is keen to emphasise in the *Institute*, reinforces faith in Christ through the proper use of the sacraments. The Spirit, active in and through the sacrament, is transparent in Himself, yet potent and powerful in bringing us into a deeper union with Christ; for it is He who has led us into a realisation of that union with Christ. The Spirit has brought us to faith in Christ through His presence in the preaching of the Word and the administration of the sacraments. At the

---

[64] *Summary of Doctrine concerning the Ministry of the Word and Sacraments*, in *Calvin: Theological Treatises*, p. 171.

[65] *Summary of Doctrine concerning the Ministry of the Word and Sacraments*, in *Calvin: Theological Treatises*, Chap. 5, p. 173.

[66] *Summary of Doctrine concerning the Ministry of the Word and Sacraments*, in *Calvin: Theological Treatises*, Chap. 7, p. 173.

[67] *Summary of Doctrine concerning the Ministry of the Word and Sacraments*, in *Calvin: Theological Treatises*, Chap. 8, p. 174.

[68] *Institute* 4.15.14, p. 1314.

same time the Spirit also secures us more firmly in our union with Christ through His ongoing presence and action in the preaching of the Word and in the sacraments.

We might summarise our observations on Calvin's understanding of the Spirit's Person and function as expressed in our union with Christ, faith and the sacraments, by noting that while the principal work of the Spirit is to effect faith, the Spirit's role for Calvin is clearly not merely that of an epistemic agent. By identifying the Spirit as the bond of our union with Christ, Calvin makes the work of the Spirit the key to the soterial centre which is in Christ. It is the Spirit who sustains us, in all our being, in union with Christ our Saviour. At the same time, Calvin is at some pains to avoid treating the Spirit's function separately from the proper objective of the Spirit's work, which is the creation and sustaining of faith within the Christian. Consequently, it is the epistemic agency of the Spirit that is repeatedly brought into focus. To understand better Calvin's motive in this, some mention must be made of the context in which he was working and writing.

3.7   The Parameters of Orthodoxy

To what degree did the reaction and opposition of Calvin both to Rome and to the radical groups of the Reformation shape his theology of the Spirit; and how did inherited Trinitarian perspectives, worked out in his thought, reinforce his opposition to their respective emphases and understanding of the Holy Spirit? Undoubtedly, Calvin's theology was forged in the context of controversy. While it is outwith the scope of our study to attempt an assessment of the overall influence of polemics in the development of Calvin's theological framework, we do note that Calvin's continual concern was to safeguard the Reformed church from radical extremes and excesses.[69] Although, as G. H. Williams observes, Calvin did not always clearly distinguish between his opponents in his polemical writings,[70] what is evident is that Calvin's concern to maintain a proper understanding of the church clearly impinges upon his doctrine of the Spirit.

The corporate integrity of the church is of major concern to Calvin. That the opening chapter of book 4 of the *Institute* is entitled 'The true church with which as mother of all the godly we must keep unity'[71] underlines Calvin's

---

[69] It remains a moot point, for example, as to the degree which Calvin's prolonged disagreement over Trinitarian and Christological matters with the anti-Trinitarian, Servetus, affected the shaping of Calvin's Christology.

[70] G. H. Williams, *The Radical Reformation*, Weidenfeld & Nicolson, London, 1962, p. 598. From 1541, Calvin produced a series of writings through which he sought to safeguard the Reformed Church from radical extremes and excesses. See *The Radical Reformation*, p. 580.

[71] *Institute*, p. 1011.

conviction that the Christian's communion in the Spirit occurs within the wider context of the Spirit's communion with the church at large. Furthermore, the church, in communion with the Spirit, is the guardian of the truth that is borne of the Spirit. Servetus, who met with his death at Geneva, was vigorously denounced by Calvin for his anti-Trinitarian[72] and 'Anabaptist' views.[73] The church had the responsibility of defending the truth of the Gospel, thereby maintaining the church's own unity:

> The Spirit of God directs that heretics be regarded as detestable, and teaches that [Christians] must be on their guard against heresies, because they cause destruction and the breaking-up of the church.[74]

Where the ministry of Word and Sacraments is properly exercised, there is found the church.[75] The church is that which issues from the bond of the Spirit between God and man, having been instituted by the Son of God manifest in the flesh and constituted by the ongoing activity of the Holy Spirit in her midst. This presence of the Spirit is expressed within the preaching of the Word and the administration of the sacraments. In focusing on the corporate nature of the church, Calvin's perspective is that of the Spirit active in the church and received by individuals as they are made members of the church. Calvin sees the church as the context wherein Christian faith is borne; it is not simply that which is constituted by those who have faith:

> By God's generosity, mediated by Christ's merit, through the sanctification of the Spirit, sins have been and are daily pardoned to us who have been received and engrafted into the body of Christ.[76]

Calvin's emphasis on the church thus constituted by the Spirit placed him in sharp contrast with more radical elements within the Reformation, especially those who looked to see the church identified as the community of the faithful alone. The conflict which this led to in defining and defending ecclesiology is well expressed by Balke in his study on Calvin's conflict with the Anabaptist radicals, where he notes,

> By his emphasis on the Lordship of Christ in His church through the Holy Spirit, a pneumatocracy, Calvin sharply rejects the atomism of the Anabaptists ... Calvin's

---

[72] *Institute* 1.13.22.

[73] Calvin styles Servetus as 'not the least among the Anabaptists - indeed, the great glory of that tribe'. *Institute* 4.16.31, p. 1353.

[74] J. Calvin, *Commentary on the Acts of the Apostles*, (Vol. 2), 24.14, translated by J. W. Fraser, St. Andrew Press, Edinburgh, 1966, p. 250.

[75] *Institute* 4.1.8.

[76] *Institute* 4.1.21, p. 1035.

thought was more organic and pneumatocratic. He wanted no part of spiritual autocracy.[77]

Balke's identification of Calvin's thought as pneumatocratic is significant. For Calvin the Spirit's presence was to be affirmed within the corporate context of the church's communion as the body of Christ on earth. The Spirit is bound to the church as the church is bound to Christ. Pneumatocracy was not to be confused with autocracy or anarchy.

The Munster experiment had demonstrably proven the perils of a spiritual autocracy which had broken free from the safeguards of an ordered ecclesiology. Calvin would have no part in it. Rejecting schism over 'nonessential matters',[78] Calvin denounced those such as the Anabaptists who,

> imbued with a false conviction of their own perfect sanctity, as if they had already become a sort of airy spirits, spurned association with all men in whom they discern any remnant of human nature.[79]

The sanctification and transformation of the church was to be understood as a process which is gradual and progressive,[80] not something immediate or completely attainable in the present life.[81] Calvin sought to reform, not to repudiate the church as it stands: it was this which set him apart from the radicals.[82] Proper doctrine and proper behaviour could and should be balanced together within the unity of the church.

Where Calvin stood against the radicals in his ecclesiology, he did at the same time self-consciously distance himself not only from the abuses of medieval Roman Catholicism but also from an understanding which conceived of the Spirit's latent action in the church, yet unrealised by the presence of faith. Where Luther had declared the priority of *sola fidei*,[83] Calvin likewise could not countenance an understanding of the Spirit's work which was hidden

---

[77] W. Balke, *Calvin and the Anabaptist Radicals*, Eerdmans, Grand Rapids, 1981, p. 235.

[78] *Institute* 4.1.12, p. 1026.

[79] *Institute* 4.1.13, p. 1027.

[80] *Institute* 4.1.17.

[81] 'Let those who imagine such perfection for themselves as would make it unnecessary to seek pardon have disciples whose itching ears mislead them into errors...' *Institute* 3.20.45, p. 911.

[82] Pelikan observes, 'It was neither Luther nor Calvin nor the Anglican Reformers, but the radicals lumped together by their opponents as "marvellous and manifold divisions and bands of Anabaptists", who put forward, as the fundamental issue of their own version of "Reformation as re-formation", the challenge to the supposed apostolic structure of the church and the substitution for it of a natural form of truly apostolic church life'. J. Pelikan, *Reformation of Church and Dogma (1300-1700)*, University of Chicago Press, Chicago, 1984, p. 314.

[83] 'By faith alone!'

in a sea of mysticism. Scholastic sacramentalism's understanding of grace dispensed *ex opere operato* was not acceptable to Calvin. In so far as the right administration of the sacraments is a mark of the church, so the sacraments 'direct and almost lead men by the hand to Christ'.[84] The facility of the sacraments lay in attesting to and ratifying God's good will towards man, which leads to faith. At the same time, Calvin did not reduce the sacraments to the status of a memorial, as did Zwingli. Calvin was jealous of the sacraments' status and facility as a means of the Spirit's operation towards the building up of the church.

It is in his attempt to ensure a doctrine of the church which maintained the parameters of Christian orthodoxy that we, once more, see Calvin as a legatee of the Western Trinitarian model. As we noted in the preceding chapter, one of the characteristics of Patristic thought in the West was a strong emphasis on the corporate integrity of the church; and Cyprian's dictum, *outside the church there is no salvation*, rang out as clearly in Calvin's ecclesiology as it did in the Patristic era. Likewise, where we saw the earlier perspective on the Spirit as *vinculum* between the Father and the Son - and derivatively as the bond between Christ and his church - reflected in Calvin's development of the *duplex cognitio Dei*, we can also detect it as a basic tenet within Calvin's ecclesiology. Moreover, as we have sought to demonstrate, it is the Spirit in His functioning as a bond between Christ and His church that provides a basis for Calvin's correlation of both Christian faith and the facility of the sacraments to their proper expression within the church. The Western Trinitarian model's emphasis on the church as bonded to Christ through the Spirit's operation as *vinculum* features large in Calvin's thought.

What, though, of that other feature which we identified as belonging to the Western Trinitarian model, an emphasis on the Spirit as an epistemic agent? Certainly we detected something of this in Calvin's *duplex cognitio Dei*. Can we also say that it is a major characteristic throughout the other areas of Calvin's thought that we have so far reviewed? An emphasis on faith as that bond which exists between the Christian and Christ was clearly identified; yet we saw that this arose from faith resting upon a foundation which is the deeper bond between Christ and His church, the bond of the Holy Spirit. Where Calvin's understanding of the Spirit's operation did appear to allow for some suprarational elements, albeit that their proper conclusion was a rational, cognitive faith in God, this precludes us from saying that the Spirit acts exclusively within an epistemic agency. Preferably, we might say that Calvin's perception appears to have embraced the Spirit's central role as being that of an epistemic agent but that this was not an exclusive role. Implicated in the Spirit's epistemic agency was both the Spirit's foundational role as the bond that is between Christ and His church and the Spirit's suprarational activity as met with in the sacraments.

---

[84] *Institute* 4.14.20, p. 1296.

Before seeking to draw further conclusions regarding Calvin's understanding of the Spirit, it remains for us to investigate one other important aspect of Calvin's thought which would help shape his legacy to Scottish theology: Calvin's understanding of the Spirit's role in his doctrine of election. It is to this that we now turn.

3.8   The Spirit and Election

Calvin deals with election in *Institute* 3.21-24, thereby making it both the logical extension and the conclusion of his concern to communicate the soterial centrality of Christ. Calvin saw the doctrine of predestination as faith's 'best confirmation':[85] consequently, Calvin's development of the theme has been fairly interpreted as arising out of his ecclesiological and pastoral concerns.[86] It is also apparent, as we shall now seek to demonstrate, that Calvin's understanding of election reinforces his Christocentric focus and leads into a significant facet of Calvin's pneumatology.

As we earlier noted, it was the soterial mission of the Son that provided Calvin with the epistemological centre for his theology in the *Institute*. Although the logical order of the *Institute* commences with the *cognitio Dei Creatoris* in book 1, it is the *cognitio Dei Redemptoris* in book 2 that provides Calvin's soteriological basis for the development of books 3 and 4. Our understanding of election is therefore centred, through our faith, upon Christ the Redeemer. It is central to Calvin that Christ is 'the mirror wherein we must, and without self deception may, contemplate our own election'.[87] The fact of our election is to be found in Christ alone. There can therefore be no looking beyond Christ for any other basis on which to establish it.

There are two features of this emphasis that are of special interest to us. Firstly, we find illustrated yet again Calvin's adherence to a Western model of the Trinity and his insistence that our communion with God be rooted in the Son of God and our participation in Him. Our communion with God as Trinity comes about through our communion with the Son of God, manifest in His Incarnation. Secondly, this concentration of interest on Christ means that there is no parallel, equivalent interest in the salvific function of the Spirit. In that election is dealt with as part of the conclusion to Calvin's doctrine of salvation, it is treated as a soteriological and therefore a Christologically centred doctrine, not a pneumatological one. Obviously, the presence of the Spirit is inferred: the Spirit is the bond which unites us to God. Our interest at this point, however, is one of emphasis. In dealing with election, Calvin's emphasis lies with the soterial centrality of the Son and not upon the Spirit. This distinction is especially important when we seek to distinguish between the fact of that

---

[85] *Institute* 3.24.9, p. 976.
[86] F. Wendel, *Calvin*, Collins, London, 1965, p. 263.
[87] *Institute* 3.24.5, p. 970.

election and our understanding of it.

We traced earlier some ambiguities relating to the Spirit's function which have arisen in seeking to interpret Calvin's *duplex cognitio Dei*. These stemmed from the logical priority which Calvin gives, in book 1 of the *Institute*, to that knowledge of God which is to be had from Creation and from the Scriptures. These problems arise again when we attempt to distinguish between the fact and the understanding of man's election. Calvin, while insisting that the fact of our election lies in Christ, points to the greater understanding of election that comes from our reading of Scripture. As Calvin states,

> For just as those engulf themselves in a deadly abyss who, to make their election more certain, investigate God's eternal plan apart from his Word, so those who rightfully and duly examine it as it is contained in his Word reap the inestimable fruit of comfort.[88]

The factual centre of election lies in Christ yet the interpretative centre lies in Scripture. Such a distinction might allow us to say that Calvin's doctrine of election provides us with two centres: one Christocentric and the other bibliocentric. The difficulty arises because these twin foci, albeit complementary, allow an ambiguous interpretation of the Holy Spirit's function in election to arise. The fact of election, centred on the soterial mission of Christ, implies the presence of the Spirit as *vinculum* between God and the elect. Calvin's continued use of the Western model of the Trinity and his concern to maintain a Christocentric soteriology does not, however, allow him to present and expound the Spirit's soterial function in explicit terms. The fact of our election is centred on Christ; yet our understanding of election is centred in Scripture. Where Calvin's emphasis on a rational and cognitive faith encourages us towards a greater understanding of our election, there is required the work of the Spirit as an epistemic agent in illumining the Scriptures. Consequently it is an emphasis on the epistemic function of the Spirit which features more highly in coming to an understanding of our election.

Calvin's perception of the Spirit bringing us to an understanding of our election was readily married to an emphasis on the Spirit as He who creates and sustains rational, cognitive faith within us. As Niesel notes, where Calvin sees the Spirit accomplishing His work, 'the receptive faculty of faith is created and strengthened in us'.[89] This was not, however, clearly related to the fact of our election, which is centred on the soterial mission of the Son. For Calvin, in using the Western model of the Trinity, there was no reason to emphasise the ontic actuality of the Spirit, for the Spirit's presence was implicit as *vinculum* in

---

[88] *Institute* 3.24.4, p. 969.
[89] W. Niesel, *The Theology of Calvin*, translated by H. Knight, Westminster Press, Philadelphia, 1956, p. 227.

union with the Son. There was no reason to expand further on the ontological relationship between the Son and the Spirit. The true relation of the Son and Spirit lay in the hiddenness of God's transcendent Being. Consequently, a disjunction appears in Calvin's thought between the fact of our election, founded upon the soterial mission of the Son and a proper understanding of that election, brought about by the epistemic function of the Spirit. The Spirit comes to be perceived as the executor of God's elective decision, opening our understanding to the fact rather than being, in Himself, the expression and assurance of it.

In book 3 of the *Institute*, where Calvin deals with election, the effectiveness of the Spirit's work is presented as contingent upon the divine decree, regenerating the elect and 'shutting off the reprobate from knowledge of his name or from the sanctification of his Spirit'.[90] The Spirit is less evidently the harbinger of salvation, in His own Being, as the revealer of truth to the elect of God. As the executor of God's elective decision in calling men to salvation, the Spirit's function in this role could too easily be taken as working independently of the Son in His soterial mission. This, when married to Calvin's distinctive emphasis on the Spirit's epistemic function in bringing us to an understanding of our election in Christ, could easily be misconstrued: election and our understanding of it could be ripped away from its reference in Christ, especially if sight were lost of Calvin's perception of the Spirit's less conspicuous place as *vinculum*, latent within the Son of God's soterial mission. We shall note that this rupture did arise within the theology of Calvin's immediate legatees. Before doing so, we turn to look in greater detail at Calvin's perception of the Spirit's epistemic agency.

3.9   The Spirit as an Epistemic Agent

In seeking to understand Calvin's treatment of the Holy Spirit's Person and function within a Trinitarian framework, we noted that Calvin's patent Christocentricity arose from his concern to emphasise the soteriological significance of Christ. In placing Christ at the centre of his theological method, Calvin's concern was to expound the soterial focus of the Son of God made manifest in human flesh, rather than to state Christ's ontological priority in manifesting the Trinity to us. To say that, for Calvin, God is revealed in Christ is to make, first and foremost, a soteriological statement, not an ontological one.

Furthermore, such statements as '[God] is shown to us not as he is in himself, but as he is towards us'[91] and 'for even if the Word in His immeasurable essence united with the nature of man into one person, we do not

---

[90] *Institute* 3.21.7, p. 931.
[91] *Institute* 1.10.2, p. 97.

imagine that he was confined therein',[92] underline Calvin's indebtedness to the Western model of the Trinity. Calvin assumed that God can legitimately be perceived as a Trinity, immanent to Himself, whose Being is manifest in and through Christ. As Wallace notes, Calvin's concern was to

> underline the wonder of the fact that it was really the eternal God who became one with us in Jesus.[93]

The difficulty which arose was that the soteriological significance of Christ's Incarnation was not expounded by Calvin in terms of a Trinitarian ontology. Calvin's Trinitarian understanding does not require an explicit connection to be made, in ontological terms, between the soterial mission of the Son of God and the ontic actuality of the Spirit, for the ontological union of the Father, Son and Spirit is neither expounded nor applied. This absence of a clear, ontological statement on the relationship of the Spirit to the Son in their salvific economy may have arisen precisely because Calvin simply assumed a Western model of the Trinity; and this assumption may itself have arisen because Calvin's main concern lay with the need to maintain a soterial focus in Christ and with the need of the church and the believer to understand the nature of that saving truth. This is reflected in the fact that the correlate, for Calvin, to the soteriological significance of the Son's mission lay in our need to comprehend what Christ has done; and it is in this context that the Spirit's epistemic function, in fashioning and forming a rational and cognitive faith, is emphasised. Consequently, Calvin's pneumatology could easily be construed as built not upon the Spirit's ontic actuality, but upon the twin pillars of Christ's soteriological significance and our need to understand the truth of God revealed to us. Where, in the former instance, the Spirit's presence is implied because of the Spirit's union with the Son, it is more clearly presented in the latter; but in a manner which requires a function of the Spirit - the epistemic function - to be focused on, rather than dealing with the ontic actuality of the Spirit's Being as central to God's salvific economy. This, combined with the assumption that an understanding of God's Triune Being is more properly to be gained from the Immanent Trinity rather than out of His salvific economy, opens the way for an understanding of the Spirit's epistemic agency to be detached from that of the Son of God's soterial mission.

Calvin's adherence to the Western model of the Trinity meant that an epistemology which assumed the priority of an Immanent Trinity could hardly be avoided. We saw this in Calvin's dealing with the doctrine of the Trinity, as found in book 1 of the *Institute* under the heading of the Knowledge of God as Creator and preceding the Knowledge of God the Redeemer as addressed in

---

[92] *Institute* 2.13.4, p. 481.
[93] R. S. Wallace, *Calvin, Geneva and the Reformation*, St. Andrew Press, Edinburgh, 1988, p. 240.

book 2. For Calvin, knowledge of God appeared to arise out of an acknowledgement of His Triune, immanent Being. The acknowledgement of God's Triune, immanent Being precedes both our benefitting from and our appreciation of the Son's soterial mission. In the logical construction of the *Institute*, commencing in *Institute* 1.1, there is a perception of God which is founded upon His immanent Being and not upon His salvific economy. This, married to an emphasis on the facility of Scripture, provided the foundation for a knowledge of God which could be taken to conflict, or at least contrast, with Calvin's soterial focus expounded in book 2. In either case we are faced with the task of constructing a pneumatology which is inferred rather than one which is developed out of an appreciation of the Spirit's ontic actuality. It is the Spirit's epistemic agency, not His Being, that is emphasised.

We see something of the marriage of the Spirit's epistemic agency to a Scriptural hermeneutic where Calvin notes,

> Scripture, gathering up the otherwise confused knowledge of God in our minds, having dispersed our dullness, clearly shows us the true God.....He has from the beginning maintained this plan for his church, so that besides these common proofs he has also put forth his Word, which is a more direct and more certain mark whereby he is to be recognised.[94]

In the Scriptures it is possible for us, through our understanding, to glimpse God's immanent Being:

> For he so proclaims himself the sole God as to offer himself to be contemplated clearly in three Persons. Unless we grasp these, only the bare and empty name of God flits about in our brains, to the exclusion of the true God.[95]

Calvin undoubtedly held Christ to be the central object of faith; but this did not mean that Calvin's soterial focus on the Incarnation shaped the logic of his theological method. What we find is that his epistemology, worked out through a biblical hermeneutical system, leaves us unsure as to where God's self-revelation to man is to be found. Is it in the Bible itself; or is it found by looking through the Bible, to Christ? The problem was not clarified for us in our examination of Calvin's Christology, where we observed that Calvin's understanding of the Son, manifest in the Incarnation of Christ and His soterial mission, pointed to an appreciation of the Son of God which centred on the Immanent Trinity and not the salvific economy. Calvin's principal interest lay in the Son of God's soterial mission and the benefits that accrue from it, rather than in an exploration of the hypostatic union. Indeed, Calvin appeared to be disinterested in seeking to explore the ontological ramifications of the Incarnation, other than as they relate to soteriology. As he states, 'But since all

---

[94] *Institute* 1.6.1, p. 70.
[95] *Institute* 1.13.2, p. 122.

Scripture proclaims that to become our Redeemer he was clothed with flesh, it is too presumptuous to imagine another reason or another end.'[96]   Calvin's Christocentric focus arose from his soterial emphasis. It is on this basis that Calvin emphasised the priority of revelation in Christ. Where his focus was lifted, as appears in book 1 of the *Institute*, to look at the Triune God Himself, Calvin's interest in pneumatology lay principally with the Spirit's epistemic function.

Where, in surveying Calvin's doctrine of election, we distinguished between the fact of our salvation and our understanding of it, we argued that there were two parallel perceptions of the Holy Spirit's Person and function. On the one hand, the Spirit is implicitly present as *vinculum* with Christ in His soterial mission; on the other hand, the Spirit is active in illumining the Scriptures, which God has established for our understanding of Him.[97] Should Calvin have taken a clearer line in grounding his epistemology in the event of the Incarnation? Surely, this was not his immediate concern. His position, however, leaves us with difficulties not only in the area of epistemology, or knowledge of God, but also in the whole discussion of the *ordo salutis* and the Holy Spirit's place therein. Given that our election is hidden in the divine decree, can there be some other ground for knowing God, other than in the ontological priority of the Incarnation? Can the doctrine of election be construed as independent and separate from the Son of God's soterial mission, or should man's election be ascertained and established in a manner contingent upon the Incarnation? On what basis can we know and experience assurance of salvation? We will return to face these questions in the following chapter, where we will look to the legacy of Calvinism in Scottish theology: for the moment, we simply note that difficulties, arising from these questions, are inherent in Calvin's treatment of pneumatology. In failing to emphasise the complementary character of the Son's soterial mission and Spirit's ontic actuality Calvin allowed, albeit inadvertently, for the possibility of a schism to develop between the Spirit's epistemic function, focused on Scripture, and the Spirit's soterial relevancy to the person of Christ. Calvin's pneumatology could easily be mistaken as reducing the Spirit's work to that of an epistemic agent, the Spirit's function being simply to bring an awareness of our election to our souls' intellectual faculty. This was seen most sharply at the beginning of book 3 of the *Institute*. We saw that faith is there presented as the fruit of the Spirit's epistemic agency, principally grounded on a proper understanding of Scripture where the Spirit has acted as illumining agent, rather than upon an appreciation of the ontic actuality of the Spirit, ever drawing us into a deeper appreciation of the Son Incarnate. The focus lies on the Spirit as interpreter of truth rather than the Spirit Himself as truth's actualiser.

Where the *Institute* provides a systematic presentation of doctrine, it must

---

[96] *Institute* 2.12.4, p. 467.
[97] *Institute* 1.7.1.

not be forgotten that Calvin himself believed that the main expression of his theology lay in his *Commentaries*. It is here that we see Calvin address once again the peculiar ministry of the Holy Spirit; but, as in the *Institute*, we see the Spirit featuring as an epistemic agent in the task of bringing the Christian into faith. It is this emphasis on the epistemic agency of the Spirit which is paramount in Calvin's usage in the *Commentaries*. It is the function of the Spirit to bring the truth of God into our hearts and minds.[98] The Spirit is the expositor of Christ and His benefits in a manner that draws us into a rational, cognitive faith.[99] The Spirit works in a confirmatory manner, building on and confirming the truths of Scripture which have been apprehended in our minds: '[The Spirit has been given] to allay our disquiet, to bring our minds to a state of tranquillity, and to stir us up to call on God with confidence and freedom.'[100] So it is that the Spirit, in bringing assurance, builds on the work of the Word. The Spirit's epistemic agency confirms to us the salvific triumph of the Son.

This perspective on the action of the Spirit is presented persuasively in the *Commentary on Ephesians*, where Calvin states,

> Our minds never become so firm that the truth of God prevails with us against all the temptations of Satan, until the Holy Spirit has confirmed us in it. The true conviction which believers have of the Word of God, of their own salvation, and of all religion, does not spring from the feeling of the flesh, or from human and philosophical arguments, but from the sealing of the Spirit, who makes their consciences more certain and removes all doubt. The foundation of faith would be frail and unsteady if it rested on human wisdom; and therefore, as preaching is the instrument of faith, so the Holy Spirit makes preaching efficacious. But here he seems to subject the sealing of the Spirit to faith. If so, faith precedes it. I answer, the effect of the Spirit in faith is twofold, corresponding to the two parts of which faith consists. It enlightens the intellect (*mens*) and also confirms the thinking (*animus*). The commencement of faith is knowledge; its completion is a firm and steady conviction, which admits of no opposing doubt.[101]

Given Calvin's emphasis on the epistemic function of the Spirit, there are implications which this carries for other areas of Calvin's pneumatology. We would note three of these.

Firstly, for Calvin, regeneration by the Holy Spirit and comprehension of the basic tenets of the Gospel are inseparably linked, such is the emphasis on the epistemic agency of the Holy Spirit. Faith involves knowledge of and communication from God; and this is through the Holy Spirit[102] expounding the

---

[98] *Commentary on John*, 15.26.

[99] *Commentary on John*, 14.25.

[100] J. Calvin, *Commentary on Romans*, 8.15, translated by R. MacKenzie, St. Andrew Press, Edinburgh, 1961, pp. 167-68.

[101] *Commentary on Ephesians*, pp. 131-32.

[102] J. Calvin, *Commentary on 1 Corinthians*, 3.16, translated by J. W. Fraser, St. Andrew Press, Edinburgh, 1960.

truths of Scriptural revelation into our lives.[103] Secondly, sanctification is also contingent on the epistemic agency of the Spirit, for sanctification is an extension and continuation of regeneration. Both regeneration and sanctification are related to the Spirit's epistemic agency:

> Faith rests upon the knowledge of Christ. And Christ cannot be known apart from the sanctification of his Spirit. It follows that faith can in no wise be separated from a devout disposition.[104]

Thirdly, given this emphasis on the epistemic agency of the Spirit, Calvin is disinclined to speak of our meeting with the Spirit in terms that might detract from the Spirit's epistemic agency. Certainly, we saw how he does acknowledge the suprarational aspect of the Spirit's work in his dealing with the sacraments. As Niesel observes, it is in the sacraments that God's acceptance of man is conveyed;[105] but Calvin, reacting against the idea that there is a latent value in the sacraments themselves, again emphasised the revelatory function of the Spirit therein.[106] Calvin was adamant in not introducing a mysticism that would detract from a clear, rational faith in Christ. As Wallace comments, Calvin was suspicious of any attempt to recognise the Spirit other than in conjunction with the Scriptural testimony.[107] Calvin thus qualified the suprarational work of the Holy Spirit in the sacraments in a manner which pointed towards the Spirit's primary role as an epistemic agent, for

> first, the Lord teaches us and instructs us by His Word. Secondly, he confirms it by the sacraments. Finally, he illumines our minds by the light of his Holy Spirit and opens our hearts for the Word and sacrament to enter in, which would otherwise only strike our ears and appear before our eyes, but not at all affect us within... .[108] Therefore, the sacraments have effectiveness among us in proportion as we are helped by their ministry sometimes to foster, confirm, and increase the true knowledge of Christ in ourselves...[109] they avail and profit nothing unless received in faith.[110]

---

[103] J. Calvin, *Commentary on the Acts of the Apostles*, (Vol. 2), 19.2.

[104] *Institute* 3.2.8, pp. 552-53.

[105] *The Theology of Calvin*, p. 224.

[106] Niesel notes Calvin's perception that 'By the preaching of the Gospel and the use of the sacraments the Holy Ghost as it were bridges the gulf between Jesus Christ and ourselves'. *The Theology of Calvin*, p. 227.

[107] 'There is no more dubious and dangerous practice, according to Calvin, than to try and make contact with the Spirit of God by turning to any other source than the Word of God'. *Calvin's Doctrine of the Word and Sacrament*, p. 129.

[108] *Institute* 4.14.8, p. 1284.

[109] *Institute* 4.14.16, p. 1291.

[110] *Institute* 4.14.17, p. 1292.

We would suggest that such an emphasis on the epistemic function of the Spirit can be seen as attributable, in some measure, to Calvin's perception of the Trinity as transcendent and separate from man. As was noted with the *extra Calvinisticum*, there is some difficulty in understanding the manner in which Calvin understood the hypostatic union of divinity and humanity in Christ and the Son of God's complete presence within His physical body. Likewise, where the sacrament is efficacious in effecting communion with Christ, this is through faith, apprehending that communion with Christ which lies in heaven, beyond this world.[111] Certainly, Calvin appeared to have wrestled with the need to communicate an understanding of the Spirit and the sacrament which is beyond human comprehension, despite his preoccupation with the need for a rational, cognitive faith: he could affirm that the communication of Christ to us is

> mystical, and incomprehensible to human reason, and spiritual, since it is effected by the Holy Spirit; to whom, since He is the virtue of the living God, proceeding from the Father and the Son, we ascribe omnipotence, by whom he joins us to Christ our Head, not in an imaginary way, but most powerfully and truly, so that we become flesh of his flesh and bone of his bone, and from his vivifying flesh he transfuses life into us.'[112]

At the same time, an emphasis on the Spirit's epistemic function in testifying to Christ as Saviour, combined with Calvin's apparent difficulty in translating the essential unity of God, in His Trinitarian immanence, into the event of God's salvific economy, would appear to lead Calvin away from developing a more comprehensive understanding of the Spirit's ontic actuality.

Calvin's preference for stressing the Spirit's epistemic agency can again be seen where he addresses the issue of *charismata* in his *Commentary on the Acts of the Apostles*. In this work, Calvin is obliged to introduce a distinction between the 'spirit of regeneration' and those 'special gifts',[113] although he does not expand on his reason for so doing, other than in the claim that such manifestations of the Spirit 'lasted only for a time'.[114] As Calvin notes,

---

[111] Wallace notes, 'Communion with the body of Christ is effected through the descent of the Holy Spirit, by whom our souls are lifted up to heaven, there to partake of the life transfused into us from the flesh of Christ'. *Calvin's Doctrine of the Word and Sacrament*, p. 206.

[112] *Summary of Doctrine concerning the Ministry of the Word and Sacraments*, in *Calvin: Theological Treatises*, p. 171.

[113] *Commentary on the Acts of the Apostles*, (Vol. 2), 19.2, p. 148.

[114] *Commentary on the Acts of the Apostles*, (Vol. 1), 2.38, translated by J. W. Fraser and W. J. G. McDonald, St. Andrew Press, Edinburgh, 1965, p. 81.

For although we do not receive the Spirit to the end that we may speak with tongues...yet it is given to us for a better use, that we may believe with the heart unto righteousness, that our tongues may be trained to true confession....[115]

Calvin's concern lay not with the *charismata* but with faith's comprehension. Sadly, his disinterest in dealing with this aspect of the Spirit's suprarational activity meant that an understanding of it would not occur within the development of Reformed theology, other than is allowed in the doctrine of the sacraments. As we shall see, Calvin's omission disallowed the development, within Scottish Reformed theology, of a theological apparatus which would be equipped to deal with the Charismatic Movement's stress upon and interest in direct, personal experience of the suprarational work of the Spirit.

3.10   Calvin's Legacy in Retrospect

Brief mention should be made of Calvin's immediate theological legacy, prior to going on to look at its effect on the early development of Scottish Reformed thought. The priority which Calvin gave to epistemology in the formulation of his theological framework, combined with the continued prominence of the Western model of the Trinity, prepared the way for the theological rationalisation of Calvin's thought which was undertaken by Beza. Where Beza fashioned the experimental *theologoumena* of Calvin into a neo-scholasticism that was to find full expression, at the Synod of Dort, in the famous 'five points of Calvinism' he was, nonetheless, building on a logical basis which arose out of Calvin's thought. Doubtless, Beza saw himself as being faithful to the legacy of Calvin. On, for example, the issue of supralapsarianism,[116] Beza's systematisation arose out of Calvin's opaqueness on the subject of the 'eternal decree'.[117] Beza's systematisation, married to Calvin's more tentative exploration of some theological themes, produced a rationalisation that was the fruit of Calvin's methodology.

In this regard, we find it difficult to endorse R. T. Kendall's criticism of Beza, that he

---

[115] *Commentary on the Acts of the Apostles*, (Vol.1), 2.38, p. 82.

[116] Bangs, in his study on Arminius, identifies Beza as supralapsarian, a position whereby 'the decrees of election and damnation have priority over the decree of permission of the Fall ... Beza's position refers to the decrees of election and damnation to man not yet considered as created'. J. Bangs, *Arminius*, Eerdmans, Grand Rapids, 1985, p. 67.

[117] As Wallace comments, 'there are occasions where Calvin does not give a clear voice on this matter'. *Calvin's Doctrine of the Word and Sacrament*, p. 251, footnote 52.

directs us not to Christ but to ourselves; we do not begin with Him but with the effects, which point us back, as it were, to the decree of election.[118]

Kendall is concerned with the implications arising from a rationalisation of Calvin's presentation of the doctrine of election which he finds in Beza, construing it as a mutation of Calvin's thought. We will turn to this complaint in a moment, but first we would seek to answer the charge that Beza's supralapsarian position is a misrepresentation of Calvin. Bangs, in defending Arminius,[119] notes that

> Perhaps everything that Beza says can be found in Calvin, but the emphasis is different. Beza lifts the doctrine of predestination to a prominence which it did not have in Calvin.[120]

Here is the point. Calvin wished to affirm the priority of *sola scriptura* in his theological method and was prepared to trust in the implications of that being worked out by the Spirit. As we have already seen, however, it is hard to trace, in Calvin, an explicit link between the epistemic function of the Spirit in expounding Scripture and Calvin's emphasis on the Son of God's soterial mission. Sadly, by failing to make a clear association between epistemology and Christology, Calvin opened the way for the development of a scriptural hermeneutic that was not Christologically centred. At the centre of his epistemological method he allowed for the possibility of a rationalisation, such as Beza's, which gave birth to the theological problem of supralapsarianism - a doctrine which lacked a clear, Christocentric reference.

In this regard the teachings of Arminius, developed by his followers in the five theses of the Remonstrant Articles, were possibly not altogether alien to the substantive theology of Calvin. According to Bangs, Arminius held the same doctrine as Luther and Calvin in seeing man as simultaneously *iustus et peccator*[121]. However, while working within the intellectual structures of the Reformed faith, Arminius developed a Christocentricity that led him to stress the process of sanctification that arises in the life of the believer and which calls for ongoing perseverance by the Christian, rather than Calvin's prioritisation of the Spirit's epistemic function centred on *sola scriptura*. Arminius posed two questions: firstly, whether it is possible for any believer, without a special revelation, to be certain or assured that he will not decline or fall away from the faith; and secondly, whether those who have faith are bound to believe that they will not decline from the faith. Bangs observes that the affirmative 'can never be accounted a catholic doctrine in the church, and the

---

[118] R. T. Kendall, *Calvin and English Calvinism to 1649*, OUP, Oxford, 1979, p. 33.
[119] Bangs argues that Arminius is wrongly thought of as a Pelagian and that his position is not, in fact, opposed to Calvin's own, early theology.
[120] *Arminius*, p. 66.
[121] 'Both saint and sinner'.

negative has never been adjudged by the church universal a heresy. In other words, there is no present assurance of final salvation'[122].

It was this conclusion of Arminius that took him on a separate course from Calvin. Like Calvin, Arminius held to a Christocentric reference: yet for Arminius the Christocentric reference was unqualified. Calvin supplemented the Christocentric reference with an emphasis on the Spirit's epistemic agency, opening the way for a doctrine of election which was not, of necessity, interpreted with a Christocentric reference. Calvin supplemented his Christocentric reference with an understanding of the Spirit functioning both as an epistemic agent and as executor of God's elective decision: perspectives on the functioning of the Spirit which in turn would issue in the conclusions of Beza.

What, though, of Kendall's accusation that the focus of Beza's supralapsarianism brought him to look to the effects of faith, rather than to a proper focus in Christ Himself, which Kendall claims to discern in Calvin?[123] Certainly the development of a doctrine of assurance is pitted with difficulties and divergences among the divines of the Reformed tradition: yet it is proper to ask whether the problem was not so much the fault of Beza but rather a weakness, found in Calvin himself, in failing to focus on the salvific economy of the Trinity. We have argued that Calvin's pneumatology presents us with a dual axis within his theological framework, both soterial and epistemic. Arminius, on the other hand, sought to stress *Christus solus*. The difficulty with both Arminius and Calvin was that neither apparently sensed a need to present a renewed emphasis upon the ontic actuality of the Holy Spirit alongwith the recovery of a Christocentric bearing. In this sense, early Reformed thought perpetuated a deficiency we detected earlier in the Western model of the Trinity. Rather than present a theology centred on the Triune God's salvific economy, stressing both the soterial mission of the Son and the ontic actuality of the Spirit, the whole action of God to man tended to be telescoped into one point of access, in the soterial mission of the Son. Consequently, Arminius could form no real doctrine of pneumatised faith and assurance, outwith the context of his Christocentric focus: and Calvin had to build his epistemology on *sola scriptura* rather than on a pneumatology founded on the Spirit's ontic actuality. Calvin, while tacitly identifying varying functions of the Spirit through stressing the Spirit's epistemic agency, in looking to the Spirit's suprarational function in the sacraments and by viewing the Spirit as executor of God's elective decision, did not appear to consider developing a unified understanding of these three functions of the Spirit. Calvin does not present us with a pneumatology whereby these three functions could be related together, arising from the Spirit's ontic actuality within the Triune God's salvific

---

[122] *Arminius*, p. 347.
[123] Kendall succinctly states, 'Faith to Calvin may be described as merely witnessing what God has already done in Christ'. *Calvin and English Calvinism to 1649*, p. 20.

economy. Calvin omitted to complement his emphasis on the Son's soterial mission with a clear exposition of the Spirit's ontic actuality.

Reformed pneumatology stood as legatee, through Calvin, to the Western model of the Trinity. A failure to explore and expound the hypostatic union and the significance of the Spirit's work within the humanity of Christ was due largely to Calvin's continued adherence to that perspective on the Trinity which we have described as the Western Trinitarian model. It did not occur to Calvin that he might embrace a Trinitarian theology which centred on God's salvific economy, expressed in a parallel concern for both the ontic actuality of the Son and the ontic actuality of the Spirit. An emphasis upon the Son which implied the presence and action of the Spirit as *vinculum*, and a stress on the Spirit functioning as an epistemic agent: these two emphases combined to be the most prominent features of the bequest which Calvin gave to pneumatology as it would develop in the Scottish context.

Chapter 4

The Scots and Westminster Confessions of Faith

4.1 Introduction

In this chapter we follow our study of Calvin's pneumatology with an examination of how Calvin's particular concerns and emphases appear to have affected the development of pneumatology in the Scottish context. In particular we look to examine how these concerns and emphases came to find expression in the *Scots Confession* of 1560 and the *Westminster Confession* of 1647. We will be concerned to establish in what way the various features which we traced within Calvin's pneumatology, following the framework of our analysis of the *Institute*, appear in these two documents.[1] We will give special attention to the development of two issues which arose in chapter 3. Firstly, we will be looking to see how any emphasis on the Spirit as an epistemic agent is countered or balanced by an understanding of the Spirit's suprarational work such as that detected in Calvin's sacramental understanding. Secondly, we will ask whether there is any further development of that distinction, which we identified in Calvin's thought, between the fact of our election which is founded on the soterial mission of the Son and a proper understanding of that election effected in us through the Spirit's epistemic agency. Before proceeding to this comparative analysis we will, however, first need to examine the pneumatological features of the *Scots* and *Westminster Confessions* and make such critical observations and comparisons as are pertinent to our investigation.

In turning to examine the *Scots Confession* and *Westminster Confession*, we enter the field of Scottish theology proper. As at least one commentator has observed, the *Scots Confession* and the beginnings of the Church of Scotland are closely associated;[2] and the *Scots Confession* would call for our investigation simply because it serves as an indicator of early Scottish Reformed thought. In a similar manner, the *Westminster Confession* would command our attention because of its status as the subordinate confessional standard of the Kirk, second to Scripture alone.

We begin with the *Scots Confession*, however, for two reasons. The first

---

[1] Topics, as they are correlated to sections in our study of Calvin in chapter 3, are highlighted in bold print in the present chapter.

[2] A. T. Innes, *The Law of Creeds in Scotland*, William Blackwood & Sons, Edinburgh, 1902, pp. 4-5.

arises from its historical, theological significance. Commissioned by the Scottish Parliament of 1560 in order to present a statement of Protestant faith, the *Scots Confession* served as an indicator of those theological principles which were seen to be distinctive of a truly reformed Christian faith. That the work was hastily composed,[3] was the work of six men[4] and most probably drafted by one, John Knox, does not diminish its helpfulness in indicating what the principal concerns of Christian faith in the Scottish Reformation were seen to be: as Henderson observes, its principal intention was 'to state the orthodox Catholic doctrine as it continued to be believed in the reformed church'.[5] Moreover, the *Scots Confession* remained, until the adoption of the *Westminster Confession* in 1647, the accepted statement of faith of the Church of Scotland.

The second reason for our looking to the *Scots Confession* lies in the interest it has aroused as a possible alternative to the *Westminster Confession* within the Kirk. This cause, more recently espoused by the late Professor James B. Torrance, formerly of Aberdeen University, has sought to promote the *Scots Confession*, free of the later interpolations of federal Calvinism present in the *Westminster Confession*, as a preferred subordinate standard of faith within the Kirk. Such a preference was earlier expressed, as Innes notes, by the Marrowmen[6] as well as in the writings of John McLeod Campbell and Edward Irving, both of whom had their reasons for reacting to the dominance of federal Calvinism current in the early part of the nineteenth century, a dominance rooted in that theology which was expressed so forcefully within the *Westminster Confession*.

We begin our review with a survey of the *Scots Confession*, going on to compare our own observations with some received, scholarly opinion, repeating the process for the *Westminster Confession*. In the final sections of the chapter we shall return to review the main features of Calvin's pneumatological legacy and to make some critical comparisons, comments and conclusions of our own.

4.2   The Scots Confession: A Survey

In seeking to determine the pneumatological significance of the *Scots Confession*, our initial critique of its 25 chapters follows the plan adopted in our investigation into Calvin's pneumatology.

In turning to consider **the Knowledge of God**, we find that the Scriptures are accorded the highest authority, this being made evident in the Preface to the *Scots Confession*, where they are styled 'the mouth of God'. As in Calvin's

---

[3] Within four days of its commission by Parliament.

[4] John Winram, John Spottiswood, John Douglas, John Row, John Willock and John Knox.

[5] G. D. Henderson, *Scots Confession*, Church of Scotland, Edinburgh, 1937, p. 16.

[6] Innes notes a preference on the part of the Marrowmen for the *Scots Confession* over the *Westminster Confession*. *The Law of Creeds in Scotland*, p. 37, footnote 1.

1559 *Institute*, the logical priority of the work is concerned with the hermeneutical question of how we can know who God is and what He has done. Where, for Calvin, this pointed to the broader priority of the *cognitio Dei Creatoris*, with both Creation and Scripture as instrumental in displaying this knowledge, the *Scots Confession* more clearly focuses upon such revelation as is in Scripture alone. The Scriptures themselves are sufficient in providing the ground of all doctrine. It is to an awareness of the truth as it is apparent from the Scriptures that God's grace enables and the Spirit strengthens us.[7] This emphatic confidence in the sufficiency of Scripture would suggest to us a possible explanation for the brevity of the ontological detail accorded to the description of God in chapter 1, where God's nature is recognised simply as being 'one in substance and yet distinct in three persons'.[8] The focus of the *Scots Confession* lies in describing God's dealing with man, as recorded and revealed in Scripture, rather than on the character of God's Being which is expressed in or gives rise to His salvific economy.

That ontological questions are not a primary concern is made further evident from the manner in which the *Scots Confession* addresses the question of **Man's union with Christ**. It is not until chapter 6 that the *communicatio idiomatum* is dealt with, and there only briefly, Christ being described as 'true God and true man, two perfect natures united and joined in one person'.[9] That the main concern lies with affirming the priority of Scripture and not with a restating or reshaping of central, Christological dogma is reflected in the fact that the *Scots Confession* is keen to affirm the norms of Christological orthodoxy without expounding them in detail, proceeding in chapter 6 to anathematise those 'as did either deny the eternity of the Godhead, or the truth of His humanity, or confound them, or else divided them'.[10] Nevertheless, the consequent structuring of the *Scots Confession* leads to some unusual classifications. It may seem strange, for instance, that the fuller implications of the Incarnation are dealt with in chapter 8, which is entitled 'Election'. There, the vicarious humanity and soterial mission of Christ are clearly identified with and rooted in the union of the Godhead with manhood which occurs in Christ Jesus, while in chapter 9 we find the sacrificial nature of Christ's suffering on our behalf expounded under the heading, 'Christ's Death, Passion and Burial'. This interpolative method of dealing with Christology and soteriology suggests that the structuring of the *Scots Confession* appears to be shaped by a desire to

---

[7] 'By the aid of the mighty Spirit of our Lord Jesus Christ we firmly intend to endure to the end in the confession of our faith' (Preface). All quotations from the *Scots Confession* are taken from J. Bulloch's translation, published by The St. Andrew Press, Edinburgh, 1960. The one adaptation which we have made is to render 'Holy Ghost' as 'Holy Spirit'.

[8] *Scots Conf.*, Chapter 1.

[9] *Scots Conf.*, Chapter 6.

[10] *Scots Conf.*, Chapter 6.

affirm a particular, interpretative approach to Scripture. Ontological considerations do not appear to be prevalent.

Where the structure of the *Scots Confession* illustrates that Scriptural hermeneutics were a prominent concern in the mind of its authors, this might have suggested to us that the epistemic agency of the Spirit, in elucidating Scriptural truths, would be emphasised. Such a perception of the Spirit does not, however, arise from an examination of the text. From the Preface of the *Scots Confession*, we saw that it is to an awareness of the truth as revealed in Scripture that God's grace enables and the Spirit strengthens us. Where the association between the **Spirit and Faith** is thus affirmed through the Spirit's work in sustaining our faith, we might expect to find an emphasis upon the Spirit's epistemic agency. This does not appear to be the case. Where, in chapter 3 of the *Scots Confession*, the formation of assured faith in the hearts of God's people is attributed to the Holy Spirit, this might be interpreted as implying the presence of a clearly articulated understanding of the Spirit's activity. This would be especially so if, bearing in mind what was noted of Calvin's understanding of the intellectual faculty's place in man's status as *imago Dei*, the *Scots Confession* was clearly a Calvinistic work, a work where the action of the Spirit in man would lead to a rational, cognitive faith. The issue, however, is by no means made clear from the text. Indeed, the wording of chapter 3,[11] where the relation of the Spirit to faith is first mentioned, allows for a distinction between the work of the Holy Spirit and the testimony which is found in the Word, a distinction that does not tear the work of the Spirit and the Word apart but which yet allows the Spirit to be distinguished from the Word. It is in the coming together of these two, the Word and the Spirit, that faith is effected in the believer's heart.[12] The work of the Spirit, however, is not restricted to that of effecting faith, nor is it suggested that the Spirit is present simply as an epistemic agent in the creation of faith. There is the possibility of allowing for a wider, suprarational work of the Spirit within the *Scots Confession*, despite its hermeneutical preoccupations.

The work of the Holy Spirit is addressed directly in chapter 12 of the *Scots Confession*.[13] Again, that distinctive ministry of the Holy Spirit, where faith arises as a consequence of the Spirit's action, is clearly stated. Faith and assurance arise from 'the inspiration of the Holy Spirit'.[14] Although we noted that there was to be found in chapter 1 of the *Scots Confession* no amplification of a bare, ontological statement on God's Triune nature, the economy and work of the Spirit, as it is spoken of in chapter 12, is not treated as hidden within the

---

[11] Entitled 'Original Sin'.

[12] 'This rebirth is wrought by the power of the Holy Spirit creating in the hearts of God's chosen ones an assured faith in the promise of God revealed to us in His Word'. *Scots Conf.*, Chapter 3.

[13] Entitled 'Faith in the Holy Spirit'.

[14] *Scots Conf.*, Chapter 12.

Trinity's perichoretic action but is clearly recognised. The Holy Spirit is cited as He 'whom we confess to be God, equal with the Father and with His Son, who sanctifies us, and brings us into all truth by His own working'.[15] Once more we see space allowed for a distinction to be drawn between the sanctifying work of the Holy Spirit and His work in opening our minds to the truths of Scripture. Indeed, the epistemic agency of the Spirit is barely referred to in chapter 12 of the *Scots Confession*, other than in His removing 'the darkness from our minds'[16] and turning our hearts towards God in obedience. Such references to the Spirit's work cannot be characterised as exclusively epistemic or rationalistic. In a similar way, where in chapter 13[17] the *Scots Confession* speaks of the Spirit as He who 'bears witness to our spirit that we are the Sons of God',[18] aiding us in our resistance to sin, there is nothing to suggest that the focus lies on the Spirit as He who shapes an explicitly rational faith. The references to the Spirit's work in chapter 13 could readily be interpreted as references to a suprarational work of the Spirit.

So far we have noted how the *Scots Confession* emphasises the agency of the Scriptures in bringing us to a clear understanding of God's grace towards us, yet does not stress the epistemic agency of the Spirit in expounding the Scriptures to our lives. On the contrary, we have noted from the references to the Spirit that a wider, suprarational work of the Spirit is presented within the text of the *Scots Confession*. Before we can attempt any further definition of the essential character of the Spirit's Person and function as it appears from the *Scots Confession*, we need to examine the vitally important section on the **Spirit and Sacraments** in chapters 21-23. Here, once more, we find the focus of the Holy Spirit's action is presented as being towards the hearts, not simply the minds, of believers. The sacraments, through the participation of believers in them,

> seal in their hearts the assurance of His promise, and of that most blessed conjunction, union, and society which the chosen have with their head, Christ Jesus.[19]

Through baptism, we are engrafted into Christ. In the Lord's Supper, the

> union and conjunction which we have with the body and blood of Christ Jesus in the right use of the sacraments is wrought by means of the Holy Spirit, who by true faith carries us above all things that are visible.... for the Holy Spirit, who can

---

[15] *Scots Conf.*, Chapter 12.
[16] *Scots Conf.*, Chapter 12.
[17] Entitled 'The Cause of Good Works'.
[18] *Scots Conf.*, Chapter 13.
[19] *Scots Conf.*, Ch. 21.

never be separated from the right institution of the Lord Jesus, will not deprive the faithful of the fruit of that mystical action.[20]

Here we have what would appear to be a suprarational work of the Spirit in the sacrament, within the stated conditions of a proper faith and a right administration of the sacrament. Once more, in chapter 23, the facility of the Spirit's work in the sacrament, distinct from His functioning as an epistemic agent, is reaffirmed; this time in the case of infant baptism, in explicit contrast to 'the error of the Anabaptists, who deny that children should be baptised before they have faith and understanding'.[21] This latter statement serves to qualify the apparent insistence, found in the polemic of chapter 22 against the Roman sacramental system, that there be a proper understanding of the sacraments both by the officiating minister and recipients of the sacrament. Here, it is not so much the epistemic agency of the Spirit that is being insisted upon, as the right and proper administration of the sacraments. The Spirit is active in the sacraments in a manner that affirms the Christian's acceptance by God in his heart, not simply in his mind.

In our survey of Calvin's pneumatology, we noted that Calvin's concern lay with the creation and sustaining of a proper faith within the Christian. Calvin repeatedly brought the epistemic agency of the Spirit into focus; and a major part of that concern, in maintaining **the parameters of orthodoxy**, lay with upholding the corporate integrity of the church. This concern is similarly found in the *Scots Confession*. The Kirk is that which is called into being and sustained by God.[22] In chapter 16, we find that the church's catholic, unitary nature is emphasised, for outwith the church 'there is neither life nor eternal felicity .... This Kirk is invisible'.[23] The presence of the true, invisible church within the visible church is determined by three signs which are laid out in chapter 18. These are, firstly, the true preaching of the Word of God, secondly, the right administration of the sacraments and, thirdly, proper ecclesiastical discipline.

Where these parameters of orthodoxy were to be upheld, a criterion for their definition was required and that definition was to be found from the Scriptures. This requirement of definition has to be borne in mind when we consider Calvin's emphasis on the Holy Spirit's epistemic agency. As noted, such an epistemic agency did not express for Calvin the whole of the Spirit's work: yet in so far as it is the Spirit that allows the parameters of orthodoxy to be discovered, in and through our reading of Scripture, the epistemic agency is bound to feature largely, if not exclusively, in an appreciation of the Spirit's Person and function. This would be especially the case where a clearer

---

[20] *Scots Conf.*, Ch. 21.
[21] *Scots Conf.*, Ch. 23.
[22] *Scots Conf.*, Ch. 5.
[23] *Scots Conf.*, Ch. 16.

systematisation of doctrine was looked for. The dependency on the Spirit's epistemic agency would then be greater. Consequently, where we might say that while the *Scots Confession* would appear to allow, as Calvin did, for a suprarational understanding of the Spirit - and indeed, in some respects, to go beyond Calvin in allowing for a suprarational dimension to the Spirit's work - the need to define the parameters of orthodoxy did, inevitably, bring the focus once more on to the need to formulate a rational and cognitive faith. Where, despite its clearly hermeneutical concerns, the *Scots Confession* did not appear to be overtly concerned with the Spirit's epistemic agency, those hermeneutical concerns together with the need to affirm an orthodox confession would lessen any likelihood of pursuing the question of how the suprarational functioning of the Spirit might be traced, other than through the true preaching of the Word of God and the right administration of the sacraments.

There remains for us to consider an area of theology which we saw, for Calvin, would significantly affect an interpretation of his pneumatology: the relationship between **the Spirit and Election**. Where Calvin dealt with the topic of election, in *Institute* 3.21-24, as the logical extension and conclusion of his concern to communicate the soterial centrality of Christ, the *Scots Confession* also associates this subject with the Person and work of Christ, dealing with it briefly in chapters 7 and 8. In chapter 7, where Christ the mediator is presented as He who is the union of the Godhead with the humanity of Christ, such a conjunction is understood as arising from 'the eternal and immutable decree of God from which all our salvation springs and depends'.[24] Chapter 8, entitled 'election', stresses the elective choice of God in making the Son Incarnate the mediator; yet at the same time, the vicarious suffering of Christ's humanity, as man on our behalf, is clearly recited there. Outwith these two chapters, the theme of election is not pursued. We should be wary, however, of drawing any definitive conclusions from this brief reference to election. As we have noted, the *Scots Confession*'s dominant concern appears to lie with emphasising the priority of Scripture and establishing proper parameters of faith. Its failure to develop other themes, such as in Christology, cannot be taken as indicating a lack of concern over them. Consequently, in assessing the importance or otherwise of election to the *Scots Confession*, we would advocate a note of caution. The *Scots Confession* appears to be less a work of systematic theology than a clarion call which invites an embracing of Scripture and an orthodoxy of confession. Indeed, lacking that logical progression and development of thought found in Calvin's work, the *Scots Confession* cannot readily be measured against Calvin's *Institute*.

Likewise we should be cautious in assessing the place accorded within the *Scots Confession* to **the Spirit as an epistemic agent**. In chapter 18 the proper interpretation of the Scriptures, as also their origin, is attributed to the Holy Spirit. The Spirit provides us with both the definition of and the ability to

---

[24] *Scots Conf.*, Ch. 7.

discern truth. In that the Scriptures are the basis of all authority within the Kirk,[25] the function of the Spirit as an epistemic agent is critical to the existence of the church; yet this is not sufficient to find or argue that the *Scots Confession* advocates the priority of the Spirit's epistemic agency. At most, we might say that the *Scots Confession* emphasises the priority of Scripture in shaping Christian doctrine and the work of the Spirit in creating, maintaining and building faith in the Christian life. The understanding of the Spirit with which this presents us is, however, far more comprehensive than that of simply an epistemic agent.

4.3 The Scots Confession: Commentators

As we noted in our introduction to this chapter, there are two reasons for our examining the *Scots Confession*: the first arises from its historical theological significance, the second is due to the interest it has aroused as a possible alternative to the *Westminster Confession* as a subordinate confessional standard within the Kirk. These two reasons are not unrelated, as the attraction of the *Scots Confession* today arises largely because of the conditions prevalent at the time of its composition, in contrast to those surrounding the *Westminster Confession*. It is to these conditions that we now briefly turn our attention.

Although the *Scots Confession* arose out of a precipitous period of Scottish history, the urgency of its commissioning and the speed of its presentation to Parliament have not detracted from an appreciation of its positive merits. As A. F. Mitchell opined,[26] the *Scots Confession* may not have been longer than four days in preparation, but its commissioning may well have been anticipated by its authors. Mitchell goes on to describe the work as having 'a framework rather historical than dogmatic, and a liberal and manly, yet reverent and cautious spirit'.[27] That the *Scots Confession* should be viewed as a response to the peculiar circumstances of the time, rather than a reflective, theological work is to be expected. Curtis described it as 'purely practical rather than theological in its terms and purpose',[28] serving as a positive declaration of the essential tenets of the Scottish Reformed faith. This perception of the *Scots Confession* as containing a primitive authenticity appealed to Edward Irving, who styled it 'the banner of the Church',[29] comparing it favourably with the *Westminster Confession*, which he described as 'the campcolours which [the Kirk] hath used

---

[25] *Scots Conf.*, Ch. 19.

[26] A. F. Mitchell, *The Scottish Reformation*, William Blackwood & Sons, Edinburgh, 1900, p. 100.

[27] Mitchell, *The Scottish Reformation*, p. 103.

[28] W. A. Curtis, *History of Creeds and Confessions of Faith*, T & T Clark, Edinburgh, 1911, p. 260.

[29] E. Irving, *The Collected Writings of Edward Irving in Five Volumes*, 1.602, edited by G. Carlyle, Alexander Strachan & Co., London.

during her days of peace'.[30] At the same time, awareness of the circumstance of its origin has not obscured an appreciation of the *Scots Confession*'s theological value. In the mid-nineteenth century Lee compared the *Scots Confession* favourably to Archbishop Hamilton's catechism of 1552,[31] while Barth chose the *Scots Confession* as the framework on which to build the theme of his Gifford lectures in 1937-38.[32]

More specifically, commentators have seen the *Scots Confession* as the vehicle of a type of theology which reflected the changing and evolving theological climate of its day. That the *Scots Confession* espouses a form of Calvinist theology has not been doubted: the question has been one of degree. Schaff declared that although the *Scots Confession* is 'Calvinistic, it is yet free from the scholastic technicalities and angular statements of the Calvinism of a later generation',[33] while Henderson viewed its Calvinism as 'mild and indeterminate as compared with later expressions'.[34] It is this argument, that the *Scots Confession* represents a form of Calvinism standing somewhere between Calvin himself and the federal scheme of Westminster theology, that is of special interest to us. As we saw from our analysis of the *Scots Confession*, its pneumatology points away from an emphasis on the Spirit's epistemic agency towards a more eclectic perspective, embracing a wider, suprarational work of the Spirit. At the same time, this was accompanied by a understanding of the Trinity which appeared to assume the transcendence of God, expressing God's Triunity in terms of His immanent Being. Can we say from this that the pneumatology of the *Scots Confession* is part of Calvin's legacy?

An acknowledgement of God's sovereignty rather than a stress on the mechanics of election, married to a presentation of the Spirit's work as a suprarational work made apparent not least in the *Scots Confession*'s teaching on the sacraments, clearly appealed to Edward Irving. Irving saw this as an antidote to an evangelicalism which made 'religion only subjective in the believer and not elective in God'.[35] Again, the absence of a systematic presentation as to how this sovereignty of God is worked out appealed to Barth, who could happily build on the *Scots Confession*'s emphasis on the integrity of the Triune God over against man. Where it is out of the mystery of His own Being that God reveals Himself to man, Barth could argue that 'God's

---

[30] *The Collected Writings of Edward Irving in Five Volumes*, 1.602

[31] J. Lee, *Lectures on the History of the Church of Scotland*, William Blackwood & Sons, Edinburgh, 1860, p. 109.

[32] K. Barth, *The Knowledge of God and the Service of God According to the Teaching of the Reformation*, Hodder & Stoughton, London, 1938.

[33] P. Schaff, *The Creeds of Christendom Vol. 1*, Harper & Bros., New York, 1878, p. 683.

[34] Henderson, *Scots Confession*, Op. cit., p. 19.

[35] *The Collected Writings of Edward Irving in Five Volumes*, 1.606.

revelation is precisely His revelation as the hidden God'.[36] Certainly the *Scots Confession*'s attractiveness to Irving and Barth does not indicate that it was anything other than Calvinistic. As Curtis observed, the treatment afforded to the doctrine of election, although brief, was characteristically Calvinistic[37] while Lee, in attributing the positive stress on the Spirit's work in regeneration and sanctification in chapter 12 to an anti-Roman polemic, does not suggest that this is anything other than Reformed in ethos.[38] The commentator A. F. Mitchell sees a parallel here, in 'the emphatic statements in the twelfth chapter regarding our entire dependence for spiritual renovation, and all good, on the Holy Spirit', to the teaching in chapter 10 of the *Westminster Confession.*[39]

That the *Scots Confession* is a development of Calvin's theology is not, however, irrefutable. Where John Knox was probably the main drafter of the work, this of itself suggests that other strands of Reformation thought may be present within it. As Kyle argues in his study on Knox, although Knox may have reflected Calvin's stress on the centrality of Scripture,[40] there were other areas of Knox's thought where this was less evidently the case. Kyle notes that Knox, unlike Calvin, did not care to stress the inner witness of the Spirit, preferring to underscore the Spirit's external work,[41] opining that the *Scots Confession*'s teaching on the sacraments may reflect the influence of Luther in Knox's thought as much as that of Calvin.[42]

Given these questions, we will be able to assess the significance of the *Scots Confession*'s pneumatology only once we have made some examination of the *Westminster Confession*. It is to this second document we now turn.

4.4   The Westminster Confession: A Survey

Having dealt briefly with the *cognitio Dei Creatoris* as echoed in creation, the first chapter of the *Westminster Confession* proceeds to lay out, clearly and unequivocally, the logical priority of Scripture. Developing this further than the succinct treatment afforded this topic in the *Scots Confession*, the *Westminster Confession* would appear to make Scripture not only its logical but also its epistemological starting point. In this respect, while chapters 1-5 of the *Westminster Confession*[43] reflect, in some measure, the subject matter found in the first book of Calvin's *Institute*, the *Westminster Confession* emphasises that

---

[36] Barth, *The Knowledge of God and the Service of God According to the Teaching of the Reformation*, p. 28.
[37] *History of Creeds and Confessions of Faith*, Curtis, Op. cit., p. 258.
[38] *Lectures on the History of the Church of Scotland*, Lee, Op. cit., p. 118.
[39] *The Scottish Reformation*, Mitchell, Op. cit., p. 110.
[40] R. G. Kyle, *The Mind of John Knox*, Coronado Press, Lawrence, 1984, p. 64.
[41] *The Mind of John Knox*, p. 45.
[42] *The Mind of John Knox*, p. 161.
[43] 1- Of the Holy Scripture; 2- Of God and the Holy Trinity; 3- Of God's Eternal Decree; 4- Of Creation; 5- Of Providence.

our starting point, in seeking **the Knowledge of God**, lies with the divinely inspired Scripture. Moreover, 'our full persuasion and assurance of the infallible truth and divine authority thereof'[44] specifically arises from the internal testimony of the Holy Spirit operating in the believer's heart. To affirm the authority of Scripture is not, in itself, sufficient. To have an understanding of the Word which leads to salvation, the 'inward illumination of the Spirit of God' is also necessary.[45]

From the opening chapter of the *Westminster Confession*, therefore, we find ourselves faced with the same logical priority given to Scripture which we deduced in Calvin, now amended with a distinct change in the epistemological priority with which we are presented. For Calvin, we noted that the *cognitio Dei Redemptoris* appeared to take epistemological priority over the *cognitio Dei Creatoris*, despite the latter's logical priority in the *Institute*. In the opening chapter of the *Westminster Confession* this is no longer the case. Both the logical and epistemological bases for what follows are rooted in the doctrine of Scripture. At the very outset of the *Westminster Confession*, the doctrine of Scripture provides both the logical and epistemological foundation for what follows and we are met with a perception of the Spirit as the illuminator of scriptural truth. The function of the Spirit is laid out as that of an epistemic agent, expounding the true meaning of the Scriptures to us. The knowledge of God, as it arises out of the Scriptures, is secured for us and in us by the Holy Spirit.

Given the foundational role accorded to Scripture and the Spirit's function in attesting to this, it is unsurprising to find that there is no development within the *Westminster Confession* of a Trinitarian model of God's Being, for this is not the basis on which subsequent theological exposition depends. In chapter 2, which deals briefly with the Trinity, the *Westminster Confession* follows the Western model of the Trinity's stress on the substantial Oneness of God, that unity expressed in 2.3 as being 'of one substance, power and eternity',[46] the Son begotten, the Spirit as proceeding 'from the Father and the Son'[47]and the Father as neither begotten nor proceeding. This statement affirming Trinitarian orthodoxy does little, however, to affect the subsequent development of the work: the Trinitarian character of God is neither expounded nor applied, with a possible exception in chapter 4, where the nature of man as *imago Dei* involves an appeal to God as Trinity in 4.1; yet how this relates to man, created 'with reasonable and immortal souls, endued with knowledge, righteousness and true holiness, after His own image'[48] remains unexplained.

Our observation that the epistemological foundation established in the

---

[44] *Westminster Conf.*, Ch.1.5.
[45] *Westminster Conf.*, Ch.1.6.
[46] *Westminster Conf.*, Ch.2.3.
[47] *Westminster Conf.*, Ch.2.3.
[48] *Westminster Conf.*, Ch.4.2.

Westminster Confession lies not with the *cognitio Dei Redemptoris* but with the Scriptures is further evidenced by the way in which **Man's union with Christ** is dealt. This is first explored in chapter 7, where we find the *Westminster Confession*'s soteriology expressly established on God's covenant promise:

> wherein He freely offereth unto sinners life and salvation by Jesus Christ; requiring of them faith in Him, that they may be saved, and promising to give unto all those that are ordained unto eternal life His Holy Spirit, to make them willing, and able to believe.[49]

We should note, however, that this soteriological focus is not Christological in character. There is no clear connection made between soteriology and Christology, other than in the identification of Christ as the harbinger[50] and the substance[51] of the covenant of grace.

Where we find that the *Westminster Confession*'s soteriology is not clearly correlated to its brief Christological statements, we should also note that while the central, Christological section, 8.2, reiterates the Chalcedonian formula, it does not emphasise the humanity of Christ as the common denominator in our association with Him. Calvin's understanding and presentation of the *communicatio idiomatum* is echoed in 8.7: yet there is no exposition in chapter 8, or elsewhere in the *Westminster Confession*, of the implications of divinity and humanity meeting in Jesus Christ, other than to note that Christ is thus 'furnished to execute the office of a Mediator and Surety'.[52] Chapter 8 is styled 'Christ the mediator'; and it is upon the central soterial event of Christ's sacrifice at the Cross that the chapter focuses. Through Christ's obedience and sacrifice, justice is executed and an everlasting inheritance purchased,[53] the application of the benefits of Christ as mediator being effected by the Spirit to the elect alone.[54] Beyond these features, there is no further exposition of any Christological significance to Christ's soterial mission.

On the basis of these observations, we would suggest that, in the *Westminster Confession*, Christological factors appear to be incidental to the focal place of Scriptural hermeneutics in formulating an epistemological base for man's knowledge of God. This emphasis upon Scriptural hermeneutics has, in large measure, led to a detachment of Christology from a consideration of soteriology. Likewise, in considering the *Westminster Confession*'s pneumatology, we find that, while suprarational aspects of the Spirit's work are attested to within the text, these remain apparently unrelated to that which appears to be the principal function of the Spirit. That is, the more prominent

---

[49] *Westminster Conf.*, Ch.7.3.
[50] *Westminster Conf.*, Ch.7.3 and 4.
[51] *Westminster Conf.*, Ch.7.6.
[52] *Westminster Conf.*, Ch.8.3.
[53] *Westminster Conf.*, Ch.8.5.
[54] *Westminster Conf.*, Ch.9.8.

feature is the epistemic agency of the Spirit in expounding the logical and epistemological priority of Scripture.

We find from the text of the *Westminster Confession* that it is in and through our union with Christ that the Spirit is acknowledged as operative in us, giving us strength through the process of sanctification.[55] The Spirit witnesses within our spirits that we are adopted through Christ,[56] filling us with peace and joy in assurance of salvation in our hearts.[57] This does not mean, however, that these aspects of the Spirit's work are integral to the theological framework of the *Westminster Confession*. On the contrary, we find that, as with the Trinitarian and Christological statements, such references to pneumatology as are present within the text of the *Westminster Confession* appear to be incidental to the theological fabric of the work.

The fabric of the *Westminster Confession*, built on the logical and epistemological priority of Scripture, weaves the relationship of the **Spirit and Faith** into the central place in the Confession's pneumatology, where the Spirit's primary role is to bring a realisation of the truth of Scripture to Christians. Faith is viewed as the gift of God to the elect, enabling them to believe: this is the critical work of the Holy Spirit, centred on the ministry of the Word.[58] Prayer, as with the sacraments, is seen to be a means of strengthening this faith.

The sacraments are referred to in the *Westminster Confession* as expressions of the covenant, the ordinances under which Christ, who is the substance of the covenant of grace, is dispensed.[59] The sacraments are presented as a means of strengthening faith,[60] made effective in communicating Christ to us by both the Spirit and 'the word of institution, which contains, together with a precept authorising the use thereof, a promise of benefit to worthy receivers'.[61] In this way the sacraments represent Christ to us and confirm our interest in Him.[62] Baptism is therefore to be understood as a sign and seal of the covenant, of the elect's engrafting into Christ.[63] The Holy Spirit is exhibited and conferred in baptism, 'to such (whether of age or infants) as that grace belongeth unto'.[64] Likewise, 'worthy receivers', partaking in the Lord's Supper, receive and feed upon, spiritually, the body and blood of Christ, which elements are 'spiritually, present to the faith of believers'.[65]

---

[55] *Westminster Conf.*, Ch.13.3.
[56] *Westminster Conf.*, Ch.18.2.
[57] *Westminster Conf.*, Ch.18.3.
[58] *Westminster Conf.*, Ch.14.1.
[59] *Westminster Conf.*, Ch.7.6.
[60] *Westminster Conf.*, Ch.14.1.
[61] *Westminster Conf.*, Ch.27.3.
[62] *Westminster Conf.*, Ch.27.1.
[63] *Westminster Conf.*, Ch.28.1.
[64] *Westminster Conf.*, Ch.28.6.
[65] *Westminster Conf.*, Ch.29.7.

A difficulty which arises, from our perspective, is in understanding how this perception of the **Spirit and Sacraments**, essentially suprarational, relates to what we have observed to be the primary pneumatological focus of the *Westminster Confession*, that of the Spirit's epistemic agency. We are invited to view the latent, suprarational action of the Spirit as present within the sacraments and objectively manifest therein. At the same time, we are presented with an underlying framework which emphasises the formation, by the Spirit, of a rational, cognitive faith among the elect. Two functions of the Spirit, the one suprarational and the other rational, stand side by side: yet how they are to be related or combined remains unexplained. Doubtless, the absence of a statement relating the rational and suprarational functions of the Spirit could be interpreted as a strength, allowing both to stand in complement of one another. The danger lies in that, where their relationship as it is founded in pneumatology remains unexplained, one function becomes emphasised while the importance of the other is diminished or lost sight of.

That the function of the Spirit in producing a conscious, rational faith is more important to the *Westminster Confession* is reinforced in the attitude adopted towards the Spirit's epistemic agency in defining the **Parameters of orthodoxy**. The *Westminster Confession* distinguishes between the invisible church of the elect[66] and the visible church,[67] affirming that it is still through the latter that salvation is normally found and that God gathers the saints to Himself.[68] However, the need to define the parameters of orthodoxy brings, as in the case of the *Scots Confession*, a focus onto rationally defined faith. The catholic church is found where 'the Gospel is taught and embraced, ordinances administered, and public worship performed more or less purely'.[69] While the existence of the visible church is viewed as important, the presence of the Spirit and His activity has to be discerned in order to determine whether the true church is also present. To this end, it is not enough to affirm that the Spirit is present and active where there is a visible church. Examination must be made as to whether the signs of the invisible church of the elect are present within the visible church. Such an exercise needs to be cognitive and rational, not intuitive and suprarational.

The danger that an over-emphasis of the epistemic agency of the Spirit might detract from other aspects of the Spirit's work is further evidenced by the manner in which the relationship between **the Spirit and Election** is dealt with. The doctrine of election is accorded a prominent place in the *Westminster Confession*, introduced in chapter 3 and thereby given a higher profile than in Calvin's *Institute*. Once again, it is through a bare appeal to Scripture that a basis for understanding election is constructed. Election is viewed as founded

---

[66] *Westminster Conf.*, Ch.25.1.
[67] *Westminster Conf.*, Ch.25.2.
[68] *Westminster Conf.*, Ch.25.3.
[69] *Westminster Conf.*, Ch.25.4.

on the Eternal Decree, whereby God ordains all things.[70] For man, this is a double decree to either life or eternal death.[71] For the elect in Christ, there is effectual calling in faith[72] and for all others, death.[73] The Spirit is the means of the elect's effectual calling to faith in Christ.[74] The effectual call is rooted in God's elective decision[75] and is executed by the Spirit,[76] who applies Christ to the elect.[77]

Where some difficulty was seen to exist in resolving the relationship of the Spirit's suprarational role in the sacraments and the Spirit's role in creating a rational and cognitive faith, so too the relationship between the Spirit as executor of God's elective decision and as an epistemic agent in the forming of faith remains enigmatic. For an understanding of the Word which leads to salvation, the 'inward illumination of the Spirit of God' is necessary:[78] the Spirit effects salvation through functioning as an epistemic agent. At the same time, the effectiveness of the Spirit in executing God's elective decision is not contingent on the ability of the recipients of God's elective decision to perceive rationally God's elective choice. The Spirit regenerates all 'who are incapable of being outwardly called by the ministry of the Word'.[79] This, however, should not be taken as an acknowledgement of the Spirit's suprarational function, but rather as an understanding of the Spirit as executor of God's elective decision.[80] It is possible to know something of the 'common operations of the Spirit'[81] without being of the elect: yet what this means in practice remains unexplored. The Spirit effects election. He also effects a rational, cognitive faith in the mind of the elect. A combined emphasis on both the epistemic and elective functions of the Spirit would make it hard to avoid a path which leads to the conclusion that the elect are those who, through a process of rational deduction, perceive themselves to be the elect of God.

4.5   The Westminster Confession: Commentators

The ongoing debate within the Church of Scotland over the status of the *Westminster Confession* as its principal subordinate standard, second only to

---

[70] *Westminster Conf.*, Ch.3.1.
[71] *Westminster Conf.*, Ch.3.3.
[72] *Westminster Conf.*, Ch.3.6.
[73] *Westminster Conf.*, Ch.3.7.
[74] *Westminster Conf.*, Ch.8.8.
[75] *Westminster Conf.*, Ch.10.1.
[76] *Westminster Conf.*, Ch.10.2 and 3.
[77] *Westminster Conf.*, Ch.11.4.
[78] *Westminster Conf.*, Ch.1.6.
[79] *Westminster Conf.*, Ch.10.3.
[80] *Westminster Conf.*, Ch.10.4.
[81] *Westminster Conf.*, Ch.10.4.

the Bible, led in 1982 to the publication of a collection of articles and essays, entitled *The Westminster Confession in the Church Today*. It is not our intention to review the accounts of the *Westminster Confession*'s place within Scottish ecclesiastical history contained therein. We do, however, note some salient points expressed in the critiques offered by James Torrance, then Professor of Systematic Theology at Aberdeen and Sinclair B. Ferguson, then associate minister of St. George's Tron in Glasgow.

Ferguson, a defender of the *Westminster Confession*, notes 3 points which are of interest to us. Firstly, Ferguson sees an emphasis on the priority of Scripture as a justifiable development of Calvin's position, given the increase in debate over the inspiration and authority of Scripture which occurred in the seventeenth century.[82] Secondly, he notes that while the *Westminster Confession* contains no chapter as such on the Holy Spirit, this could be attributed partly to the scheme of Calvin's *Institute* and partly to what he identifies as the biblical emphasis, 'in which the Spirit is seen as the agent, not as the object of faith'.[83] Thirdly, Ferguson argues that the federal theology of the *Westminster Confession* grew out of Calvin's emphasis on God's covenant grace and was developed into a twin-covenant theology.

Ferguson's third point, that the *Westminster Confession*'s theology represented an evolution from and development of Calvin's position, has been discussed by others. Leith notes that the *Westminster Confession* is 'abstract, objective, and logical in contrast to the historical, experiential, and fragmentary character' of the *Scots Confession*,[84] viewing this as a development in the inevitable process of theological rationalisation. Not all, however, have agreed with this viewpoint. James Torrance contends that the *Westminster Confession*, while seeking to apply biblical doctrines to life, shifts from a properly Christocentric focus to one where 'the emphasis moves away from what God has done for us and for mankind in Christ to what we are to do to know that we are among the elect'.[85] Consequently, Torrance sees a shifting in focus from an *ordo salutis* built on 'the Trinitarian [pattern] of the Creeds or Calvin's *Institute* of 1559'[86] to one dominated by federal theology, as characterised by the work of the English federalist, William Perkins.[87] Torrance sees Perkins as developing Beza's tendency to emphasise election over grace, and the *Westminster Confession* as a less Christocentric document than the earlier *Scots*

---

[82] *The Westminster Confession in the Church Today*, edited by A. I. C. Heron, St. Andrew Press, Edinburgh, 1982, p. 35.

[83] *The Westminster Confession in the Church Today*, p. 36.

[84] J. Leith, *Assembly at Westminster: Reformed Theology in the Making*, John Knox Press, Atlanta, 1973, p. 66.

[85] *The Westminster Confession in the Church Today*, p. 45.

[86] *The Westminster Confession in the Church Today*, p. 45.

[87] Perkins lays out the logic of an eternal and divine 'double decree' of either salvation or damnation for all mankind in *A Golden Chaine*, 1590.

Confession, 'where election is placed after the Article on the Mediator, in the context of Christology'.[88] For Torrance the decrees of election and not the grace of God were falsely formed as the *Westminster Confession*'s major premise.

The point made here by Torrance is an important one, which we noted in our own review of the *Westminster Confession*. Taking Ferguson's third point together with his first point, that an emphasis on the priority of Scripture is a justifiable development of Calvin's position, we would respond by contending that it is not sufficient to argue for the logical priority of Scripture if this means that sight is lost of the epistemological centrality of God's redemptive action, effected through the Incarnation. Biblical fundamentalism is no guarantor of Christian fundamentals. Where Calvin may have retained the epistemological priority of *cognitio Dei Redemptoris*, this appears to have been lost sight of in the *Westminster Confession*, or at least assumed under the priority afforded to Scripture. Instead, we find ourselves faced with a system which attempts to be biblical, but is questionably theological, in that it is not built on an understanding of God as He is towards us as Trinity, manifest in God's salvific economy. As Torrance rightly concludes, 'Hyper-Calvinism can lead to a new Sabellianism by implying that God is loving toward some men but not essentially in His Being'.[89]

In addressing both Ferguson's first and third points, that the *Westminster Confession*'s emphasis on the priority of Scripture is a justifiable development of Calvin's position and that its federal theology grew out of Calvin's emphasis on God's covenant grace, we find that we must differ from Ferguson, because of our observation that Calvin's epistemological focus lay with the *cognitio Dei Redemptoris* and not, as in the *Westminster Confession*, with Scripture alone. At the same time, we cannot fully embrace Torrance's viewpoint that Calvin was clearly Christocentric in his understanding and that the *Scots Confession* was, in this respect, nearer to Calvin's own position. As we noted earlier, the *Scots Confession* did not appear to hold ontological concerns as central to its fabric of thought, treating them as incidental rather than as formative in shaping its theological system.

Indeed, we might well say that the difficulties which arise in the more developed doctrinal framework of the *Westminster Confession* and which are present in embryo in the *Scots Confession* are endemic to the theology of Calvin himself. As we sought to demonstrate in the preceding chapter, a disjunction appears in Calvin's thought between the fact of our election, founded upon the soterial mission of the Son, and a proper understanding of that election, brought about by the epistemic function of the Spirit. Consequently, Calvin's pneumatology could be construed as being built not upon the Spirit's ontic actuality but upon the twin pillars of Christ's

---

[88] *The Westminster Confession in the Church Today*, p. 46.
[89] *The Westminster Confession in the Church Today*, pp. 50-51.

soteriological significance and our need to understand the truth of God revealed to us. Where, in the former instance, the Spirit's role is largely implicit, it is more clearly presented in the latter; but in a manner which requires a function of the Spirit to be focused on, rather than dealing with the ontic actuality of the Spirit as central to God's salvific economy. This interpretation would appear to be borne out by the manner in which, in the two *Confessions*, we see an increased emphasis on scriptural authority being paralleled by a stress on Christ's office as mediator and the function of the Spirit in developing faith and assurance among the elect, yet without a clear connection being made between these two aspects of God's salvific economy.

The weakness which we traced in Calvin's presentation of the Spirit's Person and function, in allowing for an understanding of the Spirit's epistemic agency to be detached from the Son of God's soterial mission, opened the way for the more developed Calvinistic theology of the *Westminster Confession*. Here, we find ourselves in some measure of agreement with R. T. Kendall, where he detects a departure from Calvin within the theology of the *Westminster Confession*, in introducing a distinction between the development of faith and the presence of assurance within the believer.[90] As we noted in our review of the *Westminster Confession*, a proper faith depends on the inward illumination of the believer, leading to a rational, cognitive faith. Kendall, having argued that 'faith to Calvin may be described as merely witnessing what God has already done in Christ',[91] concludes that, for Calvin, the beginnings of 'faith' so defined are created within the believer by the secret work of the Spirit, anterior to repentance. The Westminster Assembly, on the other hand, displayed an 'unquestioned acceptance of a distinction between faith and assurance'.[92] For Kendall, this development betrayed the ascendency of Beza's systematisation over Calvin's simpler perspective.

We would, however, wish to qualify our endorsement of Kendall's conclusions by observing that Calvin was in no small measure responsible for this distinction, which Kendall describes as one between faith and assurance. The root of the problem lay in the emphasis placed on faith's rational, cognitive content which is effected by the Spirit's epistemic agency. Working its way through the writings of Beza, the English puritans and into the *Westminster Confession*, Calvin's pneumatology allowed for a disjunction to be created between the implied presence of the Spirit's union with the Son in His atoning work and the epistemic agency of the Spirit. As we have sought to demonstrate, this distinction was nascent within Calvin's theological method, allowing for the act of justification by Christ and the Spirit's presence as *vinculum* therein to be distinguished from the more clearly emphasised epistemic agency of the Spirit. Made explicit in the *Westminster Confession*, this distinction lay latent

---

[90] *Calvin and English Calvinism to 1649*, p. 203.

[91] *Calvin and English Calvinism to 1649*, p. 20.

[92] *Calvin and English Calvinism to 1649*, pp. 195-6.

within the Trinitarian theology of Calvin himself.

Returning to Ferguson's second point, that the absence of a chapter on the Holy Spirit in the *Westminster Confession* could be attributed partly to the scheme of Calvin's *Institute* and partly to a 'biblical emphasis' in which the Spirit is seen as the agent and not as the object of faith, we would make three observations. Firstly, while the observation that the *Westminster Confession* appears to reflect Calvin's scheme in the *Institute* in not containing a chapter on the Holy Spirit may be correct, this does not serve as a theological justification of the omission. That Calvin's main concerns were not ontological does not necessarily infer that this is a strength within his theology. Secondly, to state that the biblical emphasis is one 'in which the Spirit is seen as the agent, not as the object of faith'[93] is most open ended. The *Pneumatomachi* could have stated the same! As James Torrance rightly observes, 'the tendency can be to think of the Holy Spirit in terms of efficient causality as the agent in effectual calling and applying the blessings of the Gospel'.[94] This, as we have seen, is only too evident from the manner in which the *Westminster Confession* treats the Spirit as an agent in election. Thirdly, where Ferguson argues that the federal theology of the *Westminster Confession* grew out of Calvin's emphasis on God's covenant grace, we again note James Torrance's response that the doctrine of the Spirit is, all the same, too impersonal. Torrance's solution is to advocate an expansion on the Spirit's place as 'the bond of union between the Father and the Son'.[95] For our part, we would for the moment simply note what we have already observed: that an emphasis on the Spirit as *vinculum* does not necessarily provide us with a deeper appreciation of the Spirit's ontic actuality.

4.6 Summary

At the beginning of this chapter, we identified two special issues that would concern us. Firstly, we were concerned to detect how any emphasis on the Spirit as an epistemic agent is countered or balanced by an understanding of the Spirit's suprarational work, such as that detected in Calvin's sacramental understanding. Secondly, we raised the question of whether there is any further development of that distinction, which we identified in Calvin's thought, between the fact of our election which is founded on the soterial mission of the Son, and a proper understanding of that election effected in us through the epistemic agency of the Spirit.

In the *Scots Confession* we noted that, outwith a general association with the Person and work of Christ, the theme of election is not pursued. Likewise, while recognising that the function of the Spirit as an epistemic agent is clearly important to the *Scots Confession*, this is not to say that the Spirit's epistemic

---

[93] *The Westminster Confession in the Church Today*, p. 36.
[94] *The Westminster Confession in the Church Today*, p. 53.
[95] *The Westminster Confession in the Church Today*, p. 53.

agency is advocated as its most important feature. On the contrary, we found it to be the case that the *Scots Confession* exhibited a perception of the Spirit that was not restricted simply to His epistemic agency in forming a rational faith in our minds. The *Scots Confession* clearly embraced a wider, suprarational acknowledgement of the Spirit's work. This was particularly apparent in the doctrine of the sacraments.

In looking to the *Westminster Confession*, we saw that a reference to the suprarational work of the Spirit could also be identified, especially in the doctrine of the sacraments. A framing of the relationship which should exist between the suprarational work of the Spirit and the Spirit's epistemic agency in shaping a rational and cognitive faith did, however, elude our detection. We saw that this omission, combined with the stress placed on the Spirit as executor of God's elective decision, led to a greater emphasis being placed on the value of rational understanding in not only aiding but also proving our salvation in Christ.

In addition to the difficulty that we have found in relating these various aspects of the Spirit's work to one another - the suprarational, epistemic agency and elective functions of the Spirit - we have also seen that, underlying this apparent confusion over the Person and function of the Holy Spirit, there lies a deeper failure to relate these various functions of the Spirit to an understanding of the Spirit's Person and place within the Triune God's salvific economy. True, Trinitarian and Christological orthodoxy was affirmed in the two *Confessions*, but not in a manner which related the Person and function of the Spirit to a developed understanding of the Triune God's salvific economy. In our next chapter, in turning to examine the theology of Edward Irving, we look to the work of a theologian who not only attempted to reaffirm the place of the suprarational dimensions of the Spirit's ministry but also sought to reorient an understanding of the Spirit's work to a Christocentric base. We will ask whether Irving can help us understand the connection between the Spirit's suprarational work and epistemic agency; and also whether he can help us reconcile these to that other emphasis which has emerged, of the Spirit functioning as an executor of God's elective decision.

Chapter 5

Edward Irving

5.1 Introduction

The theology of Edward Irving, who has been described as a forerunner both of Pentecostal theology[1] and the Charismatic Movement,[2] calls for our attention not only because of Irving's place within the Scottish Reformed tradition but also because of his theological works, which invite a reappraisal both of the Person and function of the Spirit and of the nature of the Trinity's salvific economy. In this chapter we will attempt to come to an understanding of how it was that Irving went about this process of reappraisal; and to assess how successful he was in reconstructing an understanding of the Holy Spirit and His place within the Trinity.

To appreciate something of what had formed within Scottish Presbyterianism and the theological tradition in which Irving stood, we turn briefly to an earlier work which was produced by two Scottish theologians, David Dickson and James Durham, and published along with the 1650 Edinburgh edition of the *Westminster Confession*. In *The Sum of Saving Knowledge*, intended by its authors to be an adjunct to the *Westminster Confession*, we find an attempted summary of the Christian faith. The result is a work in which Christ is hailed as Saviour; but it is not the *cognitio Dei Redemptoris* which provides us with the epistemological basis for an assurance of salvation. Instead, we have to recognise that the truth of our election to salvation is hidden in God's sovereign and eternal decrees. Assurance of salvation is founded on a practical syllogism, constructed as follows:

> let every watchful believer, for strengthening himself in faith and obedience, reason after this manner: 'Whosoever doth daily employ Christ Jesus for cleansing his conscience and affections from the guiltiness and filthiness of sins against the law, and for enabling him to give obedience to the law in love, he hath the evidence of true faith in himself: But I (may every watchful believer say) do daily employ Jesus Christ for cleansing my conscience and affections from the

---

[1] G. Strachan in his critical work, *The Pentecostal Theology of Edward Irving*, Darton Longman & Todd, London, 1973.
[2] By A. Dallimore in *The Life of Edward Irving: Forerunner of the Charismatic Movement*, Banner of Truth, Edinburgh, 1983.

guiltiness and filthiness of sins against the law, and for enabling me to give obedience to the law in love: Therefore I have the evidence of true faith in myself'.[3]

The Sum of Saving Knowledge invited a focus to be placed not on Christ but upon the subjective reasonings of the individual believer. It was this type of egocentric, rationalistic faith against which Irving reacted so strongly. Irving's views are well expressed in his *Notes on the Standards of the Church of Scotland*, written shortly after the Kirk's General Assembly of 1830 had deposed from the parish ministry his friend McLeod Campbell.[4] McLeod Campbell had denounced the legacy of federal Calvinism and had sought instead to found the centre of Christian assurance not, as the practical syllogism encouraged, in the subjective appreciation of the individual but in the objective manifestation of God's grace found in the Incarnation. He had attempted to reorient faith and assurance upon the person of the mediator, away from the question of the eternal decree. A renewed Christocentric reference allowed McLeod Campbell to place the evidence of God's love to man patently in the manifestation of the Son of God.[5] Irving shares McLeod Campbell's desire to affirm a Christocentric focus in seeking to understand the nature of salvation. Commenting on the *Scots Confession* as a work on which he would bestow 'the highest encomonium',[6] Irving highlights two features found in chapter 21 of that work, the section of the *Scots Confession* which is on 'the sacraments'. Firstly, Irving claims to discern a stress upon the Incarnation, expressed in the teaching that Christ's flesh possessed 'mortality and corruptibility in itself', yet received 'immortality and incorruption from the Godhead'.[7] Secondly, Irving welcomes an emphasis upon the sacraments[8] as the means whereby the gift of God in Christ is objectively conveyed to the recipient; and that the gift of Christ is conveyed to the reprobate as well as to the elect.[9] Irving repudiates the 'infidelity of Evangelicalism' in failing to appreciate the objective reality of

---

[3] *The Sum of Saving Knowledge*, bound with *The Westminster Confession of Faith*, Free Presbyterian Publications, 1973 Edition, p. 343.

[4] *The Collected Writings of Edward Irving in Five Volumes*, edited by G. Carlyle, Alexander Strachan & Co., London, 1865, 1.599 footnote. Hereafter, we will cite this compendium of Irving's works as *Collected Writings*.

[5] 'The incarnation is the foundation of the Kingdom of God, and faith in it prepares us for whatever nearness to God in love has been contemplated for those into whose nature the Son of God has come'. J. McLeod Campbell, *The Nature of the Atonement*, Macmillan & Co., London, 5th. Edition, 1878, p. xxxix. In contrast to Irving, McLeod Campbell's Christocentricity did not lead to his developing a fresh, Pneumatological perspective in his writing.

[6] *Collected Writings*, 1.608.

[7] *Collected Writings*, 1.604.

[8] *Collected Writings*, 1.605.

[9] *Collected Writings*, 1.606.

God's grace conveyed in the sacramental gift, an infidelity which falsely emphasises what is 'subjective in the believer; a religion of moods, and not of purposes and facts'.[10]

Although Irving is not himself prepared to denounce the *Westminster Confession*, his distaste of it and preference for the earlier *Scots Confession* is made quite clear. Irving is adamant in finding that the *Westminster Confession* is silent on the question of the universality of Christ's atonement. While he does not challenge the double decree to election and damnation, Irving argues that the doctrine of limited atonement is not to be found within the text of the *Westminster Confession*.[11] He affirms his own belief that the *Westminster Confession*'s silence on the universality of Christ's atonement, which Irving describes as 'a great fundamental truth of the gospel',[12] is an unfortunate omission and not a denial of the doctrine.

We should note two features in particular regarding Irving's advocacy of the *Scots Confession*. Firstly, we meet with the stress Irving places on the *Scots Confession*'s teaching on the sacraments. Irving's advocacy of the sacraments lies in their attestation of that objective reality which they signify, those things brought about through Christ's soterial mission. Irving is determined to place an appreciation of what Christ has objectively done on our behalf before us, that it might be received by us in faith. As we shall see when we return to look at Irving's understanding of the sacraments, it does not thereby follow that a suprarational function of the Spirit should take priority over the Spirit's epistemic agency. The sacraments symbolise and signify what Christ has done, while faith receives that which the sacraments signify. For Irving the concern does not lie in whether it is the epistemic agency or the suprarational work of the Spirit which takes priority. Irving's focus lies not upon the manner by which the Spirit communicates, but in human faith's apprehension and reception of that which is communicated, namely the grace of God made manifest in Christ.

Secondly, we see something of why it is that Irving is keen to lay such emphasis on the Incarnation and to expound the significance of the hypostatic union. Irving is seeking to bring the Incarnation to the centre of his theological method. Like Calvin, Irving wishes to place the *cognitio Dei Redemptoris* at the centre of his epistemology. As we shall observe, there are obvious tensions which would arise from attempting to reaffirm a Christological centre in the *cognitio Dei Redemptoris*, standing within a tradition that had come to build its epistemology on Scriptural hermeneutics and that had relegated questions of ontology, whether Trinitarian, pneumatological or Christological, to the status of an appendage. The task of revising the theological framework was, however, one upon which Irving embarked. For Irving, the critical centre of a theological

---

[10] *Collected Writings*, 1.606.
[11] *Collected Writings*, 1.641.
[12] *Collected Writings*, 1.643.

system had to lie in Christology and it is to an overview of this which we now turn.

We will proceed by first examining the nature of Irving's Christocentric focus. Thereafter, we will go on to see how this affected the development of Irving's pneumatology in the general sense, following this with a brief look at Irving's understanding of the Spirit at work in the sacraments. We conclude the chapter by offering a critique of Irving's attempted revision of the theological framework out of which he worked, reviewing how helpful his work has been in helping us towards a better understanding of the Spirit's Person and function.

5.2 Irving's Christology

The events surrounding the adverse publicity attracted by Irving's understanding of Christ's human nature have been both well chronicled and reviewed in the recent works of Strachan, Dallimore, Merricks[13] and McFarlane.[14] We will not rehearse these details here. What we shall attempt is a review of Irving's perception as to how the Person and function of the Holy Spirit are to be understood in a Trinitarian framework. In order to do this, we must first look to the Christocentric heart of Irving's theology.

To understand Irving, we need to appreciate that his focal concern is not only Christological but also Trinitarian. In this, we fully concur with McFarlane, who notes that a soteriologically centred doctrine of the Trinity stands at the heart of Irving's Christology[15]. Irving understands that it is in and through the humanity of Christ Jesus that the Godhead is manifest and that atonement with the Godhead is made possible. To effect atonement between God and man it has to be the real humanity of man, fully corruptible, that is found in Christ Jesus. It is through this humanity, which Christ shares in common with us, that the Godhead is made known and that man and God can be reconciled. That this stress on the corruptibility of Christ's flesh should become the stumbling block and ground of offence to so many of Irving's contemporaries we will return to; for the moment we simply note Irving's motivation in stressing the corruptibility of Christ's humanity. This stress on the potential corruptibility of Christ's flesh arose out of Irving's concern that the Incarnation should be understood not simply as a Christophany but as a theophany, whereby we meet not only with the Son Incarnate but also with the revelation of the Holy Spirit: as Irving himself complains in his Preface to *The Doctrine of the Incarnation opened in Six Sermons*,

---

[13] W. S. Merricks, *Edward Irving: the Forgotten Giant*, Scribe's Chamber Publications, Illinois, 1983.

[14] G. W. P. McFarlane, *Christ and the Spirit*, Paternoster Press, Carlisle, 1996. This work provides an excellent introduction to Irving's Christology.

[15] *Christ and the Spirit*, p. 13.

The point at issue is simply this: whether Christ's flesh had the grace of sinlessness and incorruption from its proper nature, or from the indwelling of the Holy Spirit.[16]

It was this stress on ontological union between God and man in the soterial event of the Incarnation that set Irving at odds with the Calvinism of his day. Contemporary Calvinism had come to set its epistemological focus on Scripture and to emphasise the epistemic agency of the Spirit at that point, acknowledging Christ as mediator and focusing on the propitiatory, sacrificial aspect of His mediatorial work, rather than on upon the inherent significance of the hypostatic union itself. Irving's approach was radical in that it turned the focus of theological enquiry back to the ontological issues: the nature of the hypostatic union and the significance of God as Trinity. In order to grasp what Irving was seeking to communicate in taking this approach, we will first outline the main features of Irving's Christological focus, thereafter going on to note some of the implications and effects which it brings.

The distinctiveness of Irving's Christocentricity is expounded in *The Doctrine of the Incarnation opened in Six Sermons*, which served as a considered response to the criticism that Irving attracted from his teaching on the corruptibility of Christ's humanity. Originally composed as a series of four sermons on the Trinity, these were edited with two further sermons added by Irving, numbers three and six, the whole being published in 1828. It is in this work that we can trace that substantial part of Irving's Trinitarian theology which is centred on a Christological pivot.

For Irving, the primary significance of Christ is that He is the manifestation of God. Outwith the Incarnation of the Son of God, we can and could have no knowledge of God:

The infinite God, who is also invisible and incomprehensible, cannot communicate Himself, or the knowledge of Himself, unto His creatures, without assuming to Himself a finite form.[17]

That finite form, through which God communicates Himself to us, is found in Jesus Christ. The focus to which God draws us is His Son, but not His Son outwith the Incarnation, in the hiddenness of eternal Deity. Our meeting with God is through the Son Incarnate, in whom all the grace and truth of God are communicated to us.[18] Jesus Christ is the only way and the full way by which God reveals and communicates Himself to man. All that comes before the Incarnation anticipates the reality of Jesus Christ, God met with man. All that follows testifies to this event whereby God is made known to man. It is through the Incarnation of the Son that the way is opened for us to apprehend the reality

---

[16] *Collected Writings*, 5.4.
[17] Sermon 6, *Collected Writings*, 5.399.
[18] Sermon 1, *Collected Writings*, 5.20.

of the Spirit and the Father, for it is in and through the Incarnation that the Triune God is made manifest and is married to mankind. The eternal Son:

> sees the whole mass and lump of fallen, sinful flesh; He submits Himself unto His Father to be made flesh; His Father sendeth the Holy Spirit to prepare Him a body.... [who] doth therewith take up, from anywhere in the lump of existing flesh, a part; and where so forming a body the eternal Son of God humbleth Himself to apprehend it, for ever to unite it to His own divine person.[19]

For Irving, it is not the humanity of Christ that constitutes Christ's individuality. That the particular personality of the eternal Son of God should join Himself to humanity: this is the means whereby the individuality of Jesus Christ is constituted. This is not to say that the divinity of the Son of God is the greater or more important part of Christ's nature, as constituted by the Incarnation. The mystery of the Incarnation is that there is a hypostatic union of divinity and humanity in the person of Jesus Christ. It is by God so manifest in union with Jesus Christ's humanity that all humanity is able to have regard to God.[20]

Where the primary significance of Christ lies in His manifesting the Trinity to mankind, the secondary aspect is that the Son of God thereby makes atonement between mankind and God by becoming united with humanity in Jesus Christ. It is the self-humiliation that is undertaken by the Son of God in this act of inhabitation within humanity that is, properly speaking, the sacrifice that is made on our behalf by the eternal Son of God,[21] the fullness of which sacrifice only the Father can truly appreciate.[22] Indeed, in all that we see in Christ Jesus, we see the self-emptying of the Son of God in the event of the hypostatic union so that man in Christ may be seen to be fulfilled, walking in total harmony with the Son of God.[23]

5.2.1   Pneumatological Implications

How is it, though, that if the humiliation and self-emptying of the Son of God in the Incarnation is so complete, the humanity of Christ can be vivified to achieve the purposes of God? Herein lies the critical significance of Irving's

---

[19] Sermon 3, *Collected Writings*, 5.159.

[20] 'By His Divine nature, I say, with the Godhead He transacteth, and by His human nature He regardeth the will and purpose and action of the Godhead intelligible, visible, and perceptible to the creature'. Sermon 3, *Collected Writings*, 5.160.

[21] 'It is not in the *kind* of life or *kind* of death; it is in *the* life and *the* death of the Man-God that we are to find the great merit of the love. The *humiliation* was the sacrifice, the *becoming* man, the *being made flesh*' Sermon 4, *Collected Writings*, 5.270.

[22] 'The greatness of this grace of self-humiliation on the part of the Son is known unto the Father only, whose bosom alone contains that fullness which is contracted into manhood's narrow limits'. Sermon 6, *Collected Writings*, 5.439.

[23] Sermon 5, *Collected Writings*, 5.319.

Christology for his pneumatology. It is the Son of God, conjoined to humanity in the person of Jesus Christ, that is the avenue whereby the Holy Spirit can be active in the humanity of Jesus Christ. Where Christ Jesus voluntarily and consciously submits in His humanity to conform to the pattern of the Son Incarnate, the means whereby He becomes effective in furthering the Father's purposes is through that humanity as it is empowered and vivified by the Holy Spirit's activity within it.[24]

Two features of this inhomination by the Spirit should be noted. Firstly, the Spirit's relation to Christ's humanity is brought about through the Spirit's prior, eternal relation to the Son of God. This derives from the basic supposition that it is the whole Trinity which is made manifest in and through the Incarnation of the Son of God. In the action of the Spirit upon the humanity of Jesus Christ, we observe the Father's will being fulfilled and the Son assenting thereto.[25] In this respect, the Holy Spirit acts as executor of the Covenant that exists between the Father and the Son, bringing us to recognise in Christ Jesus not only the Incarnate Son of God but carrying us beyond the Son, to worship the Father with whom the Son stands in covenanted relationship.[26] Irving explicitly identifies the Spirit as the *vinculum Trinitatis*. The Spirit communicates the Father's will to the Son and returns the Son's obedience to the Father;[27] in this respect, He is that *vinculum* which is between the Father and the Son.

The second feature of this inhomination by the Spirit follows from the character of the Spirit as *vinculum*, or communicator, within the Trinity. Where the Spirit is present and active in the humanity of Christ because of the Spirit's status as *vinculum* within the Trinity, expressed through the hypostatic union between God and man found in the Incarnation, that activity of the Spirit which consequently arises in Christ's humanity is centred in Christ's human will. It is in Christ's will, which is a faculty of His human soul, that the activity of the Spirit in preserving Christ's humanity as sinless is centred. It was Christ's human soul, anointed by the Holy Spirit, that resisted and rejected sin.[28] Christ's human will is directed to the Father's will[29] through the communication of the Holy Spirit. This obedience of faith was effected not without a struggle, for the flesh of Christ

---

[24] 'The humanity, sustained of the Spirit, as by the Spirit it was formed, was able to receive and unite itself to the divinity, through all the perilous voyage, from the nativity to the resurrection'. Sermon 5, *Collected Writings*, 5.321.

[25] Sermon 3, *Collected Writings*, 5.122.

[26] 'No man can receive the Spirit, merely by believing upon the redemption of Christ; for the Spirit proceedeth not from the Son only, but from the Father and the Son'. Sermon 3, *Collected Writings*, 5.184.

[27] Sermon 6, *Collected Writings*, 5.406.

[28] Sermon 3, *Collected Writings*, 5.126.

[29] Sermon 3, *Collected Writings*, 5.128.

was the middle space on which the powers of the world contended with the Holy Spirit dwelling in [Christ's] soul.[30]

It is in the triumph of the obedience of Christ, through the enabling action of the Spirit, that victory is found. Through the Son of God's sacrifice of self-humiliation, humanity in Christ is enabled to receive the Holy Spirit. Humanity, in Christ, is seen to triumph in the flesh over disobedience and death, being brought through the Holy Spirit into perfect harmony with the Father's will. Humanity is sustained in sinlessness before God through the marriage of man to God in the sinless Christ, the Son of God Incarnate.

One further feature of the Spirit's action in Jesus Christ should be underlined here. Although it is the action of the Trinity upon that `lump of fallen, sinful flesh' which is found in the hypostatic union of the Son of God Incarnate, we need to be careful in not misrepresenting Irving when he speaks of the universal implications of this. The representative character of Christ's humanity needs to be balanced by an understanding of the particularity of Christ's personhood, in that He is manifestly the one and only man who is Son of God incarnate. It is the Incarnation which guarantees Christ as a particular, individual man. Consequently, while Irving can speak of 'how God, by uniting the person of His Son to fallen humanity unto Himself, and is enabled, through Christ, to save as many as it pleaseth Him',[31] he will also speak of that particular action of the Spirit which falls upon Jesus, as distinct from the larger part of humanity. At the time of His baptism by John, when He received the baptism of the Holy Spirit, Jesus Christ began

to live a life in the power of the demonstration of the Holy Spirit ... From that time forth, accordingly, began His conflict with the spirits of darkness.[32]

We will return later to the implications of this further, empowering action of the Spirit in Christ, which is in addition to the redemptive action of the Spirit which occurs in and through the will of Christ. For the moment we note simply that the particularity of Christ is seen not only in the Son of God's Incarnation and the presence of the Spirit as *vinculum Trinitatis*, but it is also manifest in the unique action of the Spirit upon the particular humanity of Christ.

5.2.2   Soteriological Implications

It is the triumph of Christ's human will, enabled by the action of the Holy Spirit and made possible by the Incarnation of the Son of God, that is the key to man's redemption. Christ's humanity, one part of that `lump of fallen, sinful flesh', is

---

[30] Sermon 3, *Collected Writings*, 5.161.
[31] Sermon 3, *Collected Writings*, 5.115.
[32] Sermon 3, *Collected Writings*, 5.133.

so empowered by the Holy Spirit, as to be in concert with the Godhead always, and at length is crowned of the Father, and seated on the throne of His majesty.[33]

It is the humanity of Christ, sanctified and purified through the action of the Holy Spirit, that is lifted in the resurrection to be joined in eternal communion with the Trinity, conjoined to the eternal Son of God. Indeed, it is this Trinitarian focus of Irving that allows him to view the flesh of Christ in the manner in which he does. Salvation is not effected by Christ; it is effected by the Trinity. It is not the action of Christ, as He who is the hypostatic union of the divine and human, that effects redemption; it is the action of the Trinity, active in the humanity of Christ, that opens the door for all humanity to be saved. It is Christ's humanity, taken up in the *vinculum Trinitatis*, that is the avenue for all humanity to be received into eternal communion with the Triune God. In this action, Deity is in no way implicated in sin or contaminated by its involvement with that 'lump of fallen, sinful flesh' in Christ: Irving's understanding of God's grace and its effectiveness is too great for that. The influence and the salvation is unidirectional, from God to man alone. There is no possibility of God becoming contaminated by human sin through the hypostatic union.

For Irving, the Triune God remains impassable. The glory of the Triune God is exhibited in Christ, but is unaffected by Christ's humanity itself:

> The godhead cannot be tempted, and how should the Godhead suffer? The human nature of Christ alone suffered; and that is not infinite, but finite.[34]

Herein may lie a clue as to how it is that Irving can, as we saw in his attempted defence of the *Westminster Confession*, insist on the universality of atonement while at the same time maintaining a belief in a particular election from among mankind. Although the Son of God's Incarnation marries Him to the whole 'lump of fallen, sinful flesh', this takes place in the particular personhood of Jesus Christ: that person who receives the Spirit both as the *vinculum Trinitatis* and as the One who brings the baptism of the Holy Spirit, which enables 'a life in the power of the demonstration of the Holy Spirit'. Election, for Irving, must find expression within his Christocentric tautology: the elect are joined to Christ. Election can, however, also be fully and properly explained in terms of the action of the Spirit. The elect are those who are united with the will and intent of the particular personality of Christ through the action of the Holy Spirit upon them. The elect are those who receive the same Spirit who enabled Christ to live and demonstrate a life which is in the power of the Spirit, the same Spirit who enabled Christ in His own ministry. Consequently, election to either eternal life or eternal damnation can be understood both

---

[33] Sermon 3, *Collected Writings*, 5.163.
[34] Sermon 3, *Collected Writings*, 5.147.

Christologically and, as a consequence, pneumatologically. Election

> is either in the decree of God, as chosen in Jesus Christ; or it is in nature, fallen and unable to rise again.[35]

Those who are elect in Christ, because of the same action of the Spirit on their humanity as on the particular humanity of Christ, will be enabled to fulfil 'the same offices for the glory of God which Christ did'.[36] Even as God, married to man in the Incarnation, remains impassable, so too the mystery of the Father's will in electing some men and women to life remains beyond us.[37] The risen Christ dispenses the Spirit to those elect of God alone,[38] for the giving of the Holy Spirit 'is the communication to the individual of the electing love of God'.[39]

The benefits for the elect are therefore twofold. In the first instance, they can see and acknowledge that which is manifest in Christ, God's universal atonement for mankind. Secondly, they can also see what is possible for them as Christ now pours out the Spirit on God's elect as Christ Himself received the Spirit from the Father at the time of His baptism in the Jordan. What was possible for the Spirit to achieve, at work in the particular humanity of Christ, it is possible for the Spirit to achieve among God's elect. It follows that the elect in Christ should not only have a positive expectation of the Spirit's presence and action in the church's life, but should see in Christ's life the prototype of their own, an example to all who would receive the gift of God in Christ.[40]

5.2.3 Trinitarian Implications

We have already noted the clear, Trinitarian structure to Irving's thought which is exhibited in *The Doctrine of the Incarnation opened in Six Sermons*. One further point of interest to us is Irving's insistence that, in so far as we are able to give ontological description to the Trinity, we should do so in terms of that order found in the salvific economy, where we meet with the Spirit as *vinculum Trinitatis*. Likewise, Irving is clear that, as it is the Father's will that the Son should become incarnate and that the Spirit should be active upon human flesh, this will of the Father must be understood

> as preceding, both in the purpose and in the operation, the manifestation of the Son and the work of the Holy Spirit.[41]

---

[35] Sermon 2, *Collected Writings*, 5.110.
[36] Sermon 2, *Collected Writings*, 5.111.
[37] Sermon 3, *Collected Writings*, 5.179.
[38] Sermon 3, *Collected Writings*, 5.187.
[39] Sermon 3, *Collected Writings*, 5.252.
[40] Sermon 3, *Collected Writings*, 5.236.
[41] Sermon 5, *Collected Writings*, 5.347.

Where a communication of the infinite and incomprehensible God to man would not be possible without the entry, through the Incarnation, of the eternal Son into the finitude of man's existence,[42] this communication is true to God as 'a Trinity of Persons'.[43] The revelation of God in His salvific economy is true of God in that it reveals God as Trinity, for the manifestation of God through the Incarnation is the only basis by which we can speak of God: 'we can only speak from the knowledge which we have from the Godhead manifested in Christ'.[44]

At the same time, Irving remains unwilling to restrict his understanding of God's Being to that which is apparent from the Triune, salvific economy. Irving is prepared to allow God to be something in His immanent Being greater than that which we perceive Him to be through the Incarnation, for

> The Divine person of the Son is not contained in His manhood: the ocean, the round immense of space, were better said to be contained within a household dish, than that the Divine nature of the Son should be contained in manhood.[45]

The reason for this stress on apprehending the eternal Son's Being, unrestricted by the event of the Incarnation, is so that the end of worship will not be simply Christocentric but be directed beyond the humanity of Christ to the eternal Trinity, manifest to us through the humanity of Christ yet remaining essentially invisible and infinite in His Godhead as Father, Son and Holy Spirit. We are called to focus on God manifest in Christ and there to meet, as the elect of God, with the Spirit as *vinculum Trinitatis*, our worship carried in the Spirit to the Father and to the invisible and infinite reality of the Godhead. Through the salvific action of both the Son and the Spirit we are embraced by the Trinity in His salvific economy: a God, impassable and invisible, whose will cannot be known but as it is manifest towards us through and in Christ Jesus.

5.3   Irving's Pneumatology

In reviewing Irving's Christology, we have seen that it is through the life of Christ that we discover the key to understanding the work of the Spirit in humanity. Irving's pneumatology was, from the outset, interrelated with and dependent on his Christological thinking. Consequently, the difficulties encountered in his Christological thinking would profoundly affect his development of pneumatology. This is particularly noticeable in two areas of Irving's thought: his affirmation of the sinlessness of Christ's vicarious humanity and the status given to the divine *hypostasis* of the Son in the person

---

[42] Sermon 6, *Collected Writings*, 5.399.
[43] Sermon 6, *Collected Writings*, 5.404.
[44] Sermon 6, *Collected Writings*, 5.433.
[45] Sermon 6, *Collected Writings*, 5.412.

of Jesus Christ.

Where Irving saw himself as defending the historic, catholic doctrine of the Lord's human nature against docetic or reductionist philosophies, it was integral to his thesis that Christ's humanity was exactly the same as ours. The difficulty that arose for him was essentially an interpretative one: while he asserted that the particular humanity of Christ was *potest non peccare*,[46] his presentation of this was formulated within the context of a Calvinist tradition which affirmed man's total depravity: *non potest non peccare*.[47] This, combined with an acknowledgement of God's sovereign election in salvation and the limited jurisdiction allowed to the free will of man in salvation, caused Irving's emphasis on the peccability of Christ to trap him in a position whereby his *potest non peccare* was drowned out by what his Calvinistic contemporaries imagined themselves to be hearing: that Christ shared the condition of depraved humanity, *non potest non peccare*. Irving, in perceiving himself to be an advocate of the Reformed position, could only but affirm man's total depravity and therefore the total depravity of Christ's own flesh.

Certainly Irving's position is not unclear. As we have seen, for Irving the Incarnation is a Trinitarian event whereby the Spirit is present with the humanity of Christ as *vinculum Trinitatis*; the Spirit's activity, which is centred in Christ's will, preserving Christ's humanity as sinless. Where difficulty arises is when an attempt is made to explain, without reference to the action of the Spirit, how it is that impeccable divinity can be married to totally corrupted humanity. This point, relating to the marriage of Christ's divine and human natures, brings us to our second area of difficulty: the question of the status given, by Irving, to the divine *hypostasis* of the Son within the person of Jesus Christ.

Throughout Irving's thinking, through to his last major work, *The Day of Pentecost*, there is a clear emphasis on the Incarnation as a perichoretic event: he sees Christ Jesus not simply as the Son of God made flesh, but as the One who arises out of the Triune God's involvement in the Incarnation. The difficulty with Irving's approach lies in that, while emphasising the perichoretic activity of the Godhead within the real humanity of Christ, he does not further develop his understanding of the significance of the Son of God's marriage to human flesh, other than to note that sacrifice which is inherent in the self-abasement of the Incarnation. It is through the Incarnation that the Son opens an avenue for the Spirit, *vinculum Trinitatis*, to enter and dwell within corruptible humanity. Irving does not, however, differentiate between the presence of the Son Incarnate in Christ and the action of the Holy Spirit upon His humanity, other than to state that the Son undertakes, in the Incarnation, a sacrificial act of self-abasement and humiliation. More importantly, Irving does not make a distinction between the operation of the Spirit occuring in the

---

[46] 'Able not to sin'.

[47] 'Unable to avoid sinning'.

particular humanity of Christ and that action of the Spirit which takes place within the humanity of the elect. Perhaps, for Irving, the second part of the problem was not relevant; yet the answer might well matter if we seek to discern the relation of the Spirit to the Son in the life of Christ.

This potential problem is apparent in Irving's final Christological work, *Christ's Holiness in Flesh: The Form and Fountainhead of All Holiness in Flesh*. The treatise is opened with Irving restating the pivotal dogma of Christ's shared humanity with mankind and His consequent sharing of man's sinful condition. A chastened Irving reemphasises that sinfulness is not a property inherent to the Christ, for

> he was under no law till he became man by generation of the virgin, in the power of the Holy Ghost. Up to that time, he had no responsibility, and could have no sin.[48]

Through the event of Incarnation, the Son of God comes to share the sinful nature of man, though not sharing the event of man's sin:

> His body had our sins in it; not on as a cloak, but in it as a weakness, and a property, and a law, yet was he without any sin or guile.[49]

It remains unclear how Irving understands, beyond the humiliation of Incarnation, the function of the *hypostasis* of the Son of God within Christ's life: if he believes there to be any ongoing function at all. In his defence against the accusation that he held there to be sin in the Son of God, Irving appears to be contending against advocates of a *Logos-sarx* Christology, where the human nature of Christ is subsumed within the coming of the divine; but what, for Irving, is the subsequent role of the Logos in the ministry of Jesus? Christ's vicarious humanity is exemplary, as the paradigm for sinful man, indwelt and led by the Holy Spirit, 'generate of flesh and regenerate of the Spirit at the same instant'.[50] Irving's insistence on the shared, corrupt humanity of Jesus leads him to contend for the possibility of our walking in actual holiness in this life, for Christ has done so: to contend otherwise would be to deny the reality of the Incarnation.[51]

In so emphasising the work of the Spirit, without further defining how this

---

[48] E. Irving, *Christ's Holiness in Flesh: The Form and Fountainhead of All Holiness in Flesh*, John Lindsay & Co., Edinburgh, 1831, p. 5.

[49] *Christ's Holiness in Flesh: The Form and Fountainhead of All Holiness in Flesh*, p. 2.

[50] *Christ's Holiness in Flesh: The Form and Fountainhead of All Holiness in Flesh*, p. 8.

[51] 'If any one ... will stand up and say, that this body and soul of ours cannot become holy in this life, he understands not the glory of the power of God in the Holy Spirit, and asserteth that man's nature is not only too much for me to reclaim, but also too much for the Holy Spirit'. *Christ's Holiness in Flesh: The Form and Fountainhead of All Holiness in Flesh*, p. 8.

relates to the two natures of Christ, there is the possibility of Irving laying himself open to the charge of either Nestorianism or a Spirit-flesh binitarianism. Is it right that, in emphasising the capacity of the Holy Spirit to work in 'sinful flesh', Irving should make this identification without further qualifying the presence of the Logos in man? For Irving himself, there is certainly no apparent problem here, not least because the action of the Trinity is always perichoretic, with the Spirit, Son and Father working together in harmonious conjunction. The Incarnation is the means of anchoring the Triune God's involvement in the condition of man:

> It is the person of the Son of God acting within the limits of manhood, and so become man, and ever brought thereinto by the Holy Ghost, who, upon finding Himself man, doth find himself at once a spiritual and a fleshly man, born of God and born of flesh, whereof he sanctifieth the latter by the hand of the former; and so approveth himself worthy and able, as man, to use the Holy Ghost, for the destruction of sin in the flesh, and the defeat of temptation from the devil and the world.[52]

Irving makes recourse to the doctrine of perichoresis to ground and validate the manner in which he goes on to speak of the Holy Spirit. Here, indeed, we have a masterly reversal of how the doctrine had come to be used in the Reformed tradition: where the Spirit's action had been held, by the federal Calvinists, as implicit by virtue of the Word of God's interaction with us, so Irving uses the same doctrine to imply the activity of the divine Son, while emphasising the action of the Spirit on human flesh. Is this sufficient? McFarlane is content with such an appeal to the perichoretic operation of the Trinity.[53] We would be more cautious, questioning whether this sufficiently safeguards an understanding of both the Son and the Spirit's salvific economy. This is an issue we will revisit as we continue to review the legacy of the Western Trinitarian model.

A correlation between the action of the Spirit upon Christ and the action of the Spirit upon the humanity of the elect is further demonstrated from the manner in which Irving approaches the *schema* of the Spirit's manifestation in the church. Irving longs for a suprarational work of the Spirit in the believer's life, specifically characterised by a display of God's power, 'in order to convince an unbelieving and ignorant world'.[54] Irving looks to a manifestation which is subsequential to the conviction of God's love in the believer's heart; yet this work of the Spirit is to be understood as part of the outworking of the life of Christ Himself in the body of Christ, the church. In this, the Spirit effects within normal human life that which He sustained and enabled in the humanity

---

[52] *Christ's Holiness in Flesh: The Form and Fountainhead of All Holiness in Flesh,* p. 9.
[53] *Christ and the Spirit,* p. 76. McFarlane adopts an analysis that does not invoke a distinction between Western and Eastern models of the Trinity, as described in our study.
[54] *Collected Writings,* 5.559.

of Christ Jesus Himself. The Spirit brings together, or works coherence into, men and women, imparting to them the principle of life that is in Christ,[55] going on to suffuse the church with that life, in the Spirit, that was and is true of Christ's humanity:

> The church is to be not only the container of the manifested God, but she is the actor of his works, and the utterer of His wisdom: and to accomplish this, Christ, when he ascended up on high, received the Seven Spirits, the fullness and completeness of the vital, active Godhead. This is his occupation in heaven, to build the spiritual temple of the Lord out of the materials which He hath impregnated with His own life.[56]

Irving longs for a manifest demonstration of the power of God through the *charismata*, advocating the cultivation of a desire and a pursuit of *glossolalia* by Christians as part of this; but he marries this appeal for pneumatological phenomena to his determinedly Christocentric model. The church is to be pneumatised, looking to the life of Christ himself as a paradigm of humanity under the control of the Spirit: at the same time, the risen Christ is the agent whereby the fullness of the Spirit is released into His continuing body on earth.

The evolution towards a balance in Irving's thought between Christological and pneumatological considerations is best demonstrated in *The Day of Pentecost or The Baptism With The Holy Ghost*. Irving opens this work with the affirmation that the Baptism with the Holy Ghost is the ultimate expression of the ministry of Jesus, His *nobile officium*. This work of the Holy Spirit is intrinsically bound up with the resurrected Christ. The resurrected Christ has entered into a position that allows a work of the Holy Spirit through Him that was not possible in the days of his Incarnation:

> The whole work of the Son of Man, until the Resurrection, consisteth in the taking of this mortal life, and offering it without one sin upon the cross, to end it forever; but the work of the Holy Ghost is not to manifest a mortal life, no, nor even such a life as Adam was created withal, but that inexhaustible and glorious and eternal life into which Christ entered at the Resurrection.[57]

Christ, who was able to sin (*potest peccare*) but did not, now stands over against man the sinner; yet in this gulf there remains the uniting bond of Christ's humanity, a bond forged forever in the hypostatic union. Christ's life as lived on earth remains a paradigm for us, demonstrating the real potential of how the Spirit would indwell and work in man; but the present ministry of the Spirit towards us is not to duplicate the specific ministry of Jesus in our lives.

---

[55] *Collected Writings*, 5.517.

[56] *Collected Writings*, 5.518.

[57] E. Irving, *The Day of Pentecost or The Baptism With The Holy Ghost*, John Lindsay & Co., Edinburgh, 1831, p. 3.

The Spirit's ministry is now to bring the benefit of the reign of the transformed and resurrected Christ into our yet untransformed condition, the Holy Spirit acting as 'the substance in the Godhead for cleansing the spirit'.[58]

This distinction is important, for there is, for Irving, a difference in the status of the resurrected Christ from that held during His ministry on earth. The present function of the Spirit among the elect is not simply to duplicate the earthly life of Christ. The potential of the Christological paradigm in the life of the elect will only be fully realised in and among them eschatologically. The catalyst for the present work of the Spirit towards that end is the shared humanity of the Risen Christ with those who await such a transformation:

> Resurrection is not Adam's life restored; but another life, conferred by God, of an infinitely more excellent kind, in which is contained the fullness of the Godhead in a body. This life, equal in dignity and in power to the headship, lordship, and sustentation of all creatures; this life, possessed of all capacities equal to the sitting on God's own throne, and wielding the sceptre of the world; this life, conscious to the mind of God, possessed of the energy of God, inhabited by the light and love and goodness and power of God; is that which Christ entered into by resurrection, and communicates to the church by baptism with the Holy Ghost.[59]

In what way is Christ's life paradigmatic, then? The paradigm of Christ's life remains important to us in that it allows us to distinguish between the different actions of the Spirit's present work among the elect, prior to their own resurrection. The actions of the Spirit in and on the elect are to be associated with what has already occurred in the humanity of Jesus. These actions, while being integrally part of our inheritance, are made effective through our baptism and our appropriating faith by the Spirit.[60] Threefold, these actions can be distinguished as creation, regeneration and glorification[61] and can be, in turn, associated with the birth, life and resurrection of Christ.

In holding to this paradigmatic model, Irving makes use of it both to affirm the perichoretic action of the Trinity and also to identify three distinct stages which can be detected in the Spirit's operation on our humanity. The first action, which corresponds to the birth of Christ, is the 'creation of being', as effected in the act of Christ's generation and, for us, paralleled in our regeneration by the Spirit. This first stage is properly understood as the action of the Father, for it finds expression in the Father's act of electing us to salvation and eternal life. The second action, corresponding to the life of Christ,

---

[58] *The Day of Pentecost or The Baptism With The Holy Ghost*, p. 3.

[59] *The Day of Pentecost or The Baptism With The Holy Ghost*, pp. 4-5.

[60] 'The Holy Spirit [is] the substance and life of each operation; for the Father doeth nothing without the Holy Ghost, and the Son doeth nothing without the Holy Ghost'. *The Day of Pentecost or The Baptism With The Holy Ghost*, p. 18.

[61] *The Day of Pentecost or The Baptism With The Holy Ghost*, p. 54.

is found in the 'sustentation of being in all its capacities'[62] which, again, is paralleled in the Christian life by 'our nourishment upon the flesh and blood of Christ'.[63] This arises out of the accomplishment in Christ's life of living in holiness and obedience to the Father. The work in this second stage is properly designated as that of the Son, because it occurs by merit of the Son's Incarnation.

The third action is the 'baptism of the Holy Spirit'. This corresponds to the Holy Spirit issuing from the present, resurrection life of Christ and it is properly the work of both the Father and the Son, whereby

> the Holy Ghost doth bring to every believer the presence of the Father and the power of the Holy Ghost, according to that measure, at the least, in which Christ during the days of his flesh possessed the same.[64]

The distinction between these three stages of the divine economy is important, for it allows Irving to express his conviction that the church has been devoid of the operation of the third, particular work of the Spirit for too long. The church has grieved and erred in not looking for the action of the Spirit in this third stage but yet has remained Christian, by merit of its participation in the first and second stages. It is to this third stage that Irving calls the church:

> His disciples in the days of his flesh received a share of the powers then possessed by him; and when he received new powers, 'the gift of the Holy Ghost', on his ascension to the Father, they received on the day of Pentecost the full share thereof, to the extent of this body's power to contain, and of this world's power to bear the sight and hearing of them.[65]

Where Irving develops the pneumatology already present in his earlier, Christological works, it is to allow for a distinction between the different aspects of the Spirit's economy towards us. He does this while seeking to retain the perichoretic integrity of the Trinity's salvific economy, expressed and made manifest to mankind in the Incarnation. Where the paradigmatic metaphor of Christ's life and ministry is sustained, it is within the context of the resurrected Christ's agency in sending the Spirit upon the church.

Earlier, we noted that it could be argued that Irving allows insufficiently for a distinction between the action of the Spirit and that of the eternal Son conjoined to humanity in Christ. Likewise, it might be questioned whether it is appropriate to draw such a close parallel between the presence of the Spirit in the earthly life of Christ and the Spirit's activity in the life of the church today. For the moment it will suffice to note that Irving, in emphasising that it is our

---

[62] *The Day of Pentecost or The Baptism With The Holy Ghost*, p. 24.
[63] *The Day of Pentecost or The Baptism With The Holy Ghost*, p. 25.
[64] *The Day of Pentecost or The Baptism With The Holy Ghost*, p. 39.
[65] *The Day of Pentecost or The Baptism With The Holy Ghost*, p. 36.

shared humanity with Christ which serves as the basis whereby we realise the Spirit's presence in our own life, does maintain a distinction between the corruptible Christ and corrupted humanity. He seeks to distinguish between the unique Christ, who is the Son of God made man and who is inhabited by the Spirit, and our corrupted humanity which receives the Holy Spirit, by merit of Christ's atoning work. Whether that distinction is adequate is a matter we will return to shortly.

5.4   The Spirit and the Sacraments

What is of special interest in Irving's tripartite categorisation of the Spirit's work, in correlating the three actions of the Spirit to the birth, life and resurrection of Christ, is the manner whereby he associates the second action of the Spirit with our nourishment upon the flesh and blood of Christ: an apparent allusion to the sacrament of the Lord's Supper. The facility of the sacrament is associated with a particular action of the Spirit.

We earlier noted how, in his commentary on the *Scots Confession*, Irving had welcomed an emphasis upon the sacraments as a means whereby the gift of God in Christ is conveyed objectively to the recipient, in that the sacrament signifies the manifestation of Christ both to the reprobate and to the elect. Here we can better understand something of Irving's reasoning. As God's mercy is manifested to all men in and through the Incarnation, so the visible token of that manifestation is freely offered in the sacrament. The efficacy of the sacrament is, however, bound up with the further action of the Spirit, first in election to salvation by the Father and subsequently by imparting to us, in the Spirit's second action, the nourishment of Christ's life. In the sacrament the gift of God in Christ is objectively conveyed to the recipient, while by the action of the Spirit we are enabled to receive that which the sacrament signifies.

In seeking to understand this perspective, we would note that Irving does not appear to be consciously embracing a suprarational work of the Spirit in the sacrament in preference to a rational perception of the Spirit's work arising from the Spirit's epistemic agency. Irving was acting in a manner true to his time: the contemporary, theological context did not require Irving to affirm further the value of the Scriptures in explaining the truth of God's salvation. The importance of the Spirit's epistemic agency, in opening our minds to understand the Scriptures, could be assumed. Irving's concern was that the focus of our theology should lie beyond man's rational understanding and subjective moods, to be founded instead on that which occurs in the objective manifestation of the Triune God's grace in Christ. That which was to be apprehended is that to which the Scriptures attest, namely the Triune God's soterial mission manifest in Christ. The means by which this is apprehended is a rational, cognitive faith in the believer directed towards God in Christ. In Irving's presentation of the sacraments, linking them as he does to the need for a rational and cognitive faith in the believer, we might say that there is a dovetailing together of both the suprarational work and epistemic agency of the Spirit.

That Irving's desire is to encourage a Christian faith which arises from the substantial communication of Christ to us, as represented in the sacraments, is expressed in the short discourse, *Idolatry of the Sacraments*.[66] The sacraments are outward signs which signify the communication of an inward grace,[67] signifying the communication of spiritual grace by the Holy Spirit to 'those who receive them with a spiritually enlightened mind'.[68] While there is no facility in the sacrament outwith the presence of faith[69] and while grace can be communicated to us apart from the sacraments,[70] the sacraments do represent the communication of the grace of God to us in Christ, physical tokens which point to God's gift to us. The importance of the sacraments lies in that they signify that our communion with the Triune God occurs through the physical body of Christ.[71] It is because the sacraments speak so clearly of Christ that their presence is essential to the existence of the visible church.[72] As Irving explains in his *Homilies on Baptism*, the sacraments plainly communicate the Son of God manifest; and it is their ability to take the true doctrine and 'declare it to the sense of man'[73] wherein lies their facility.

Irving, through relating the Spirit's work in the sacrament to God's grace manifest in Christ, presents us with a view of the Spirit's work which apparently avoids dichotomising the Spirit's suprarational work and epistemic agency. The sacraments, as do the Scriptures, expound Christ to us. That we are able to respond in faith because we are elect of the Father does not detract from the significance of the sacraments as a means of declaring to the world the fact that God's grace is made manifest and known through Christ.

5.5   Critique

There are four aspects of Irving's pneumatology, as outlined above, that have a particular bearing on the development of our thesis. These, which we offer by

---

[66] *Collected Writings*, 4.86ff.. This short work exhibits the same understanding of the sacraments as Irving expressed in his larger collection of *Homilies on Baptism*.

[67] Baptism appealing to man's sense of sight, the Lord's Supper 'to a closer faculty of our nature than any of the five senses ... whereby the body ... converteth [the elements] into a living union with itself'. *Collected Writings*, 4.88.

[68] *Collected Writings*, 4.87.

[69] *Collected Writings*, 4.91-2.

[70] Which are but the signs which signify: see *Collected Writings*, 4.87.

[71] It is through our communication with the physical body of Christ that we are assured of God's grace, for 'His body was the only sinless thing which had been in the world since the fall ... the manifest germ of a new creation, the parent of a new family, the source of a new light, the spark of a new life.' *Collected Writings*, 4.89.

[72] *Collected Writings*, 4.91.

[73] *Collected Writings*, 2.252.

way of conclusion to this chapter as a brief critique, are the Spirit and Christology, the Spirit and the Trinity, the Spirit and the Doctrine of election and the Spirit and the Resurrected Christ.

5.5.1 The Spirit and Christology

In affirming the central importance of Christ's humanity, Irving exposed a weakness which was inherent in Reformed Christology. As we argued when reviewing Calvin's Christology in chapter 3, there was in Calvin a tendency to focus on the Incarnation as a theophany. That theophany was expressed through the manifestation of the Son in His soterial mission, yet without the accompaniment of a clearly developed understanding of the Spirit's role therein. Consequently, one way of viewing Irving's understanding of the Holy Spirit at work in Christ's humanity would be to see him as presenting us with nothing other than what was undeveloped yet implicit in Calvin's Christology. Where Irving differs from Calvin is in that he explicates the status and function of the Holy Spirit, as the Spirit is made manifest to us through the Son's Incarnation. Irving develops and expounds the dogma that the Incarnation is not a theophany accomplished through the Son alone, but a manifestation of the Trinity's salvific economy towards mankind, made patent by the activity of the Spirit in that humanity which has become married to the Son in the Incarnation.

Following this line of reasoning, we could go on to view Irving's account as offering an alternative exposition of Calvin's legacy to that traced in chapter 4, where we detected a growing tendency within the development of Scottish theology, as reflected in the pneumatology of the *Scots Confession* and *Westminster Confession*, to emphasise the Spirit's epistemic agency in a manner apparently unrelated to ontological considerations. Irving's exploration into the significance of the Spirit's action in Christ's humanity would thereby be seen to correct a tendency to neglect either pneumatological or Trinitarian aspects of the Incarnation.

Difficulties do arise from Irving's model, however, should we attempt to go on to distinguish between what was accomplished in Christ by merit of His status as the Son Incarnate and what was accomplished through the Spirit's activity within Christ's corruptible humanity. Although this question might not have arisen for Irving, it may occur to us should we want to pursue the question of what relationship can exist between the Spirit at work in Christ's humanity and the Spirit at work in our humanity today. Irving's understanding of the Spirit as *vinculum* caused him to see the relationship of Christ to us in terms of our humanity, finding a paradigm and example of the Spirit's operations in Christ's humanity. It follows that the Spirit is active in our humanity in the same way as He was active in Christ's humanity during His ministry on earth, in so far as the only operation of the Spirit we can experience is that which arises from our participation in Christ's humanity and our consequent participation in His experience of the Spirit as *vinculum* between God the Father and God the Son. Whether this understanding of the Spirit's action upon our humanity is adequate, or whether it leaves insufficient room for a distinction to be retained between us and the Son of God Incarnate is a question we will return to in chapter 7. For the moment we note that Irving, by reaffirming the full significance of the Son's Incarnation, illustrated the need to give ontological definition to an understanding of the Spirit's function in the Trinity's salvific economy.

5.5.2   The Spirit and the Trinity

There is a further way in which Irving, by appealing to an understanding of the Spirit as *vinculum Trinitatis*, reflects Calvin's thought. In chapter 3 we suggested that Calvin's Trinitarian focus appeared to centre not on God's salvific economy but on the immanent character of God's Triune Being. Irving echoes this through stressing that the transcendence and impassability of God, which are essential characteristics of God's immanent Being, are definitive features in seeking to come to an understanding of God in His communion with man in the Incarnation. Again, as in Calvin, we find repeated the Western Trinitarian model's perception of the Spirit as *vinculum*, the Spirit as bond between the Father and the Son; but now more fully developed and made more central to an understanding of the Son's soterial mission, through Irving's exposition of the significance for humanity of the Spirit's eternal communication between the Father and the Son.

There is, however, a lacuna that arises within Irving's thought at this point. A tension occurs between his appeal to the eternal relations of the immanent Godhead and his appreciation of the Trinity's salvific economy. It is from the salvific economy that we are to form our understanding of the Trinity as He is both in His economy and eternal nature. Irving wants to present an understanding of the Trinity's perichoretic action which is founded soundly on the Incarnation of the Son: an understanding of God that arises from His salvific economy. At the same time, he wishes to preserve the notion that God is, in His immanent Being, greater than and beyond any perception of Him which we can form out of His salvific economy. For Irving, the Trinity as met with in the salvific economy is the eternal Trinity; yet God, in His eternal Being, is greater than that which He is perceived to be when made manifest to us in the Incarnation.

The difficulty that arises for us out of this distinction is that it can create a dichotomy in our understanding of the Spirit's Person and function. We have noted how there had developed, out of Calvin's thought, a distinction between the epistemic agency of the Spirit and the Spirit's function as executor of God's elective decision, whereby both of these functions could be and had been detached from an appreciation of the Spirit's involvement in Christ's soterial mission. These two functions of the Spirit were not necessarily to be interpreted with a Christocentric reference, as was apparent from our analysis of both the *Scots Confession* and the *Westminster Confession*. Irving, appealing to the function of the Spirit as *vinculum*, reaffirmed the pivotal significance of Christ for our understanding of the Spirit's actions. It was, however, possible that these two functions of the Spirit would remain detached and hidden in the eternal relations of the inscrutable Godhead, unless they were to be explicitly associated with the Spirit's economic action upon the humanity of Christ. An understanding of the Spirit as epistemic agent at work in the elect of God could remain distinguished from an appreciation of the Spirit's presence, as *vinculum*, with the Son in the Son's soterial mission. Likewise, an understanding of the Spirit as *vinculum* could become detached from an understanding of the Spirit as executor of God's elective decision.

We would suggest that such a detachment does appear to have occurred in Irving's understanding: or more precisely, it was a detachment which Irving perpetuated, inherited by him from the tradition in which he stood. Irving was able to speak of the hidden, elective choice of God as separate from the love of God as manifested to all humanity through the Incarnation. For Irving's part, it is unlikely that the existence of this dichotomy would be conceded, because of the way he framed his understanding of the Trinity's participation in that elective process. It is to Irving's understanding of the Spirit in election that we now turn.

5.5.3   The Spirit and the Doctrine of Election

That the Spirit should function as executor of God's elective decision, in securing our election, does not appear to have been interpreted by Irving as a function of the Spirit as *vinculum Trinitatis*. The elective decision appears to have been held to be outwith the salvific economy of God, as expressed in the Incarnation: so it was that Irving could hold both to universal atonement and also double election. Atonement was manifest in the Incarnation, election was not. While maintaining a strong Christocentricity, Irving manages to keep the decision of election outwith God's salvific economy and retain it within the hidden, inscrutable will of the Father. It may well be that this should be interpreted not as a weakness in Irving's thought but a strength: a proper balance to the fact of God's salvific economy made manifest in Christ, yet God remaining essentially inscrutable and unintelligible to man. Further, it could be argued that Irving has overcome the problem by appealing to the three actions of the Spirit which are related to the birth, life and resurrection of Jesus, the first of these being the Father's act of election to salvation and eternal life. There are, however, difficulties which arise, not from the Trinitarian model but from the underlying theological supposition.

In chapters 3 and 4 we traced the doctrine of election in Calvin and its early development in the *Scots* and *Westminster Confessions*, observing that this doctrine did not appear to arise from an epistemology centred on either the *cognitio Dei Redemptoris* or from a consideration of God's Being as Trinity, but from an epistemology based on and shaped out of Scriptural hermeneutics. The stress on God's elective decision arose from a view of God's sovereignty formed out of an epistemology founded on Scripture, not one based on ontological considerations. Consequently it was possible for the relationship between the Spirit's economic function and the Spirit as the executor of God's elective decision to remain opaque. This appears to be the case in Irving's work, where an understanding of the Spirit as the executor of God's elective decision appears unrelated to the Spirit's economic function within the *vinculum Trinitatis*, founded firmly on the *cognitio Dei Redemptoris* in Christ. While Irving's Trinitarian model attempts to integrate the different functions of the Spirit, it does not provide a unified, ontological foundation for our understanding of them. Without wishing to repudiate the facility of Scripture in giving testimony to God's salvific economy, we would suggest that it may be fruitful were we to explore further the possibility of establishing a unified, ontological model of the Spirit's functions whereby all three functions - the Spirit's epistemic agency, suprarational work and function as executor of God's elective decision - may be perceived not only within a Trinitarian context but also as aspects of the Spirit's ontic actuality. This we shall touch on in chapters 6 and 7, returning to the issue once again in chapter 8.

5.5.4   The Spirit and the Resurrected Christ

A significant feature of Irving's pneumatology lies in the importance attached to the resurrection and ascension of Christ in His human body, with the effect this has in shaping our present communion with the Holy Spirit. Two important aspects of this are Irving's interpretation of the Spirit's activity in the sacraments and that work of the Spirit which he describes as the 'baptism of the Holy Spirit'.

Irving understands the Spirit's communication to us through the sacraments to occur because of our union with the physical body of the resurrected Christ, through that humanity which Christ shares in common with us. Where baptism conveys our acknowledgement of and participation in the washing and consecration of Christ's humanity on our behalf, it is in the Lord's Supper that our communion with Christ is made more fully apparent, through the use of the physical symbols of the bread and wine. The elements signify not only the gift of the Son of God in His soterial mission but serve as an affirmation that it is through the present gift of Christ's humanity, eternally married through the hypostatic union to the Son of God and now ascended in heaven at the Father's right side, that we receive the gift of eternal life in our own humanity. Our participation in the symbols of His body and blood is our participation, through faith, in His life and the empowering of the Holy Spirit therein. Christ's present life is ours to share in and participate in.

The potential of our being enabled out of the glorious communion that Christ's humanity now shares with the Father in heaven is complemented by the gift not only to live in the strength of Christ, but also to enjoy the outpouring of the Spirit from the ascended Christ. The Spirit comes, not only to nourish us out of the life of Christ but to bring us to share in the glories of Christ's eternal inheritance, now that He has been raised from death and is ascended on high. The 'baptism of the Holy Spirit' is an infusion of the Spirit, as He was present in the earthly life of Christ, so far as we can bear His presence within our humanity. Here, in speaking of an infusion into the Christian of the empowering which was Christ's, we come closest to discerning in Irving's pneumatology what we identified in chapter 1 as the distinctive emphasis of the Charismatic Movement: an emphasis on a suprarational, experiential action of the Spirit, which we have described as arising from the ontic actuality of the Spirit. Caution should be exercised, however, in drawing too close a parallel. Irving, like Calvin, understood the central aspect of the Spirit's economy to be the formation of a rational, cognitive faith in the human mind, and saw this third action of the Spirit as consequential to faith's formation. We saw Irving's insistence on the prerequisite of faith reflected in the importance that he attached to a conscious appreciation of what Christ had done in our receiving benefit from the sacraments. What is of special interest in Irving's account is the way in which the empowering action of the Spirit is specifically associated with the resurrected and ascended Christ, consequential upon the completion of His earthly ministry. Far from being detached from Christ, the action of the Spirit is seen as contingent upon Him in enabling the church to continue in Christ's ministry. This stress on the significance of Christ's present ascension in seeking to understand the ontic actuality of the Spirit is something we will return to in chapter 8.

Irving, living in the early nineteenth century, sought after an understanding of the Spirit and the Trinity which was centred on the person of Christ, seeking to break false strictures which he perceived to exist within the Scottish theological tradition. A similar quest was embarked upon by the twentieth century Scottish dogmatician, Thomas F. Torrance. It is to Torrance's work that we now turn.

Chapter 6

Thomas F. Torrance

6.1 Introduction

There are two reasons for us now turning to examine the Trinitarian theology of T. F. Torrance. Firstly, Torrance's tenure as a Professor at New College in Edinburgh,[1] together with his significant influence as both an interpreter and advocate of Reformed theology, spanned a period of time, traced in chapter 1, that witnessed the emergence and development of the Charismatic Movement in Scotland. Although Torrance was neither directly involved in nor influenced by the Charismatic Movement, his work is of interest to us in so far as his writings reflect something of the theological issues which had come to influence Scottish theology during and immediately prior to the period of the Charismatic Movement's emergence in Scotland. Secondly, in looking to Torrance we find a theologian who attempts, as in the case of Irving, to tackle the question of how we are to understand the ontological character of God's Trinitarian Being. Torrance is a Scottish theologian who wrestles with the fundamental theological issues which affect our perception of the Holy Spirit within a Trinitarian framework. In this chapter we will examine the main themes which fashion an understanding of the Holy Spirit's Person and function in Torrance's writings. We begin with a brief outline of the theological background to Torrance's work.

Torrance's work can be described in part as a reaction to the legacy of nineteenth century liberal thought. By the early years of the twentieth century Hegelian idealism had come to find expression in Scottish theology by means of the same wave of post-enlightenment German philosophy which had brought to it Schleiermacher's perspective, that theology was properly an expression of the Christian community's corporate piety. Inevitably, this had moved the centre of theological enquiry towards an anthropocentric axis. The view of God expressed in the *Westminster Confession* had become increasingly unacceptable to the theologically literate. Dogmatic assertions which were once treated as axiomatic were no longer exempt from the bar of reason and empirical examination. The transcendent God had increasingly come to be viewed as one who should also be a reasonable God.

---

[1] Professor of Church History from 1950-52 and of Christian Dogmatics from 1952-79.

Some tensions could arise, however, between a quest in pursuit of a reasonable explication of Christian belief and the desire to maintain traditional, catholic dogma. We see something of these tensions in the work of one of Torrance's teachers and predecessors at New College, H. R. Mackintosh,[2] of whose work the church historians Bulloch and Drummond opined,

All the old names of Scottish theology had vanished from his pages. So far as he was concerned Protestant Theology might have begun in Germany half a century or so before his birth, and in this he was representative of his generation.[3]

Was such a harsh judgement warranted? In Mackintosh there appears a confidence in the profundity and the absolute truth of the Christian revelation,[4] with the rich wells of the fullness of the Christian Gospel, as yet beyond the ready confines of our comprehension, spanning out from the midst of the Christian community as an invitation to all mankind. For Mackintosh, Jesus is the manifestation of the truth concerning God, the Fatherhood of God patently being 'present in the tangible personality of Jesus'.[5] At the same time, Mackintosh had difficulty with aspects of dogma which, from an empirical perspective, could be difficult to explain. We see this in his attitude to the Trinity, the Chalcedonian formulation of the two natures of Christ and his perception of the Holy Spirit.

The doctrine of the Trinity, for Mackintosh, is an expression of Christian monotheism.[6] Christianity, as heir to the Old Testament, is 'a form of ethical monotheism which yet has learned to conceive God in a new way'.[7] The doctrine of the Trinity is to be seen as the economic unveiling of God, expressing a dynamic in God whereby Creation, Redemption and Renewal are the respective phases of God's self-disclosure;[8] but not the self-disclosure of a God whom we can describe, in His immanent being, as Triune. The doctrine of the Trinity may well be an attempt to frame an absolute background of reality out of which the gift of Christ is given to us,[9]

---

[2] Professor of Systematic Theology, 1904-36.

[3] A. L. Drummond and J. Bulloch, *The Church in Late Victorian Scotland 1874-1900*, St. Andrew Press, Edinburgh, 1978, p. 215.

[4] 'God, for the Christian mind, is the Father corresponding to Jesus as Son: we see Him reflected, without break or shadow, in the Redeemer's soul'. H. R. Mackintosh, *The Originality of the Christian Message*, Duckworth & Co., London, 1920, p. 39.

[5] *The Originality of the Christian Message*, p. 53.

[6] *The Originality of the Christian Message*, p. 32.

[7] H. R. Mackintosh, *The Doctrine of the Person of Christ*, T & T Clark, Edinburgh, 1912, p. 508.

[8] *The Doctrine of the Person of Christ*, p. 512.

[9] *The Doctrine of the Person of Christ*, p. 517.

Yet it is in the unity of God as known in Christ that our minds come finally to rest. The triune life is apprehended by us for the sake of its redemptive expression, not for the internal analysis of its content. The problem can never be one of ontology mixed with arithmetic.[10]

This reticence to allow for categories of expression which are not amenable to empirical analysis is further evidenced in Mackintosh's attitude to the Chalcedonian formula's two natures of Christ. This formula was seen as importing into the life of Christ 'an incredible and thorough going dualism. In place of that perfect unity which is felt in every impression of Him, the whole is bisected sharply by the fissure of distinction.'[11] What remains critical, for Mackintosh, is faith in Christ; but this is not to be confused with that 'adhesion to a particular Christological formula, and that ... doctrine of the two natures [which], in the rigid abstract shape given it by tradition, is detachable from the believing estimate of our Lord.'[12]

The difficulty of owning dogma which did not appear amenable to empirical analysis was further evidenced in Mackintosh's treatment of the Holy Spirit, whose presence can best be described as 'but a higher mode of Christ's transcendent influence, the climax of His work'.[13] Mackintosh further remarks that,

> Between the Spirit and Christ in the heart no experimental distinction can be made.... The glorified Jesus is identical with the Jesus who sojourned on earth, and the work resumed under larger conditions, with an access of divine power, is but the continuation of His earthly task, in the light of which it must be interpreted.[14]

In Mackintosh there is no explicit attack on confessional orthodoxy: the difference lay in that statements regarding God's transcendent being could not easily be accommodated within a scheme of theology formed on the axis of empirical analysis. As Mackintosh stated,

> In faith, as in science, there is an objective reality to be known; for faith that reality is revelation, for physical science it is what may be called, broadly, Nature.[15]

Where we can trace, as early as 1921 in *The Divine Initiative*, Mackintosh's insistence on the need to see Jesus Christ as the expression of God's revelatory action towards mankind rather than an expression of man's religiosity, we can

---

[10] *The Doctrine of the Person of Christ*, p. 526.
[11] *The Doctrine of the Person of Christ*, p. 294.
[12] *The Doctrine of the Person of Christ*, pp. 298-99.
[13] *The Doctrine of the Person of Christ*, p. 511.
[14] *The Doctrine of the Person of Christ*, p. 374.
[15] H. R. Mackintosh, *The Christian Apprehension of God*, SCM, London, 1929, p. 42.

also identify a reason for Mackintosh's amenability to Barth's *krisis* theology, his appreciation of which is expressed most fully in his final work, *Types of Modern Theology*.[16] In a similar manner, Torrance's search has been for an understanding of God's revelation which, as in the study of science, was open to empirical analysis. As Mackintosh sought to form a presentation of the Gospel appropriate to the philosophical and cultural milieu of his time, we find also in Torrance's work a wrestling with the legacy of nineteenth century liberal thought and the need to declare the certitudes of Christianity in a manner appropriate to a scientific age. In this quest after an understanding of an objectively revealed God, we can recognise the help Torrance found in the teaching of Karl Barth.

Barth's *Der Römerbrief*, first published in 1919, marked a turning point in dogmatic thinking and methodology. Barth's fundamental thesis was that the transcendent God reveals Himself to us only in and through the Incarnation. This thesis Barth would pursue throughout his prolific writings. Such change or development as can be traced in Barth's writings was but a transition in interest from investigating the nature of that divine transcendence made manifest through the Incarnation to an exploration, in Barth's later writings, into the implications of God's revelation and salvific economy towards mankind as it is found in the mediation of the One, Triune God in the event of the Incarnation. Barth stressed the social immanence of the Trinity within God's own transcendent Being; and that theophany, which is always a Christophany, made apparent through the central event of God's self disclosure in and through Christ Jesus.

In his *Prolegomena* to *Church Dogmatics*, we see how Barth is at pains to establish the Oneness of God in Trinity. That God is an Immanent Trinity is fundamental to the revelation of His nature, which can only be perceived by us as we meet with the revelation of His One Being.[17] It is when God is recognised by us in His unity and otherness that the way is opened for a proper understanding of God as Trinity.[18] Where, then, did this leave Barth's understanding of the Holy Spirit, given this emphasis on God's transcendent, ontological unity? In Barth's own words,

---

[16] Mackintosh did not have the opportunity to develop further his thinking in this area.

[17] 'As regards the name, Father, Son, and Holy Spirit, we have to distinguish *alius - alius - alius*, but not *aliud - aliud - aliud*, as if it were a case of parts of a whole or individuals of a species...It is a case, with the so called "Persons", of a *repetitio aeternitatis in aeternitate*; therefore not of a threeness of eternity *extra se*, but of a threeness of eternity *in se*'. K. Barth, *Church Dogmatics*, Vol. 1, Part 1, translated by G. T. Thomson, T & T Clark, Edinburgh, 1936, p. 402.

[18] 'It is to the one single essence of God, which is not to be tripled by the doctrine of the Trinity, but emphatically to be recognised in its unity, that there also belongs what we call today the "personality of God"...[a concept which, of itself] is a product of the struggle against modern naturalism and pantheism.' *Church Dogmatics*, Vol. 1, Part 1, p. 403.

Manifestation must be added as something special, as a special act of the Father or the Son or both, to the givenness of the revelation of the Father in the Son... This special element in revelation is undoubtedly identical with what the NT usually calls the Holy Spirit, as the subjective side in the event of revelation.[19]

The impact of this perspective on pneumatology would be significant. Barth's reaffirmation of the total transcendence and unknowability of God, qualified by the event of the Incarnation alone, would reinforce the necessity of holding a Christocentric focus to all our theology, with an equivalent reappraisal of the Spirit's place in the economy of God. This, in Barth's thinking, was doubtless as much a reaction against a misconstruction of the nature of 'Spirit', the *Geist* of Hegelian thought,[20] as it was a desire to recapture the centrality of Jesus as the basis of a truly theocentric theology and to provide a legitimate basis for our speech about and understanding of God. This method, however, formed a predisposition not to focus directly on the Person and function of the Holy Spirit. To do so might have risked detracting from the ontological and epistemological focus we are called to in the Incarnation.

The effect of Barth on Torrance, as the latter sought to reaffirm the central dogmas of Christian faith in a manner amenable to modern, scientific enquiry, has been considerable. Torrance shares Barth's radical Christocentricity, a focus which is evident in every area of Torrance's work. Our primary interest lies in tracing how this radical Christocentricity shapes Torrance's understanding of the Spirit's Person and function in three central components of his theology: God's self-revelation as Trinity, the soterial relevance of the hypostatic union and the significance of the sacraments. We proceed to examine each of these in turn.

6.2   The Spirit and the Trinity

In the preface to his doctoral thesis, submitted in 1947 to the University of Basel, Torrance stated a belief that was to characterise his theological mission:

> It is my firm conviction that the misunderstanding of the Gospel which took place as early as the second century, with the consequent relapse into non Christian ideas, has resulted in a doctrine that is largely unbiblical, and that has been only

---

[19] *Church Dogmatics*, Vol. 1, Part 1, p. 514.

[20] A reaction echoed by Torrance, who observes, 'We have the great error of modernism which finds the truth of salvation in the religious subject himself, and which identifies the Holy Spirit with the depths of man's own spirituality and personality. This has been accentuated in German thought by the fact that the word *Geist* stands both for the Spirit and for the reason, so that for a great deal of modern Protestant theology the Spirit of God means little more than subjective awareness of God or religious self understanding...'. T. F. Torrance, *Theology in Reconstruction*, SCM, London, 1965, p. 231.

partially corrected by the work of Augustine and the Reformers. The great mistake has been to detach the thought of grace from the *person* of Jesus Christ.[21]

It is in and through the person of Christ that we are met with by God and therefore can come to apprehend the reality of God and the character of God's gracious disposition towards us. The involvement of God in this act of Incarnation is complete, for in it we are faced with the act of God's self-commitment to mankind, through His personal intervention in human history in Christ.[22] For Torrance, not only the initiative but the total and final expression of God's grace is found in Christ Jesus.[23] This means that any focus by man upon God would be a false one, were it not centred on Christ alone. To seek after God the Father, or even the Holy Spirit, other than in and through Jesus Christ will produce a false focus and a consequent distortion in our understanding of God.[24] It is only to the One who is manifest in the flesh of Jesus Christ that we can look to find the reality of God.

Thus far, we might observe that Torrance's stress on the centrality of the Incarnation is not dissimilar to that of Edward Irving, in that both Torrance and Irving espouse a theology founded on the epistemological basis of *cognitio Dei Redemptoris*. Where they differ is in Torrance's insistence that this theophany which is evident in God's salvific economy in Christ is, in fact, eternally true of God in His immanent Being. We noted that Irving, despite his emphasis and focus on the Incarnation, did not proceed to affirm that the infinite reality of the Godhead becomes, through our participation in Christ's humanity, apprehended by us as He is in His immanent, Triune Being. The immanent Being of God remains, for Irving, ultimately strange to us. Torrance, on the other hand, insists that it is precisely because this theophany, which we meet with in the Incarnation, is true of God as He is in His infinite and immanent Being, that we can be assured that in our apprehension of and speech about God we are able to form an understanding of Him as He truly is. As Torrance states in *Space, Time and Incarnation*,

---

[21] T. F. Torrance, *The Doctrine of Grace in the Apostolic Fathers*, Oliver & Boyd, Edinburgh, 1948, p. v.

[22] 'God has personally intervened in human history in such a way that the ground of man's approach to God, and of all his relations with God, is not to be found in man's fulfilment of the divine command, but in a final act of self-commitment on the part of God in which He has given Himself to man through sheer love and in such a fashion that it cuts clean across all questions of human merit and demerit.' *The Doctrine of Grace in the Apostolic Fathers*, p. 21.

[23] *The Doctrine of Grace in the Apostolic Fathers*, p. 133.

[24] *The Doctrine of Grace in the Apostolic Fathers*, p. 139.

the Incarnation of the Son of God in the realm of space and time means that He assumes created truth and rationality and makes them His own although He is distinct from them.[25]

When we meet with God's salvific economy in Christ, we are faced with none other than the reiteration of God's eternal, immanent Being towards us. This has been made possible because the eternal Trinity has broken into the strictures of human rationality and containment in space and time through the event of the eternal Son's Incarnation. It is not that we can rationalise the Being of God because of this divine invasion: it is that God can declare Himself as He truly is, in His eternal Being, towards us. Torrance's theological perspective does not allow us to imagine that we might deduce the reality of the immanent, Triune Being of God from the event of the salvific economy. Torrance wishes rather to stress that the initiative lies not with our comprehension but with God's self-revelation. It is because God has embraced man that our perception of God, unveiled within His salvific economy, can arise. The Trinity in His salvific economy is the self-exposition of the Immanent Trinity in His grace towards man.

Given this Trinitarian perspective, two consequences follow for the manner in which we can speak of the Person and function of the Spirit. First of all, there can be no recognition by us of our meeting with the Spirit other than in and through the Son's meeting with us in the Incarnation. To say otherwise would be to deny the ontological priority of the Son's Incarnation and the declaration by God of that which He is towards us in Christ. The Spirit does nothing to detract our attention from the Son. As Torrance puts it in *God and Rationality*,

> By His very mode of being as Spirit He hides Himself from us so that we do not know Him directly in His own hypostasis ... Yet because it is through Him that the Word of God was made flesh and through Him that the Word continues to be heard and believed ... we know Him as no less Lord God than the Father and the Son.[26]

The second consequence which follows from Torrance's Trinitarian perspective is that our appreciation of the Spirit in God's salvific economy arises from that reiteration of God, as He is in His immanent Being, in His salvific economy. The Spirit expounds to us our relationship to the Father which is brought about through the Son. In so doing, the Spirit demonstrates His own part in that relationship as *vinculum Trinitatis*. Torrance presents the perception of the Spirit as *vinculum Trinitatis* as a revelation of God's immanent Being which is made apparent to us in and through Christ's soterial mission. It is through our meeting with and participating with God in Christ that we come to participate

---

[25] T. F. Torrance, *Space, Time and Incarnation*, OUP, London, 1969, p. 65.
[26] T. F. Torrance, *God and Rationality*, OUP, London, 1971, p. 167.

in the Spirit. We find this clearly illustrated in a sermon broadcast by Torrance on radio in 1956, after Billy Graham's All Scotland Crusade. Torrance desires to root the Christian disciple in an appreciation of the prevenient grace of God focused on Christ: he speaks of God's grace and His love in Jesus as being one and the same thing. From this, there follows his understanding of the Holy Spirit:

> The communion of the Spirit means that we are yoked together with Jesus Christ in love, and for ever made to share with Him in the riches of His grace and in the love of God. Apart from union with Christ through the power of the Holy Spirit, all that the Gospel has to say of the grace of the Lord Jesus and the love of God would be useless to you. The communion of the Spirit is the bond of love which actually binds us to God and makes us share in the grace of Jesus Christ. If you wish to enter, or enter more fully, into this communion of the Spirit....pray that the Lord Jesus will bring you into living communion with Him. When you do that you will find that He will come and breathe His Spirit upon you and give you to share in the riches of His grace and in the eternal love of God.[27]

Torrance here expounds clearly the practical implications of the eternal *vinculum Trinitatis*. We come to participate in the Spirit because God in Christ has reached out and joined Himself to us. Our participation in the Spirit is therefore to be understood, not as separated from or consequential to our relationship to Christ, but as integral thereto, even as the Spirit is eternally and inseparably united to the Son in the immanent Triunity of the Godhead.

Torrance insists that there can be no recognition by us of our meeting with the Spirit other than in and through the Son's meeting with us in the Incarnation. This, combined with his understanding of the *vinculum Trinitatis* as revelatory of God's immanent Being, leads him to affirm the importance of the *Filioque* clause within the Nicene-Constantinopolitan creed in clarifying 'the Lordship of the Spirit and the propriety of the Spirit to the Son'.[28] Such an emphasis on the self-exposition of God serves as an antidote to that tendency in liberal thought to tear apart the Spirit from the Son, confusing the Holy Spirit with man's spirit and substituting eternal verities with human predilections. Our meeting with the Spirit is clearly set in the context of the Spirit as bond between the Father and the Son.

One further aspect relating to our awareness of the Spirit's working should be noted at this point. While it is because of the Incarnation that humanity has access to participation in the Spirit, Torrance's understanding is that a proper appreciation of this participation can arise only by our looking, not to the Spirit's action upon ourselves, but to Jesus. The action of the Spirit calls us to focus attention outwith ourselves and upon Jesus:

---

[27] T. F. Torrance, 'A Sermon on the Trinity', in *Biblical Theology*, 6, (1956), p. 44.

[28] T. F. Torrance, *Theology in Reconstruction*, p. 229.

We are to think of the work of the Spirit ... as opening us up within our subjectivities for Christ in such a radical way that we find our life not in ourselves but out of ourselves, objectively in Him ... This is the objectivity that will not allow us to confuse the Holy Spirit with our own spirits, or to confound his objective activity with our own subjective states.[29]

Consequently, our perception of the Spirit's Person and function has to be interpreted in terms of the Spirit's action in and on the life of Christ.

6.3   The Spirit and the Hypostatic Union

In our analysis of Irving's pneumatology, we detected a potential difficulty in Irving's understanding of the relationship of the Son of God to the Spirit within the earthly ministry of Jesus. For Irving, the focus of divine activity lay in the work of the Holy Spirit, active upon and within Christ's humanity. Other than as providing an enabling role in establishing the hypostatic union, the person of the Son of God within the hypostatic union is not perceived by Irving as relevant to the ongoing earthly ministry of Christ. Through the Incarnation the Son of God enables the Spirit to be active in the life of Christ as man. The Spirit sustains and enables Christ's humanity to walk in conformity to the will and purposes of God. Likewise, in the resurrection, the marriage of divinity to humanity in the hypostatic union allows Christ's humanity to be raised to eternal communion with the Trinity. The main focus for Irving lies, however, in the ministry of the Holy Spirit upon Christ's humanity. Irving interpreted Christ's divinity as serving the role of catalyst for the Spirit's action upon humanity.

In this approach, Irving offered an interpretation of the *communicatio idiomatum* which was, in one sense, clearer than that which was inherited within Scottish Reformed theology from Westminster Calvinism. As we noted in chapter 3, Calvin assigned some properties of Christ to His divinity, some to his humanity and some to both; and this analysis was reiterated in the *Westminster Confession*. Such distinctions within the hypostatic union did, however, herald the danger of inviting further, unwelcomed distinctions between the full participation of the Son of God within the Immanent Trinity and the nature of His presence within the soterial event of the Incarnation.

For Torrance, any distinction made between the Son of God's status within the Immanent Trinity and that revealed in the hypostatic union would be quite unacceptable. The Son of God, in His participation in the salvific economy, was there as fully present as the Son of God as He is in the eternal, immanent Triunity of God's Being. To say otherwise would be to deny the central tenet of Torrance's theology, that the Trinity in salvific economy is none other than God's immanent Being expounded to man in grace. Torrance required to take

---

[29] *Theology in Reconstruction*, p. 238.

the doctrine of the two natures and reaffirm it in a manner that overcame Mackintosh's criticism of the `rigid abstract shape given it by tradition`. The way Torrance overcame this difficulty was by developing the radical Christocentricity which he had learnt from Barth.

Torrance saw that it was not enough to look at the hypostatic union as a static event. The Incarnation stood for the becomingness of God towards man, in that God opened Himself in vulnerability by His total commitment in the Son's soterial mission, which was equally - because of the *vinculum Trinitatis* - the commitment of the Father and the Spirit towards man. The Incarnation represented the dynamic self-giving of the Triune God towards man. At the same time, the humanity which the Son of God assumed was representative of all mankind's humanity. The hypostatic union therefore represented the lifting up of humanity, from incarnation through to resurrection and ascension, into communion with the very Being of God. Consequently, the hypostatic union and *communicatio idiomatum* should not be understood in rigid, abstract terms but in a dynamic, fluid sense. The Incarnation and all that follows in the life of Christ represents the dynamic action of God's declaration and commitment of His Being to man and of man's reciprocal response of surrender, obedience and participation in the purposes of God: and both of these, the self-giving of God to man and the responsive surrender of man to God, are fully manifested and declared to all in and through the person of Jesus Christ. Torrance succinctly explains it thus:

> Neither an approach to Jesus starting from his humanity, nor an approach starting from his deity, is in place: we must approach Jesus simultaneously on both levels in the space-time field in which he and we encounter each other; from the very start of our theological interpretation, therefore, we must learn to think conjunctively of him as God and man in the one indivisible fact of Jesus Christ.[30]

This aspect of divine and human reciprocity which is found in Christ is critical to our gaining a proper understanding of Torrance's pneumatology. In common with Irving, Torrance emphasises the inclusiveness of Christ's humanity as that humanity which is assumed by God on behalf of all mankind. In this regard, in their understanding of the dynamic movement of Christ's humanity in being taken up into communion with God, Irving and Torrance are at one. Where they differ is in their understanding of the other part of that equation, the dynamic movement of Christ's divinity towards man. For Irving, it is sufficient that the Son of God becomes incarnate, thereby allowing that the Spirit might have access to and communion with the humanity of Christ. Torrance, however, does not distinguish the divine action on the humanity of Christ in this way. The Incarnation does not simply open a venue, or means of access to humanity, for the Spirit. At all times there is but one action of God towards man which is

---

[30] T. F. Torrance, *Theology in Reconciliation*, Geoffrey Chapman, London, 1975, p. 281.

from the Father, through the Son and by the Spirit. The Spirit is never other, in God's salvific economy, than that which He is in God's immanent Being: the *vinculum Trinitatis*, reaching out to embrace humanity in the name of the Father and the Son. Rather than emphasise the function of the Spirit, as Irving did, Torrance seeks to maintain a focus upon Christ and to present the Spirit's activity within the context of the perichoretic, salvific economy of the Trinity. Consequently, Torrance is unwilling to seek to identify the action of the Spirit upon the humanity of Christ in any way that will detract from a central focus upon the dynamic reciprocity between the Triune God and man which is expressed in the hypostatic union. As we saw illustrated in his 1956 radio broadcast, Torrance will not allow the Spirit to be spoken of other than as He who is active in man's union with God through Jesus Christ.

From a pneumatological perspective, the question that must arise from Torrance's understanding of the Spirit's activity within the hypostatic union is whether he has, in fact, anything distinctive to say at all regarding the Spirit. Torrance's focus lies upon the action of the Triune God manifest in the Son. We can participate in the Spirit only because Christ Himself has participated before us: in this sense, our interaction with the Spirit is consequential to our interaction with the Son, flowing from the hypostatic union of God and man in the Incarnation. We will return to this question later in the chapter: for the moment we note that Torrance's distinctive and dynamic interpretation of the hypostatic union leads to an understanding of the Spirit which is far less focal than that found in Irving.

6.4   The Spirit and the Sacraments

In seeking to trace an understanding of the Spirit's relationship to the sacraments in Calvin's thought, we noted the possibility of some tension arising between an emphasis on the suprarational nature of the Spirit's action in the sacraments and Calvin's understanding of the sacraments' facility as an aid towards the strengthening of faith. The legacy of Calvin faced us with the challenge of balancing an understanding of the Spirit's suprarational work with an understanding of the Spirit's function as an epistemic agent in the formation of a rational, cognitive faith. This tension appears to have been continued in the early development of Scottish theology where, as we saw from the *Scots Confession* and *Westminster Confession*, a theology of the sacraments is presented in both documents in such a manner that we are invited to embrace an understanding of the Spirit which assigns Him a suprarational function, as more than that of an epistemic agent; yet at the same time there is in both documents a stress on the Spirit's role in creating a rational and reasoned faith, centred not simply in the heart but formed clearly in the mind. This was not only the case among hyper-Calvinists, as with the authors of the *Sum of Saving Knowledge*. It was clear also from Irving's writings that the facility of the sacraments was seen to lie in their ability to declare the truth of God in Christ to man's senses. The sacraments, as with the Scriptures, expound Christ to us. Where Irving's approach differed from what had gone before was that he stressed the Spirit's work through both the sacraments and Scripture in calling us to focus on Christ Himself. Irving sought to overcome any tension between the suprarational character of the Spirit's action in the sacraments and the Spirit's epistemic agency in forming a rational, cognitive faith by emphasising that both these functions of the Spirit point us towards God's grace manifest in Christ.

This approach of Irving, in looking beyond the particular function of the Spirit towards that which is communicated in Christ Himself, to whom the sacraments testify and whose grace they signify, is found also in Torrance's writings. In presenting a theology of the sacraments, Torrance continues his mission of lifting our eyes to the activity of God's grace in the Incarnation, focusing our attention through and beyond the sacraments to gaze through 'sacramental transparence'[31] on Christ alone. Our interest in this section is to observe how Torrance develops his understanding of Christocentricity in the sacraments as a continuation of his polemic against the subjectivism which he sees arising not only in nineteenth century liberal theology but also in hyper-Calvinism.

For Torrance, the sacraments are validated by the Christ to whom they direct us in that both sacraments, baptism and the Lord's Supper, are appointed by God as 'the divinely instituted forms of human response vicariously provided in Jesus Christ'.[32] We are drawn to participate in the sacraments in that they are given to us by God in order that we might be drawn into that which Christ has done on our behalf. Here, we are reminded of the hypostatic union and the response of Christ's humanity to God's act of grace in the Incarnation of the Son of God. It is that which Christ has fulfilled on behalf of all humanity within the hypostatic union, in the dynamic of God's gracious self-giving towards man and man's freely-given response to God, which the sacraments speak of and invite us to participate in. This can be illustrated by looking in greater detail at Torrance's understanding of the two sacraments.

The act of baptism speaks, above all else, of the baptism undergone by Christ in His vicarious humanity. For a Christian to be baptised is, fundamentally, not a statement concerning that Christian's faith or condition but a statement about what Christ has done on behalf of that person and all humanity. By this we come to understand that the action of the Spirit which is married to the sacrament of baptism is there not because of any latent, spiritual power in the sacrament itself, but because of what has occurred in Christ's life, in Christ's reception of the Spirit at His baptism in the Jordan. Because Christ received the Spirit in His baptism, we receive the Spirit in our baptism out of our participation in Christ's humanity: Christ receives the Spirit 'actively and

---

[31] *Theology in Reconstruction*, p. 258.
[32] T. F. Torrance, *The Mediation of Christ*, Paternoster Press, Exeter, 1983, p. 99.

vicariously as Redeemer, the Church passively and receptively as the redeemed Community'.[33] Here again, we see how Torrance will not allow us to speak of the grace of God or determine an act of the Spirit which is other than rooted in the person of Christ. For Torrance, it is critical to our understanding of baptism that the Spirit is manifest upon Christ at the point of Christ's clear identification with sinners. It is at the point of Christ's identification with us that we can receive the Spirit, for the Spirit will testify to none other than Christ. In this sense, it is Christ and not the Spirit who is baptism's 'material content and its active agent'.[34]

Torrance's theology of baptism is that the sacrament is a visible exposition of the Spirit's place as *vinculum Trinitatis*, the Spirit united to us through Christ's identification with us in His baptism. This is not to say that the sacrament of baptism, because of its transparency, becomes an empty symbol. Where baptism signifies what Christ has done, the sacrament actively enrols us into union with Christ. Because the Spirit is present with Christ in His baptism, we are called to realise the Spirit's presence with us in our baptism as we are identified with the Christ who has so fully identified with us. Through the Spirit's presence we 'enter into the inheritance of Christ'.[35] The Spirit, in baptism, thereby works to actualise in us that which Christ has done and to enable us to participate with Christ in His union with the Father.[36]

Likewise, in the Lord's Supper, we are faced with no mystery there signified other than the mystery of Christ Himself.[37] The Lord's Supper is truly eucharistic, a thanksgiving act, in that we there participate in celebrating that which Christ has vicariously undertaken on behalf of all. Because the Lord's Supper is a celebration of Christ Himself we can affirm His real presence with us in the sacrament, for in participating in this act of thanksgiving we do so as those who, having been baptised, participate with Christ in all things. As Torrance puts it,

> union with Jesus Christ in his vicarious humanity and participation in his vicarious self-offering to the Father must constitute the fundamental determinants in our understanding of both the real presence and the eucharistic sacrifice.[38]

Once again, as we saw in Torrance's interpretation of the hypostatic union, it is the whole, dynamic action of Christ's humanity, as it is lifted through the Son in the *vinculum Trinitatis* of the Spirit to the Father, that we celebrate in the Lord's Supper and of which we are participants. Our participation is not limited to a celebration of our union with the humanity of Christ: at this point we see

---

[33] *Theology in Reconciliation*, p. 87.
[34] *Theology in Reconciliation*, p. 84.
[35] *Theology in Reconciliation*, p. 84.
[36] *Theology in Reconciliation*, p. 100.
[37] *Theology in Reconciliation*, p. 106.
[38] *Theology in Reconciliation*, pp. 111-12.

the difference between Torrance and Irving. Irving emphasised that our participation with the Triune God is effected in the Lord's Supper through sharing in Christ's common humanity and the Spirit's activity within that humanity. For Torrance, in the dynamic reciprocity of Christ's vicarious life there is both the divine initiative and the human response. Our participation in the Lord's Supper is both with God and man in Christ, for it is only through our participation with the whole Trinity's self-giving in Christ that we have any participation with God through the vicarious humanity of Christ. The Lord's Supper signifies not only our participation with Christ's humanity but also our being taken up, in the *vinculum Trinitatis*, in the Son's communion with the Father through the Spirit:

> Our participation through the Spirit [is] in what the whole Christ, the incarnate, crucified, risen and ascended Son, is in himself in respect both of his activity from the Father towards mankind and of his activity from mankind towards the Father.[39]

It is because the Lord's Supper speaks so patently of the One who is God come to man and man brought to God that Torrance can speak of Christ, who has instituted the Lord's Supper, as being really present, bringing us into participation with the Spirit.[40] Indeed, so absolute is this commitment of Christ to His sacrament that Torrance would have us understand the Lord's Supper as being, until Christ's parousia, 'the form of his actual and active presence among us'.[41] Our participation in the sacrament is the measure of our participation with Christ prior to the *eschaton*.[42] Consequently, we can say that our participation in the Spirit is found through our participation with Christ: in the Lord's Supper we fully participate in the Spirit:

> such an immediate self-giving of God to us in his own divine Being and life through Jesus Christ must be understood as one that takes place in the Holy Spirit who is not just an emanation from God but the immediate presence and activity of God in his own divine Being, the Spirit of the Father and the Son, himself the Lord and giver of life.[43]

With such an understanding of the sacrament's presentation of Christ - and thereby the Triune God - to us, it comes as no surprise to find Torrance

---

[39] *Theology in Reconciliation*, p. 109.
[40] 'It is Christ himself who is really present pouring out his Spirit upon us, drawing us into the power of his vicarious life'. *Theology in Reconciliation*, p. 107.
[41] *Theology in Reconciliation*, p. 120.
[42] T. F. Torrance, *Space, Time and Resurrection*, Handsel Press, Edinburgh, 1976, p. 149.
[43] *Theology in Reconciliation*, p. 132.

speaking of the sacraments as proclaiming in act[44] the Gospel to man. In the sacraments the objectivity of the Gospel is secured. The sacraments, in communicating Christ, are truly evangelical and may properly be described as 'converting ordinances', for through them we are drawn into the life of Christ and His eternal communion with the Triune God.[45] In his interpretation of the sacraments, Torrance allows no room for either liberal or evangelical subjectivity. Torrance will not even allow us to speak of our own faith, for even that must arise in us out of Christ's vicarious faith: it is not I, but Christ in me that has faith.[46]

From the perspective of our study, there are problems that arise from Torrance's approach. As demonstrated in his radically Christocentric interpretation of the sacraments, Torrance will not allow us to discuss the Spirit's activity within or among us, other than in terms of our inclusion in Christ's vicarious humanity. It is not enough to say that the Spirit leads us to Christ: such a preparatory act of the Spirit would involve some appeal to our human subjectivity, which Torrance will not allow. There is no meeting with the Spirit for man other than in the event of God's meeting with man in the Incarnation. In the vocabulary of our thesis, Torrance would have us say that our personal realisation of the Spirit and experience of the Spirit in His ontic actuality must arise out of and remain as a consequence of the Son of God's soterial mission. There is, for Torrance, no parallel ontic actuality of the Spirit to be set alongside that of the Son. Our meeting with the ontic actuality of the Spirit must come in and through our participation with the ontic actuality of the Son, the Spirit always being the *vinculum Trinitatis*.

In Torrance's theology of the sacraments we meet with a pneumatology which is consistent with both his Trinitarian focus and interpretation of the hypostatic union. Torrance's radical Christocentricity causes him to insist that there is no knowledge of the Trinity outwith our knowing of Christ; and no knowing of Christ other than as He who is God come to man and man taken to God. Consequently, there can be no experience of the Spirit's ontic actuality other than through our participation in Christ. Having identified this approach to the Spirit's Person and function by Torrance, we can now proceed to investigate the strengths and weaknesses of Torrance's case and to note its implications for the development of an appropriate Trinitarian model.

6.5   The Person and Function of the Spirit

In chapter 3 we argued that Calvin, developing an epistemology out of the *duplex cognitio Dei*, focused on an epistemological centre in Christ, from whom we gain a *cognitio Dei Redemptoris*. The primary function of the Spirit,

---

[44] *The Mediation of Christ*, p. 105.

[45] *The Mediation of Christ*, p. 107.

[46] *The Mediation of Christ*, pp. 107-8.

as an epistemic agent, was more clearly identified with the complementary *cognitio Dei Creatoris*. We then developed our thesis to note that while the epistemic agency of the Spirit appeared to be the Spirit's primary function, two other functions were apparent. The first of these appeared to be a suprarational work of the Spirit which was associated with the operation of the sacraments. We noted that this function appeared to complement, in an ancillary manner, a primary emphasis on the Spirit's epistemic agency. In addition to these two functions of the Spirit, we further deduced a third, arising from Calvin's method in dealing with the question of election. That is, we noted the Spirit depicted as the executor of God's elective decision. We argued that these three functions of the Spirit - the epistemic agency, the suprarational work of the Spirit and the Spirit as the executor of God's elective decision - were all treated as distinguishable from the Person, or Being, of the Spirit. Rather than emphasise the Being or ontic actuality of the Spirit, Calvin was seen to be more concerned with the Spirit's function. Moreover, we argued that this failure to focus on the Spirit's ontic actuality was paralleled by a further weakness in the manner in which Calvin viewed the Son's soterial mission. We found that Calvin did not sufficiently stress a full meeting with the Son's ontic actuality in and through the Incarnation, citing the *extra Calvinisticum* and Calvin's understanding of the *communicatio idiomatum* as illustrative of a Trinitarian theology which preferred to construe the Son's Being not in terms of His economy but in relation to God's immanent Being. Calvin's understanding of the Being of both the Son and the Spirit appeared to arise from his acceptance of the Western model of the Trinity rather than from any further exploration into alternative models of the ontic actuality of the Son and the Spirit, arising from the Triune God's salvific economy.

In Torrance we find a compelling, alternative approach to Calvin, in viewing the Person and function of the Spirit within a Trinitarian framework. By centring his theology on the Incarnation and the revelation of the Trinity, which is manifest through the dynamic interaction of God and man in Christ's hypostatic union, Torrance brings the focus firmly back onto the ontic actuality of the Son which is made manifest to us in and through the Incarnation alone. For Torrance, it is still the Immanent Trinity that is looked to; yet God in His immanence cannot be understood outwith the Son's Incarnation. The Immanent Trinity cannot be spoken of other than in relation to the salvific economy of God that issues in Christ. Furthermore, through our union with Christ we meet also with the Being of the Spirit, the *vinculum Trinitatis*, in the communion of the Father with the incarnate Son. Consequently, we find that for Torrance there can be no clear distinction introduced as to the separate functions of the Spirit: for we meet fully with the ontic actuality of the Spirit in our union with Christ. Torrance brings together all three functions of the Spirit which we deduced in Calvin; and roots them in the Being of the Spirit, whom we meet with and are embraced by through our union with God in Christ. In this, we might favourably compare Torrance to Irving. Irving attempted to hold together the functions of the Spirit's epistemic agency and suprarational work, through a focus on Christ's common humanity; yet the Spirit's function as executor of God's elective decision was held apart from these, hidden in the mystery of God's transcendent will. There is no such hidden, transcendent function of the Spirit for Torrance. Following Barth, Torrance views election not in an individualistic sense, but as arising out of the inclusiveness of Christ's humanity, the elect man for all men. Our election is not hidden in the Father's will but is made patent to us in Christ. By emphasising our communion with the Being of the Spirit as arising from our union with Christ, Torrance sustains all three functions of the Spirit - the epistemic agency, the suprarational work of the Spirit and the Spirit as executor of God's elective decision - within the one focus upon Christ. All that the Spirit effects in us and for us arises out of our meeting with His Being through our communion in Christ.

With such an emphasis placed on the Being of the Spirit met with in Christ, does this mean that Torrance has no use for functional distinctions regarding the Spirit's Being and operation? We have already noted how the Christian's election is, for Torrance, to be interpreted as occurring within Christ's election. Outwith this Christocentric context, we cannot speak of an elective work of the Spirit. Likewise, any attempt at distinguishing between an epistemic agency and suprarational work of the Spirit becomes largely redundant for, in one sense, all the action of the Spirit is suprarational, in that He animates within us the revelation of God that is in and through Christ alone. As Torrance puts it,

> We are prevented from entertaining a notion of the Spirit as the rational principle that informs all things with order or imparts to human being form from out of Himself... Rather we must think of the Spirit as actualizing within creation its bond of union with the *Logos*.[47]

As the Spirit is at work within us and as we are faced with the testimony of Scripture and 'sacramental transparence', it is Christ that we are brought to focus upon, the Spirit bringing us to be conscious of Christ alone: the Spirit 'hides Himself from us so that we do not know Him directly in His own hypostasis'.[48]

While Torrance does not stress any particular function of the Spirit, his understanding of the manner of the Spirit's effect upon us is significant. The anonymity of the Spirit is, for Torrance, so complete that we cannot identify the ontic actuality of the Spirit other than in terms of the Spirit's testimony to Christ. We have already noted that, for Torrance, there must be no room allowed for human subjectivity: we would not expect Torrance to subscribe to the notion that any subjective, human phenomena might alert us to the Spirit's presence and activity, other than through the assurance of the Spirit's presence

---

[47] *God and Rationality*, p. 172.
[48] *God and Rationality*, p. 167.

in the dominically instituted sacraments. Torrance is not willing to suggest any effect of the Spirit which does not point past the Spirit's own anonymous, ontic actuality to the inherent rationality and order that lies at the heart of the Triune God's self-revelation, in and through the Incarnation of the Son, the Word of God. The action of the Spirit, married to the Incarnation of the Word, testifies to the inherent rationality at the heart of God's self revelation in and through the Word. Through the *vinculum Trinitatis*, the suprarational work of the Spirit brings us into communion with God through the inherent rationality of the Word made flesh in Christ. Thus, although our communion with the Spirit can be described as suprarational, through the Spirit we are led to the inherent rationality of the Son's Incarnation. We are thereby led towards 'objective cognitive content'.[49]

For Torrance, the requirement of sustaining an objective Christocentricity means that our communion with the Spirit, while being understood in terms of the Spirit's Being and not His function, testifies to the inherent rationality of the Son. As such, although it is not the epistemic agency of the Spirit that is highlighted by Torrance, we might well ask whether the final effect of Torrance's method is, essentially, any different from the emphasis on the epistemic agency of the Spirit which we traced in Calvin, in that it is the cognitive or rational content of God's self-revelation that is here emphasised. More than that, it gives rise to a further question. Given that Torrance's pneumatology arises out of our communion with the Spirit in Christ and that he does not seek to develop, independent of Christ, an understanding as to the function of the Spirit, how can we seek to speak in any way of the Spirit's ontic actuality as distinct from that of the Son? Torrance's answer is that we cannot: nor should we attempt to. We can only speak of participation in the Spirit in terms of Jesus' own participation in the Spirit. At the same time, this participation is not simply vicarious. Through the Spirit's action, our lives are further orientated to the life of Christ:

> We are to think of the work of the Spirit not simply as the actualizing within us of what God has already wrought for us in Jesus Christ once and for all, but as opening us up within our subjectivities for Christ in such a way that we find our life not in ourselves but out of ourselves, objectively in him.[50]

Where we do not attempt to split off the Spirit from Christ, and thereby seek to alienate the work of the Spirit from our meeting with God through the vicarious humanity of Christ, Torrance would allow us to seek to identify the presence and work of the Spirit which arises from our inclusion in Christ: yet such a mission ultimately can only bring us back to a deeper and truer communion with and consciousness of Christ.

---

[49] *God and Rationality* p. 17.
[50] *Theology in Reconstruction*, p. 238.

6.6   Critique

Should Torrance's interpretation of the Spirit's Person and function be correct, it would follow that the perception of the Spirit which we deduced as present among advocates of the Charismatic Movement in Scotland would be untenable. To speak, as we did in chapter 1, of the primary means of our realising the ontic actuality of the Spirit as being through our experience would be unacceptable. For Torrance, our meeting with the Spirit can only be understood in terms of our participation in the humanity of the Son and the Spirit's witness to this fact. Such a meeting with God cannot properly be defined as suprarational or lacking the possibility of rational explication, for the substantive content of the meeting is not the Spirit but Christ, the Son of God Incarnate. Moreover, Torrance's emphasis on the need to sustain the objectivity of God's dealing with us, free from any contingency upon our own subjective perspective, is antithetical to our suggestion in chapter 1 that a Charismatic perspective on the Spirit prioritises a suprarational experience of God, allowing a rational, cognitive faith to arise as a consequence of the Spirit's suprarational work.

In the light of our earlier overview of Patristic pneumatology, we can view this conflict of perspectives in a different way. In chapter 2 we argued that a characteristic of the pre-Nicene model of the Trinity was a parallel emphasis upon the ontic actuality of both the Son and the Spirit. In this model, the Son's ontic actuality is expressed in the Incarnation, the Spirit's ontic actuality being understood as actualised along with that work of the Son which is in and through the Incarnation, yet the Spirit's work remaining peculiarly His own and not confused with that of the Son. This pre-Nicene model of the Trinity invites comparison with the theological framework that, as we suggested in chapter 1, was representative of an understanding of the Spirit present within the Charismatic Movement. Both the pre-Nicene model and the Charismatic perspective would perceive the ontic actuality of the Spirit as complementary to yet distinct from the ontic actuality of the Son, expressed in the Son's soterial mission. Likewise, Torrance's approach to pneumatology finds a parallel in Athanasius' stress upon the Son as *homoousios* with the Father, the event of the Son's Incarnation affording the basis for our apprehension of God. For Athanasius, as with Torrance, this sets the basis of our interaction with God and our appreciation of His ontological nature within the context of the Son's Incarnation: yet with Athanasius, we noted the difficulty that could arise from a sharper focus on the Incarnation was a possible obscuring of the Spirit's ontic actuality within our immediate experience. Could the same be true of Torrance and do the questions, raised in chapter 2, regarding the reservations which need to be expressed over Athanasius' theology, equally apply to Torrance? Does Torrance takes sufficiently seriously the ontic actuality of the Holy Spirit; or does his radical Christocentricity actually rob him of a properly Trinitarian perspective, as we might seek to understand it in terms of the pre-Nicene model?

For Torrance the critical centre of theology must lie with the Incarnation and the affirmation of both the Son's relationship to the Father, the *homoousion* which Athanasius stated in the fourth century and Barth reaffirmed in the twentieth century;[51] and the Son's relationship with man, as expressed in Torrance's interpretation of the hypostatic union. Nothing should detract from the centre of theological enquiry afforded by the Incarnation, for the ontic actuality of the Son is the key to the development of Trinitarian theology. In chapter 2, while noting Torrance's conviction that Athanasius provides, through his focus on the event of the Son's Incarnation, a key to eternal relations and distinctions within the immanent Being of God, we argued that Athanasius did not in fact develop a model of the Trinity which combined an understanding of the incarnate Son's consubstantial relationship to the Father with a developed, ontological matrix of relationships between Father, Son and Holy Spirit. In contrast, we have seen that Torrance himself has succeeded in developing an integrated model of the Trinity. Torrance has avoided any misunderstanding over the Holy Spirit which might distract us from the objective centre of theology that lies with the Son and His Incarnation. His reason in doing so may be partly explained in that, where Athanasius addressed the threat of the Arian challenge, Torrance has sought to respond to the erosive effects on Christian dogma of liberal theology. Torrance will not allow the priority of Christ as the epistemic centre to our knowledge of God to be endangered by opening a way for a return to that subjectivity which was found in liberal theology. Torrance's polemic against liberal theology has, consequently, prevented him from exploring that aspect of experience - suprarational experience and not simply subjective experience - which might properly belong to an understanding of the Spirit's ontic actuality.

In the next chapter we will compare two Scottish theologians who, in contrast to Torrance, have in some measure formed their theological framework and pneumatological perspectives by way of a response to the call of the Charismatic Movement to address, in a fresh way, how the Person and function of the Holy Spirit may be affirmed within a Trinitarian framework.

---

[51] T. F. Torrance, *Karl Barth: Biblical and Evangelical theologian*, T & T Clark, Edinburgh, 1990, pp. 160ff..

Chapter 7

Tom Smail and James Dunn

7.1 Introduction

In this chapter of our study we come to examine the work of two theologians, both with Scottish roots, who have attempted to develop an understanding of the Person and function of the Holy Spirit. Tom Smail and James Dunn are of interest to us not simply because of their Scottish origins but because they have approached this task in contrasting ways. Smail has chosen an explicitly Trinitarian framework, continuing to develop the Western model of the Trinity and seeking to elucidate the significance, for us, of immanent relations within God's Triune Being. Dunn takes as his starting point the experience of the Spirit within the life of Jesus, seeking to develop and explore the significance of this for our own experience and understanding of God. In turning to Smail and Dunn we look to two theologians who have sought to explore the possibilities of what, in chapter 1, we observed to be contrasting approaches to pneumatology raised in the debate over the Charismatic Movement in Scotland. That is, on the one hand, a Trinitarian model which starts from a suppositional understanding of the Immanent Trinity and, on the other, one which seeks to speak of God out of the context of human experience of the Holy Spirit. Having offered in this present chapter a critique of Smail and Dunn, we will then proceed, in the final chapter of this study, to explore the possibility of an alternative way forward, drawing on observations we have made in Patristic pneumatology and developments in Scottish pneumatology. There we will seek to develop a Trinitarian model which expresses the perception of the Spirit which we identified as belonging to the Charismatic Movement in Scotland and which can be perceived as lying within the parameters of the catholic faith of the Christian church.

7.2 Tom Smail

Canon Tom Smail, possibly more than any other figure we have mentioned, demonstrates an evolving, Trinitarian perspective on pneumatology that has been shaped on the anvil of the Charismatic Movement's development from the early 1960s until the present day. Now a retired Anglican canon, Smail was actively engaged in the parish ministry of the Church of Scotland from 1953 to

1968. Smail identifies his formative Charismatic experience as occurring during a period of his ministry at Wishaw: Thornley Church, from 1962-68.[1] His background and theological training are both Scottish and Reformed. Smail's three main publications, *Reflected Glory* (1975), *The Forgotten Father* (1980) and *The Giving Gift* (1988), reflect the interaction of this background with the development of the Charismatic Movement. The significance of these works of critical reflection to our study is enhanced when we recall Smail's contribution both to the early development of the Charismatic Movement in Scotland and, later, as Director of the Fountain Trust.[2] In looking at Smail, we will try to understand the context within which his theology takes shape, identifying the emphases which have remained constants in his thought and also trace the correctives that he has introduced to his understanding of the Spirit and the Trinity, as his perception has changed.

Smail's first book, *Reflected Glory*, was published at the height of the Charismatic Movement and, for Smail, at the point of his deepest involvement as the director of the Fountain Trust. This work, while carrying emphases which reflected his perspective as it was in the mid 1970s, also laid out features which can be traced as central throughout the development of his thought. These features are threefold: the sovereign character of God's prevenient Grace, the corporate context within which the Spirit operates and the conviction that theology is properly Trinitarian, with a Christocentric focus.

7.2.1 The Sovereign Character of God's Prevenient Grace

From the first, Smail's understanding was that men and women receive God's gift of salvation through faith, and that this is the result of a sovereign act of God. It is God, not the believer, who takes the initiative.[3] In this respect, Smail was aware that his perception, which he sees as reflecting his Scottish background, clashed with the deeply Arminian roots of the Pentecostals.[4] Indeed one of the reasons given by him for the styling of the Holy Spirit as, in the title to his third book, *The Giving Gift*, was that it helped convey that the Holy Spirit comes to us out of God's initiative, in no way contingent upon us.[5]

7.2.2 The Corporate Context within which the Spirit Operates

The primary context wherein the action of the Holy Spirit is realised is, for Smail, the church. The church is the *terminus ad quid* of the Spirit's operations.

---

[1] Recorded interview: 22 March 1990.
[2] By 1975 Smail had served as Director of the Fountain Trust for three years. In 1980 he had just left that position to teach theology. In 1988 he had been serving as an Anglican rector in the south of London for three years.
[3] T. A. Smail, *Reflected Glory: The Spirit in Christ and Christians*, Hodder & Stoughton, London, 1975, p. 82.
[4] Recorded interview: 22 March 1990.
[5] T. A. Smail, *The Giving Gift*, Hodder & Stoughton, London, 1988, pp. 17-22.

It is out of the church that the corporate context of the Spirit's mission is realised and the individual's experience of the Spirit is derived.[6] It is through and in the church as an identifiable, generic whole, that the Spirit's glory and presence is to be found:

> Not the individual 'I' but the corporate 'we' are being changed into Christ's likeness.[7]

For Smail, the individual's experience of the Spirit is secondary to the church as the context wherein the Spirit is active. In that the Spirit mirrors the glory of Christ, this can only adequately be mirrored in the church as a whole.[8] The Spirit does not relate to us in an isolated way, that can ever make the church a simple addendum to our individual Christian experience; rather, the Spirit leads us into a relatedness with the church around us.[9]

7.2.3 Theology as Trinitarian, with a Christocentric Focus

Through Smail's emphasis on the prevenience of grace and the priority of the church, we see a rejection of any individualistic philosophy which might emphasise the priority of human action or experience in establishing or verifying the work of God in our lives. Likewise, Smail is resolved to emphasise the ontological priority of God's immanent Triunity over our appreciation of God in His salvific economy. An appreciation of the truth of God, together with the inherent rationality that such truth contains, cannot simply arise out of human reason or theological formulation. On the contrary, it is God's revelation of Himself to us that allows the apprehension and comprehension of His reality to be formed within our understanding. From this perspective, Smail emphasises that theology should be both Trinitarian and Christocentric.

God can never be other than what He is towards us: in Smail's understanding, there is no distinction possible between a *Deus Revelatus*[10] and a *Deus Absconditus*.[11] What needs to be affirmed is that all we say of God in Himself must be faithful to God as He has shown Himself to be. This revelation is not contingent on our appreciation or experience of it: its truth, apprehensible to man, is objectively secured. This objectivity is anchored in the person of Jesus Christ. The phrase, 'Christ institutes, the Spirit constitutes'[12] conveys not only something of the necessary role of the Holy Spirit, but also the critical, ontological priority of the Incarnation in providing us with a point of reference

---

[6] *Reflected Glory*, p. 21.
[7] *Reflected Glory*, p. 126.
[8] *Reflected Glory*, p. 28.
[9] *The Giving Gift*, p. 185.
[10] 'God as revealed to us'.
[11] 'God absent or beyond our cognitive or experiential verification'.
[12] *The Giving Gift*, p. 191.

in our relationship to God. Where there is no knowledge of God but through the Incarnation, there is no God but He who is manifest as Trinity. For Smail, the great end of renewal is to bring the church into a deeper appreciation not simply of the Holy Spirit but of the Trinitarian God.[13]

In examining Smail's thought, we shall be reviewing why it is that he retains these three central pillars within his thesis. We begin, however, by looking at the shape of his thought as it appears to develop through the progression of his three books.

7.3   *Reflected Glory*

The publication of *Reflected Glory*, a work which affirmed the need for a Christocentric focus to Christian faith, came at a time when the crest of optimism over the Charismatic Movement was at its height in Scotland. There was, as we have seen, excitement and hope over what effect renewal might have. Furthermore, the Fountain Trust was well established in its work of promoting Renewal throughout the denominational church and Tom Smail was now its Director. That the Charismatic Movement would lead to the renewal of the church as a whole and not simply be identified as the aggregate of individuals who had entered into the Charismatic experience, and that it be seen as brought by God to awaken and inspire the whole body of Christ on earth: this was the evident hope expressed in Smail's first book. Where the earlier part of the Charismatic Movement had a Neo-Pentecostal emphasis on *glossolalia*, the focus now lay on the place of community: the church as the community of faith, fashioned by the Holy Spirit:[14] more than that, the church as the community which belongs to Jesus Christ, vivified by the Spirit in Jesus' name.[15]

It was on this catalyst of the church as Jesus' community, the creation of the Spirit, that Smail founded his understanding of the believers' experience of the Spirit. Where it is by the Spirit that the Christian is moved further towards Christ,[16] then to experience the Spirit is to experience the inheritance which is in the church and that comes from our union with Jesus Christ.

Smail's emphasis on the corporate dimension of the Spirit's work appeared to mirror the renewed emphasis, clearly being made within the Charismatic Movement at that time, upon the church as the context wherein we might identify the Spirit's activity. Additionally, however, it needs to be remembered that Smail also wrote as one raised in the Reformed tradition. This is reflected

---

[13] 'I want to see a Trinitarian renewal and not a Charismatic renewal.' Recorded interview: 20 March 1990.

[14] *Reflected Glory*, p. 128.

[15] *Reflected Glory*, p. 16.

[16] *Reflected Glory*, p. 13.

in the way he speaks of the mystery of the Spirit's presence within the church[17] and emphasises that it is through a rational, cognitive faith that the Spirit's presence is recognised. For Smail, it is faith that precedes and leads to experience, not experience that leads to faith.[18] More than that, faith and the concomitant experience of the Spirit are but the outward sign of God's election and our regeneration, which is wrought in us by God's grace alone.

Looked at another way, Smail's thesis allows us to affirm that the Spirit is active within us, in leading us to the point of faith: however, prior to faith, the Spirit remains anonymous and transparent. The view of Himself to which the Spirit leads us is that expressed in and through Christ alone. Smail, despite his support of the Charismatic Movement, will not allow faith to be derived from the individual's subjective experience. Experience is, indeed, valuable;[19] but faith remains rooted in our election by a sovereign God, whose Spirit moves anonymously in our lives, leading us to our appropriation of Christ by faith. That faith is a conscious, rational state of awareness.

Smail's emphasis on the importance of the church, Christ's community, as the *locus operandi* of the Holy Spirit, may have owed something to the influence of both a contemporary emphasis in the Charismatic Movement and his inherited Reformed perspective. There were, however, also contemporary pneumatological perceptions which Smail wanted to challenge, especially where he considered these to be the product of a theological disjunction which had been introduced between the work of Christ and that of the Spirit. This he found in the experientially conditioned theology of the Pentecostals. Pentecostalism appeared to Smail, in advocating two separate events of 'salvation' and 'baptism in the Spirit', to challenge his central tenet of God's singular, sovereign grace in and through Jesus as the only basis of man's salvation.[20] For Smail, it was evident that the doctrine of the Spirit needed to be viewed within another context, that of a proper understanding of Christ's vicarious humanity. Consequently, a parallel emphasis to the Spirit's action in the life of Christ should be identified for Christians: the church is identified as the *locus operandi* of the Spirit. The Spirit's work in the collective humanity of the Christian community is seen as derived from His work in the vicarious humanity of Jesus.[21] As the locus of the Spirit's action is found in the life of God's Son incarnate, so we understand that the Spirit at work in our humanity will always lead us further towards God's Son.

---

[17] *Reflected Glory*, pp. 36ff..

[18] 'What we do not believe in Christ we cannot go on to experience in Christ.' *Reflected Glory*, p. 29. 'Concentration on Christ, unveiled openness to Christ, faith in Christ ... puts us in the place where experience of Christ may start'. *Reflected Glory*, p. 82.

[19] 'The *object* of faith is Christ, but, because Christ is who he is and promises what he promises, the *end* of faith is experience'. *Reflected Glory*, p. 31.

[20] *Reflected Glory*, p. 47.

[21] *Reflected Glory*, p. 72.

In emphasising the derived nature of the church's communion with the Spirit, Smail presented his pneumatology within a framework consonant with the received Western model of the Trinity which, as we traced in Calvin through into the *Scots Confession* and *Westminster Confession*, emphasised the place of the church as the community of Christ, the *locus operandi* of the Spirit's operation, in the Spirit's reciprocal relationship of love between the Father and the Son. Emphasising with Irving and Torrance the importance of Christ's humanity, we can already identify at this stage of Smail's thought an understanding of the church as sharing the Son's relationship to the Father in so far as the Son has come to share the church's humanity. Implicit to Smail's understanding of the Spirit at work in the church is a view of the Spirit as *vinculum* between the Father and the Son.

A less typically Reformed perspective appeared in the second distinctive feature of Smail's thought at this time, in his understanding that there is within the economy of the Trinity an order of subordination. This does not involve a subordination of Being, but a subordination of function.[22] Here Smail sought to break with a perspective of God who, even in the Incarnation, stands over against and apart from a humanity which exists in the depravity of a sinful condition. True, the Spirit is ontologically inseparable from the Father and the Son; yet it is the Spirit who is the effective agent in creating an awareness of the Triune God within us, who shares in the same humanity which Christ took to Himself in the Incarnation.

This stress on the dynamic nature of God's salvific economy towards us, rooted in and through the Incarnation,[23] may well reflect the nature of Smail's own discovery of the Spirit's experienced reality in his own life in and through a personal sense of the Spirit's immediate action upon him: Smail does not comment on this. He does, however, stress the need to present God's revelation of Himself as a dynamic communication of His own Being towards us, in order to overcome a notion of God distant and remote. At the same time, Smail wishes to preserve a proper sense of God's 'otherness'.[24] Smail's concern was that the Charismatic Movement, in reacting to the notion of a distanced and remote Trinity, had instead deserted the reality of God's Trinitarian revelation for an experientially centred theology, insufficiently concerned with the functional priority of the Father: that is, of the Father whose desire the Son came to fulfil and whose will the Spirit executes.

7.4 *The Forgotten Father*

This sense of disquiet grew to fuller expression in Smail's second work, *The*

---

[22] *Reflected Glory*, p. 45.

[23] *Reflected Glory*, p. 26.

[24] Smail complains against 'a complacent and unambiguous identification of the Lord with his people.' *Reflected Glory*, p. 124.

Forgotten Father. Published shortly after Smail joined the staff of St. John's Nottingham, this book reflected something of Smail's disillusionment with the development of the Charismatic Movement in the later 1970s. What had been, for many, the hoped for integration of the Renewal within the historic churches had not occurred. On the contrary, there appeared to be growing cases of schism and the accompanying rise of new, independent Fellowships. In *The Forgotten Father*, Smail developed his Christocentric focus to place what he perceived to be a proper understanding of the Spirit within the context of the Incarnate Son's relationship to the Father. In so far as the Spirit is the harbinger of experience of God, that experience would have to be grounded in a proper understanding of the relationship between the Father and the Son.[25] In his first work, Smail had already established that the Incarnate Son's relation with the Holy Spirit was paradigmatic of our own experience of the Spirit,[26] the Spirit bringing to expression within the church the complete life of Christ.[27] Now that dynamic, of the Spirit's relation to us through the Son, was to be set in the fuller, Trinitarian context of the Son's relationship to the Father. Where Smail had earlier distanced himself from the Pentecostals, whom he had seen as driving a wedge between the Son and the Spirit, now he further sought to affirm the necessity of holding to a Christology which also fully stressed the Father-Son relationship; and that this Father-Son relationship should provide the context wherein experience of the Spirit is found and understood.[28] In this regard, Smail is rigorous in his assault on those theologians whose pneumatology he saw as having weakened this Father-Son perception of the Trinity. D. M. Baillie, among others, is perceived as failing to have emphasised that it is because Jesus is the Son of the Father that he can consequently be called the 'man full of grace'.[29]

While stressing the priority of the relation of Father-Son as the basis of our understanding of and participation with the Spirit, Smail is, at the same time, keen not to abandon his stress, seen in *Reflected Glory*, on the dynamic nature of God's salvific economy towards us. Appealing to Barth's exposition of both the ontological equality of the Father and the Son[30] and the reality of the Incarnation, Smail calls for 'a functional as against an ontological subordination'.[31] Where, however, in *Reflected Glory*, Smail would allow himself a description of the work of the Holy Spirit as 'only the last stage in a

---

[25] T. A. Smail, *The Forgotten Father*, Hodder & Stoughton, London, 1980, p. 25.
[26] 'He poured out the power of the Spirit on his own humanity in order that by the same Spirit it should be conveyed to ours.' *Reflected Glory*, p. 101.
[27] *Reflected Glory*, p. 106.
[28] *The Forgotten Father*, p. 104.
[29] *The Forgotten Father*, p. 97.
[30] *The Forgotten Father*, p. 106.
[31] *The Forgotten Father*, p. 107.

great divine descent',[32] he is now more careful to place his appreciation of the Spirit within the Father-Son relationship.[33] The ontological priority of the Triune God's immanent Being must be maintained, for the communion of the Father and the Son needs to be seen as an eternal one.[34]

To understand Smail's theological development here, we need to appreciate that, beyond the basic tenets which we have identified throughout his writings, his method can properly be described as reactive rather than as proactive. That is, like any theologian who addresses contemporary issues, his theology is seen to be shaped by his experience and reflection thereon. His affirmation, seen in *Reflected Glory*, that a Christocentric focus to our understanding of the Spirit need be asserted was, in some measure, an attempted corrective to the lack of theological reflection which characterised the Charismatic Renewal. Likewise, his purpose in *The Forgotten Father* was to bring a corrective to what he perceived to be a weakness, not only in the Charismatic Movement, but in theology as a whole: that is, the failure to give a proper place to the Father in seeking to explicate the relationship of the Son to the Spirit. This progression thereby led him to address further concerns, firstly in pneumatology and Christology, and then concerning the ontology of the Trinity. What began as an attempt to lay a theological framework for the Charismatic Movement led to an exploration into the essential character of the Trinity.

It is possibly because of this reactive factor in Smail's theology that we can see a tension emerge. There is, on the one hand, an emphasis upon the absolute sovereignty of God who remains as He who Is, apart from His Creation. This was seen in Smail's liking for Barth's presentation of the ontological priority of God within His own immanent Being and His essential separation from us. Certainly it was probably the case that this perspective and presentation of the otherness of God was reinforced by other factors. Smail was reacting against aspects of the Charismatic Movement, where it seemed to him that insufficient place was being given to a proper focus on the Son or the Father, along with the Spirit. Further, he wanted here to emphasise the unique place of Jesus as part of the Trinity: the Son through whom we might gain an inheritance, yet whose status we can never properly share.[35] More than that, Smail wanted to root the context wherein we speak of the Spirit within the Father-Son relationship prior to addressing the issue of the Spirit's engagement with us. In contrast to all of this, we have also seen Smail's desire to emphasise the salvific economy of God's action towards us and the ontic actuality of the Spirit as a dynamic action of the Spirit from the Father towards us, a subordination of the Spirit in function if not in Being that is apparent within the Trinity as perceived and experienced by us.

---

[32] *Reflected Glory*, p. 26.
[33] *The Forgotten Father*, p. 98.
[34] *The Forgotten Father*, p. 103.
[35] *The Forgotten Father*, p. 138.

This tension between God's unique otherness and His dynamic, ontic actuality in relation to us is important to grasp, in that it possibly helps us understand what might be construed as a weakness in Smail's approach. Smail, reflecting, as does Torrance, a radical Christocentricity learnt from Barth, would appear to disallow any functional distinction between the work of the Spirit and the presence of the Incarnate Son in the person of Jesus. In Smail's thought, the Spirit is certainly dynamic in His relation towards us, but that dynamic has to be interpreted within the ontological priority of the Father-Son relationship. The Spirit can only properly be understood in his action upon Jesus, not upon us. The church is enabled by the Spirit, through the shared humanity which Christ has in common with us, to enter into communion with God. The church must, however, be distinguished from the Son and not be viewed as an extension of the Incarnation, as has sometimes been allowed.[36] We can understand our relationship to the Spirit only as He bridges our partial appreciation of what it is to have our true inheritance in Christ, bringing us into an appreciation of what we are to hope and look for in that relationship with the Father. The basis of our inclusion within this relationship lies, however, not with the Spirit but in the common humanity which Christ shares with us. The Spirit brings us to an appreciation of what we share through Christ's common humanity with us.

In this, the question arises as to what significance Smail attaches to our communion with the Spirit Himself, other than allowing the Spirit to function in a manner similar to that which we traced in Torrance's thought, as an anonymous and transparent witness to the Son. Smail himself was quite aware of the need to clarify his presentation of the Spirit's Person and function within his Trinitarian model;[37] and this was the issue which he addressed in his third book, *The Giving Gift*.

7.5   *The Giving Gift*

In *The Giving Gift*, whilst going on to develop his explanation of the Spirit's distinctive operation, Smail was keen to reaffirm two principles. The first, established in *The Forgotten Father*, was that our understanding of the Spirit needs to be rooted in the reciprocity of relationship which is between God the Son and God the Father.[38] The second, established in *Reflected Glory* and a consequence of his third basic tenet that theology is Trinitarian with a Christocentric focus, was that God cannot be, in Himself, other than what He is in His revelation to us. Both of these principles will, as we shall see, lead Smail's thought in a clear direction. In addition to these, however, he introduces a further insight: Smail now perceives the Spirit as personal.

---

[36] *The Forgotten Father*, p. 134.
[37] *The Giving Gift*, pp. 13-14.
[38] *The Giving Gift*, p. 92.

The Spirit is to be understood not simply as an agent or communicative medium of the relationship between the Father and the Son. The Spirit must be understood as personal, both in Himself and towards us. That is, the Spirit, like the Father and the Son, is

> one who reveals Himself as the source and centre of the kind of actions and relationships that, by analogy with ordinary human experience, we recognise to be personal.[39]

This perception of the Spirit is critical to Smail's expanded thesis. Well aware of a tendency in the Western Trinitarian tradition to depersonalise the Spirit[40] and reduce Him to a relational principle, Smail wishes to assert that, in the Spirit's concourse with the Father and the Son and in their mutual relationship of one to the other, the Spirit needs to be seen not simply as *vinculum Trinitatis* but as He who, in His own person, acts personally and creatively.

The context of the Spirit's personal action is the relationship of the Father and the Son; yet within this the Spirit will manifest Himself in different ways and at different times, as He did in the life of Jesus.[41] Here we must understand that, in emphasising the character of the Spirit as personal, Smail retains the Western model of the Trinity's perspective that the context of the Spirit's Being and action, albeit as a third centre and source of action within the Trinity,[42] is found in the reciprocal relationship of the Father and the Son. That is, Smail does not have a quarrel with the Western emphasis on the Spirit's place within the reciprocity of the Father and the Son; rather, Smail wishes to correct the tendency, as he perceives it, to rob the Spirit of His personal, sovereign nature. This said, Smail is also determined that the personality of the Spirit should always be seen in terms of the Father-Son relationship: so it is that he describes the Spirit as a different sort of Person from the Father and the Son, in that His character is determined by the interrelationship of the Father and the Son. As Smail puts it,

> The being of the Spirit *originates* in the self-giving of the Father to the Son, and is further characterised by the responsive self-giving of the Son to the Father.[43]

In so emphasising the personality of the Spirit, rooted in the relationship of the Father and the Son, Smail achieves two positive results. Firstly, he preserves the emphasis, maintained throughout his thought, on the need for a clearly Christocentric reference for our understanding of the Spirit's action. Secondly,

---

[39] *The Giving Gift*, p. 33.
[40] *The Giving Gift*, p. 21.
[41] As in the conception (*The Giving Gift*, pp. 97-98), baptism (*The Giving Gift*, pp. 98 and 102) and transfiguration (*The Giving Gift*, p. 104) of Jesus.
[42] *The Giving Gift*, pp. 34-35.
[43] *The Giving Gift*, p. 157.

he counters a weakness which he now discerns to be present in *Reflected Glory*: that is, a tendency to subordinate the work of the Spirit to that of the Son.[44]

A second, fresh perspective on the Spirit which Smail identifies in the *Giving Gift*, in addition to emphasising the Spirit as personal, is that of the Spirit's creativity.[45] This aspect provides us, through Smail's presentation, with yet another facet of how a proper understanding of the Spirit needs to be set within the context of the Father-Son relationship. The Spirit, in creating within us both responsiveness[46] and purposefulness,[47] calls us to accede, within our own being, to the example of Christ: Christ who Himself demonstrates the purposefulness of the Father through the life of the Son of God and the responsiveness of the Son of God to the Father.

Thus far, we have seen Smail's assertion that the Spirit needs to be construed both as a personal, creative Being and also within terms of the Father-Son relationship. To this, Smail introduces a further characteristic of the Spirit: that there is, within the terms of the Spirit's sovereign, personal action, a refusal to violate our human personality. The Spirit cannot be manipulated by us to be something other than Himself; yet, at the same time, He Himself does not come to us as an autocrat.[48] The Spirit liberates us to say 'Yes' to God:[49] He does not force us. Here, Smail wishes to allow the object of God's grace the place of freely choosing to embrace and confess the personal action of the Holy Spirit.[50]

How, though, are we to allow this place for personal, human freedom without leaning towards Smail's dreaded Arminianism? Is Smail contradicting his first, basic tenet, that God acts in and through sovereign, prevenient grace? Indeed not, for Smail brings to his aid that other foundational concept in his thought: the corporate dimension of the church, in which the Spirit operates. It is the church, not the individual, which is reaffirmed as the context of the Spirit's glorification of the Son.[51] Moreover, in that the Spirit deals personally with those found to be in union with the vicarious humanity of the Son, it is within the corporate context of the Spirit's action, united to Christ's humanity - that is, within the church - that the *locus operandi* of the Spirit is found and His presence affirmed.[52] The corporate character of the church and the Spirit's presence therein, the second of Smail's basic tenets, is thus reaffirmed as an integral and critical part of Smail's Trinitarian model. It is through the medium

---

[44] *The Giving Gift*, p. 44.

[45] *The Giving Gift*, p. 180.

[46] *The Giving Gift*, pp. 170ff..

[47] *The Giving Gift*, pp. 175ff..

[48] In contrast to the authoritarianism which Smail finds in both Roman Catholicism and Protestantism. *The Giving Gift*, pp. 69-70.

[49] *The Giving Gift*, p. 174.

[50] *The Giving Gift*, p. 72.

[51] *The Giving Gift*, p. 85.

[52] *The Giving Gift*, p. 20.

of the church that the personality of the Spirit is met with, His creativity discovered. It is through the individual's adoption into the corporate community, the community that shares and acknowledges the vicarious humanity of Christ, that experience of the Spirit is grounded and validated.

Does it follow that the Spirit is tied of necessity to the locus of the confessing community, the church? Emphatically not. It may well be that the consequence of the personal actions of the Spirit and the Son is that the church is the location wherein the Spirit's work is identified; but this is due, not to a doctrine of necessity whereby the Spirit is reduced to the role of an agent, but to a principle of reciprocity which is at work. That is, the sovereign, personal action of the Son and the Spirit complement one another. Within their personal action, both are operative within our humanity. The Son of God came to take our humanity to Himself. The Spirit comes with spontaneity and creativity, drawing us ever further into our relationship with Christ and our Father:

> It is this giving and receiving between Son and Spirit that achieves the Father's purpose in His creation.[53]

Here, we see Smail come closest, in his understanding of God's dynamic action, to an affirmation of that which we identified in the pre-Nicene model, in the notion that there is a parallel between the ontic actuality of the Spirit and the Son in the salvific economy. For Smail, the nature of this parallel action of the Son and the Spirit does require to be clearly expounded. Firstly, while the Son and the Spirit can be described as the two hands of God they are, while working together, unambiguously interlocked.[54] There can be no locus for the action of the Spirit other than that which is forged through the Son's Incarnation. Thus, although there is not a subordination of the Spirit to the Son, the Spirit is at work within the community of the church among those who are married to God through Christ's vicarious humanity; and it is the church that provides the context through which the Spirit's personal, sovereign action is made apparent.[55] Secondly, although the Son and the Spirit both act personally in their reciprocal, creative work on mankind, the locus of that work is not to be viewed as being found, primarily, within the human predicament but is bound up in the relationship of the Father and the Son.[56] Jesus Christ is not simply the paradigm of a truly human relationship with God in the Spirit, as mirrored in *Reflected Glory*, but is now the Redeemer who has gone before us and also made a way in the Spirit possible for us. The church cannot duplicate the unique ministry of Jesus, the Son of God Incarnate, for the personality of the

---

[53] *The Giving Gift*, p. 87.

[54] *The Giving Gift*, p. 125.

[55] *The Giving Gift*, p. 135.

[56] 'The distinctive work of the Spirit is to communicate the life that is in the Father and the Son, so that we actually share and experience it in ourselves.' *The Giving Gift*, p. 167.

church and its members is separate from that of both the Son and the Spirit; yet it is for the Spirit to work in us both the responsiveness and the self giving which was forged by Christ on our behalf.[57]

It is this evolution in Smail's pneumatology, from an earlier appreciation of the need for a functional subordination in order to facilitate an expression of the dynamic economy of the Spirit, through to a focus on the reciprocity of relations between the Father and the Son founded in the Immanent Trinity, that leads us to conclude that Smail does not fully succeed in breaking out from the lacuna imposed, in seeking to understand the ontic actuality of the Spirit, by the Western model of the Trinity. Smail is constrained by the need to explicate the Spirit's ontic actuality in terms of an Immanent Trinity. Smail's thought, as reflected in the *Giving Gift*, suggests a return to a perspective which stresses the immanence of God's Being over against and prior to His involvement in salvific economy with us. In some ways, this development should come as little surprise. As we saw, two fundamental tenets of Smail's thought from the beginning had been that God's grace is sovereign and prevenient and that God must be, in Himself, what He is towards us in His self-revelation: Trinitarian and Christocentric. Smail remains what he always was, a Scottish theologian nurtured in Calvin and tutored by Barth. Did not, though, his involvement in the Charismatic Movement bring him to a deeper appreciation as to the functional subordination of the Spirit's ontic actuality? Indeed, but as we saw, this led to a tension with his deepening emphasis on, firstly, the Father-Son relationship and, consequently, a perception of the Spirit and His relationship within God's Triunity formed out of the reciprocity which is between the Father and the Son. Perhaps most significantly, Smail's qualification regarding the Person of the Spirit, differentiated from the Father and Son in their status as Persons, betrays a further distancing from a Trinitarian perception built on the ontic actuality of the Trinity's salvific economy, to be replaced with a focus on the Spirit as *vinculum* within an Immanent Trinity.

In *The Giving Gift*, the clearest indication of Smail's underlying Trinitarian perception lies in his stated conviction that the Gospel is concerned with inducting us into a knowledge of God, not simply as He is in His salvific economy, but as He is within Himself.[58] Indeed, it is by understanding how the three Persons of the Godhead are related to one another that we are to see how it is that God relates to us, for we are related to all three Persons in a manner that is appropriate to their relation to one another.[59] Likewise, where there is a place for understanding the dynamic of the Spirit, the focus is away from the salvific economy and is upon inter-Trinitarian relationships. The Spirit's operation on us must therefore be anticipated in terms of the Spirit's relationship to the Son of God within the immanent Triune Being. Our

---

[57] *The Giving Gift*, p. 171.

[58] *The Giving Gift*, p. 145.

[59] *The Giving Gift*, p. 146.

perception of the Spirit upon Jesus of Nazareth should be derived from our perception of the Immanent Trinity. As Smail puts it,

> Because Jesus is the eternal Son made man, in his human story we see being acted out the eternal interplay of Father, Son and Spirit within the life of God.[60]

In tracing Smail's pneumatology, we have seen it develop as he has reflected upon contemporaneous aspects of the Charismatic Movement and theology at large. Smail, consciously outworking his pneumatology in a Trinitarian context, presents us with a model of the Trinity which depicts both the Son and the Spirit as proceeding from the Father, with both the Son and Spirit reaching out to one another in a reciprocal relationship.[61] We note three questions which arise from this perspective on the Trinity.

Firstly, in emphasising the action of the Spirit on the Son of God, has Smail failed to engage with the fact that, when we are met with the ontic actuality of the Spirit, we have no other immediate reference other than our own reference which is anthropocentric and, for those within the Charismatic Movement, experiential? Even though we may wish to affirm the objective reality of God's self-revelation, is it proper for us to do this in a way that abstracts from our own predicament? The challenge that Smail appears to circumvent is that, even although he allows for the Spirit to create and induce a response of faith within us, he gives us no real reference in terms of our own experience. In terms of Jesus' experience, Smail is so resolved to emphasise the uniqueness of the Spirit's concourse with the Son, within the Father-Son relationship, that he cannot attempt to explain the meeting between the Spirit and humanity, even the vicarious humanity of Christ, other than in terms of the eternal Son's Incarnation.

Secondly, is Smail in fact limiting the creativity of the Spirit, in not allowing the fact that, in his action upon us, the Spirit might bring about effects that contrast with those experienced by Jesus? That is, while there may be vital aspects of the Spirit's presence among us which follow from the viatorial triumph of Christ the Redeemer in human flesh, is it not possible that there are other aspects of the Spirit's ontic actuality which arise among us simply because of the difference between Christ's humanity and ours? By refusing the possibility of any anthropocentric reference outwith Christ's own humanity, Smail could be accused of not taking seriously the reality of the Spirit's action upon our humanity. Smail's discomfort in dealing with the phenomena which arise from the Spirit's ontic actuality, or the confrontation arising between our own humanity and the Holy Spirit, leads him to retreat from the challenge of individual experience. We might well wish to agree with Smail in affirming that phenomena are not the measure of the Spirit's presence; but this is not to

---

[60] *The Giving Gift*, p. 148.
[61] *The Giving Gift*, p. 171.

say that they can be disregarded, in the formation of our pneumatology, as a proper result and accompaniment of it.

The third question which arises, therefore, is whether Smail actually succeeds in escaping from that depersonalisation of the Spirit within the Trinity which he himself detected in the inherited Western model of the Trinity. Despite his attempt to reaffirm the Spirit in personal terms, as in his comparison of the Spirit's status to that of a child within its parents' union,[62] it is open to question whether Smail does, in fact, present us with an understanding of the Spirit which conceives of the Spirit in terms any less impersonal than those inherited from our Western model of the Trinity. Smail speaks of the personal action of the Spirit in relation to the Incarnate Son yet, because his focus is on the inter-trinitarian relationships of God's immanent Being, he can provide us with only limited help in formulating a fresh understanding of the Spirit's ontic actuality.

7.6   James Dunn

James Dunn, a graduate of Glasgow University and a Church of Scotland minister,[63] is currently Professor of Divinity in the University of Durham. His contribution is important to our study in that Dunn has addressed the issues raised by the Pentecostal and Charismatic revivals from the perspective of a New Testament theologian. More specifically, he has sought to address the question of how a proper place can be given to an understanding of the Spirit in the Christian life, without having recourse to the traditional categories of dogmatic interpretation. In this respect, Dunn offers us an alternative perspective to that of Smail, who is more self-consciously seeking to build on the inherited categories of dogmatic thought.

7.7   The Priority of Experience

The most striking feature of Dunn's approach is his starting point. For Dunn, an examination of the place of the Spirit does not begin with a proposition regarding the nature of God, but with the experience of God or, more particularly, experience of God as Spirit. This position was laid out by Dunn in his earliest work, *Baptism in the Holy Spirit*,[64] where he sought to demonstrate that it was experience of the Spirit in a personal, identifiable moment which was the critical mark in the commencement of faith[65] within the membership of the early Christian community. Here we need to be clear that Dunn's perception of this experience is precisely that: it is an experience. Dunn's understanding of

---

[62] *The Giving Gift*, p. 199.
[63] Licensed to preach by the Presbytery of Glasgow in 1964.
[64] A revised form of Dunn's Ph.D. thesis, presented in 1968.
[65] J. D. G. Dunn, *Baptism in the Holy Spirit*, SCM, London, 1970, p. 4.

experience of the Spirit is not to be confused with a Schleiermachian interpretation, where the Spirit is perceived as the community's or individual's awareness of God. For Dunn, the experience is, in its very character, both decisive and climactic. It is an experience which gives rise to an immediate sense of existential awareness: but the experience is not, of itself, reducible to that sense of awareness.

In this regard, Dunn's method of theological formation, in approaching pneumatology, cannot be said to originate from a cognitive or epistemic foundation. For Dunn, the basis is formed in the birth of an existential conviction within the individual, which may create a correlative intellectual conviction; but the experience is not reducible to epistemic terms, simply because the experience of the Spirit is greater than an intellectual awareness alone.

Having established the priority of experience, Dunn goes on, seeking to identify the type of that experience found in the life of Jesus Christ. At this point, it is clear that the importance of Christ is typological rather than representative, in that Christ is to be acknowledged as being a fully human being, but one whose humanity is in no way vicarious or necessarily a catalyst for our induction into Christ's own experience. People become Christian through a response to Jesus,[66] a response made to the proclamation of the Gospel regarding the Christ who heralds the New Age and New Covenant.[67] In this regard, Jesus' own experience of the Spirit is vital, for it is this which is seen to initiate him into the role of harbinger of the New Age. This experience is identified by Dunn as occurring at the point of Jesus' baptism in the Jordan by John, an experience which had

> epochal significance for Jesus, even though that significance may only have been fully grasped after some reflection by Jesus.[68]

Having established, in his first work, the priority of experience, Dunn proceeded to examine in its sequel, *Jesus and the Spirit*, the significance of Jesus' own experience of the Spirit. Here, we see two factors which reinforce the methodological path taken by Dunn.

Firstly, as we have noted, Dunn attaches considerable importance to investigating the nature of Jesus's own experience of the Spirit. More specifically, Dunn's early method focuses on exploring the experience of Jesus as a man, regardless of any metaphysical or ontological questions that might arise concerning his nature. Christology is not, initially, Dunn's immediate

---

[66] 'That man is a Christian who has received the gift of the Holy Spirit by committing himself to the risen Jesus as Lord, and who lives accordingly'. *Baptism in the Holy Spirit*, p. 229.
[67] *Baptism in the Holy Spirit*, p. 32.
[68] J. D. G. Dunn, *Jesus and the Spirit*, SCM, London, 1975, p. 65.

concern. Jesus' uniqueness is to be found in his experience and the emergent consciousness that this induced, firstly in Jesus himself and then, derivatively, in his followers. It is the character of that interpretation which Jesus attaches to his own experience which, in Dunn's schema, allows Jesus to be perceived, typologically, as a paradigm for human experience of and response to God as Spirit.

A second reason lying behind the methodology adopted by Dunn lies with his own epistemology. Following on the axiom of Rudolf Bultmann, that faith in an individual can only arise from the recognition by that individual of the activity of God in his own life,[69] Dunn has a further reason for attempting to define the nature of Jesus Christ's own faith. Seeking to determine how Jesus' experience relates to his belief in God, Dunn is led further into exploring Jesus' own self-awareness of God. It is only by being able to interpret Jesus' understanding as to the nature of his own faith in God that we can discuss the nature of Jesus' relation to God. For Dunn, the identity of Jesus' relation with God needs to be addressed from the perspective that Jesus Himself holds.[70] To adopt any other approach would be to ignore the typological significance of Jesus.

Dunn's perception of Jesus' self-consciousness centres on two features: the sense of God as his Father and the Spirit as his enabler. Dunn notes that

> Jesus thought of himself as God's son and as anointed by the eschatological Spirit, because in prayer he experienced a power to heal which he could only understand as the power of the end time and as an inspiration to proclaim a message which he could only understand as the gospel of the end time.[71]

It was this sense of intimacy with God as his Father which gave Jesus a sense of compulsion in seeking to share this relationship with others.[72] The sense of enabling that came from his experience of the Spirit was, for him, understood as eschatological reality breaking into the present order of creation.[73]

While the experience of Jesus is taken as typologically paradigmatic for Christian experience as a whole, the special character of Jesus' own experience does, however, limit the availability of this experience to others. Certainly Jesus Himself appears to have recognised 'a distinctiveness and even unique element in his own experience of God'.[74] Interestingly Dunn does not develop this aspect of Jesus' self-consciousness, a sense of his own uniqueness, as a qualifier to his perception of Jesus' typological significance for Christians as a

---

[69] *Jesus and the Spirit*, p. 1.

[70] *Jesus and the Spirit*, p. 92.

[71] *Jesus and the Spirit*, p. 67.

[72] *Jesus and the Spirit*, p. 41.

[73] *Jesus and the Spirit*, pp. 44ff..

[74] *Jesus and the Spirit*, p. 90.

whole: it may be that Dunn understands this as a non-rational element within Jesus' experience.[75] Whatever, it is apparent that Dunn perceives the specialness of Jesus to lie, more obviously, in the quality of his experience of God. Jesus' disciples may participate in his awareness of God[76] and the experience of the early Christian community may have included experiences like Jesus' own experience;[77] but Jesus' experience, both in the sense of sonship and the consciousness of the eschatological Spirit which he enjoyed, is perceived by Dunn as being much richer than that of the first Christians. Expressing this in his subsequent work, *Unity and Diversity in the New Testament*,[78] Dunn states,

> Jesus' experience of God was at a profounder level, in a much more immediately personal relationship, in a more direct individual disclosure 'below the surface'.[79]

Dunn rationalises this difference, between the experience of Jesus and that of his followers, through distinguishing between the Charismatic and the Enthusiast. Jesus is perceived to be Charismatic in that

> his ministry was characterised by a power and authority which was neither learned in any school nor bestowed by any human agency but which came to him and through him in direct and spontaneous manner.[80]

Where the early Christians came to empathise with this experience of Jesus, the true Charismatic, their experience is more properly described as being that both of the Charismatic and the Enthusiast.[81] For Dunn, the Enthusiast's behaviour may signify the convictions held regarding the Enthusiast's own experience and comprehension of God,[82] but lacks the accurate and complete correlation to the experience of the Spirit found in the case of Jesus. In contrast, the two chief characteristics of the Enthusiast are his assertion of the immediacy of the Spirit's revelation and the emphasis placed on the value of religious ecstasy.[83] Identifying the earliest form of Christianity as essentially enthusiastic,[84] Dunn is able thereby to distinguish the experience of Jesus from that of the

---

[75] 'Jesus' experience of God embraced non rational as well as rational elements - *dunamis* to heal as well as *exousia* to proclaim - and he regarded both as valid and important manifestations of God's Spirit'. *Jesus and the Spirit*, p. 89.

[76] *Jesus and the Spirit*, p. 38.

[77] *Jesus and the Spirit*, p. 195.

[78] First published in 1977.

[79] J. D. G. Dunn, *Unity and Diversity in the New Testament*, SCM, London, 2nd edition, 1990, p. 189.

[80] *Unity and Diversity in the New Testament*, p. 186.

[81] *Jesus and the Spirit*, p. 194.

[82] *Jesus and the Spirit*, p. 157.

[83] J. D. G. Dunn, 'Rediscovering the Spirit (2)', *Expository Times* 94 (1982-3), p. 9.

[84] *Unity and Diversity in the New Testament*, p. 176.

early church, while at the same time affirming the typological relevance of Jesus to the church through the common experience of the charismatic. The early Christian may have been a Charismatic and an Enthusiast but Jesus was the true Charismatic. The early Christians' experience of the Spirit, expressed in and through their collectively enthusiastic identity, required to be challenged to a greater degree of proximation to the truly charismatic faith of Jesus. For Dunn, the early Christian understanding of Jesus is, above all, significant in experiential terms, in that the yardstick of true, charismatic experience is Jesus. This, certainly, is his understanding of Paul's approach[85] and is that which Dunn wishes to commend as a model to the modern church.[86]

The implications of Dunn's basic thesis for our study are evident when it comes to examining his understanding of what we have already established as a fundamental issue in theological debate on the place of the Holy Spirit, the relation of Christology to pneumatology. Dunn's early response to Christology was radical, in that he presented his experiential model as the primary model in understanding the significance of Jesus' relationship to God the Father and the Spirit. Dunn saw that, for the early church, experience of the Spirit was fundamental both to its self-understanding and its understanding of Jesus. This thesis, laid out in *Baptism in the Spirit* and developed, through examining the nature of Jesus' own understanding of his experience of the Spirit, in *Jesus and the Spirit*, led Dunn to interpret Jesus' relationship with the Father and the Spirit in exclusively experiential terms. Dunn identified two aspects to Jesus' experience, in both a sense of filial belonging to the Father and eschatological commissioning by the Spirit. Jesus' uniqueness lay both in his own sense of this dual relationship, with the Father and the Spirit; and also in the early church's recognition of that uniqueness, in so far as it came to share something of Jesus' charismatic experience.

It was this emphasis which led to Dunn's attack on the Chalcedonian formula, specifically in approaching discussion of Christ in terms of 'two natures'. In a paper published in 1973 he declared,

We must pass behind the wooden, artificial phrases of the traditional Chalcedonian formulation of the two natures of Christ, to the living, human experience of the Spirit possessing and empowering Jesus in remarkable and unique degree. Whatever its value in past centuries, the static Christology of Chalcedon does no justice to the dynamic Christology of the New Testament. If, however, we persist with the Chalcedonian formula, then it would be better to express the theory of the two natures in the Pauline terms of flesh and Spirit (from which it ultimately derives) - and recognise that what we call the deity of Jesus was no more and no less than the Spirit of God in Him.[87]

---

[85] *Jesus and the Spirit*, p. 319.
[86] *Jesus and the Spirit*, p. 360.
[87] J. D. G. Dunn, 'Rediscovering the Spirit', *Expository Times* 84 (1972-3), p. 11.

For Dunn, a preoccupation with the metaphysic of that relationship between the divine and human detracted from the dynamic reality of both Jesus' relationship with the Father and the Spirit and, importantly, the church's understanding of its own relationship with the Father and the Spirit, brought about through Jesus. The method of Chalcedon could, in Dunn's eyes, only divert the church from the need to experience the Spirit[88] and thereby come to an appreciation of both the Fatherhood of God and the immediate, eschatological sense which the Spirit brings.[89]

In taking this approach, Dunn felt that other problems, arising from a metaphysical Christology, could be overcome. Dunn detected a tension between exponents of 'exemplarist Christology',[90] where the place of the Christian's imitation of Christ is emphasised, with 'kerygmatic Christology', where Jesus is presented as the object of faith.[91] Dunn's alternative method, of presenting Christ as a typological paradigm, sought to overcome this divide by bringing together both the filial aspects of exemplarist Christology with the eschatological dimension of kerygmatic theology, both founded in the experience of Christ and, derivatively, in the experience of the early Christians.[92]

Where his approach disallowed the development of a clear model of the Trinity with objective, ontological relationships being set between the Father, Son and Spirit, Dunn viewed this not as a weakness but as a strength. Dunn's observation was that the New Testament understanding of Jesus, together with his relationship with the Father and the Spirit, was heterogeneous and diverse, inevitably conflicting with any model which could be interpreted as exclusivist and static. This issue, explored in *Unity and Diversity in the New Testament*, led the way to a more detailed exploration of the Christological theme in Dunn's fourth major work, *Christology in the Making*.[93]

In this work, Dunn argued the case that the Christology owned by the early church developed out of its experience of the reality of Christ: that is, its appreciation of the reality of Christ as proximated to through the church's experience.[94] Consequently, Dunn criticised what he perceived to be an overemphasis, in dogmatic theology, on the 'Incarnational model',[95] by which he understood the search for an understanding of Christ as 'God made man'. The preoccupation with such a static model served, in Dunn's understanding, to

---

[88] 'Rediscovering the Spirit', *Expository Times* 84 (1972-3), p. 43.
[89] 'Rediscovering the Spirit', *Expository Times* 84 (1972-3), p. 12.
[90] Dunn understands this to be the main emphasis of nineteenth century liberal theology: *Jesus and the Spirit*, p. 13.
[91] *Jesus and the Spirit*, p. 14.
[92] *Jesus and the Spirit*, p. 342.
[93] First published in 1980. The second edition, revised with an extended, apologetical foreword added, was published in 1989.
[94] J. D. G. Dunn, *Christology in the Making*, SCM, London, 2nd edition, 1989, p. 265.
[95] *Christology in the Making*, p. 267.

detract from the more dynamic and fluid understanding of Christ which the New Testament presented.

In the preface to the second edition of *Christology in the Making* it is clear that Dunn, in the vigorous criticism which he faced after the first edition's publication and his critics' accusation that he had rejected classical Christology, felt badly misunderstood: Dunn defends himself against the criticism that he had, in the first edition, paid too little attention to the Incarnational model.[96] Certainly, shortly after publishing the first edition of *Christology in the Making*, Dunn did state his wish to reformulate some of his earlier conclusions, especially those relating to the priority of a Spirit Christology,[97] where such an emphasis could be interpreted as precluding the existence of other valid, Christological models. It is important to see, however, that Dunn's basic thesis regarding the priority of experience has remained constant throughout his writings. With his foundation set firmly on the priority of experience, Dunn can affirm the need to allow competing, even contrasting, assessments of Christ, to coexist, where

> the truth of Christ will be found in the individual emphases of the different New Testament formulations as much as in that which unites them.[98]

It is out of the context of the mutual interaction of these different New Testament formulations of Christ, and the need to resolve their differing emphases, that Dunn sees early credal developments emerging. Trinitarian thought is rooted in the tension between the experience of Christ's lordship and the activity of the Spirit.[99] Likewise, where the critical issue of early Christology was whether or not Christianity could be conceived of as being, as with Judaism, a monotheistic faith, Dunn understands that the attempt to resolve this debate led to the emergence of Logos Christology as the dominant model. Monotheism having been established, the early church could then go on to explore and express, as it did in the Nicene formula, the relation of God as Father and Son, a process of discovery which itself was born out of the dominance of Father-Son language.[100]

For Dunn, however, these developments can be viewed as consequential and secondary to the central issue which he invites us to address. Although these dogmatic formulations are legitimate expressions, arising from the need to address apologetical issues facing the early church, the priority of the experiential and the model of Christ as the typological paradigm still stand as foundational elements in the Christian life.

---

[96] Dunn did, however, concede that not enough attention had been paid to St. John's Gospel: *Christology in the Making*, p. xxvi.

[97] 'Rediscovering the Spirit (2)', *Expository Times* 94 (1982-3), pp. 15-16.

[98] *Christology in the Making*, p. 267.

[99] 'Rediscovering the Spirit (2)', *Expository Times* 94 (1982-3), p. 17.

[100] *Christology in the Making*, pp. xxx-xxxi.

Dunn's emphasis on the experiential and his focus on the Spirit, in seeking to understand the development of early Christianity, led him to a radical review of ecclesiology. His sharpest criticism of the church comes in his earlier period of writing, when his focus lay on the need to assert the priority of experience for the Christian life. Dunn saw the experiential emphasis of early Christian faith quenched by two extremes found within the contemporary church:

> the mechanical sacramentalism of extreme Catholicism and the dead biblicist orthodoxy of extreme Protestantism.[101]

In Dunn's understanding, the Reformation had served as a reaction against extreme sacramentalism and sacerdotalism[102] by which, in the western church, an appreciation of the Spirit had become confounded by that perspective which had presented the church as the vehicle of the Spirit's action. Where the Reformers had countered this with an emphasis on personal faith and the authority of Scripture, this corrective had not restored a proper understanding of the Spirit's role in the Christian life. In both Catholic and Reformed traditions, the continued sacramental use of baptism and clericalism inhibited a true understanding of the Spirit's dynamic within the church.[103] Dunn asserts that the church must be seen as the creation of the Spirit, the context established by the Spirit's action, the dynamism and creativity of the Spirit lying at the very heart of the church's existence, rather than peripheral to it or contingent upon it.[104]

In contrast to the dullness of inherited ecclesiology, Dunn found the Pentecostals' rediscovery of the Spirit, in terms of experience, a sign of hope.[105] While rejecting their tendency to distinguish two stages in the work of the Spirit in the believer,[106] he saw the possibility of the Pentecostals' experience being married to the inherited perspectives of the wider church, thereby injecting a more vital and vivacious element into contemporary Christianity.[107]

Dunn did, however, have another reason for commending the Pentecostal and Charismatic Movements: they illustrated the validity of his thesis that experience lay at the centre of Christian faith. The presence of contemporary experiential phenomena invited comparison with similar phenomena mentioned in the biblical accounts.[108] This comparison worked not only to validate Dunn's thesis regarding the essentially experiential nature of Christianity, but allowed

---

[101] *Baptism in the Holy Spirit*, p. 4.
[102] *Baptism in the Holy Spirit*, pp. 224-25.
[103] *Rediscovering the Spirit*, p. 41.
[104] *Rediscovering the Spirit*, p. 43.
[105] J. D. G. Dunn, 'Spirit-Baptism and Pentecostalism', *Scottish Journal of Theology*, 23, (1970), p. 406.
[106] 'Spirit-Baptism and Pentecostalism', p. 404.
[107] 'Spirit-Baptism and Pentecostalism', p. 407.
[108] *Jesus and the Spirit*, p. 5.

him to apply the lessons of first century Christian life to the present. Certainly, it should be said that it is hard to tell whether it is Dunn's observations of contemporary Christianity or his conclusions regarding New Testament characteristics that are more influential in shaping his opinions; however, Dunn sees that safeguards were introduced by the early church which would prove useful for the church today.[109] Two, in particular, are pertinent for the purposes of our study.

Firstly, Dunn sees that the unity of the early Christians, within their participation in the new life and common experience of the Spirit, led to a stress on the corporate dimension of religious experience.[110] The experience of the Spirit is not to be understood as sanctioning an individualistic piety: the action of the Spirit needs to be concretised in the reality of corporate Christian living.[111] Secondly, in that the typological paradigm of charismatic life is Jesus, then only that power experienced and causing the Christian to become more like Jesus can be acknowledged as being that of the Holy Spirit.[112] For the early Christians, their experience of the Spirit identified with their experience of Jesus. In the light of the resurrection of Jesus, the association between Jesus and the Spirit was established.[113]

Dunn's review of ecclesiology is significant in that it reverses the relationship, presumed within the Reformed tradition, between the church and the Spirit. Dunn provides an alternative to that perception of the church which can arise from the Western model of the Trinity whereby the church, as recipient of grace, receives the Spirit as *vinculum Trinitatis*. In the Western model, the relationship between the Father and the Son becomes reflected in the relationship between God and His church. There, we saw the presence of the Spirit assumed, implicit to an understanding of the church as the vehicle whereby Christ is represented upon earth. In that Smail built his understanding of the Spirit on the Western model, he viewed the Spirit's action as subsequential to or contingent upon the Son's Incarnation: the Spirit constitutes that which the Son institutes. In contrast, Dunn's thesis presents us with an understanding of the Spirit, along with the Son, as institutor of the church. The call to unity of love within the church and the adoption of an eschatological focus are predicated by the common experience of the Spirit and do not precede that experience. Dunn offers a model whereby the action of the Spirit can be seen as leading to the creation of church as that community which shares a common experience of the Spirit and faith in Christ.

A second area where Dunn offers a radical alternative to the Western model lies in his understanding of the Trinity. As already noted, Dunn's approach is

---

[109] *Jesus and the Spirit*, p. 360.
[110] *Jesus and the Spirit*, p. 260.
[111] *Jesus and the Spirit*, p. 297.
[112] *Jesus and the Spirit*, p. 320.
[113] 'Rediscovering the Spirit (2)', *Expository Times* 94 (1982-3), p. 16.

not easily accommodated to traditional Trinitarian language. His starting point, in the experience of Jesus of Nazareth, means that he is concerned with construing Jesus neither in terms of the hypostatic union of God and man, nor in terms of the ontology of God's own immanent Being. In adopting this approach, Dunn appears to circumvent many of the difficulties inherent in language arising from the dogmatic structures of Patristic and later debate. The apparent advantage of avoiding ontological language does, though, produce its own difficulties. Dunn's insistence on founding his theological method in the experience of Jesus causes him to relativise other aspects of God's Being, in that these can only be perceived in relation to and through that experience. Thus, although Dunn may affirm the immediacy of the Spirit in and to the experience of Jesus, he cannot speak of the Spirit as possessed of His own Being, other than as that which characterises the Spirit's place within the experience of Jesus. Likewise, he cannot properly speak of the Being of the Father, other than as that which is established in the filial appreciation of the Son. Given Dunn's methodology it becomes illegitimate, for example, to speak of the Spirit's relation to the Father, other than where this can be determined from the experience of Jesus of Nazareth.

In what sense, then, can Dunn formulate an understanding of the Trinity? For Dunn, the Trinity can only be that which becomes apparent in and through the experience of Jesus himself. The doctrine of the Trinity has to be seen as a theologoumenal development which communicates the early Christians' understanding of the relation, as discovered through Jesus' own experience, between Jesus and the Father and Jesus and the Spirit. At the same time, because the Christian can only proximate towards the charismatic awareness of Jesus, the doctrine of the Trinity must, at best, be but a proximation to that reality which is anchored in the experience of Jesus alone.

We might summarise Dunn's understanding of the Christian perception of God as Trinity by envisaging two parallel relationships between man and God. The first relationship represents that experienced by Jesus. The second relationship expresses that existing between the Christian and God. The Christian experiences the Spirit. This experience awakens his existential awareness and proximates to that of Jesus, the typological paradigm of man, who also experiences the Spirit. The Christian experience of the Spirit is, however, qualitatively different from that of Jesus Himself, for as Jesus' relationship is truly charismatic, the Christian experience is a compound of the charismatic and enthusiastic. The two relationships, that of Jesus and the Christian, are parallel yet separate.

In his own experience of the Spirit, the Christian is drawn into a deeper proximation to Jesus' relationship and experience of the Spirit, the Christian being conscious that his own experience is founded on and contingent upon that experience which is true to Jesus himself. So it is that as the Christian experiences the Spirit in his relationship with God, he proximates more closely to Jesus' relationship to God. For the Christian, a true understanding of what it means to experience the Spirit is found only through looking at what that experience meant for Jesus, for whom it brought a sense of both deep, filial appreciation of God as Father and eschatological empowering by the Spirit. It is in the experience of Jesus that the Christian finds the deeper significance and purpose of his own experience of the Spirit.

Dunn himself sees the effect of the Christian's experience of the Spirit as producing a triangular relationship in which the Christian stands at the apex, with experience of the Spirit pointing to dual termini in the Father and the Son. It is a relation brought about by the Christian's experience of the Spirit which causes the Christian to relate both to the Father in sonship and to the Son in service.[114]

What are the strengths and weaknesses of this approach, in providing us with a Trinitarian model which might help to explain the Charismatic experience? Firstly, while allowing that the Spirit is personal in His relation to us, Dunn's approach has the advantage of not leading us to an anthropomorphized notion of the Spirit as a person, analogous to human personhood. Dunn's critique presents an understanding of the Spirit which preserves a sense of the Spirit's dynamic in coming from the Father and the Spirit's ontic actuality as realised, personally, within Christian experience. Secondly, the emphasis on the typological significance of Jesus, as one man among mankind, avoids the conflict we have seen arise from differing understandings of Christ as the representative of mankind. That is, Dunn avoids any tension which might arise between viewing Christ as representative in terms of His vicarious humanity, as advocated by Edward Irving and T. F. Torrance, and in terms of His sacrificial death, as emphasised in the *Westminster Confession*. Thirdly, Dunn's Trinitarian model clarifies the fact that it is the Spirit Himself who is the agent of our experience of God.

These strengths, arising from Dunn's attempts to construe the relationship of pneumatology to Christology through stressing the self-consciousness of Jesus, help circumvent some of the difficulties which an 'objectivising' analysis of Jesus' hypostatic identity might produce: that is, as in Smail's method, where an exploration of Jesus' communion with the Spirit is set within the framework of the Immanent Trinity. Dunn's approach provides, on the face of it, an experiential understanding of the Christian life which, combined with Dunn's understanding of the relation of pneumatology to ecclesiology, might commend his approach as a means of interpreting the Charismatic experience.

On the other hand, there are disadvantages to Dunn's method. The principal weakness in Dunn's thesis is that he does not allow for a clear identification between the Christian's experience of the Spirit and that which was true to the experience of Jesus Himself. Further, Dunn does not attempt to argue for an essential link within the Christian's life between the activities of the Spirit and an acknowledgement of Jesus. Dunn views the experience of the Spirit as

---

[114] *Jesus and the Spirit*, p. 326.

consequential to the Christian's acknowledgement of Christ in faith, such being evident to him from the New Testament data. However, by taking 'experience' as the criterion in assessing the nature of the gift of the Spirit within the Christian life, Dunn does not demonstrate why confession of Jesus and the experience of the Spirit need be associated. Dunn criticises the tendency, in Pentecostal thought, to speak of different stages in the reception of the Spirit and his category of 'experience' does counter this tendency: yet, while consolidating the manner by which we speak of the Spirit, Dunn neglects to show why the character of that experience, induced by the Spirit, is specifically Christian.

Dunn's thesis is weakest when subjected to the critical question of why Christian experience should be specifically associated with Jesus. His argument is based on the observation of that experience which arose within the early Christian community, without any exploration of why this should be peculiar to the Christian revelation. Perhaps Dunn does not see a need to explore why the Spirit should be specifically associated with Jesus. While, however, this may be legitimate within the parameters of New Testament theology as a singular discipline, it is insufficient in providing an answer when the particularity of Christian revelation is brought within the wider arena of apologetical debate and philosophical analysis. Faced with claims by others to divine, spiritual experience, Christian pneumatology needs to offer some understanding as to why the Charismatic experience needs to be associated with the God who is manifest in and through Jesus Christ. Certainly, Dunn notes that experiential religion was not unique to Christian circles[115] and that the early church, as with Paul, had to introduce critical criteria in evaluating the legitimacy of experience.

It is of interest that Dunn does not explore the possibility that experience of the Spirit is, in some measure, self-validating in its orientation and testimony to Jesus Christ. As we noted in chapter 1, it appeared to be the case among some Charismatics that the Spirit, in the ontic actuality of His coming, might be understood as bearing an implicit testimony to Jesus Christ. In such circumstances, the Spirit could be viewed as He who comes from the Father in the name of the Son, yet remaining distinct from Him. The action of the Holy Spirit appears, in the experience of the Charismatics, to be associated with Jesus. Dunn offers us no help in explaining why this should be so.

One further difficulty which we might note as arising from Dunn's analysis lies in the distinction made between the experience of the Christian and Jesus, as that of the Enthusiast and the Charismatic. Dunn does not present any clear argument for introducing this distinction. Indeed, it would appear that Dunn is, at this point, appealing to his observations of contemporary Christian movements as much as to the biblical record. On what basis does he claim that Jesus' own experience of the Spirit was not as thoroughly ecstatic as that of the

---

[115] *Jesus and the Spirit*, pp. 304ff..

first Christians? Or on what grounds does he assert that manifestations found among either the early or contemporary charismatic community are not induced by the Spirit in the same way that Jesus Himself experienced? Dunn leaves himself open to the criticism that he perpetuates a romantic model of Jesus, removed from the experience of contemporary Christians, living a life of unknowable and inaccessible communion with the Father and in the Spirit; and that, having set the criterion of experience as formative in the theological understanding of the early church, he fails to allow a clear association between the experience of Christians and the communion with the Spirit enjoyed by Jesus Christ.

7.8   Smail and Dunn in Context

We have observed that Smail, in seeking to present an understanding of the Spirit's Person and function, focused on the Spirit's presence in God's immanent Triunity and appeared to retreat from the challenge of the Charismatic experience; while Dunn, in emphasising the keystone of experience, has distanced himself from a traditional Trinitarian understanding of God.[116] The question arises as to whether it is possible to hold to an understanding of the Spirit's Person and function which, while allowing for and recognising our direct experience of His Being, can be expressed in a Trinitarian framework. In attempting to resolve this difficulty, we begin by reviewing what we have established regarding the development of pneumatology within Scottish Theology.

Where, in our study, we have in some measure attempted to evaluate the development of an understanding of the Person and function of the Holy Spirit within the Scottish tradition, we have observed that Christological considerations did not prove to be a significant factor in that process. This is important when we remember that a charge, to which the Charismatic Movement is susceptible, is that it has placed too much emphasis on the Spirit's ministry, in isolation from the central issue of Christ, revealer of God and redeemer of man. It does not appear, however, that in the immediate post-Reformation era a critical, causal link between Christology and pneumatology was seen as important. The main focus lay with soteriology and with various functions of the Spirit, as evident in the area of epistemology. The nature of the Spirit's Person, or Being, appeared to be of interest only in so far as a Trinitarian theology necessitated some description of the Spirit's functions. It was not until the issue of Christ's vicarious humanity was raised, as evidenced in our study of Irving, that the question of the relationship of Christology to the Person of the Spirit was addressed; and the perilous position of Westminster

---

[116] That is, from one formulated in abstracted terms 'from above'. Dunn's quarrel is with an abstracted view of God, not with a Trinitarian confession. See Dunn, *The Christ and the Spirit*, Vol.1, pp. 377-8, T & T Clark, Edinburgh, 1998.

Calvinism in treating Christ's humanity as practically incidental to our understanding of His soterial ministry became apparent. Even then the question of how the Incarnation of the Son should be related to the presence of the Spirit within His humanity was not developed. This failure to address the relationship of the Son and the Spirit was partly due to the issue being raised upon the catalyst of soteriological, not ontological, concerns; and partly because, with the growing influence of German theological paradigms, there was a shift in focus from the objective nature of God's self-revelation onto, on the one hand, the subjective awareness of man and, on the other, the existential and noetic ideal to be found in God. There was, in the later part of the nineteenth century, no apparent interest within Scottish theology in exploring the character of God's ontic actuality in His relationship towards us.

It is not until the mid twentieth century, in the theology of Torrance, that we see the nature of God's Being, as it becomes apparent from His salvific economy, examined more seriously. In Torrance, however, pneumatology is absorbed within his focus upon the dynamic of the Incarnation, a Christocentric tautology which dominates his whole theological perspective, including his understanding of the Spirit. It is the central role of the Son incarnate which, for Torrance, predicates his understanding of the Spirit. Torrance's pneumatology is not so much influenced by Christology, as controlled by and subsumed within it. In this respect, Torrance perpetuated a weakness which had become inherent within Scottish theology, the failure to maintain a perspective on both pneumatology and Christology, without subsuming the first within the soterial implications of the second.

Because of this background, it is not surprising that, in beginning to explore the dimensions of the Spirit's work, the early participants in the Charismatic Movement in Scotland made no ready connection between a rediscovered pneumatology and the Trinitarian models offered to them out of the tradition of Scottish theology. Instead, the Charismatic Movement came to be founded on a monopneumatic ontology borrowed from the Pentecostals. Charismatics presented an experiential, sensory explanation in their advocacy of the Spirit's ministry, and had no readily available theological mechanism which might enable them to do otherwise. It remained the case that patterns of indigenous theology in Scotland offered the Charismatics no adequate pneumatological understanding to which they could relate their experience.

The absorption of pneumatological concerns within Christology and the consequent neglect of pneumatology which we have traced in Scottish theology should not, however, surprise us. Patristic Christology had been developed as a field of dogmatics separated from pneumatological considerations. Scottish Reformed thought, where it followed Calvin's adoption of the Western model of the Trinity, developing this to emphasise the epistemic function of the Spirit, creating an environment where it became possible to engage in Christological reflection largely independent of pneumatological considerations. Consequently, an embracing of Neo-Pentecostalism and a devotional emphasis on the economy of the Spirit among Charismatics did not lead, of necessity, to a reconsideration of Christology or Trinitarian thought. The pneumatology of the Scottish context appeared, in fact, to encourage the development of a pneumatology among the Charismatics which was separated from Christological considerations. Developments in pneumatology were free to take whatever form they might, largely unrestricted by Christological considerations.

Paradoxically, where the Charismatic Movement did not offer a direct challenge to the theology which undergirded church structures, there was no persuasive, theological reason why the Charismatic Movement should have led to schism within and from the established denominations. Furthermore, given that the received Western model of the Trinity also presented ecclesiology in predominantly Christological terms, the Charismatic Movement did not appear at an early stage as a threat to traditional ecclesiastical structures. Indeed, if the development of the Charismatic Movement had not taken the course it did when, in the mid 1970s, there came to be an increasing degree of schism within Charismatic groupings, there appears to be no pneumatological reason why schism from the established denominations should have been inevitable.

Outwith the Reformed tradition, the greater emphasis on pneumatology current in the Wesleyan and Pentecostal traditions, together with their growing currency within the Scottish church and especially among those who were engaged in evangelism and outreach, pointed the way towards the Charismatic Movement adopting, in large measure, an alien interpretative framework within the Scottish context.[117] Charismatics were among those who adopted an apparently respectable theology from the Wesleyan tradition; but it was not one which was easy to reconcile with the broader context of Reformed, pneumatological understanding in Scotland. Consequently, the growth of the Charismatic movement tended to be associated more with the adoption of popularising methods and innovative theology, occurring largely independently of critical, theological reflection and the main Reformed tradition of Scottish theology.

This did not mean that a need to explore further the relationship of pneumatology to Christology was not perceived. The possibility of

---

[117] John Wesley's doctrine of Christian perfection, as expounded in *A Plain Account of Christian Perfection* (1766) and the notion that entire sanctification can be received and experienced in the Christian life, bringing the Christian to a place whereby *potest non peccare*; this, together with John Fletcher's use of the expression 'the baptism of the Holy Spirit' to describe the process of sanctification and accompanying assurance of spiritual well-being, was foreign to the Scottish Reformed tradition. Such notions, however, were present in the thought of those who were, as noted in chapter 1, precursors of the Charismatics. Likewise, the Finneyite revivalism which arose in the 'Tell Scotland' Campaign of the 1950's - as it found expression in Billy Graham's All Scotland Crusade and the personal, experiential piety of men such as D. P. Thomson of Crieff - all this aroused a quite different perspective on the Christian life.

pneumatology being affected by the Christological models to which we adhere had been seen, perhaps most clearly, in the writing of Irving, where the implications of the relationship between the Spirit's action on Christ's humanity and the inhomination of the Son was, in some measure, tackled. It was apparent from Irving's thought that a Christology which clearly emphasised the common humanity of both Jesus and ourselves might cause us to review our understanding of the Spirit, were the activity of the Spirit seen as focal to Jesus' life and ministry. What remained unclear was the best method of reviewing the relationship. In the approaches of Smail and Dunn, we are presented with two alternative methods in tackling this issue as to the relationship of the Spirit of God, active in the humanity of Christ, and the activity of the Logos incarnated in Jesus.

Smail, standing in the tradition of both Barth and Torrance, has sought to affirm the ministry of the Holy Spirit and the importance of such within the church through stressing the ontological characteristics of God within the immanence of His Triune Being. Such a perspective has, however, limited Smail's ability to speak of the Spirit in terms of His own ontic actuality. Smail's insistence on presenting an understanding of the economy of the Spirit in terms which derive from a model of God's immanent Triunity leads him to view the interaction of the Spirit with humanity within a perspective which focuses our understanding of the Spirit's action upon humanity in terms of His action upon the particular humanity of Christ. The humanity of Jesus, the Son of God, is thereby made not only the catalyst but also the criterion for evaluating the authenticity of any claim to perceive the Spirit's present operation on humanity. This led Smail to hold to a high expectation of what it means for the Spirit to be active in and among us; and consequently, it has led him to retreat in large measure from continued participation in the Charismatic Movement. Smail's discontent with those who claim an experience of and revelation from the Spirit arises from the conviction that the Spirit's action on our humanity should reflect that action of the Spirit which was upon Jesus.

Smail's continued adherence to a Western model of the Trinity, with its perspective on the Spirit as *vinculum Trinitatis*, also led him into difficulties when he sought to convey something of the Spirit's dynamic towards us. Where, in his earlier work, an appreciation of the dynamic of the Spirit's economy was an important feature, this changed as he proceeded to work through the implications of his Trinitarian theology. Smail mitigated his emphasis on the dynamic action of the Spirit towards the humanity of Christian believers, stressing instead the action of the Spirit upon and within Christ's vicarious humanity and emphasising how this arises from the eternal communion of the Father and the Son. Consequently, we saw that Smail increasingly moved away from stressing the dynamic of the Spirit within God's salvific economy towards an emphasis on the Spirit as He who is reciprocal within the relationship of the eternal Father and Son. For Smail, it has become the case that a proper appreciation of God's immanent Being should precede an evaluation of the Spirit's ontic actuality.

Where Smail starts with the axiom of the Trinity's ontological integrity, Dunn has adopted a contrasting approach, not denying the objectivity of the existential reality of God; but seeking to root our understanding of that reality within the experience of humanity and verifiable by mankind. Where Smail starts with that reality which is hidden in the objectivity of God, yet manifest to us, Dunn begins with human experience as the point upon which our appreciation of God's reality is founded. As with Smail, however, Dunn insists on presenting Jesus Christ as the prototype of the Charismatic. Where Dunn differs from Smail is in that he does not insist that Christ's experience of the Spirit should arise out of, or be derived from, His status as the divine Son. The affirmation of one particular Christological model is not Dunn's interest. Instead, for Dunn, a truer focus lies in the special character of Christ's experience of the Spirit. What both Smail and Dunn share is their insistence that the experience of the Spirit enjoyed by Jesus is indicative of a true experience of the Spirit by humanity.

For Smail, this has led to an increasing degree of disillusionment with the Charismatic Movement. For Dunn it has meant a distinction and, indeed, a disjunction being introduced between the experience of the true Charismatic, Jesus, and that of Christians who, as Enthusiasts or ecstatics, can but imperfectly reflect that elusive paradigm founded in Christ. Dunn thereby makes Himself vulnerable to the accusation that he allows for an insufficient identification between Jesus and ourselves, in the common work of the Spirit in Jesus's humanity and ours. Dunn will not allow us the same experience as that of Jesus.

In their preoccupation with the Christological paradigm, Smail and Dunn both appear to perpetuate the failure of the Scottish Reformed tradition to marry a functional pneumatology to their Christology. For both Smail and Dunn, their pneumatology is contingent on their Christological understanding, radically different though their approaches be. Both present an idealised understanding of the Spirit's action, which derives from their Christological perspectives. For both, the action of the Spirit found in the church is but a poor reflection of that patterned in Christ Jesus.

Such a measure of distrust, regarding the nature of our present experience of the Spirit, does not appear to be typical of those interviewees whose accounts were noted in chapter 1 and who have been central participants in the Scottish Charismatic Movement. Neither Smail nor Dunn offer a theology which mirrors the positive expectation of those who believe that a direct and immediate experience of the Holy Spirit may be realised, and who claim to experience such a thing, actualised in their own lives. Having identified the apparent weakness within Scottish theology of subordinating pneumatology to Christology, we must therefore ask whether it is possible for us to redress this deficiency, thereby reaching towards a pneumatological understanding which more adequately conveys that to which the Charismatic Movement testifies. We seek to address this question in the final chapter of our study.

Chapter 8

Towards the Trinity

8.1 Review

In seeking to establish a theological framework within which we might examine the Person and work of the Holy Spirit, we noted in the opening chapter of our study that the Charismatic Movement's emphasis upon experience of God faced us with four questions. We open our final chapter by reviewing these questions in the light of what has been discussed in the intervening chapters.

The first question raised related to the propriety of ontic actuality as a descriptor. In chapter 1, we conceived of this expression to denote the activity of God as met with in Charismatic experience, noting that within the Charismatic Movement God is perceived as being met with in His ontic actuality, apprehended as God actualises His own Being towards us. Consequently, our ability to comprehend or speak of God is contingent on God meeting with us in His ontic actuality.

Our study would lead us to suggest that ontic actuality is a descriptor that can be fitted into the framework of the Scottish tradition. That the initiative should lie with God in revealing Himself, and that this self-revelation is to be received by mankind, is integral to the thought of Calvin and firmly rooted in Scottish Reformed theology. Where the focus of the Scottish tradition differs from that of the Charismatic Movement is in regard to what is central to that revelation. As argued in chapters 3 and 4, the emergent Scottish tradition was more concerned with maintaining a theological framework structured on a system of Scriptural hermeneutics than with one dominated by ontological concerns. In contrast, the Charismatic Movement has tended to view the authority of Scripture, albeit axiomatic, as ancillary to the primary emphasis of experiencing God in His ontic actuality. The primary concern of the Charismatic Movement, on the other hand, has been an ontological one. The Charismatic Movement has been concerned with affirming and exploring the relationship that exists between the Person of the Holy Spirit and Christians.

This is not to say that the Scottish tradition has disallowed a place for meeting with God other than in mankind's understanding of God gained through the Scriptures. As we noted throughout our discussion of developments in Scottish pneumatology, the sacraments have featured as a means of God's communion with His church. Likewise, the resurgence of dialectical theology in the twentieth century, as evidenced in the work of Karl Barth and T. F. Torrance, brought the issue of ontology to the centre of the theological agenda. The Christocentric focus expressed in the sacraments and in renewed ontological interests did not, however, provide a framework in which the Charismatic Movement's focus on the Spirit could readily find expression. An emphasis on celebrating the sacraments has not been a central feature of the Scottish Charismatic Movement;[1] and an objective focus on the person of Christ did not meet the need to explain the real and personal appropriation of the Spirit which occurred, in a suprarational manner, within the experience of the Charismatic Movement.

Where we are to present a Trinitarian model true to the Scottish tradition, we recognise that this model should have a clearly Christocentric reference. At the same time, if our model is to be true to the Charismatic experience, it has to offer an anthropocentric reference in addition to that found in the Incarnation. It is necessary to present a perception of God met with and experienced in His ontic actuality by mankind, as well as in the meeting of mankind by God in the person of Jesus Christ. We require to establish a perception of the Trinity which has an anthropocentric as well as a Christocentric reference.

The second question raised in our opening chapter follows from the first but is more specifically pneumatological in tenor. We noted that there was a need to explore whether it is theologically legitimate to speak of the Holy Spirit, as distinct from the Father and the Son, as He who is met with by us in God's ontic actuality. In our subsequent survey of the development of pneumatology in the Patristic period, we saw that such a notion of the Spirit's ontic actuality appeared to be present in the pre-Nicene period, the Spirit's ontic actuality acting in a manner complementary to the ontic actuality of the Son expressed in and through the Son's Incarnation. What emerged in the post-Nicene period was a concern to define relations within the Triunity of God, a process which led in the West to an understanding of the Spirit as *vinculum Trinitatis*. From this, we deduced that developments in post-Nicene Trinitarian thought appeared to diminish a full appreciation of the Spirit's ontic actuality.

It follows that reservations over that tendency in the Charismatic Movement, to emphasise the ontic actuality of the Spirit as opposed to that of the Son, may well be legitimate. An emphasis on the Spirit does not readily fit with the post-Nicene model developed in the West. At the same time, any failure within the Charismatic Movement to grapple with the relationship of the Spirit to the ontic actuality of the Son is paralleled by that tendency, which we have traced in the Scottish tradition, to evade the issue of ontology as a whole. Furthermore, the dominant Western emphasis on the *vinculum Trinitatis* has meant that when the

---

[1] With the noticeable exception of Charismatic Renewal within the Roman Catholic church in Scotland which, as we noted in chapter 1, has followed its own distinctive course.

question of the nature of God's Being made manifest in salvific economy has been addressed, it has been handled primarily as a Christological issue. The *vinculum Trinitatis* serves to implicate and imply the Spirit's presence and activity when the fact of the Incarnation is addressed. Indeed, so strong is this assumption that, where the nature of the Spirit's ontic actuality is addressed separately from that of the Son, this could be - and has been - mistakenly taken as tantamount to a denial of the priority of the Incarnation and the salvific mission of the Son.

Where we speak of the ontic actuality of the Spirit we must therefore seek to do so in a manner that does not detract from the Son's Incarnation and soterial mission, but which can be seen to parallel and complement it. While seeking to avoid subsuming the ontic actuality of the Spirit within the event of the Son's Incarnation, we need to develop a Trinitarian model which allows us to maintain the central significance of the Son's Incarnation while also conveying the full sense of the Spirit's present participation with us. We would argue that such an approach is justified by those perspectives established and traced by us in pre-Nicene pneumatology. This approach is also required in the light of the difficulties we noted as arising in the attempts by both Smail and Dunn to establish a fresh understanding of the Spirit, the former appealing to a foundation in the Incarnation where the Spirit is perceived as *vinculum Trinitatis*, and the latter to an experience-centred pneumatology linked to a more opaque Christology. What is required is a Trinitarian model that will help us comprehend how the Son's Incarnation and the Spirit's ontic actuality are complementary aspects of the divine economy, expressing the ontic actuality of both the Son and the Spirit.

Thirdly, in so far as we have identified that a relationship should exist between our suprarational experience of the Spirit and our rational appreciation of God, we raised the question of the nature of this relationship, querying whether it could be legitimate to predicate rational appreciation of God from suprarational experience. It has been evident from our review of developments in Scottish theology that where some place has been given, principally through the vehicle of the sacraments, to the suprarational work of the Spirit, primary emphasis has been upon rational appreciation of God. Furthermore, the Charismatic Movement's emphasis on suprarational experience carries separate connotations from those associated with the Spirit's work in the sacraments. A tendency in the Charismatic Movement towards the ecstatic and phenomenal contrasts with a more subtle and implicit understanding of the Spirit's suprarational work in those areas of Scottish sacramental theology we have looked into. To devise a model that might allow us to view our rational appreciation of God as arising out of a suprarational experience of the Spirit might seem improbable, in that the Scottish tradition has been weighted in favour of a rational appreciation of God.

At the same time, we would also observe that certain aspects of the way the Spirit has been dealt with in Scottish theology render such a reorientation of thought not entirely untenable. As we noted, it was possible to identify in Calvin's thought three functions of the Spirit - the epistemic agency, the suprarational work of the Spirit and the Spirit as the executor of God's elective decision - all of which, we argued, appeared to be distinguishable from the Person of the Spirit. Consequently there did not appear to be any clear development of these functions in a manner which would associate them with the ontic actuality of the Spirit. Would it not be possible to consolidate these three functions of the Spirit, treating them as proper functions of the Spirit's Being? We saw this approach, marrying the Being and functions of the Spirit, in the work of T. F. Torrance. Torrance, however, chose to emphasise the Spirit's ontic actuality within the context of the *vinculum Trinitatis,* preferring to stress the priority of the Son's Incarnation in the salvific economy. Should we succeed in constructing a Trinitarian model amenable to both the Scottish tradition and the Charismatic perspective, we will have to find a way of presenting the Spirit's ontic actuality which denotes these functions of the Spirit, without subsuming the Spirit's ontic actuality within an Incarnational tautology. At the same time, our presentation of the Person and function of the Spirit should complement and not detract from the Son's ontic actuality.

Where, for the Charismatic, the primary means of realising the ontic actuality of the Spirit is through present experience, the appropriation of rational or propositional truth regarding God is predicated by this meeting with the Spirit. God's communication to us is a communication of His Being actualised towards us. What is required of us is that we present a model whereby the functions of the Spirit - the epistemic agency, the suprarational work of the Spirit and the Spirit as the executor of God's elective decision - can be seen to arise from the ontic actuality of the Spirit in a way that is complementary to the ontic actuality of the Son.

Finally, we noted that we would have to ask whether the importance attached by participants within the Charismatic Movement to relationship, both with God and with other Christians, assists us in improving our understanding of the Person and function of the Holy Spirit. We observed, within Patristic thought, the development of Trinitarian models which emphasised relationships within God's immanent Being. The possibility arises that we might reconstruct a Trinitarian model centred on the ontic actuality of both the Son and the Spirit, allowing us to perceive divine-human and human interpersonal relationships as integral to our perception of God. In other words, the existence of relationship between God and people, and among people, should itself be constitutive of our understanding of the Trinity and our communion with the Holy Spirit, as He embraces us in His ontic actuality.

Our task in this final chapter is to outline a Trinitarian model which has a clear anthropocentric reference, allowing us to form a balanced perspective of the complementary functions of the Son and the Spirit, present in their ontic actuality and constitutive of the Triune God's salvific economy. Our model should lead us towards an understanding of our communion with the Spirit which allows the Spirit's function to be seen as integral to the Spirit's communion with us, presenting us with a perception of divine-human relationality which neither creates a dualism between mankind and God, nor reduces the doctrine of the Trinity to the status of an anthropomorphism.

In the next section of this chapter we will look at the issue of relationality and ontology. We will examine how we might best approach the question of relationality within the Trinity, where this is to be combined with an anthropocentric reference. We will consider some alternative ways of viewing relationality within the Trinity, having consideration for our need to form a Trinitarian model which depicts the Spirit's ontic actuality. We will then posit a model that allows us to view Triune relationality with an anthropocentric reference. Following this, we will proceed to examine how we might relate the operation of the Spirit upon mankind to the paradigm of the Spirit's operation in Jesus. Finally, we will go on to conclude our study by exploring briefly how our revised model of the Trinity might help us towards gaining a fresh perspective on the Person and function of the Holy Spirit.

8.2   The Question of Relationality

Through our study in the development of early Trinitarian thought in chapter 2, we observed some of the difficulties that can arise in attempting to develop a Trinitarian model out of an understanding of relationships within the Immanent Trinity. We noted a tendency in Patristic thought to develop an expression of relationships with a focus on the Immanent Trinity coming to take priority over an appreciation of God's Triune Being in salvific economy. Consequently, the perceived ontology of the Economic Trinity could come to be viewed as arising out of a proper appreciation of the Immanent Trinity. Pre-Nicene Trinitarian thought was formed from an appreciation of God's salvific economy. It was largely the need to determine the issue of the *homoousion* and define the relationship of the Father and Son that drew the focus of thought onto immanent Trinitarian relationships. We also observed that the development of models of the Immanent Trinity took place within a mindset shaped by Plato and his successors, which tended to emphasise mankind's rational awareness of the Triune God's Being; a God whose Being could so easily be interpreted as eternally set apart from mankind and creation.

In identifying the priority given to an immanent model of the Trinity in Calvin and in the early development of Scottish theology, we have argued that this focus on the Immanent Trinity has detracted from an awareness of the ontic actuality of the Spirit, met with in the experience of people. This observation should not lead us, of necessity, to advocate that a theology of the Immanent Trinity should be abandoned in favour of a singularly economic perspective. We acknowledge that the search for an appropriate description of the relationship between an Immanent and Economic Trinity is a concern of contemporary Trinitarian theology. From the perspective of our study, we simply note the danger of beginning with the axiom of an Immanent Trinity. A focus on the Immanent Trinity may diminish our awareness of the Spirit's ontic actuality. Is it not fair to ask whether a developed understanding of the Economic Trinity should not, in fact, be given priority over a developed understanding of the Immanent Trinity? In our study, we have suggested that the primary concern of the Charismatic Movement is an ontological one, in that Charismatics have a legitimate concern in affirming and exploring the relationship which exists between the Holy Spirit and mankind.

A fresh perspective on the Person and function of the Holy Spirit within a Trinitarian framework may well be gained by exploring further the nature of relationality within the relationship brought about between the Triune God and mankind. In looking to the question of relationality, we will restrict ourselves to looking at some of the differing attempts, met with in our study, to analyse the nature of relationality between God and mankind. Two approaches to the question of relationality can readily be identified. These we will describe as expositions of *immanent relationality* and *economic relationality*. We met with the first of these in chapter 6, championed by Karl Barth. Central to this method is the conviction that the key to understanding relationality lies in expounding the interpersonal relationships of the Godhead. There are those who have continued, beyond Barth, in seeking to develop an understanding of the implications of *immanent relationality* within the Being of God, endeavouring to expound and apply the significance of immanent Trinitarian relations in helping to understand mankind's relationship to God and human relationships themselves.[2]

One such theologian is the late Colin Gunton of King's College, London, whose criticism of Augustine was noted in chapter 2.[3] In a series of publications through the 1990s up to his sudden death in 2003, Gunton continued to explore and develop the implications of the intrinsic relationality that is in God's Triune Being. Following Barth, Gunton affirms that our knowledge of God can only be had through God's acts towards us. Gunton's particular Patristic preference lies with the Cappadocians and, whilst aware of

---

[2] A comprehensive examination of these and other contemporary developments lies outwith the compass of this study, but reference can be had to the following works. A review of European Trinitarian thought from the mid 1970's to mid 1990's from a broad, Reformed perspective is found in John Thomson's *Modern Trinitarian Perspectives*, OUP, Oxford, 1994. An even broader review of work to date, from an Anglican perspective, is David S. Cunningham's *These Three Are One*, Blackwell Publishers, Oxford, 1998. One particular development of Karl Barth's thought, taking a philosophical theological approach, is Alan Torrance's *Persons in Communion*, T&T Clark, Edinburgh, 1996.

[3] Others have sought to develop further the Augustinian *vinculum*: Smail, in *The Giving Gift*, especially commends the work of H. Muhlen (*The Giving Gift*, pp. 154ff..), who seeks to correct a tendency within the Augustinian tradition to depersonalise the Spirit.

the dangers of romanticising the Eastern Tradition,[4] he sees in their work a basis for conceptual development. He finds in the Cappadocians a coherent description of God in His acts, which he summarises as 'all of God's acts take their beginning in the Father, are put into effect through the Son and reach their completion in the Spirit'.[5] While the Economic Trinity provides us with our basis for making positive statements about God,[6] from this Gunton sees that we can go on to speak of God as He is in His Immanence.[7]

Gunton invites us to view the Trinity in terms of interpersonal relatedness, allowing the relationships which exist between the Persons of the Trinity to qualify, ontologically, the character of the three Persons.[8] From this basic premise, an understanding of personhood is established as a central key to Gunton's understanding of divine and human relationality. Gunton deduces that it is from the dynamic relation of particularity and separateness among the three Persons of the Trinity that personhood is constituted.[9] It is from the basis of this foundational Trinitarian ontology that Gunton can claim to perceive the relationship which exists between mankind and God. Where mankind is God's creation, human beings exist both in relatedness and community, yet with a separateness that affirms their distinctive personhood. We see from this that, for Gunton, the study of ontology calls us to examine the relatedness of persons rather than questions of substance, or *ousia*. In terms of mankind's communion with God, his interest lies in studying mankind's relatedness to the Divine, rather than examining the nature of mankind's substantial participation with the divine *ousia*.

The nature of this relatedness within God and by mankind to God has also been developed, along parallel lines to those of Gunton, by John Zizioulas.[10] As Zizioulas puts it, 'the ontology of God is not subject to the necessity of the substance'[11]. Mankind can share that relationship with God which, in freedom and love, as Son of the Father conjoined to mankind through the Incarnation,

---

[4] C. E. Gunton, *The Promise of Trinitarian Theology*, T & T Clark, 1991, p. viii.

[5] C. E. Gunton, *Act and Being*, SCM Press, London, 2002, p. 77.

[6] Ibid.. pp. 76-93. Gunton, noticeably in his later work, gives recogniton to the importance of Irenaeus's depiction of the divine economy, taking this as pointing the way towards the fuller Trinitarian synthesis of the Cappadocians. *Vide* C. E. Gunton, *Father, Son and Holy Spirit*, T & T Clark, London, 2003, pp. 77, 81.

[7] Because, Gunton reasons, 'He is triune as he presents himself to us in our time, and that this tri-unity is eternal'. *Act and Being*, Op. cit., p. 94.

[8] C. E. Gunton, *Augustine, the Trinity and the Theological Crisis of the West*, in *The Scottish Journal of Theology* 43(1), 1990, pp. 44-45.

[9] 'Otherness and relation continue to be the two central and polar concepts here. Only where both are given due stress is personhood fully enabled'. C. Schwoebel and C. E. Gunton (Editors), *Persons, Divine and Human*, T & T Clark, Edinburgh, 1991, p. 59.

[10] Formerly Professor of Systematic Theology at Glasgow University and presently Orthodox Metropolitan of Pergamon.

[11] J. Zizioulas, *Being as Communion*, DLT, London, 1985, p. 46.

Christ has with the Father[12]. Again, where relationship within the Triune God is permanent and unbreakable, ontology is made into a matter of relationship[13].

The effect of this on our understanding of the church's participation in the Holy Spirit is to foster a perception of the Holy Spirit as He who liberates us into true personhood, both in particularity and in freedom, hence realising and bringing us into that personhood which arises from our union with Christ. The Spirit is He who effects our communion with God, thereby releasing us into personhood. As Gunton aptly phrases it, the Spirit

> is God present to the world as its liberating other, bringing it to the destiny determined by the Father, made actual, realised, in the Son.[14]

This perception of the Spirit as He who liberates us has the advantage of allowing us to view the Spirit eschatologically, reaching out to us and shattering the confines of what Gunton denounces as the 'non-eschatological Platonic triad'[15] which features so large in Western Trinitarian thought. Gunton views this false perspective on the Trinity as arising from what we styled, in chapter 2, a Western model of the Trinity. Where we put this Western model behind us, we can come to realise that the Spirit is embracing us in His own relationality, the Spirit constituting within the church a communion which is reflective of that communion which is true of the Triune God's immanent relationality.

The question which faces us is whether this approach to pneumatology gives sufficient expression to an understanding of mankind's communion with the substantial reality - the *ousia* - of the Spirit. The perspectives of Gunton and Zizioulas offer us an alternative to the Western model of the Trinity in much the same way as the Eastern Trinitarian model, which we identified in chapter 2, offers an alternative model in post-Nicene developments. The Spirit is perceived as reaching out; but the nature of that communion with mankind is founded on the relatedness of persons arising from God's triunity. Ultimately, the model offered remains one founded on a perception of the Immanent Trinity, not one shaped by the ontic actuality of the Son and the Spirit, in the actualisation of God's Being towards us. For our purposes, in seeking to express how the Being of the Spirit can be actualised in human experience, this approach is of limited assistance. The area where it might prove to be of most help is in offering a perspective which affirms the importance of relationality in understanding Trinitarian and divine-human ontology, in a manner that identifies the Spirit acting in freedom and relatedness. We will return to this

---

[12] *Being as Communion*, p 56.
[13] *Persons, Divine and Human*, p. 41.
[14] A.I.C. Heron (Editor), *The Forgotten Trinity* Vol. 3, Council of Churches for Britain and Ireland, London, 1991, p. 130.
[15] *The Forgotten Trinity*, p. 132.

aspect later.

An alternative way of viewing relationality within the Trinity and the Triune God's relationship to mankind is to expound the Trinity in terms of *economic relationality*. By this we understand a method whereby a perception of the Immanent Trinity is extended to describe that Trinity's threefold relatedness as Father, Son and Spirit in terms that explicate the nature of the Spirit's economy. An understanding of the Triune God is extended to emphasise distinctive aspects of the divine economy which can be associated with each of the three Persons. Relationality is perceived as an attribute not only of the divine Persons among themselves, but is expressed in the distinctive nature of the Triune God's salvific economy towards mankind.

One example of this approach arose in our study of Edward Irving's pneumatology. There we noted that Irving traced three distinct stages which can be detected in the Spirit's operation on our humanity. The first action, seen in our regeneration by the Spirit, was that of the Father; the second action, of sustaining us in holiness and obedience to the Father, that of the Son; the third action, the 'baptism of the Holy Spirit', corresponded to the Holy Spirit issuing from the present, resurrection life of Christ. What was not evident in Irving's perception of the Triune God's economic relationality was how this was to be correlated to his understanding of the Immanent Trinity, an understanding which was developed in terms of the traditional Western model's perception of the Spirit as *vinculum Trinitatis*. This question, although not addressed by Irving, has been taken up more recently in the writings of the German theologian, J. Moltmann. In *The Trinity and the Kingdom of God* Moltmann laid out his understanding that the radical commitment of God to mankind, the foundation of which was expounded in his earlier work, *The Crucified God*, requires that any doctrine of the Trinity must be related to an understanding of the salvific economy. There is a clear relationship that exists between our experience of God in His salvific economy and God as He is in His immanent Being, a relationship that will be fully clarified in the eschatological fulfilment of God's Kingdom.[16] In that there is an eschatological aspect to a full understanding of the Trinity, our present understanding is a qualified one, whereby we are called to understand and identify the actualisation of the Spirit in temporal terms. This corresponds to that ongoing history and experience of salvation which is realised among men prior to the full coming of God's Kingdom to earth. Moltmann appeals for a 'Trinitarian doctrine of the Kingdom' in a tripartite scheme that he appropriates from the works of Joachim of Fiore.[17] Three expressions of the Kingdom, bearing a striking similarity to Irving's three stages, are envisaged. The first, that of the Father, pertains to the

---

[16] 'The economic Trinity completes and perfects itself to immanent Trinity when the history and experience of salvation are completed and perfected'. J. Moltmann, *The Trinity and the Kingdom of God*, SCM, London, 1981, p. 161.

[17] *The Trinity and the Kingdom of God*, pp. 203-5.

creation and preservation of the world; the second, that of the Son, to redemption from sin; the third, that of the Spirit, brings us to experience the energies of the new creation.[18] These three kingdoms together point towards 'the eschatological kingdom of glory'[19] which awaits upon God for its final realisation.

The difficulty arising from Moltmann's approach is that, in identifying these three forms of the kingdom as an exposition of the Triune God's nature made manifested to us, Moltmann maintains that God, in His essential, immanent Being, remains other than what He is perceived to be in His salvific economy. As Moltmann reminds us in a more recent work on the Holy Spirit, *The Spirit of Life*, our knowledge of the Holy Spirit 'is always an indirect knowledge, and remains tied to the experiences which are its point of departure'.[20] God's essential Being is accessible to us through our praise in the trinitarian doxology,[21] yet remains ever beyond our definition. Certainly, Moltmann would invite us to form an understanding of how it is that God deals with us by His Spirit in the present and this he would have us hold to in a Trinitarian framework; but he does not argue for a clear, metaphysical picture of the Immanent Trinity. Instead, he appeals to the notion of God who, in His essential Being, stands over against us, the 'primordial Trinity'[22] who remains unknowable, yet without whom there can be no meaningful identification of the Triune, salvific economy and of the Spirit's activity. To speak of God in His economic relationality we require this perception of a primordial Trinity who is 'from eternity an *open* Trinity ... open for human beings, open for the world, and open for time'.[23]

Herein lies the difficulty that confronts us in seeking to understand the Person and function of the Holy Spirit in terms of the Triune God's economic relationality. Whatever economic model of the Trinity is devised by this method, there is perceived to be an antecedent reality within God's Being. We may, with Moltmann, insist that this reality is open, accommodating all that has been and is wrought through the divine, salvific economy; yet our assurance, that in meeting with the Spirit we are meeting with Him in His ontic actuality, must always be dulled by the knowledge that the essential Being of God remains beyond us. Certainly such an approach ensures a sustained awareness that God is truly self-defining. It remains open to question whether such an understanding of God's Triune Being is of help to us in constructing a Trinitarian model that will demonstrate adequately the nature of the Spirit's Person and work.

---

[18] *The Trinity and the Kingdom of God*, p. 211.
[19] *The Trinity and the Kingdom of God*, p. 212.
[20] J. Moltmann, *The Spirit of Life*, SCM, London, 1992, p. 289.
[21] *The Spirit of Life*, pp. 301ff..
[22] *The Spirit of Life*, p. 292.
[23] *The Spirit of Life*, p. 294.

Present within both approaches to the question of relationality that we have outlined, *immanent relationality* and *economic relationality*, is the conviction that there should be an eschatological dimension to our perception of the Trinity. That is, a distinction is made between our present knowledge and experience of God and that which will be realised by mankind beyond the *eschaton*. In the first approach, a proper appreciation of Triune, immanent relationality was seen as releasing us into a realisation of what we are called to be, from present beginnings, within the eschatological dimension. In the second approach, an awareness of God in present, temporal reality is qualified by the realisation that beyond the temporal we are yet to be met by God in the eternal dimension. We would suggest that a third approach might be pursued. God, in meeting with us in our temporal dimension, can be understood as inviting us to participate in that which we could not be without Him; but at the same time He is calling us to realise that the Triune God is no other than that which He manifests Himself to be in His ontic actuality, active in His salvific economy towards us now.

In seeking to relate our perception of the Trinity to ourselves, rather than in pursuing an exclusively Christocentric focus as insisted upon by Torrance, we follow the path opened for us by Dunn. We look for an explanation of our meeting between mankind and the Spirit of God in terms that will not lead us, of necessity, to subsume our understanding of this meeting within a Christocentric tautology: a problem that we found to be inherent within the Western model of the Trinity, as evidenced in the work of Smail. In looking to develop an understanding of the Spirit's presence and action upon us, we therefore seek to expand further our Trinitarian understanding and reference to our humanity, distinct yet not detached from humanity vicariously met with by God in Christ. We come to introduce an anthropocentric reference to our model of the Trinity, a reference which is supplementary to that established for mankind in and through the Incarnation. In the following section we begin to explore this alternative approach more fully.

8.3   An Anthropocentric Reference in Perceiving the Trinity

In suggesting that we seek to establish a point of an anthropocentric reference to our understanding of the Trinity, we are not looking to reintroduce the agenda of the liberal theological quest of the nineteenth century, built on a foundation of Schleiermachian subjectivity which Barth and Torrance, among others, have sought so strenuously to overcome. Rather, we are attempting to recognise and respond to a needful distinction, noted in our discussion of Smail and Dunn, between the vicarious humanity of Christ - who is uniquely the Son Incarnate - and the humanity of those who, albeit experiencing the same Holy Spirit as Jesus Christ, stand apart from the individual man who is Jesus Christ.

In one sense, the need to establish an anthropocentric reference for our understanding of the Trinity occurs because of the focal importance of the

Incarnation. Both our Pre-Nicene and Western Trinitarian models illustrate this. In the Pre-Nicene model as exemplified by Irenaeus, the Spirit is joined to humanity in the church, wherein we are met with Jesus Christ: the 'two hands of the Father', the Spirit and the Son, coinciding there together - hence the doctrines of recapitulation[24] and the vicarious humanity of Christ. Again, in the Western model, the Augustinian emphasis on the Spirit as the 'bond' between the Father and the Son allows the Godhead a relationship with mankind through the event of the Incarnation while, at the same time, anchoring our appreciation of the Spirit to a Christocentric focus in the Son. The difficulty arising from both approaches is that neither properly allows our humanity's communion with the Spirit to be readily differentiated or distinguished from the Spirit's presence and activity in Christ's humanity. This was the inescapable problem that confronted Irving when he sought to stress our humanity's communion with God: his critics had grasped that Christ's humanity was conjoined to God, but failed to understand how our own humanity was implicated in that communion with God through Christ's humanity. While the evolving development of Trinitarian models in the Patristic era led to a view of the Immanent Trinity that could truly be said to arise from the salvific economy of God, an appreciation of humanity met with in the ontic actuality of both the Son and of the Spirit came to be lost sight of where increasing attention was given to the Immanent Trinity and the character of the *homoousion*. As we noted in chapter 2, it was possibly in part a reaction to this process that brought trouble to Arius in the fourth century, where he attempted to emphasise the full significance of Christ's human nature, as did Irving in the nineteenth century. Furthermore, even when the universal significance of Christ's humanity has been stressed, as we observed in the work of T. F. Torrance, there is still the danger, in holding to a singularly Christocentric reference in describing our humanity's communion with and experience of the Holy Spirit, that we fail to distinguish between Jesus Christ's own communion with God and that communion which is established and enabled by Him, through His atoning work, for all mankind. In order to counter any tendency to telescope all human experience of the Spirit into the experience of Christ Himself, we must therefore determine a further anthropocentric reference to mankind's communion with the Triune God, a corollary to the Christocentric reference. Our suggestion is that in order to reach towards an understanding of relationality both in the Triune Being and in God's relationship to humanity, there has to be a point of reference taken to mankind beyond the moment of revelation that is in and through the Incarnation.

It needs to be stressed, at this point, that we are not seeking to diminish or detract from the soteriological focus that is upon Jesus Christ, *homoousion* with the Father and hypostatically united in His divinity and humanity. Nor are we

---

[24] The understanding, found in Irenaeus, that the whole of humanity is summed up, or encapsulated, in the life of Jesus Christ.

suggesting that salvation is to be found anywhere other than in and through the Son Incarnate. What we are seeking to establish is a point whereby mankind meets with and realises the ontic actuality of the Spirit beyond the Spirit's presence and action in the humanity of Jesus Christ Himself. What is under review is how the Holy Spirit expresses Himself both towards Jesus Christ and towards those He is calling and drawing to Jesus Christ.

We require to develop a Trinitarian model which preserves a symmetrical balance between the ontic actuality of the Son, as met with in the Incarnation, and the ontic actuality of the Spirit, as made evident in Charismatic experience. This bifocal symmetry, focusing upon the ontic actuality of the Son expressed in the Incarnation and the ontic actuality of the Spirit realised through our anthropocentric reference, will be a critical feature of our revised Trinitarian model. By this means we will seek to distinguish our understanding of God's self-revelation from that met with in Torrance, who presented us with a Christocentricity which could be falsely mistaken as a form of Christomonism. Likewise, we would determinedly seek to avoid a Father-Spirit binitarianism as found in Lampe's *God as Spirit*[25] and the consequent danger of circumventing or minimising the significance of the Son's Incarnation. We look to establish a bifocal symmetry, focusing on both the ontic actuality of the Son as met with in the Incarnation and the ontic actuality of the Spirit identified through our anthropocentric reference. Through this bifocal symetry we will seek to express the distinctive identities of the Son and the Spirit in the salvific economy which is from the Father, without subrogating the ontic actuality of either the Spirit or the Son through focusing on one in preference to the other.

It is at this point that our search for a revised Trinitarian model brings us to depart most radically from the approach fostered by the traditional Western model. Kilian McDonnell, in exploring possibilities within the traditional approach and while arguing the need for an understanding of the Son and Spirit's mutuality in the salvific economy, cautions against the possibility of viewing the two missions of Son and Spirit as 'two foci at the ends of an elongated circle', insisting instead that their mutuality be viewed as that of two concentric circles which, while apparently superimposed, remain distinct from one another.[26] From this, McDonnell argues that the Spirit fulfils the 'contact function' between God and mankind, drawing mankind to the Father through Christ and through the church. In our search for a revised Trinitarian model we would argue that, in contrast, the ontic actuality of the Son and the Spirit can be viewed precisely as 'two foci at the ends of an elongated circle', with the qualification that the Spirit is present in the first focus as He who is upon the Son Incarnate in Jesus Christ; and in the second focus as He who is upon and active in mankind other than in and through the humanity of Jesus Christ. From

---

[25] G. W. H. Lampe, *God as Spirit*, Clarendon Press, Oxford, 1977.
[26] K. McDonnell, 'Trinitarian Theology of the Spirit', *Theological Studies* 46 (1985), p. 210.

our perspective, with the first focus the emphasis lies upon the Incarnate Son, who has become a specific human being, for us.

Jesus Christ, in and through the hypostatic union, undertakes to save us, vicariously embracing our humanity in and through his own humanity. In this first focus upon Jesus Christ, we recognise the Holy Spirit's presence and activity in His humanity. The focus is on the vicarious humanity of Jesus Christ, hypostatically united to the Son of God in salvific purposefulness. We might represent this first focus, diagrammatically, as follows:

First focus:

The Triune God

manifest through

the Incarnation

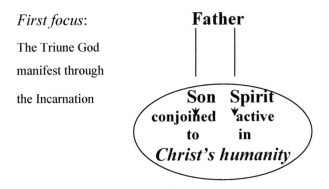

With the second focus, the emphasis lies with the Spirit who comes to mankind, energising us, informing us and drawing us into a lateral movement of discovery and surrender to the Son of God, irretrievably yoked to our humanity through the Incarnation. We might represent this second focus, diagrammatically, as follows:

Second focus:

The Triune God

met with in the

Spirit's

salvific economy

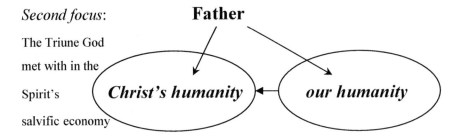

By emphasising the bifocal symmetry of the Son and the Spirit in their ontic actuality, we can hopefully present a perception of the distinctiveness of both the Son and the Spirit in their salvific economy. While maintaining the catholic tradition of focusing on that theophany which is in Christ Jesus, we wish to identify a further point of relationship in the salvific economy, not only identifying the Incarnation as the point of God's meeting with mankind; but also acknowledging mankind, outwith Christ, met with in the Spirit.

Two advantages accrue in pursuing this bifocal symmetry. Firstly, there is here a perspective of the Trinity which is focused on Christ together with an appreciation of the Spirit as He who is manifest and met with in and through the Incarnate Son. Secondly, there is a complementary perspective which arises from our present experience and participation in the Holy Spirit. Both foci are Trinitarian, in that the Father is recognised as the sender of both the Son and the Spirit. In the Incarnation, where we are confronted with the ontic actuality of the Son, we also meet with the Spirit's activity in the humanity of Christ. At the same time, through our present reception of the Spirit, we are brought to a sharper awareness of the Son who is now risen, glorified and with the Father. Through holding to this bifocal symmetry, we retain a viewpoint that is at once both Christocentric, in that it is centred on the Incarnation, and anthropocentric, in that it is focused on our present reception of the Spirit.

Given that we seek to establish a bifocal symmetry to our Trinitarian model, the question arises of how the ontic actuality of the Spirit, as related to our anthropocentric reference, can be correlated to the Spirit's relationship with the Son's ontic actuality, as realised in the Incarnation. It is to this issue that we now turn.

8.4   Relating the Spirit in us to the Spirit in Jesus

In what way can our experience of the Spirit be related to the experience of the Spirit in Jesus? At one extreme, we met with T. F. Torrance's conviction that all human experience of God must be focused on Jesus and the awareness of the Trinity into which His life inducts us. As Torrance puts it,

> The devout and accurate way to know the Holy Spirit is not by beginning with manifestations or operations of the Spirit in creaturely existence which is external to God but from the propriety of the Spirit to the eternal being of God, as the Spirit of the Father and the Son, and thus from His internal relations within the Godhead.[27]

An alternative approach can be attempted, using the method of Irving. We earlier saw Irving expand on his understanding of how Christ, in sharing in a common humanity with mankind, became the catalyst for our reception and experience of the Spirit. For Irving, such a reception of the Spirit by mankind is made possible through the Son of God's Incarnation. Herein lies a key to help us distinguish between our present experience of the Spirit and that experience of the Spirit which was true for Jesus. Irving identified that the Christian shares in both a common humanity with Jesus Christ and in the common work of the Spirit upon that humanity. That which makes Jesus different from all others is that He is uniquely the Christ, the Son of God incarnate. The difficulty which

---

[27] *The Trinitarian Faith*, p. 208.

arose for Irving was that, in holding to the Western model of the Trinity, he perceived the Incarnation itself as providing the grounds for humanity's reception of the Spirit. Irving understood that the Son, by becoming incarnate, allowed for all mankind the potential of sharing in Christ's communion in the Spirit.

In the light of our observations on the development of Pre-Nicene thought, we would now ask whether this approach could not be bettered by adapting it to allow for the existence of a mutuality between the ontic actuality of the Son and the Spirit. That is, instead of emphasising the Incarnation as the catalyst of the Spirit's coming to the church, we might view the ontic actuality of the Son and of the Spirit with a bifocal symmetry, as discussed in the preceding section. By adopting this alternative approach, we can affirm the common humanity of both Christ and the Christian, as well as perceiving the Spirit's presence and influence upon both Christ and the Christian. Furthermore, by breaking away from the Western model of the Trinity which Irving assumed, we are freed to identify the one characteristic of Jesus which distinguishes Him from those whose humanity and reception of the Spirit He shares: His identity as Son of God Incarnate. At the same time, we can still acknowledge that humanity and experience of the Spirit which he shares with His church. The uniqueness of Jesus can now be perceived in terms of His being the Son of God Incarnate.

From Irving we see how a perception of the Spirit that is built on the Western Trinitarian model can cause some confusion when we look to identify the distinguishing features of Jesus as both the Christ and Son of God. Too easily the presence of the Spirit upon Jesus can be taken as the distinguishing feature of His being the Son of God: a feature which we traced in Dunn's work. That the Spirit was upon Jesus in a special, or even unique, manner is not in dispute. What we do challenge is that syllogism which combines the fact of the Spirit's presence upon Jesus with a Western model of the Trinity, thereby arriving at the conclusion that it is because of the Incarnation that the church is enabled to receive the Spirit. This questionable assumption arises when we lose sight of the bifocal symmetry, created by the mutuality that exists between the ontic actuality of the Son and that of the Spirit. When this symmetry is regained, we are freed to recognise that the Spirit's action upon our humanity is complementary to that reception of the Spirit which is in the life of Christ; but our reception of the Spirit is not, as understood from the Western model's perception of the Spirit as *vinculum Trinitatis*, necessarily predicated by it.

Where we approach the operation of the Spirit in us and the Son of God incarnate with a bifocal symmetry, we are able to observe a mutual correlation between the ontic actuality of the Son in the Incarnation and the Spirit in our present experience. Both arise from the ontic actualisation of the Son and the Spirit from the Father, and therefore find their harmony in that which is purposed by the Father. Furthermore, the ontic actuality of both the Son and the Spirit have the effect of bringing glory to the Father through Christ Jesus. Foundational to our understanding of this latter point is an empirical observation, gained from our study of the Charismatic Movement in Scotland in chapter 1. An experience of the Spirit, as understood in terms of the Charismatic Movement, appears to lead to a greater appreciation of and desire to approximate to the God whose gift of salvation is brought to us in Jesus Christ. That is, although the Spirit is to be apprehended by us through an anthropocentric reference, the Spirit does not cease to be related to the Son but, in fact, draws us closer towards Him. An acknowledgment and reception of the Spirit in His ontic actuality does not detach us from the Son; rather, it attracts us more deeply into participation with Him. The Spirit informs and calls us into our humanity's full salvation, enabled and realised in and through the humanity of the incarnate Son of God.

In this we note a second characteristic of our revised Trinitarian model. Where, in maintaining the perspective of bifocal symmetry, the Christocentric reference and the anthropocentric reference are to be distinguished, the relationship between the Son and the Spirit has the effect upon us of drawing us into the mutuality which exists between the Son and Spirit, arising from their salvific mission from the Father. Where the ontic actualisation of the Son finds expression through the birth, life, death and resurrection of Jesus of Nazareth as the Christ, so the ontic actualisation of the Spirit, found in an anthropocentric reference, calls mankind to a deeper and greater proximation to the human being who is Christ Jesus. It calls us into a purposeful life of discipleship, into sharing in His sufferings and also in His resurrection empowerment. The Spirit, although realised in our experience as having an anthropocentric reference, turns our awareness beyond ourselves to participation in the life of Jesus Christ.

Two further points should be noted here. In chapter 7 we saw how Dunn identified ecstasy as a feature of early Christian experience which distinguished the church from Jesus, thereby introducing a distinction between the early Christians' experience of the Spirit and Jesus' experience of the Spirit. We would suggest that the bifocal symmetry of our revised model helps to counter Dunn's objection to Christian ecstasy being interpreted as truly charismatic. That Christians should manifest the presence of the Spirit in a manner different from that of Jesus does not require us to insist that there is a different experience of the Spirit, only that the Spirit is manifest differently in those who are other than the Son of God Incarnate. Secondly, it is here that we might invoke that feature of the Gunton-Zizioulas approach which stressed both the freedom and relatedness of the Spirit. The Spirit, while free to relate to us in His own Being, also maintains a relation to the Son. While we may receive the Spirit in our humanity, the Spirit is also manifestly present in the humanity of Jesus Christ, the Son of God incarnate; and calls our humanity into a deeper and more profound relationship to that humanity which is inhabited by the Son of God incarnate. The Spirit may no longer be interpreted as *vinculum Trinitatis*; but the Spirit, active in His own freedom, draws us towards that same Jesus Christ in whom the Son's ontic actuality is realised and brought to completion. The symmetry found in the ontic actuality of both the Son and the

Spirit calls us to proximate more deeply to the humanity that is met with in Jesus Christ.

Thus far, we have identified two features of our revised Trinitarian model. Firstly, we have stressed the importance of maintaining a bifocal symmetry, corresponding to Christocentric and anthropocentric references in apprehending the ontic actuality of the Spirit. Secondly, we have identified that the Spirit, while freely actualised towards us in His Being, is mutually related to the Son whose mission finds full realisation in the person of Jesus Christ. Consequently, the Spirit, meeting with mankind in an anthropocentric reference, brings us to proximate towards the person of Jesus Christ. From these two features, we may deduce a third: that of the procession of the Spirit upon both Christ and our humanity. Where we have introduced a distinction between Christocentric and anthropocentric references for the Spirit, it is necessary to elaborate on how the ontic actuality of the Spirit upon mankind is related to the Spirit's communion with the Son of God incarnate in Jesus Christ. In so far as we have noted the need to maintain a bifocal symmetry to our understanding of the Trinity, we might describe this procession as twofold. In the following section, we will explore further the nature of this twofold procession of the Spirit.

8.5   The Twofold Procession of the Spirit

Earlier in this chapter, we noted the importance of establishing an eschatological dimension to our perception of the Trinity when seeking to understand the nature of relationality as it exists in the Triune God's relationship towards mankind. Having established the need to maintain a bifocal symmetry in viewing the ontic actuality of the Son and the Spirit, we have further noted how the Spirit calls mankind towards a deeper proximation to Jesus Christ. The question which now faces us is how it can be possible to affirm the Spirit's action upon the humanity of Christ without having recourse to a doctrine of relations within an Immanent Trinity. While we are able to affirm the ontic actuality of the Son from the Incarnation and the ontic actuality of the Spirit from His activity in our present experience, we require to resolve how it is possible to affirm that the same Spirit is active in Jesus Christ as is active in our experience.

It is at this point that an eschatological dimension to our understanding of the Trinity requires reaffirmation. Once more, we have recourse to Irving in order to help us form our thinking here. We earlier saw how Irving emphasised the importance of the sacraments in signifying that our communion with the Triune God occurs through the physical body of Christ. Irving affirmed that it is through our communion with the physical body of Christ that we are assured of God's grace. The critical feature of our present communion with Christ is that through it we can share in the benefits that arise for our humanity out of the glorified, resurrected humanity of Jesus Christ. Our present relationship to Christ is not that of humanity related to the Son of God incarnate among us on earth; but of humanity called into relation to the humanity in Christ that is glorified and enthroned in the heavenlies, forever conjoined in hypostatic union to the Son of God.

As we noted in chapter 5, in Irving's account the empowering action of the Spirit upon mankind is specifically associated with the resurrected and ascended Christ, consequential to the completion of His earthly ministry. The present action of the Spirit was seen to be contingent upon Christ in enabling the church to continue in Christ's ministry. We would adapt this aspect of Irving's thought to suggest that, when we are called through the Spirit into communion with Christ, we are called into communion with One whose glorified humanity presently receives and knows the Spirit's ontic actuality in a manner which is eschatologically remote from us, but whose communion with and reception of the Spirit is substantially the same as ours. The Spirit whom Christ receives in His glorified humanity is the same Spirit, sent from the Father, who meets with us in our present experience. The difference between Christ's humanity and ours is in that His experience and communion with the Father is unsullied and unspoilt by human sin. We might say that the resurrected Christ and we who are restrained, to use T. F. Torrance's terminology, within the space-time continuum, receive the same Spirit and in the same manner. Christ's glorified humanity and ours receive the same Spirit, sent from the Father and met with in His ontic actuality; but Christ's reception of the Spirit is eschatologically distinguishable from our own.

It is this eschatological distinction which arises in perceiving humanity's present reception of the Spirit that helps us towards an understanding of the third distinguishing feature of our revised Trinitarian model: the twofold procession of the Spirit. Our communion with the Spirit is substantially the same as that communion experienced by Christ, except in one respect: Christ, unsullied by sin on earth and now glorified in heaven, enjoys a communion with the Spirit qualitatively different from that communion found among sinners. We might say that Christ's reception of the Spirit is that of a humanity uncorrupted by sin, while our reception of the Spirit is that of a humanity whose ability to commune with God has been impaired by sin. It is in relation to this distinction that the significance of the Charismatic experience of 'baptism in the Spirit' might be understood. Central to Irving and, as we have seen, to the main tradition of Scottish theology, has been the role of the sacraments in bringing people to a deeper realisation of Jesus Christ. This focus on the sacraments has not been a central feature of the Charismatic Movement. We would, however, suggest that the Charismatic Movement's emphasis on experiencing the Spirit can be seen as a corollary to and complement of the sacramental focus in the Scottish, Reformed tradition. The Charismatic experience of 'baptism in the Holy Spirit' might be interpreted as that experience of the Spirit which arises when the Father, through the Spirit, brings us to experience in some measure our share and inheritance in the eschatological triumph of the Son of God Incarnate, who shares a humanity in common with us. On the basis of both a humanity shared in common with Christ and the activity of the Spirit in both Christ and us, 'baptism in the Spirit' might therefore be interpreted as an action of the Spirit whereby we come to experience a measure of communion with the Spirit that belongs to the glorified humanity of Christ, a communion unspoilt by the defilement of sin. We might therefore describe 'baptism in the Spirit' as a moment of proleptic, eschatological realisation effected in us by the Spirit, allowing us a foretaste of that which is our full inheritance through faith in Jesus Christ.

In this sense, we are enabled to speak of a twofold procession of the Spirit, reflecting the bifocal symmetry of our revised Trinitarian model. Firstly, in that there is a procession of the Spirit from the Father to the Son Incarnate, we witness Jesus Christ's complete experience of the Spirit, unsullied by sin and demonstrated as eternal through the resurrection of Christ. This is the experience of the Spirit's ontic actuality known to Christ, the Son Incarnate, a relationship that is as permanent as the present marriage of Christ's humanity to the divinity of the Son. Secondly, there is a procession of the Spirit from the Father to humanity whereby, in being brought by the Spirit into an increasing degree of proximation to Christ, we are enabled by the Spirit to anticipate Christ's relationship with the Father through the Spirit. We should not forget that this second procession of the Spirit is no less an experience of the Holy Spirit than that which is Christ's, for the Spirit leads us towards the fuller, unsullied relationship that is Christ's. That is, our experience of the second procession of the Spirit will lead us in the direction of the first procession. Put another way, both processions of the Spirit are interrelated in that the first procession is realised in and through the ontic actuality of the Son's Incarnation and atonement and the second is our present experience of the ontic actuality of the Spirit. The second procession points the way towards the full, eschatological realisation of the first.

Thus far, we have traced three distinguishing features of our revised Trinitarian model: firstly, the requirement of bifocal symmetry; secondly, the effect of the Spirit in bringing about a proximation of people towards Christ; and thirdly, the twofold procession of the Spirit. We now proceed to explore some ways in which our revised model of the Trinity can help us in bringing a fresh perspective to our understanding of the Person and function of the Holy Spirit.

8.6 The Person and Function of the Spirit

It has been remarked that one of the enduring difficulties associated with the Western model of the Trinity has been a reluctance to admit to a special mission of the Holy Spirit, for such recognition might be seen to detract from a proper focus on Christ.[28] In our attempt to form a revised model of the Trinity, we have not sought to interpret the Holy Spirit's mission by further exploring an understanding of the Spirit as *vinculum Trinitatis*. Instead, we have sought to maintain a Christocentric focus supplemented by an anthropocentric focus, thereby affirming that the Spirit can be and is actualised in His Being towards us. From this perspective of bifocal symmetry, we have sought to demonstrate how the ontic actuality of the Spirit serves as a corollary to that of the Son in His Incarnation, the Son and the Spirit both proceeding from the Father in the Triune God's salvific economy towards mankind.

An important consequence of maintaining a bifocal symmetry in our Trinitarian understanding is that we are thereby freed to speak of the Person and function of the Spirit. In focusing on the ontic actuality of the Spirit towards mankind we have recognised that the Person, or Being, of the Spirit is distinguishable from the Person of the Son in His meeting with us. In so distinguishing the Spirit from the Son and by identifying the Spirit in His ontic actuality, we are able to acknowledge the function of the Spirit as it arises out of His own Being. That is, we are enabled to discuss the function of the Spirit in terms of the Spirit's substantial Being and to acknowledge that the Spirit's Being is at one with His function. The Spirit, in His ontic actuality, is functional. Consequently we can speak of any functions of the Spirit as aspects of but one function, that of the Spirit's own Being as He meets with us. Properly speaking, we should therefore refer not to the *functions* but to the *function* of the Spirit; for the function of the Spirit arises from our meeting with the Being of His Person. The proper subject of our examination has been the Person and function of the Holy Spirit.

In so discussing the Person and function of the Spirit in His ontic actuality and His effect upon mankind, we would suggest that it is important to distinguish between those aspects of Christian experience which give rise to special symptoms and an ongoing experience of the Spirit which is foundational to our true communion with God. As we observed in chapter 1, one of the difficulties which arose from the strands of Finneyite, Holiness and Pentecostal thought which appeared within the Charismatic Movement and which were presumed, in critiques that were made of it, to be formative in its theology, was that experience of the Spirit tended to be viewed as 'crisis experience', focusing on momentary climaxes of communion with the Holy Spirit. While not seeking to deny the legitimacy and value of such moments and accompanying phenomena such as glossolalia, we are inclined to interpret these as symptoms occurring within people and arising out of our ongoing communion with the Spirit. Such experiences may well be interpreted, as was mooted in the previous section, as moments of proleptic, eschatological realisation effected in us by the Spirit and which allow us a foretaste of that

---

[28] D. M. Coffey, 'A Proper Mission of the Holy Spirit', *Theological Studies* 47 (1986), p. 227.

which is our full inheritance through faith in Jesus Christ. These incidents should not, however, be taken as indicators of the Holy Spirit establishing first contact with people. Instead, having acknowledged that the Spirit does seek to commune with us in His own Being and having conceded that this might well produce moments of personal crisis and fresh realisation within people, we would seek to outline an integrated understanding of the Spirit's function which arises out of His Being and His ontic actuality, as He is active in the Triune God's salvific economy towards us.

In chapter 1 we noted that the Charismatic Movement has stressed the significance of the Holy Spirit in effecting a personal, suprarational experience of God, thereby inducting the Christian into a conscious communion with the Divine. We there set ourselves the task of examining whether such an understanding of the Person and function of the Holy Spirit could be validated without violating the central tenets of Trinitarian theology. In the light of our study, we would suggest that it is indeed possible to frame a Trinitarian model which does stress the need to experience the Holy Spirit in the Christian life. We can and should speak of our need of the Holy Spirit as He who, in meeting with us in His ontic actuality, brings us into an experience of God and also moves us towards Jesus Christ. What must be questioned, in view of our deductions regarding the Person and function of the Spirit, is whether a personal, suprarational experience of God is the primary aspect of the Spirit's function, or but one among others.

In the opening section of this chapter, we noted the need to present a model whereby what we earlier identified as three functions of the Spirit - the epistemic agency, the suprarational work of the Spirit and the Spirit as the executor of God's elective decision - could be seen as arising from the ontic actuality of the Spirit. That is, we saw the need to correlate that relationship which exists between the Person of the Holy Spirit, whose Being is met with in His ontic actuality, and such aspects of the Spirit's function that we can identify as arising from His meeting with us. Where our criticism of the Scottish Reformed tradition has centred on the emphasis which has been placed on the epistemic agency of the Spirit, we would also observe that a weakness evident in the Charismatic Movement lies in the danger of a facile and exclusive identification of that aspect of the Spirit's function which gives rise to a suprarational experience of God - the suprarational work of the Spirit - with the ontic actuality of the Spirit. In both the Scottish Reformed tradition and the Charismatic Movement there is the possibility of confusing one aspect of the Spirit's function with the Person and function of the Spirit in His totality. In the light of what we have noted regarding the Person and function of the Spirit, participants within the Charismatic Movement should perhaps seek to reappraise their perception of the Holy Spirit in the light of this distinction; and go on to ask whether the epistemic and elective aspects of the Spirit's function are not as critically important to our reception of and communion with the Spirit as is suprarational experience. In that the Scottish tradition has stressed an epistemic functioning of the Spirit, it would certainly be the case that one possible way forward would be to explore how the Charismatic Movement's emphasis on personal, suprarational experience and that aspect of the Scottish tradition which has most demonstrated an appreciation of the Spirit's suprarational work - the Reformed understanding of the sacraments - might be more effectively married in the worship of the church. We would suggest that the vitality of the Charismatic Movement may be better consolidated within the Scottish context if it were married to a better understanding of sacraments in celebrating the Triune God's communion with mankind.

At the same time, the damage wrought in Scottish theology through identifying the Spirit in terms of varying functions rather than by maintaining a focus on the unitary nature of His Person and function should not be ignored. In seeking to develop a fresh pneumatological perspective we require to realign our understanding of the three, particular aspects of the Spirit's function mentioned above. These three 'functions' require to be viewed in terms of the Spirit's ontic actuality, arising as varying aspects of the Person and function of the Spirit as He meets with mankind. Where we acknowledge that the function of the Spirit can arise only from our meeting with the Being of His Person, we are more likely to acknowledge that suprarational experience, greater understanding and deeper assurance of salvation in Christ can only arise out of a deeper and profounder desire within us to meet with the Spirit who leads us towards and into a deeper participation with the humanity found in the Son of God Incarnate, Jesus Christ.

8.7   Conclusion

In this study we have not set out to justify or test the validity of a Christian doctrine of God as Trinity. Rather our task has been one of examining how it is that we view the Triune Being of God as we are embraced in His grace and saving love. More particularly we have concerned ourselves with seeking to determine how we might describe our communion with the Holy Spirit, as He meets with us; and to review how this meeting might best be explained and interpreted, that the church might better appreciate that inheritance which belongs to her.

To this end we have engaged in an examination of the dogmatic structures within which our perception of the Spirit's Person and function takes shape. We concluded our initial review of the Charismatic Movement in Scotland by setting out some questions with which the Charismatic Movement, as it appeared within the Scottish context, confronted us. Thereafter we proceeded to review the nature of those Trinitarian structures which evolved in the Patristic era, observing the development of an emphasis on and the priority of a Trinitarian framework which focused on the Immanent Trinity and which, in the West, came to emphasise the identity of the Spirit as *vinculum Trinitatis*. Where we saw that this Western model of the Trinity appeared to be treated as axiomatic in Calvin's thought and in the early development of Scottish theology, we noted how its continued use and interpretation led to a restricted view of the Holy Spirit and a disjunction being introduced to the manner in which the Person and function of the Holy Spirit was perceived: varying functions of the Spirit appeared to be given greater emphasis while in some measure sight was lost of the unitary nature of the Spirit's Being and our communion with Him.

At the same time, we identified that a different Trinitarian perspective could be traced in the pre-Nicene period, observing that an apparently more primitive Trinitarian framework, which focused on the complementary nature of the Son and the Spirit in the divine economy, need not necessarily be interpreted as one which was inferior or preparatory to that which, after Nicea, superseded it. In the work of Irving, Smail and Dunn we traced attempts to reinstate a proper perspective on the Person and function of the Holy Spirit. We have observed, however, that to overcome the weaknesses inherent within the Western model of the Trinity and its interpretation in the Scottish context, it is not enough simply to tamper with an understanding of the Spirit as *vinculum Trinitatis*: a more radical approach is called for. Such an approach, we have argued, requires us to reaffirm the complementary nature of the Spirit's ministry to that of the Son within God's salvific economy. As T. F. Torrance has argued, the Incarnation must be central to our theology: yet so too, we would suggest, must be a renewed understanding of the Spirit's ontic actuality. A fresh appreciation of the Trinity is required, one which grasps and maintains a bifocal symmetry in our reception of and communion with the Triune God: an approach which reflects a perspective on the Trinity which was present in pre-Nicene Trinitarian theology. Developing this bifocal symmetry, we have argued for a fresh pneumatological perspective, looking to both the Spirit's presence with the Son in His Incarnation, and also recognising the ontic actuality of the Spirit as met with in our own, present experience.

In seeking to explicate the nature of the Christian's communion with the Holy Spirit, we have sought to avoid straying towards a monopneumatic or binitarian theology. On the contrary, we have been concerned to relate our understanding of the Spirit's Person and function to the central focus of Christian devotion which must lie in Jesus Christ. In taking this approach, we have argued for a revised model of the Trinity which is, unashamedly, economic: centred on the salvific economy of the Triune God which is from the Father and met with by people in the ontic actuality of both the Son and the Spirit. In this revised Trinitarian model, we have spoken of bifocal symmetry, the proximation of mankind towards Christ and the twofold procession of the Spirit. Where our revised model of the Trinity may leave questions regarding the nature of God's immanent Being unexplored, we have sought to address what we believe to be the more pressing issue: how Christians, embraced in the ontic actuality of the Spirit and brought together, are in fact brought towards a participation with the Trinity, drawn into deeper devotion and proximation to the Son of God Incarnate.

In this study we have pursued the goal that, through revising the manner in which we approach an understanding of God as Trinity, we might better come to appreciate the ministry of the Holy Spirit in our midst today. Our prayer is that the fresh perspective on the Person and function of the Holy Spirit which our revised model offers may help to stimulate discussion and shape an agenda whereby the whole church might seek to bring greater glory to the Father through Jesus Christ His Son; and that Christians together, in looking to live more fully in the presence of the Spirit, may cry out with renewed expectancy, 'Come, Holy Spirit!'

Glossary of Theological
and Other Specialist Terms

Ad extra	To the outside.
Apophatic	A means of describing God in terms of what He is not.
Axiom	A self-evident truth.
Binitarianism	The notion that there are but two persons in the Godhead, leading us to disregard either the Son or the Spirit as a distinct, divine person.
Cartesian	That strain of individualistic thinking that developed in post-Reformation European thought, exemplified by the dictum of the philosopher Descartes, 'I think therefore I am'.
Cataphatic	A description of God in terms of His positive attributes.
Christology	The study of the Person of Jesus Christ and the relationship of His divinity to His humanity.
Christomonism	The notion that all of God is subsumed in the person of Jesus Christ.
Cognitio Dei Creatoris	Knowledge of God as Creator.
Cognitio Dei Redemptoris	Knowledge of God as Redeemer.
Communicatio idiomatum	Literally, 'the communion of idioms', referring to the relationship between the divine and human attributes of Christ's person and nature, as defined and distinguished in the Chalcedonian definition of 451 AD.
Cosmology	The study of the whole creation.
Deus Absconditus	God absent or beyond our cognitive or experiential verification.
Deus Revelatus	God as revealed to us.
Docetism	The belief that Jesus Christ only *appears* to be human like us, whilst in fact remaining singularly and substantially Divine.
Dogma	A fundamental truth.
Duplex cognitio Dei	A twofold knowledge of God that comes to us from, one the one hand, recognising God as our Creator and, on the other hand,

	recognising God as our Redeemer.
Economic Trinity	The nature of God as He is towards His creation.
Epistemic	Pertaining to rationally formulated, cognitive knowledge and understanding.
Epistemic agent	Applied to the Holy Spirit, His work in bringing and shaping an understanding of God within our human intellect.
Epistemology	The science of understanding, investigating the way knowledge is gained.
Eschatological	Pertaining to the end of the present age and the full inbreaking of the Kingdom of God.
Ex opere operato	The notion that God's grace is communicated in the action of administering the sacrament, whether or not faith is present.
Extra Calvinisticum	The notion, in the writings of Calvin, that while the Son of God fully becomes incarnate in human flesh in the person of Jesus Christ, there is also a way in which the Son of God continues to abide in heaven, even during that time of Christ's earthly life.
Federal theology	A theological system founded on an interpretation of the covenants of God.
Filioque	Pertaining to the phrase, found in the western, Latin rendering of the Nicene Constantinopolitan Creed, describing the Holy Spirit as 'proceeding from the Father and the Son'.
Glossolalia	An ecstatic speaking in foreign languages or 'tongues', either human or angelic, enabled by the direct action of the Holy Spirit upon the Christian believer.
Hermeneutical	Relating to the style and method of interpretation.
Homoousion	The descriptor of Jesus Christ as Son of God, sharing in the divine Being (<u>Greek</u>: *ousia*) of God the Father. Clearly stated in the Nicene Creed of 325 AD.
Hypostatic union	The union of two natures, the divine and human, in Jesus Christ.
Imago Dei	Image of God: referring to mankind's creation in God's likeness.
Immanent Trinity	The nature of God as He is to and within Himself.

Inhomination	Coming into humanity.
Kerygma	The truth of the gospel of Jesus Christ, as it is proclaimed in Jesus' name
Kirk	Within the Scottish context, the national, Presbyterian Church of Scotland.
Locus operandi	The place of operation or activity.
Logos	The eternal, pre-incarnate identity of the Word of God who, born of Mary, became Jesus Christ.
Logos-sarx framework	An interpretative model of God, focusing on the incarnation of the Word of God in human flesh.
Logos ensarkos	The Word of God conjoined to human flesh, as described in John's Gospel 1.14.
Modus operandi	The means by which a work is brought about and made effective.
Monarchianism	The notion that all of God is subsumed in the monarchy of God as Father.
Neo-Pentecostal	A new expression of classic Pentecostal beliefs found outside the historic Pentecostal churches, emphasising baptism in the Holy Spirit followed and evidenced by speaking in tongues.
Nestorianism	The teaching that Jesus Christ is not indivisibly one person but is the conjunction of two persons, one divine and one human, who yet become indivisible in Christ.
Noetic-sensible divide	A dualistic notion, arising from Platonic thought, of an absolute gulf between the spiritual world of ideas (the noetic realm) and the carnal, material world which our bodies exist in (sensible realm).
Ontic actuality	Applied to God, this describes the becomingness of God towards us in His own Being.
Ontological	Pertaining or relating to primitive or essential Being.
Opus operandi	The nature of a work undertaken.
Ordo salutis	the way salvation is ordered and made effective for people by God.
Ousia	The Greek word for Being.
Perichoretic	Pertaining to the developed notion of the interrelatedness or interpenetration of the Persons of the Trinity towards one another.

Pneumatology	The study of the Person, function and works of the Holy Spirit
Pneumatomachi	'Spirit fighters': a derogatory term applied to those who understood the Spirit as agent of, not sharer in, the Being of God.
Sabellianism	A belief that to speak of different persons within the Trinity is merely to discuss facets of God's oneness.
Salvific economy	God's dealing with us in His saving purpose, presence and power.
Soterial /soteriological	Pertaining to salvation
Soteriology	The study of the means and method of salvation.
Spirit-flesh binitarianism	The belief that Christ is constituted by the divine initiative of the Spirit and the Father, there being no further, third divine person who might be styled 'the Son'.
Subordinationism	A doctrinal formulation that represents the Son or Holy Spirit as subordinate to the Father within the Godhead
Supralapsarianism	A belief that God's decrees of election and predestination precede mankind's Fall.
Suprarational	While not being irrational, that which is apprehended by the rational but not fully embraced or comprehended by it.
Terminus ad quid	The objective goal towards which activity is focused.
Theologoumenon	A theological conviction which reflects personal opinion as distinct from fundamental dogma.
Vinculum	A Latin term for 'bond', used by Augustine when speaking of the Holy Spirit's relationship to the Father and the Son, as the 'bond of love' between them. The *vinculum Trinitatis* designates the Spirit as the 'bond' between Father and Son in the Trinity.

Bibliography

1 - Patristic Sources (Chapter 2), Primary
2 - Patristic Sources (Chapter 2), Secondary
3 - Books: General
4 - Articles: General
5 - Confessions of Faith
6 – Reports
7 - Other Sources

1. Patristic Sources (Chapter 2), Primary

Ambrose of Milan, *The Holy Spirit, FOTC*, Vol. 44

Athanasius, *Against the Arians, NPNF*, Vol.4.

— *Letters to Serapion*, C. R. B. Shapland (Trans.), Epworth, London, 1951.

Augustine of Hippo, *De Trinitate*, in *Library of Christian Classics*, Vol. 8, translated by J. Burnaby, SCM, London, 1965.

Basil of Caesarea, *Basil the Great on the Holy Spirit*, translated by G. Lewis, Religious Tract Society, London, 1888.

Clement, *The Apostolic Fathers*, translated by J. B. Lightfoot, MacMillan, London, 1893.

Denys the Areopagite, *The Complete Works of Pseudo-Dionysius*, translated by C. Luibheid, SPCK, London, 1987

Gregory of Nyssa, *From Glory to Glory: Texts from Gregory of Nyssa's Mystical Writings*, edited and translated by H. Musurillo, with an introduction by J. Danielou, John Murray, London, 1962

Hermas, *The Shepherd of Hermas*, translated by C. H. Hoole, Rivingstons, London, 1870.

Hilary of Poitiers, *De Trinitate, FOTC*, Vol. 25.

Irenaeus, *The Early Christian Fathers*, edited and translated by H. Bettenson OUP, London, 1956.

Origen, *The Writings of Origen*, Vol.1, T & T Clark, Edinburgh, 1869

— *Commentary on John, The Fathers of the Church*, Vol. 80, translated by R. E. Heine, CUA, Washington, 1989.

Tertullian, *The Writings of Tertullian*, Vol.2, T & T Clark, Edinburgh, 1870.

Compendia

Ignatius, Irenaeus and Justin, in *The Ante-Nicene Fathers* Vol. 1, A. Roberts and J. Donaldson (Editors), Eerdmans, Grand Rapids, 1884.

Basil of Caesarea, Cyril of Jerusalem, Gregory of Nazianzus, Gregory of Nyssa, in *The Later Christian Fathers*, edited and translated by H. Bettenson, OUP, London, 1974

2. Patristic Sources (Chapter 2), Secondary

Campenhausen, H. von *The Fathers of the Greek Church*, Pantheon, New York, 1959.

Cross, F. L. *The Early Christian Fathers*, Duckworth, London, 1960

Crouzel, H. *Origen*, T & T Clark, Edinburgh, 1989.

Danielou, J. *The Origins of Latin Christianity*, DLT, London, 1977.

Drewery, B. *Origen and the Doctrine of Grace*, Epworth Press, London, 1960.

Fairbairn, D. *Eastern Orthodoxy through Western Eyes*, Westminster John Knox Press, Louisville, 2002.

Glimm, Marique and Walsh, *The Apostolic Fathers*, CUA, Washington, 1947.

Grillmeier, A. *Christ in Christian Tradition*, Vol. 1, Mowbrays, London, 1975.

Gunton, C. E. 'Augustine, the Trinity and the Theological Crisis of the West', *Scottish Journal of Theology* (43.1), 1990.

— *The Promise of Trinitarian Theology*, T & T Clark, Edinburgh, 1991

Hanson, R. P. C. *The Search for the Christian Doctrine of God*, T & T Clark, Edinburgh, 1990.

Hart, T. A. 'Incarnation and Apotheosis', PhD thesis, Aberdeen , 1989.

Kelly, J. N. D. *Early Christian Doctrines*, 5th Edition, A & C Black, London, 1985.

Lightfoot, J. B. *The Apostolic Fathers*, MacMillan, London, 1893.

— *The Apostolic Fathers*, Pt.2, Vol.2, Sct.1, MacMillan, London, 1885.

Louth, A. *The Origins of the Christian Mystical Tradition*, OUP, Oxford, 1981.

Mackey, J. P. *The Christian Experience of God as Trinity*, SCM, London, 1983.

Meredith, A. 'Clement of Alexandria', in *The Study of Spirituality*, edited by C. Jones, G. Wainwright and E. J. Yarnold, SPCK, London, 1986.

Pelikan, J. *The Emergence of the Catholic Tradition*, University of Chicago Press, Chicago, 1971

Robinson, J. A. *St. Irenaeus: the Apostolic Preaching*, MacMillan, New York, 1920.

Stevenson, J. (Editor) *Creeds, Councils & Controversies*, SPCK, London, 1973.

Thomson, J. *Modern Trinitarian Perspectives*, OUP, Oxford, 1994.

Torrance, A. *Persons in Communion*, T&T Clark, Edinburgh, 1996.

Torrance, T. F. *The Trinitarian Faith*, T & T Clark, Edinburgh, 1988.

Wallace-Hadrill, D.S. *Christian Antioch: A Study in Early Christian Thought in the East*, CUP, Cambridge, 1982.

Williams, R. D. *Arius: Heresy and Tradition*, DLT, London, 1987.

3. Books: General

Balke, W, *Calvin and the Anabaptist Radicals*, Eerdmans, Grand Rapids, 1981.

Bangs, J. *Arminius*, Eerdmans, Grand Rapids, 1985.

Barth, K. *Church Dogmatics*, Vol. 1, Part 1, translated by G. T. Thomson, T & T Clark, Edinburgh, 1936.

— *The Knowledge of God and the Service of God According to the Teaching of the Reformation*, Hodder & Stoughton, London, 1938.

Bennett, D. *Nine O'Clock in the Morning*, Kingsway, Eastbourne, 1978.

Black, H. *Reflections on the Baptism of the Holy Spirit*, New Dawn Books, Greenock, 1987.

— *The Clash of Tongues with Glimpses of Revival*, New Dawn Books, Greenock, 1988.

— *Reflections on the Gifts of the Holy Spirit*, New Dawn Books, Greenock, 1988.

Bloch-Hoell, N. *The Pentecostal Movement*, Universitetsforlaget, Copenhagen, 1964.

Calvin, J. *Calvin: Institutes of the Christian Religion*, Edited by J. T. McNeill & translated by F. L. Battles, The Westminster Press, Philadelphia, 1960.

— *Calvin: Theological Treatises*, Edited by J. K. S. Reid, The Westminster Press, Philadelphia, 1954.

— *Commentary on John*, translated by T. H. L. Parker, St. Andrew Press, Edinburgh, 1959.

— *Commentary on the Acts of the Apostles*, (Vol. 1), translated by J. W. Fraser and W. J. G. McDonald, St. Andrew Press, Edinburgh, 1965.

— *Commentary on the Acts of the Apostle*,(Vol. 2), translated by J. W. Fraser, St. Andrew Press, Edinburgh, 1966.

— *Commentary on Romans*, translated by R. MacKenzie, St. Andrew Press, Edinburgh, 1961.

— *Commentary on Ephesians*, translated by T. H. L. Parker, St. Andrew Press, Edinburgh, 1965.

— *Commentary on 1 Corinthians*, translated by J. W. Fraser, St. Andrew Press, Edinburgh, 1960.

— *Commentary on 2 Corinthians*, translated by T. A. Smail, St. Andrew Press, Edinburgh, 1964.

— *Commentary on 1 Peter*, translated by W. B. Johnston, St. Andrew Press, Edinburgh, 1963.

Campbell, J. McLeod. *The Nature of the Atonement*, Macmillan & Co., London, 5th. Edition, 1878.

Cunningham, D. S. *These Three Are One*, Blackwell Publishers, Oxford, 1998.

Curtis, W. A. *History of Creeds and Confessions of Faith*, T & T Clark, Edinburgh, 1911.

Dallimore, A. *The Life of Edward Irving: Forerunner of the Charismatic Movement*, Banner of Truth, Edinburgh, 1983.

Dickson, D. and Durham, J. *The Sum of Saving Knowledge*, bound with *The Westminster Confession of Faith*, Free Presbyterian Publications, 1973 Edition.

Dowey, A. E. *The Knowledge of God in Calvin's Theology*, Columbia University Press, New York, 1952.

Drummond, A. L. Bulloch, J. *The Church in Late Victorian Scotland 1874-1900*, St. Andrew Press, Edinburgh, 1978

Dunn, J. D. G. *Baptism in the Holy Spirit*, SCM, London, 1970.

— *Christology in the Making*, SCM, London, 2nd edition, 1989.

— *Jesus and the Spirit*, SCM, London, 1975.

— *The Christ and the Spirit*, Vol.1, T & T Clark, Edinburgh, 1998.

— *Unity and Diversity in the New Testament*, SCM, London, 2nd edition, 1990.

Fiddes, P. S. *Participation in God*, DLT, London, 2000.

Finney, C. *Lectures on Revivals of Religions*, W. G. McLoughlin (Editor), Harvard University Press, Cambridge, Mass., 1960.

Gee, D. *Wind and Flame*, Heath Press, Croydon, 1967.

Gunton, C. E. *Act and Being*, SCM Press, London, 2002

— *Father, Son and Holy Spirit*, T & T Clark, London, 2003

Harper, M. *As at the Beginning*, Hodder & Stoughton, London, 1965.

Henderson, G. D. *Scots Confession*, Church of Scotland, Edinburgh, 1937.

Heron, A. I. C. (Editor) *The Forgotten Trinity* Vol. 3, Council of Churches for Britain and Ireland, London, 1991.
— *The Westminster Confession in the Church Today*, St. Andrew Press, Edinburgh, 1982.
Hocken, P. *Streams of Renewal*, Paternoster Press, Exeter, 1986.
Innes, A. T. *The Law of Creeds in Scotland*, William Blackwood & Sons, Edinburgh, 1902.
Irving, E. *The Collected Writings of Edward Irving in Five Volumes*, edited by G. Carlyle, Alexander Strachan & Co., London, 1865.
— *Christ's Holiness in Flesh: The Form and Fountainhead of All Holiness in Flesh*, John Lindsay & Co., Edinburgh, 1831.
— *The Day of Pentecost or The Baptism With The Holy Ghost*, John Lindsay & Co., Edinburgh, 1831.
Kendall, R. T. *Calvin and English Calvinism to 1649*, OUP, Oxford, 1979.
Kyle, R. G. *The Mind of John Knox*, Coronado Press, Lawrence, 1984.
Lampe, G. W. H. *God as Spirit*, Clarendon Press, Oxford, 1977.
Lee, J. *Lectures on the History of the Church of Scotland*, William Blackwood & Sons, Edinburgh, 1860.
Leith, J. *Assembly at Westminster: Reformed Theology in the Making*, John Know Press, Atlanta, 1973.
McDonnell, K. *John Calvin, the Church, and the Eucharist*, Princeton University Press, Princeton, 1967.
McFarlane, G. W. P. *Christ and the Spirit*, Paternoster Press, Carlisle, 1996.
Mackintosh, H. R. *The Christian Apprehension of God*, SCM, London, 1929.
— *The Doctrine of the Person of Christ*, T & T Clark, Edinburgh, 1912.
— *The Originality of the Christian Message*, Duckworth & Co., London, 1920.
Merricks, W. S. *Edward Irving: the Forgotten Giant*, Scribe's Chamber Publications, Illinois, 1983.
Mitchell, A. F. *The Scottish Reformation*, William Blackwood & Sons, Edinburgh, 1900.
Moltmann, J. *The Spirit of Life*, SCM, London, 1992.
— *The Trinity and the Kingdom of God*, SCM, London, 1981.
Niesel, W. *The Theology of Calvin*, Translated by H. Knight, Westminster Press, Philadelphia, 1956.
Parker, T. H. L. *Calvin's Doctrine of the Knowledge of God*, Oliver & Boyd, Edinburgh, 1969.
Peckham, C. and M. *Sounds from Heaven*, Christian Focus, Fearn, 2004.
Pelikan, J. *Reformation of Church and Dogma (1300-1700)*, University of Chicago Press, Chicago, 1984.
Schaff, P. *The Creeds of Christendom Vol. 1*, Harper & Bros., New York, 1878.
Schwoebel, C. and Gunton, C. E. (Edit.) *Persons, Divine and Human*, T & T Clark, Edinburgh, 1991.
Sherrill, J. *They Speak with Other Tongues*, Hodder & Stoughton, London, 1965.
Strachan, G. *The Pentecostal Theology of Edward Irving*, Darton Longman & Todd, London, 1973.
Smail, T. A. *The Forgotten Father*, Hodder & Stoughton, London, 1980.
— *The Giving Gift*, Hodder & Stoughton, London, 1988.
— *Reflected Glory: The Spirit in Christ and Christians*, Hodder & Stoughton, London,

1975.

Thomson, J. *Modern Trinitarian Perspectives*, OUP, Oxford, 1994.

Torrance, A. *Persons in Communion*, T&T Clark, Edinburgh, 1996.

Torrance, T. F. *God and Rationality*, OUP, London, 1971.

— *Karl Barth: Biblical & Evangelical theologian*, T & T Clark, Edinburgh, 1990.

— *Space, Time and Incarnation*, OUP, London, 1969.

— *Space, Time and Resurrection*, Handsel Press, Edinburgh, 1976.

— *The Doctrine of Grace in the ApostolicFathers*, Oliver & Boyd, Edinburgh, 1948.

— *The Mediation of Christ*, Paternoster Press, Exeter, 1983.

— *Theology in Reconciliation*, Geoffrey Chapman, London, 1975.

— *Theology in Reconstruction*, SCM, London, 1965.

Wallace, R. S. *Calvin's Doctrine of the Christian Life*, Oliver & Boyd, Edinburgh, 1959.

— *Calvin's Doctrine of the Word and Sacrament*, Oliver & Boyd, Edinburgh, 1953.

— *Calvin, Geneva and the Reformation*, St. Andrew Press, Edinburgh, 1988.

Wendel, F. *Calvin*, Collins, London, 1965.

Wilkerson, D. *The Cross and the Switchblade*, Random House Inc., New York, 1963.

Williams, G. H. *The Radical Reformation*, Weidenfeld & Nicolson, London, 1962.

Willis, E. D. *Calvin's Catholic Christology*, Brill, Leiden, 1966.

Woosley, A. *Duncan Campbell: A Biography*, Hodder & Stoughton, London, 1974.

Zizioulas, J. *Being as Communion*, Darton Longman & Todd, London, 1985.

4. Articles: General

Coffey, D. M. 'A Proper Mission of the Holy Spirit', *Theological Studies* 47 (1986).

Dilworth, M. 'Charismatic Renewal and Scottish Catholics', Unpublished Paper, Undated.

— 'Renewal and Scottish Catholics in Renewal', *Renewal* 86 (1980).

Dunn, J. D. G. 'Rediscovering the Spirit', *Expository Times* 84 (1972-3).

— 'Rediscovering the Spirit (2)', *Expository Times* 94 (1982-3).

— 'Spirit-Baptism and Pentecostalism', *The Scottish Journal of Theology* 23 (1970).

McDonnell, K. 'Trinitarian Theology of the Spirit', *Theological Studies* 46 (1985).

Pendrich, S. 'Is God doing a new thing?', *Scottish Baptist*, December 1982.

Russell, A. 'Grass not so green in non-denominational fellowships', *Scottish Baptist*, December 1984.

Torrance, T. F. 'A Sermon on the Trinity', *Biblical Theology* 6 (1956).

5. Confessions of Faith

Scots Confession, translated by J. Bulloch, St. Andrew Press, Edinburgh, 1960.

The Westminster Confession of Faith, Free Presbyterian Publications, Glasgow, 1973.

6. Reports

The interim report of the Panel on Doctrine on 'The work and gifts of the Holy Spirit', *Assembly Reports*, 1973.

Report of the Panel on Doctrine on 'The Charismatic Movement within the Church of Scotland', *Assembly Reports*, 1974.

'Scottish Baptists and the Charismatic Renewal Movement', Baptist Union of Scotland Publications, Undated.

7. Other Sources

Editorials, *Renewal* 45 (1973), 53 and 54 (1974)

Church of Scotland, *Assembly Reports*, 1971,1972,1973,1976.

Baptist Union of Scotland, *Scottish Baptist Year Book*, 1979,1982.

Transcriptions of recorded interviews with:

David Black on 24 November 1989

Stewart Brunton on 5 December 1989

Hugh Clark on 17 November 1989

Brian Hayes on 20 November 1989

Tom Smail on 22 March 1990

Unpublished correspondence and records of Scottish Churches Renewal (SCR) by courtesy of Douglas Flett, formerly of Bishopbriggs Christian Centre.

Index

Ambrose, 56, 60.
Apophatic, 22, 67, 68.
Arius, 43-47, 50, 219.
Athanasius, 45-50, 53, 60-62, 64, 73, 174-
175.
Augustine, 54, 56-60, 65, 67-70, 75-76,
82, 161, 213-214.

Bangs, J. 108-109.
'baptism in the Spirit', 1-13, 15, 18-20,
23-25, 28, 139-140, 146-148, 154-155,
180, 190, 194, 216, 226-227.
Barth, K. 81, 120-121, 159-160, 165, 172,
175, 182-184, 188, 205, 209, 213, 218.
Basil of Caesaria, 51-53, 74.
Black, D. 7, 9-11, 23.
Black, H. 3-6, 28.
Binitarian, 50, 61, 145, 220, 231.

Calvin, J. 15, 28-29, 78-111, 112-115,
117-118, 120-123, 125, 127-130, 134,
151-153, 155, 164, 166, 170-171, 173,
181, 188, 203, 208, 211-212, 231.
Campbell, D. 4-5.
Campbell, J. McLeod. 113, 133.
Cataphatic, 22.
Christology, 27, 31, 51, 55, 60-62, 64, 75,
79, 84-87, 92, 93, 99, 103, 109, 114,
123-124, 128, 131, 134-136, 138, 141,
142, 144, 146-148, 151, 158, 182, 183,
191, 194-196, 200, 202-206, 210.
Christomonism, 220.
Clement, Apostolic Father, 33.
Clement of Alexandria, 41-42.
Cognitio Dei Creatoris, 80-85, 87-88, 99,
114, 121-122, 171.
Cognitio Dei Redemptoris, 80-81, 83-85,
87-88, 99, 122-123, 128, 132, 134,
153-154, 161, 170.
Communicatio idiomatum, 79, 85, 87, 114,
123, 164-165, 171.
Cosmology, 46.

Cyril of Jerusalem, 50-51.

Denys the Areopagite, 65, 69-70.
Dilworth, M. 10, 13.
Deus Absconditus, 178.
Deus Revelatus, 178.
Docetism, 62, 72, 143.
Dowey, A.E. 81, 83.
Dunn, J.D.G. 176, 190-207, 210, 218,
223-224, 231.
Duplex cognitio Dei, 79, 80-81, 83, 85,
93, 98, 100, 170.

Economic Trinity, 32, 37-38, 43, 54, 56-
58, 60, 71, 153-154, 157, 212-214,
216-218, 231.
Epistemic, 34, 100-102, 104-105, 107,
109-110, 116, 126, 128, 174, 191, 203,
229.
Epistemic agent, 79, 84, 87, 93, 95, 98,
100-107, 110-111, 112, 115-120, 122,
124-126, 129-131, 134, 136, 149-154,
166, 167, 171-173, 211, 229.
Epistemology, 27-29, 134, 153, 102-104,
108-110, 170, 192, 202.
Eschatology, 147, 192-195, 198, 200, 215-
218, 225-228.
Ex opere operato, 98.
Extra Calvinisticum, 79, 85-87, 107, 171.

Federal Theology, 127-128, 130.
Filioque, 59, 163.

Gee, D. 3.
Glossolalia, 2-3, 5, 7, 9,12, 18, 23-24,
146, 179, 228.
Gregory of Nazianzus, 51-53, 74.
Gregory of Nyssa, 51, 53, 62, 65.
Grillmeier, A. 61-62.
Gunton, C.E. 57, 213-215, 224.

Hanson, R.P.C. 45, 48, 53.

Hermas, 32-33.
Hermeneutics, 19, 50, 103, 109, 114-115,
    118, 123, 134, 153, 208.
Hilary of Poitiers, 54-55, 59.
Homoousion, 31, 44-51, 53-55, 57, 59-61,
    65, 71-73, 76, 175, 212, 219.
Hypostatic union, 86, 103, 107, 111, 134,
    136-140, 146, 154, 160, 164-168, 170-
    172, 175, 199-200, 219, 221, 226.

Ignatius, 34.
Imago Dei, 67, 70, 75, 79, 82-84, 91-92,
    115, 122.
Immanent Trinity, 31, 37-39, 41-43, 46-
    60, 64-65, 67-68, 71-72, 75-76, 79, 83-
    84, 86-87, 102-103, 120, 142, 152,
    157, 159, 161-164, 166, 171, 175, 176,
    178, 183, 188-190, 199-200, 202, 205,
    211-213, 215-219, 225, 230-231.
Irenaeus, 36-39, 72-73, 76, 214, 219.
Irving, E. 16, 113, 119-121, 131, 132-155,
    156, 161, 164-167, 169, 171, 181, 200,
    202, 205, 216, 219, 222-223, 225-226,
    231.

Justin Martyr, 35-36, 38.

Kelly, J.N.D. 43-44.
Kendall, R.T. 108-110, 129.

Logos-sarx, 61-62, 144.
Logos ensarkos, 61.

Mackey, J.P. 40-41, 43-44, 57, 71.
Mackintosh, H.R. 157-159, 165.
McDonnell, K. 92-93.
McFarlane, G.W.P. 135, 145.
Moltmann, J. 216-217.
Monarchianism, 40, 50, 52, 72.

Neo-Pentecostal, 2, 5-8, 14, 15-18, 21, 25,
    28.
Nestorianism, 86, 145.
Noetic-sensible, 36, 40, 64-65, 67, 69, 75,
    83, 86, 203.

Ontic actuality, 22-24, 26, 28-29, 32, 34-
    39, 41-42, 44-46, 50, 52-56, 58-61, 64-

    65, 67-68, 70-76, 84, 86-87, 100, 102-
    104, 107, 110-111, 128-130, 154-155,
    170-175, 183-184, 187-190, 200-201,
    203, 205-206, 208-213, 215, 217-231.
Ontology, 32, 37-38, 40-43, 45-47, 50, 53,
    55-56, 58-60, 63-75, 84, 101-103, 114-
    115, 128, 130, 134, 136, 141, 151-152,
    154, 156, 158-160, 162, 174-175, 178,
    181-184, 191, 195, 199, 203, 205-206,
    208-209, 212-215.
Ordo salutis, 104, 127.
Origen, 42-43, 46.
Ousia, 44-46, 53, 65, 72, 76, 214-215

Parker, T.H.L. 81, 83.
Pentecostal, 1-10, 12, 15, 17, 21.
Perichoretic, 64, 68, 74, 76, 115, 143,
    145, 147-148, 152, 166.
Pneumatology, 12, 15-16, 18-19, 21, 24,
    27-28, 31, 35-36, 40, 51, 61, 69, 70,
    72, 75, 78-79, 83, 86, 92, 99, 102-105,
    110-111, 112-113, 117-118, 120-121,
    123-125, 128-129, 134-135, 137-138,
    141-142, 146, 148, 150-151, 154-155,
    160, 164-166, 170, 173-175, 176, 180-
    183, 188-191, 194, 200-206, 208-210,
    215-216, 230-231.
Pneumatomachi, 48, 51, 130.

Sabellianism, 56, 128.
Salvific economy, 31-53, 56-60, 63-65, 67-
    68, 70-72, 74, 76, 80, 84-85, 87, 99,
    102-103, 105, 107, 110-111, 114, 128-
    129, 131, 132, 141-142, 145, 148, 151-
    154, 159, 161-162, 164, 166, 171, 178,
    181-183, 187-188, 203, 205, 210-212,
    216-221, 224, 228-229, 231.
Smail, T.A. 7-8, 92, 176-190, 198, 200,
    202, 205-206, 210, 218, 231.
Soteriology, 41, 46, 53-54, 67, 71-73, 85,
    87, 99-103, 114, 123, 129, 135, 139,
    202-203, 219.
Subordinationism, 36, 39-41, 43-45, 52,
    57, 63, 71-72, 181-183, 187-188.
Supralapsarianism, 108-110.
Suprarational, 1, 6, 8, 15-16, 19-29, 32,
    90-92, 98, 106, 108, 110, 112, 115-
    118, 120, 123, 125-126, 130-131, 134,

145, 149-150, 154-155, 166-167, 171-
175, 209-211, 229-230.

Tertullian, 39-40, 42, 54.
Torrance, J. 127-128, 130.
Torrance, T.F. 47, 53, 82-83, 113, 155,
156-175, 181, 184, 200, 203, 205, 209,
211, 218-220, 222, 226, 231.

Vinculum, 59-60, 75, 79, 84, 90, 98, 100-
101, 104, 111, 129-130, 138-143, 151-
154, 162-163, 165-166, 168-171, 173,
181, 185, 188, 198, 205, 209-211, 216,
223-224, 228, 230-231.

Wallace, R.S. 89, 91, 92, 102, 106.
Wallace-Hadrill, D.S. 62.
Williams, R.D. 43, 46.
Willis, E.D. 85-86.

Zizioulas, J. 214-215, 224.

Paternoster Biblical Monographs

(All titles uniform with this volume)
Dates in bold are of projected publication

Joseph Abraham
Eve: Accused or Acquitted?
A Reconsideration of Feminist Readings of the Creation Narrative Texts in Genesis 1–3
Two contrary views dominate contemporary feminist biblical scholarship. One finds in the Bible an unequivocal equality between the sexes from the very creation of humanity, whilst the other sees the biblical text as irredeemably patriarchal and androcentric. Dr Abraham enters into dialogue with both camps as well as introducing his own method of approach. An invaluable tool for any one who is interested in this contemporary debate.
2002 / 0-85364-971-5 / xxiv + 272pp

Octavian D. Baban
Mimesis and Luke's on the Road Encounters in Luke-Acts
Luke's Theology of the Way and its Literary Representation
The book argues on theological and literary (mimetic) grounds that Luke's on-the-road encounters, especially those belonging to the post-Easter period, are part of his complex theology of the Way. Jesus' teaching and that of the apostles is presented by Luke as a challenging answer to the Hellenistic reader's thirst for adventure, good literature, and existential paradigms.
2005 / 1-84227-253-5 / approx. 374pp

Paul Barker
The Triumph of Grace in Deuteronomy
This book is a textual and theological analysis of the interaction between the sin and faithlessness of Israel and the grace of Yahweh in response, looking especially at Deuteronomy chapters 1–3, 8–10 and 29–30. The author argues that the grace of Yahweh is determinative for the ongoing relationship between Yahweh and Israel and that Deuteronomy anticipates and fully expects Israel to be faithless.
2004 / 1-84227-226-8 / xxii + 270pp

Jonathan F. Bayes
The Weakness of the Law
God's Law and the Christian in New Testament Perspective
A study of the four New Testament books which refer to the law as weak (Acts, Romans, Galatians, Hebrews) leads to a defence of the third use in the Reformed debate about the law in the life of the believer.
2000 / 0-85364-957-X / xii + 244pp

Mark Bonnington
The Antioch Episode of Galatians 2:11-14 in Historical and Cultural Context
The Galatians 2 'incident' in Antioch over table-fellowship suggests significant disagreement between the leading apostles. This book analyses the background to the disagreement by locating the incident within the dynamics of social interaction between Jews and Gentiles. It proposes a new way of understanding the relationship between the individuals and issues involved.

2005 / 1-84227-050-8 / approx. 350pp

David Bostock
A Portrayal of Trust
The Theme of Faith in the Hezekiah Narratives
This study provides detailed and sensitive readings of the Hezekiah narratives (2 Kings 18–20 and Isaiah 36–39) from a theological perspective. It concentrates on the theme of faith, using narrative criticism as its methodology. Attention is paid especially to setting, plot, point of view and characterization within the narratives. A largely positive portrayal of Hezekiah emerges that underlines the importance and relevance of scripture.

2005 / 1-84227-314-0 / approx. 300pp

Mark Bredin
Jesus, Revolutionary of Peace
A Non-violent Christology in the Book of Revelation
This book aims to demonstrate that the figure of Jesus in the Book of Revelation can best be understood as an active non-violent revolutionary.

2003 / 1-84227-153-9 / xviii + 262pp

Robinson Butarbutar
Paul and Conflict Resolution
An Exegetical Study of Paul's Apostolic Paradigm in 1 Corinthians 9
The author sees the apostolic paradigm in 1 Corinthians 9 as part of Paul's unified arguments in 1 Corinthians 8–10 in which he seeks to mediate in the dispute over the issue of food offered to idols. The book also sees its relevance for dispute-resolution today, taking the conflict within the author's church as an example.

2006 / 1-84227-315-9 / approx. 280pp

Daniel J-S Chae
Paul as Apostle to the Gentiles
His Apostolic Self-awareness and its Influence on the Soteriological Argument in Romans
Opposing 'the post-Holocaust interpretation of Romans', Daniel Chae competently demonstrates that Paul argues for the equality of Jew and Gentile in Romans. Chae's fresh exegetical interpretation is academically outstanding and spiritually encouraging.
1997 / 0-85364-829-8 / xiv + 378pp

Luke L. Cheung
The Genre, Composition and Hermeneutics of the Epistle of James
The present work examines the employment of the wisdom genre with a certain compositional structure and the interpretation of the law through the Jesus tradition of the double love command by the author of the Epistle of James to serve his purpose in promoting perfection and warning against doubleness among the eschatologically renewed people of God in the Diaspora.
2003 / 1-84227-062-1 / xvi + 372pp

Youngmo Cho
Spirit and Kingdom in the Writings of Luke and Paul
The relationship between Spirit and Kingdom is a relatively unexplored area in Lukan and Pauline studies. This book offers a fresh perspective of two biblical writers on the subject. It explores the difference between Luke's and Paul's understanding of the Spirit by examining the specific question of the relationship of the concept of the Spirit to the concept of the Kingdom of God in each writer.
2005 / 1-84227-316-7 / approx. 270pp

Andrew C. Clark
Parallel Lives
The Relation of Paul to the Apostles in the Lucan Perspective
This study of the Peter-Paul parallels in Acts argues that their purpose was to emphasize the themes of continuity in salvation history and the unity of the Jewish and Gentile missions. New light is shed on Luke's literary techniques, partly through a comparison with Plutarch.
2001 / 1-84227-035-4 / xviii + 386pp

Andrew D. Clarke
Secular and Christian Leadership in Corinth
A Socio-Historical and Exegetical Study of 1 Corinthians 1–6
This volume is an investigation into the leadership structures and dynamics of first-century Roman Corinth. These are compared with the practice of leadership in the Corinthian Christian community which are reflected in 1 Corinthians 1–6, and contrasted with Paul's own principles of Christian leadership.
2005 / 1-84227-229-2 / 200pp

Stephen Finamore
God, Order and Chaos
René Girard and the Apocalypse
Readers are often disturbed by the images of destruction in the book of Revelation and unsure why they are unleashed after the exaltation of Jesus. This book examines past approaches to these texts and uses René Girard's theories to revive some old ideas and propose some new ones.
2005 / 1-84227-197-0 / approx. 344pp

David G. Firth
Surrendering Retribution in the Psalms
Responses to Violence in the Individual Complaints
In *Surrendering Retribution in the Psalms*, David Firth examines the ways in which the book of Psalms inculcates a model response to violence through the repetition of standard patterns of prayer. Rather than seeking justification for retributive violence, Psalms encourages not only a surrender of the right of retribution to Yahweh, but also sets limits on the retribution that can be sought in imprecations. Arising initially from the author's experience in South Africa, the possibilities of this model to a particular context of violence is then briefly explored.
2005 / 1-84227-337-X / xviii + 154pp

Scott J. Hafemann
Suffering and Ministry in the Spirit
Paul's Defence of His Ministry in II Corinthians 2:14–3:3
Shedding new light on the way Paul defended his apostleship, the author offers a careful, detailed study of 2 Corinthians 2:14–3:3 linked with other key passages throughout 1 and 2 Corinthians. Demonstrating the unity and coherence of Paul's argument in this passage, the author shows that Paul's suffering served as the vehicle for revealing God's power and glory through the Spirit.
2000 / 0-85364-967-7 / xiv + 262pp

Scott J. Hafemann
Paul, Moses and the History of Israel
The Letter/Spirit Contrast and the Argument from Scripture in 2 Corinthians 3
An exegetical study of the call of Moses, the second giving of the Law (Exodus 32–34), the new covenant, and the prophetic understanding of the history of Israel in 2 Corinthians 3. Hafemann's work demonstrates Paul's contextual use of the Old Testament and the essential unity between the Law and the Gospel within the context of the distinctive ministries of Moses and Paul.
2005 / 1-84227-317-5 / xii + 498pp

Douglas S. McComiskey
Lukan Theology in the Light of the Gospel's Literary Structure
Luke's Gospel was purposefully written with theology embedded in its patterned literary structure. A critical analysis of this cyclical structure provides new windows into Luke's interpretation of the individual pericopes comprising the Gospel and illuminates several of his theological interests.
2004 / 1-84227-148-2 / xviii + 388pp

Stephen Motyer
Your Father the Devil?
A New Approach to John and 'The Jews'
Who are 'the Jews' in John's Gospel? Defending John against the charge of antisemitism, Motyer argues that, far from demonising the Jews, the Gospel seeks to present Jesus as 'Good News for Jews' in a late first century setting.
1997 / 0-85364-832-8 / xiv + 260pp

Esther Ng
Reconstructing Christian Origins?
The Feminist Theology of Elizabeth Schüssler Fiorenza: An Evaluation
In a detailed evaluation, the author challenges Elizabeth Schüssler Fiorenza's reconstruction of early Christian origins and her underlying presuppositions. The author also presents her own views on women's roles both then and now.
2002 / 1-84227-055-9 / xxiv + 468pp

Robin Parry
Old Testament Story and Christian Ethics
The Rape of Dinah as a Case Study

What is the role of story in ethics and, more particularly, what is the role of Old Testament story in Christian ethics? This book, drawing on the work of contemporary philosophers, argues that narrative is crucial in the ethical shaping of people and, drawing on the work of contemporary Old Testament scholars, that story plays a key role in Old Testament ethics. Parry then argues that when situated in canonical context Old Testament stories can be reappropriated by Christian readers in their own ethical formation. The shocking story of the rape of Dinah and the massacre of the Shechemites provides a fascinating case study for exploring the parameters within which Christian ethical appropriations of Old Testament stories can live.

2004 / 1-84227-210-1 / xx + 350pp

Ian Paul
Power to See the World Anew
The Value of Paul Ricoeur's Hermeneutic of Metaphor in Interpreting the Symbolism of Revelation 12 and 13

This book is a study of the hermeneutics of metaphor of Paul Ricoeur, one of the most important writers on hermeneutics and metaphor of the last century. It sets out the key points of his theory, important criticisms of his work, and how his approach, modified in the light of these criticisms, offers a methodological framework for reading apocalyptic texts.

2006 / 1-84227-056-7 / approx. 350pp

Robert L. Plummer
Paul's Understanding of the Church's Mission
Did the Apostle Paul Expect the Early Christian Communities to Evangelize?

This book engages in a careful study of Paul's letters to determine if the apostle expected the communities to which he wrote to engage in missionary activity. It helpfully summarizes the discussion on this debated issue, judiciously handling contested texts, and provides a way forward in addressing this critical question. While admitting that Paul rarely explicitly commands the communities he founded to evangelize, Plummer amasses significant incidental data to provide a convincing case that Paul did indeed expect his churches to engage in mission activity. Throughout the study, Plummer progressively builds a theological basis for the church's mission that is both distinctively Pauline and compelling.

2006 / 1-84227-333-7 / approx. 324pp

David Powys
'Hell': A Hard Look at a Hard Question
The Fate of the Unrighteous in New Testament Thought
This comprehensive treatment seeks to unlock the original meaning of terms and phrases long thought to support the traditional doctrine of hell. It concludes that there is an alternative—one which is more biblical, and which can positively revive the rationale for Christian mission.
1997 / 0-85364-831-X / xxii + 478pp

Sorin Sabou
Between Horror and Hope
Paul's Metaphorical Language of Death in Romans 6.1-11
This book argues that Paul's metaphorical language of death in Romans 6.1-11 conveys two aspects: horror and hope. The 'horror' aspect is conveyed by the 'crucifixion' language, and the 'hope' aspect by 'burial' language. The life of the Christian believer is understood, as relationship with sin is concerned ('death to sin'), between these two realities: horror and hope.
2005 / 1-84227-322-1 / approx. 224pp

Rosalind Selby
The Comical Doctrine
The Epistemology of New Testament Hermeneutics
This book argues that the gospel breaks through postmodernity's critique of truth and the referential possibilities of textuality with its gift of grace. With a rigorous, philosophical challenge to modernist and postmodernist assumptions, Selby offers an alternative epistemology to all who would still read with faith *and* with academic credibility.
2005 / 1-84227-212-8 / approx. 350pp

Kiwoong Son
Zion Symbolism in Hebrews
Hebrews 12.18-24 as a Hermeneutical Key to the Epistle
This book challenges the general tendency of understanding the Epistle to the Hebrews against a Hellenistic background and suggests that the Epistle should be understood in the light of the Jewish apocalyptic tradition. The author especially argues for the importance of the theological symbolism of Sinai and Zion (Heb. 12:18-24) as it provides the Epistle's theological background as well as the rhetorical basis of the superiority motif of Jesus throughout the Epistle.
2005 / 1-84227-368-X / approx. 280pp

Kevin Walton
Thou Traveller Unknown
The Presence and Absence of God in the Jacob Narrative
The author offers a fresh reading of the story of Jacob in the book of Genesis
through the paradox of divine presence and absence. The work also seeks to
make a contribution to Pentateuchal studies by bringing together a close reading
of the final text with historical critical insights, doing justice to the text's
historical depth, final form and canonical status.
2003 / 1-84227-059-1 / xvi + 238pp

George M. Wieland
The Significance of Salvation
A Study of Salvation Language in the Pastoral Epistles
The language and ideas of salvation pervade the three Pastoral Epistles. This
study offers a close examination of their soteriological statements. In all three
letters the idea of salvation is found to play a vital paraenetic role, but each also
exhibits distinctive soteriological emphases. The results challenge common
assumptions about the Pastoral Epistles as a corpus.
2005 / 1-84227-257-8 / approx. 324pp

Alistair Wilson
When Will These Things Happen?
A Study of Jesus as Judge in Matthew 21–25
This study seeks to allow Matthew's carefully constructed presentation of Jesus
to be given full weight in the modern evaluation of Jesus' eschatology. Careful
analysis of the text of Matthew 21–25 reveals Jesus to be standing firmly in the
Jewish prophetic and wisdom traditions as he proclaims and enacts imminent
judgement on the Jewish authorities then boldly claims the central role in the
final and universal judgement.
2004 / 1-84227-146-6 / xxii + 272pp

Lindsay Wilson
Joseph Wise and Otherwise
The Intersection of Covenant and Wisdom in Genesis 37–50
This book offers a careful literary reading of Genesis 37–50 that argues that the
Joseph story contains both strong covenant themes and many wisdom-like
elements. The connections between the two helps to explore how covenant and
wisdom might intersect in an integrated biblical theology.
2004 / 1-84227-140-7 / xvi + 340pp

Stephen I. Wright
The Voice of Jesus
Studies in the Interpretation of Six Gospel Parables
This literary study considers how the 'voice' of Jesus has been heard in different
periods of parable interpretation, and how the categories of figure and trope may
help us towards a sensitive reading of the parables today.
2000 / 0-85364-975-8 / xiv + 280pp

Paternoster
9 Holdom Avenue,
Bletchley,
Milton Keynes MK1 1QR,
United Kingdom
Web: www.authenticmedia.co.uk/paternoster

July 2005

Paternoster Theological Monographs
(All titles uniform with this volume)
Dates in bold are of projected publication

Emil Bartos
Deification in Eastern Orthodox Theology
An Evaluation and Critique of the Theology of Dumitru Staniloae
Bartos studies a fundamental yet neglected aspect of Orthodox theology:
deification. By examining the doctrines of anthropology, christology, soteriology and ecclesiology as they relate to deification, he provides an important
contribution to contemporary dialogue between Eastern and Western
theologians.
1999 / 0-85364-956-1 / xii + 370pp

Graham Buxton
The Trinity, Creation and Pastoral Ministry
Imaging the Perichoretic God
In this book the author proposes a three-way conversation between theology,
science and pastoral ministry. His approach draws on a Trinitarian
understanding of God as a relational being of love, whose life 'spills over' into
all created reality, human and non-human. By locating human meaning and
purpose within God's 'creation-community' this book offers the possibility of a
transforming engagement between those in pastoral ministry and the scientific
community.
2005 */ 1-84227-369-8 / approx. 380 pp*

Iain D. Campbell
Fixing the Indemnity
The Life and Work of George Adam Smith
When Old Testament scholar George Adam Smith (1856–1942) delivered the
Lyman Beecher lectures at Yale University in 1899, he confidently declared that
'modern criticism has won its war against traditional theories. It only remains to
fix the amount of the indemnity.' In this biography, Iain D. Campbell assesses
Smith's critical approach to the Old Testament and evaluates its consequences,
showing that Smith's life and work still raises questions about the relationship
between biblical scholarship and evangelical faith.
2004 / 1-84227-228-4 / xx + 256pp

Tim Chester
Mission and the Coming of God
Eschatology, the Trinity and Mission in the Theology of Jürgen Moltmann
This book explores the theology and missiology of the influential contemporary theologian, Jürgen Moltmann. It highlights the important contribution Moltmann has made while offering a critique of his thought from an evangelical perspective. In so doing, it touches on pertinent issues for evangelical missiology. The conclusion takes Calvin as a starting point, proposing 'an eschatology of the cross' which offers a critique of the over-realised eschatologies in liberation theology and certain forms of evangelicalism.
2006 / 1-84227-320-5 / approx. 224pp

Sylvia Wilkey Collinson
Making Disciples
The Significance of Jesus' Educational Strategy for Today's Church
This study examines the biblical practice of discipling, formulates a definition, and makes comparisons with modern models of education. A recommendation is made for greater attention to its practice today.
2004 / 1-84227-116-4 / xiv + 278pp

Darrell Cosden
A Theology of Work
Work and the New Creation
Through dialogue with Moltmann, Pope John Paul II and others, this book develops a genitive 'theology of work', presenting a theological definition of work and a model for a theological ethics of work that shows work's nature, value and meaning now and eschatologically. Work is shown to be a transformative activity consisting of three dynamically inter-related dimensions: the instrumental, relational and ontological.
2005 / 1-84227-332-9 / xvi + 208pp

Stephen M. Dunning
The Crisis and the Quest
A Kierkegaardian Reading of Charles Williams
Employing Kierkegaardian categories and analysis, this study investigates both the central crisis in Charles Williams's authorship between hermetism and Christianity (Kierkegaard's Religions A and B), and the quest to resolve this crisis, a quest that ultimately presses the bounds of orthodoxy.
2000 / 0-85364-985-5 / xxiv + 254pp

Keith Ferdinando
The Triumph of Christ in African Perspective
A Study of Demonology and Redemption in the African Context
The book explores the implications of the gospel for traditional African fears of occult aggression. It analyses such traditional approaches to suffering and biblical responses to fears of demonic evil, concluding with an evaluation of African beliefs from the perspective of the gospel.
1999 / 0-85364-830-1 / xviii + 450pp

Andrew Goddard
Living the Word, Resisting the World
The Life and Thought of Jacques Ellul
This work offers a definitive study of both the life and thought of the French Reformed thinker Jacques Ellul (1912-1994). It will prove an indispensable resource for those interested in this influential theologian and sociologist and for Christian ethics and political thought generally.
2002 / 1-84227-053-2 / xxiv + 378pp

David Hilborn
The Words of our Lips
Language-Use in Free Church Worship
Studies of liturgical language have tended to focus on the written canons of Roman Catholic and Anglican communities. By contrast, David Hilborn analyses the more extemporary approach of English Nonconformity. Drawing on recent developments in linguistic pragmatics, he explores similarities and differences between 'fixed' and 'free' worship, and argues for the interdependence of each.
2006 */ 0-85364-977-4 / approx. 350pp*

Roger Hitching
The Church and Deaf People
A Study of Identity, Communication and Relationships with Special Reference to the Ecclesiology of Jürgen Moltmann
In *The Church and Deaf People* Roger Hitching sensitively examines the history and present experience of deaf people and finds similarities between aspects of sign language and Moltmann's theological method that 'open up' new ways of understanding theological concepts.
2003 / 1-84227-222-5 / xxii + 236pp

John G. Kelly
One God, One People
The Differentiated Unity of the People of God in the Theology of
Jürgen Moltmann
The author expounds and critiques Moltmann's doctrine of God and highlights
the systematic connections between it and Moltmann's influential discussion of
Israel. He then proposes a fresh approach to Jewish–Christian relations building
on Moltmann's work using insights from Habermas and Rawls.
2005 / 0-85346-969-3 / approx. 350pp

Mark F.W. Lovatt
Confronting the Will-to-Power
A Reconsideration of the Theology of Reinhold Niebuhr
Confronting the Will-to-Power is an analysis of the theology of Reinhold
Niebuhr, arguing that his work is an attempt to identify, and provide a practical
theological answer to, the existence and nature of human evil.
2001 / 1-84227-054-0 / xviii + 216pp

Neil B. MacDonald
Karl Barth and the Strange New World within the Bible
Barth, Wittgenstein, and the Metadilemmas of the Enlightenment
Barth's discovery of the strange new world within the Bible is examined in the
context of Kant, Hume, Overbeck, and, most importantly, Wittgenstein.
MacDonald covers some fundamental issues in theology today: epistemology,
the final form of the text and biblical truth-claims.
2000 / 0-85364-970-7 / xxvi + 374pp

Keith A. Mascord
Alvin Plantinga and Christian Apologetics
This book draws together the contributions of the philosopher Alvin Plantinga to
the major contemporary challenges to Christian belief, highlighting in particular
his ground-breaking work in epistemology and the problem of evil. Plantinga's
theory that both theistic and Christian belief is warrantedly basic is explored and
critiqued, and an assessment offered as to the significance of his work for
apologetic theory and practice.
2005 / 1-84227-256-X / approx. 304pp

Gillian McCulloch
The Deconstruction of Dualism in Theology
With Reference to Ecofeminist Theology and New Age Spirituality
This book challenges eco-theological anti-dualism in Christian theology,
arguing that dualism has a twofold function in Christian religious discourse.
Firstly, it enables us to express the discontinuities and divisions that are part of
the process of reality. Secondly, dualistic language allows us to express the
mysteries of divine transcendence/immanence and the survival of the soul
without collapsing into monism and materialism, both of which are problematic
for Christian epistemology.
2002 / 1-84227-044-3 / xii + 282pp

Leslie McCurdy
Attributes and Atonement
The Holy Love of God in the Theology of P.T. Forsyth
Attributes and Atonement is an intriguing full-length study of P.T. Forsyth's
doctrine of the cross as it relates particularly to God's holy love. It includes an
unparalleled bibliography of both primary and secondary material relating to
Forsyth.
1999 / 0-85364-833-6 / xiv + 328pp

Nozomu Miyahira
Towards a Theology of the Concord of God
A Japanese Perspective on the Trinity
This book introduces a new Japanese theology and a unique Trinitarian formula
based on the Japanese intellectual climate: three betweennesses and one
concord. It also presents a new interpretation of the Trinity, a co-
subordinationism, which is in line with orthodox Trinitarianism; each single person of the Trinity is eternally and equally subordinate (or serviceable) to the
other persons, so that they retain the mutual dynamic equality.
2000 / 0-85364-863-8 / xiv + 256pp

Eddy José Muskus
**The Origins and Early Development of Liberation Theology in
Latin America**
With Particular Reference to Gustavo Gutiérrez
This work challenges the fundamental premise of Liberation Theology, 'opting
for the poor', and its claim that Christ is found in them. It also argues that
Liberation Theology emerged as a direct result of the failure of the Roman
Catholic Church in Latin America.
2002 / 0-85364-974-X / xiv + 296pp

Jim Purves
The Triune God and the Charismatic Movement
A Critical Appraisal from a Scottish Perspective
All emotion and no theology? Or a fundamental challenge to reappraise and realign our trinitarian theology in the light of Christian experience? This study of charismatic renewal as it found expression within Scotland at the end of the twentieth century evaluates the use of Patristic, Reformed and contemporary models of the Trinity in explaining the workings of the Holy Spirit.
2004 / 1-84227-321-3 / xxiv + 246pp

Anna Robbins
Methods in the Madness
Diversity in Twentieth-Century Christian Social Ethics
The author compares the ethical methods of Walter Rauschenbusch, Reinhold Niebuhr and others. She argues that unless Christians are clear about the ways that theology and philosophy are expressed practically they may lose the ability to discuss social ethics across contexts, let alone reach effective agreements.
2004 / 1-84227-211-X / xx + 294pp

Ed Rybarczyk
Beyond Salvation
Eastern Orthodoxy and Classical Pentecostalism on Becoming Like Christ
At first glance eastern Orthodoxy and classical Pentecostalism seem quite distinct. This ground-breaking study shows they share much in common, especially as it concerns the experiential elements of following Christ. Both traditions assert that authentic Christianity transcends the wooden categories of modernism.
2004 / 1-84227-144-X / xii + 356pp

Signe Sandsmark
Is World View Neutral Education Possible and Desirable?
A Christian Response to Liberal Arguments
(Published jointly with The Stapleford Centre)
This book discusses reasons for belief in world view neutrality, and argues that 'neutral' education will have a hidden, but strong world view influence. It discusses the place for Christian education in the common school.
2000 / 0-85364-973-1 / xiv + 182pp

Hazel Sherman
Reading Zechariah
The Allegorical Tradition of Biblical Interpretation through the Commentary of Didymus the Blind and Theodore of Mopsuestia
A close reading of the commentary on Zechariah by Didymus the Blind alongside that of Theodore of Mopsuestia suggests that popular categorising of Antiochene and Alexandrian biblical exegesis as 'historical' or 'allegorical' is inadequate and misleading.
2005 / 1-84227-213-6 / approx. 280pp

Andrew Sloane
On Being a Christian in the Academy
Nicholas Wolterstorff and the Practice of Christian Scholarship
An exposition and critical appraisal of Nicholas Wolterstorff's epistemology in the light of the philosophy of science, and an application of his thought to the practice of Christian scholarship.
2003 / 1-84227-058-3 / xvi + 274pp

Damon W.K. So
Jesus' Revelation of His Father
A Narrative-Conceptual Study of the Trinity with Special Reference to Karl Barth
This book explores the trinitarian dynamics in the context of Jesus' revelation of his Father in his earthly ministry with references to key passages in Matthew's Gospel. It develops from the exegeses of these passages a non-linear concept of revelation which links Jesus' communion with his Father to his revelatory words and actions through a nuanced understanding of the Holy Spirit, with references to K. Barth, G.W.H. Lampe, J.D.G. Dunn and E. Irving.
2005 / 1-84227-323-X / approx. 380pp

Daniel Strange
The Possibility of Salvation Among the Unevangelised
An Analysis of Inclusivism in Recent Evangelical Theology
For evangelical theologians the 'fate of the unevangelised' impinges upon fundamental tenets of evangelical identity. The position known as 'inclusivism', defined by the belief that the unevangelised can be ontologically saved by Christ whilst being epistemologically unaware of him, has been defended most vigorously by the Canadian evangelical Clark H. Pinnock. Through a detailed analysis and critique of Pinnock's work, this book examines a cluster of issues surrounding the unevangelised and its implications for christology, soteriology and the doctrine of revelation.
2002 / 1-84227-047-8 / xviii + 362pp

Scott Swain
God According to the Gospel
Biblical Narrative and the Identity of God in the Theology of Robert W. Jenson
Robert W. Jenson is one of the leading voices in contemporary Trinitarian theology. His boldest contribution in this area concerns his use of biblical narrative both to ground and explicate the Christian doctrine of God. *God According to the Gospel* critically examines Jenson's proposal and suggests an alternative way of reading the biblical portrayal of the triune God.
2006 / 1-84227-258-6 / approx. 180pp

Justyn Terry
The Justifying Judgement of God
A Reassessment of the Place of Judgement in the Saving Work of Christ
The argument of this book is that judgement, understood as the whole process of bringing justice, is the primary metaphor of atonement, with others, such as victory, redemption and sacrifice, subordinate to it. Judgement also provides the proper context for understanding penal substitution and the call to repentance, baptism, eucharist and holiness.
2005 / 1-84227-370-1 / approx. 274 pp

Graham Tomlin
The Power of the Cross
Theology and the Death of Christ in Paul, Luther and Pascal
This book explores the theology of the cross in St Paul, Luther and Pascal. It offers new perspectives on the theology of each, and some implications for the nature of power, apologetics, theology and church life in a postmodern context.
1999 / 0-85364-984-7 / xiv + 344pp

Adonis Vidu
Postliberal Theological Method
A Critical Study
The postliberal theology of Hans Frei, George Lindbeck, Ronald Thiemann, John Milbank and others is one of the more influential contemporary options. This book focuses on several aspects pertaining to its theological method, specifically its understanding of background, hermeneutics, epistemic justification, ontology, the nature of doctrine and, finally, Christological method.
2005 / 1-84227-395-7 / approx. 324pp

Graham J. Watts
Revelation and the Spirit
*A Comparative Study of the Relationship between the Doctrine of Revelation
and Pneumatology in the Theology of Eberhard Jüngel and of
Wolfhart Pannenberg*
The relationship between revelation and pneumatology is relatively unexplored.
This approach offers a fresh angle on two important twentieth century
theologians and raises pneumatological questions which are theologically crucial
and relevant to mission in a postmodern culture.
2005 / 1-84227-104-0 / xxii + 232pp

Nigel G. Wright
Disavowing Constantine
*Mission, Church and the Social Order in the Theologies of John Howard Yoder
and Jürgen Moltmann*
This book is a timely restatement of a radical theology of church and state in the
Anabaptist and Baptist tradition. Dr Wright constructs his argument in dialogue
and debate with Yoder and Moltmann, major contributors to a free church
perspective.
2000 / 0-85364-978-2 / xvi + 252pp

Paternoster
9 Holdom Avenue,
Bletchley,
Milton Keynes MK1 1QR,
United Kingdom
Web: www.authenticmedia.co.uk/paternoster

July 2005